Criminal Justice Case Briefs

Significant Cases in Criminal Procedure

Craig Hemmens
Boise State University

John L. Worrall
California State University, San Bernardino

Alan Thompson
The University of Southern Mississippi

Roxbury Publishing Company
Los Angeles, California

Library of Congress Cataloging-in-Publication Data
Hemmens, Craig.
Criminal justice case briefs. Significant cases in criminal procedure / Craig Hemmens, John L. Worrall, Alan Thompson.—1st ed.
p. cm.
Includes bibliographical references and index.
ISBN 1-931719-23-3
1. Criminal procedure—United States—Cases. I. Title: Significant cases in criminal procedure. II. Worrall, John L. III. Thompson, Alan, 1968– IV. Title.

KF9630.A7H46 2004
345.73'0522—dc21   2003009739 CIP

Publisher: Claude Teweles
Managing Editor: Dawn VanDercreek
Production Editor: Sacha A. Howells
Production Assistant: Josh Levine
Typography: SDS Design, info@sds-design.com
Cover Design: Marnie Kenney

Printed on acid-free paper in the United States of America. This book meets the standards for recycling of the Environmental Protection Agency.

ISBN 1-931719-23-3

ROXBURY PUBLISHING COMPANY
P. O. Box 491044
Los Angeles, California 90049-9044
Voice: (310) 473-3312 • Fax: (310) 473-4490
Email: roxbury@roxbury.net
Website: www.roxbury.net

Acknowledgments

The authors would like to thank Claude Teweles of Roxbury Publishing and all the members of his staff. Without his prompting and their encouragement, this project would never have come to fruition. We thank them for their patience and faith in us.

Craig Hemmens would like to thank Mary, Emily, Sera, Amber, and Snowball for their love and support.

To my father, Don Worrall, for always being there. I miss you more than words can say.

—John L. Worrall

Alan Thompson would like to thank his wife Leslie as well as the criminal justice faculty at Sam Houston State Universtiy for their continued support, collective wisdom, and enduring friendship.

The authors would also like to thank the reviewers who helped shape this book: John S. Dempsey, Suffolk Community College; Robert A. Harvie, St. Martin's College; Raymond G. Kessler, Sul Ross State University; Patrick Mueller, Stephen F. Austin State University; Jim Ruiz, Pennsylvania State University–Harrisburg; Lawrence C. Trostle, University of Alaska–Anchorage; Marian Williams, Bowling Green State University. ✦

Contents

Chapter One: The Exclusionary Rule

Chapter Two: What Constitutes Probable Cause?

Chapter Three: When Has a Seizure Occurred?

Chapter Four: Arrest

Chapter Five: Standards for the Use of Force

Chapter Six: Searches With Warrants

Chapter Seven: The Knock and Announce Rule

Chapter Eight: Stop and Frisk

Chapter Nine: Search Incident to Arrest

Chapter Ten: Consent Searches

Chapter Eleven: Plain View Searches

Chapter Twelve: Open Fields Searches

Chapter Thirteen: Vehicle Searches

Chapter Fourteen: Regulatory Searches

Chapter Fifteen: Electronic Surveillance

Chapter Sixteen: Pretrial Identification Procedures

Chapter Seventeen: Right to Counsel

Chapter Eighteen: The Development and Scope of the *Miranda* Warnings

Chapter Nineteen: What Constitutes Interrogation?

Chapter Twenty: Entrapment

Chapter Twenty-One: Asset Forfeiture

Preface

This book is intended to serve as a supplement to an undergraduate criminal justice textbook on search and seizure and interrogations, or as it is better known in law schools, "criminal procedure." It may also be used by a graduate student in criminal justice or a law-school student struggling to understand the law while wading through the myriad (and often contradictory) opinions contained in the typical law-school casebook.

While nothing substitutes for reading the original case opinion, the reality is that only those with a passion for the subject and plenty of time can afford to always go first to the source. This book is intended to assist those who are trying to read the original opinion, and to provide more detail than can be contained in a typical textbook.

The book is divided into sections that mirror the typical criminal justice textbook and law-school casebook approach to the subject, so that students and instructors can easily refer to related cases. All the significant United States Supreme Court cases are included, through the 2002–2003 term.

Each case brief follows the same basic format: Facts, Issue, Holding, Rationale, and Case Significance. The *Facts* section includes the relevant facts of the case that led to the eventual Supreme Court decision, as well as a brief explanation of the decisions in the lower courts. The *Issue* is the question presented to the Supreme Court for its ruling. The *Holding* is the result, the decision by the Supreme Court. The *Rationale* section contains the explanation of the Supreme Court for its decision. The *Case Significance* section contains a discussion of why the case matters to criminal justice.

We hope that this book is of use to instructors and students seeking to understand the often arcane world of criminal procedure. We welcome any comments or suggestions that readers have. ✦

Case Holdings

Chapter One: The Exclusionary Rule

Weeks v. United States, 232 U.S. 383 (1914): Evidence that is seized in violation of the Fourth Amendment by federal law enforcement officers is not admissible in a federal criminal trial.

Rochin v. California, 342 U.S. 165 (1952): Evidence obtained as the result of a search which "shocks the conscience" is inadmissible in a criminal trial because the search violates the due process clause of the Fourteenth Amendment.

Mapp v. Ohio, 367 U.S. 643 (1961): The exclusionary rule applies to all state criminal trials.

Wong Sun v. United States, 371 U.S. 471 (1963): Evidence that is obtained indirectly as a result of an illegal search by the police (known as "fruit of the poisonous tree") is excluded from a criminal trial unless the taint of the illegal search is subsequently purged by the police.

United States v. Crews, 445 U.S. 463 (1980): An in-court identification which occurs after an illegal pretrial identification is admissible if the witness's recollection is independent of the illegal pretrial identification.

Nix v. Williams, 467 U.S. 431 (1984): If police can demonstrate that evidence they obtained illegally would inevitably have been obtained through lawful means, that evidence may be admitted at a criminal trial.

United States v. Leon, 468 U.S. 897 (1984): Evidence seized by officers who act in good-faith reliance on a search warrant that is later declared invalid may be admitted at a criminal trial.

Massachusetts v. Sheppard, 468 U.S. 981 (1984): Evidence seized by officers who act in good-faith reliance on a search warrant that is later declared invalid may be admitted at a criminal trial.

Murray v. United States, 487 U.S. 533 (1988): Evidence seized by officers who act in reasonable reliance upon a search warrant that is later declared invalid may be admitted at a criminal trial, if the officers can demonstrate an independent source for their determination of probable cause.

Minnesota v. Olson, 495 U.S. 91 (1990): A warrantless, nonconsensual entry of a residence to arrest an overnight guest, without an exigent circumstance, violates the Fourth Amendment.

Arizona v. Evans, 514 U.S. 1 (1995): Evidence seized in violation of the Fourth Amendment, where the violation was the result of erroneous information received from court employees, is admissible in a criminal trial.

Chapter Two: What Constitutes Probable Cause?

Beck v. Ohio, 379 U.S. 89 (1964): Probable cause to arrest exists when the police have reasonably trustworthy information that would warrant a person of "reasonable caution" to believe a crime is taking place or has taken place.

Draper v. United States, 358 U.S. 307 (1959): Information supplied by an informant that is later corroborated by the police can establish probable cause to arrest.

Aguilar v. Texas, 378 U.S. 108 (1964): An affidavit for a search warrant based on information supplied by an informant must contain sufficient details about how the informant reached his or her conclusions and how he or she knows what he or she knows.

Spinelli v. United States, 393 U.S. 410 (1969): A search warrant cannot be issued when the affidavit on which it is based contains insufficient information concerning how the informant learned of the suspected criminal activity in question.

Illinois v. Gates, 462 U.S. 213 (1983): A totality of circumstances analysis is required for the purpose of determining whether information supplied by an informant constitutes probable cause to search.

Chapter Three: When Has a Seizure Occurred?

Schmerber v. California, 384 U.S. 757 (1966): The warrantless "seizure" of one's blood is constitutional.

Cupp v. Murphy, 412 U.S. 291 (1973): The warrantless seizure of evidence that is likely to disappear does not violate the Fourth Amendment.

Michigan v. Chesternut, 486 U.S. 567 (1988): Following a person does not constitute a seizure within the meaning of the Fourth Amendment.

Brower v. County of Inyo, 489 U.S. 593 (1989): A roadblock used by the police to stop a fleeing felon constitutes a seizure within the meaning of the Fourth Amendment.

California v. Hodari D., 499 U.S. 621 (1991): A Fourth Amendment seizure of a person does not take place unless the suspect submits to the officer or the officer uses physical force to apprehend the suspect.

Florida v. Bostick, 501 U.S. 429 (1991): The appropriate test for determining whether a person on a bus is seized is whether a reasonable passenger would feel free to decline officers' requests or otherwise terminate the encounter.

Bond v. United States, 529 U.S. 334 (2000): It is a violation of the Fourth Amendment for police officers, without any suspicion, to physically manipulate bus passengers' luggage.

Kyllo v. United States, 533 U.S. 27 (2001): It is a violation of the Fourth Amendment for the police to scan, without a warrant, the details of a home with a device that is not in general public use.

Illinois v. McArthur, 531 U.S. 326 (2001): An officer's refusal to let a person into his or her residence, knowing that the person will destroy evidence therein, does not violate the Fourth Amendment.

Chapter Four: Arrest

Frisbie v. Collins, 342 U.S. 519 (1952): The forcible apprehension of a defendant in a state other than that where he is to stand trial does not deprive the court of jurisdiction to hear the case.

United States v. Santana, 427 U.S. 38 (1976): A warrantless arrest in a private residence is constitutional if the arrest originates in a public place.

United States v. Watson, 423 U.S. 411 (1976): A warrantless arrest in a public place is constitutional, so long as the police have probable cause.

Dunaway v. New York, 442 U.S. 200 (1979): A person cannot be seized and transported to a police station without probable cause.

Payton v. New York, 445 U.S. 573 (1980): Absent exigent circumstances, it is unconstitutional to make a warrantless entry into a private place for the purpose of effecting an arrest.

Welsh v. Wisconsin, 466 U.S. 740 (1984): The Fourth Amendment does not permit the warrantless arrest of a person in a private residence when the arrestable offense is not jailable.

Winston v. Lee, 470 U.S. 753 (1985): A compelling government need must be demonstrated before a person can be forced to undergo surgery for the purpose of removing a bullet.

United States v. Alvarez-Machain, 504 U.S. 655 (1992): A foreigner can be forcibly abducted from his or her country of origin and brought to the U.S. for trial, provided the abduction does not violate any treaties.

Atwater v. City of Lago Vista, 532 U.S. 318 (2001): It is not a violation of the Fourth Amendment to arrest a person for an offense that carries no jail term.

Chapter Five: Standards for the Use of Force

Tennessee v. Garner, 471 U.S. 1 (1985): It is a violation of the Fourth Amendment for the police to use deadly force to apprehend an unarmed fleeing felon.

Graham v. Connor, 490 U.S. 396 (1989): Use of force claims against the police must be judged from a Fourth Amendment objective reasonableness standpoint.

Chapter Six: Searches With Warrants

Coolidge v. New Hampshire, 403 U.S. 443 (1971): Attorneys general cannot issue search warrants because they are not considered "neutral and detached magistrates."

Zurcher v. Stanford Daily, 436 U.S. 547 (1978): A warrant can be issued for the search of premises controlled by an innocent third party, provided that probable cause is present.

Mincey v. Arizona, 437 U.S. 385 (1978): If no exigent circumstances exist, a warrant must be obtained to search a homicide scene.

Steagald v. United States, 451 U.S. 204 (1981): Police officers can search the home of a third party for a person for whom they have an arrest warrant, but a separate search warrant must be obtained.

Michigan v. Summers, 452 U.S. 692 (1981): A warrant carries with it the authority to detain residents of houses to be searched pursuant to a valid warrant.

Maryland v. Garrison, 480 U.S. 79 (1987): Evidence is admissible when officers mistakenly and in good faith execute a search warrant at a location not authorized in the warrant.

California v. Greenwood, 486 U.S. 35 (1988): Items placed in the trash for collection on a public street may be searched without a warrant or probable cause.

Minnesota v. Carter, 525 U.S. 83 (1998): A person who is in another's apartment with consent and for the purpose of doing business does not enjoy an expectation of privacy.

CHAPTER SEVEN: THE KNOCK AND ANNOUNCE RULE

Wilson v. Arkansas, 514 U.S. 927 (1995): Unless exigent circumstances exist, the Fourth Amendment's reasonableness clause requires that officers knock and announce their presence when serving search or arrest warrants.

Richards v. Wisconsin, 520 U.S. 385 (1997): The Fourth Amendment does not permit a blanket exception to the knock and announce requirement for felony drug warrants.

United States v. Ramirez, 523 U.S. 65 (1998): The Fourth Amendment does not require a heightened showing of "more specific inferences of exigency" before law enforcement officials can conduct a no-knock entry that will cause destruction of property.

CHAPTER EIGHT: STOP AND FRISK

Terry v. Ohio, 392 U.S. 1 (1968): The police may stop and frisk individuals with reasonable suspicion that criminal activity is afoot.

Adams v. Williams, 407 U.S. 143 (1972): A police officer may conduct a stop and frisk based on information provided by a reliable informant.

United States v. Cortez, 449 U.S. 411 (1981): The assessment of police action under *Terry* must be based on "the whole picture" and should take into account "all of the circumstances" surrounding the case.

United States v. Sharpe, 470 U.S. 675 (1984): A forty minute detention for the purpose of a limited investigation does not violate the Fourth Amendment, provided that reasonable suspicion is present.

United States v. Hensley, 469 U.S. 221 (1985): The police may conduct an investigative stop of an individual who is the subject of a "wanted" flyer.

United States v. Sokolow, 490 U.S. 1 (1989): It is not a violation of the Fourth Amendment to stop someone based on a "drug courier profile," provided that reasonable suspicion exists.

Alabama v. White, 496 U.S. 325 (1990): An anonymous tip, corroborated by the police, creates "reasonable suspicion" to justify a stop and frisk.

Minnesota v. Dickerson, 508 U.S. 366 (1993): The police may seize contraband detected through the sense of touch during a protective pat-down search only if the contraband is immediately apparent and no manipulation takes place.

Florida v. J. L., 529 U.S. 266 (2000): The Fourth Amendment does not authorize police to undertake a warrantless frisk based solely upon an anonymous tip.

Illinois v. Wardlow, 528 U.S. 119 (2000): An individual's sudden flight from a high-crime area creates reasonable suspicion, justifying a stop and frisk.

United States v. Arvizu, 534 U.S. 266 (2001): The appropriate Fourth Amendment standard for assessing the legality of an investigative stop is one that takes into consideration a totality of the circumstances.

CHAPTER NINE: SEARCH INCIDENT TO ARREST

Warden v. Hayden, 387 U.S. 294 (1967): The prohibition on the seizure of items of only evidential value and allowing seizure of instrumentalities, fruits, or contraband is no longer accepted as being required by the Fourth Amendment.

Chimel v. California, 395 U.S. 752 (1969): The police may search the area within the immediate control of an arrestee in order to discover any weapons or to prevent the destruction of evidence.

Vale v. Louisiana, 399 U.S. 30 (1970): The police may not conduct a warrantless search of a suspect's home when the suspect is arrested outside the home and exigent circumstances are not present.

United States v. Robinson, 414 U.S. 218 (1973): A police officer may conduct a full search of an arrestee, even when the officer does not fear for his or her safety.

United States v. Edwards, 415 U.S. 800 (1974): A search incident to arrest can take place several hours after the arrest.

United States v. Chadwick, 430 U.S. 1 (1977): The warrantless search of a moveable container is unconstitutional so long as exigent circumstances do not exist.

Illinois v. LaFayette, 462 U.S. 640 (1983): Shoulder bags can be searched incident to a lawful arrest.

Maryland v. Buie, 494 U.S. 325 (1990): A police officer can conduct a warrantless "protective sweep" of an area where a suspect is arrested.

CHAPTER TEN: CONSENT SEARCHES

Stoner v. California, 376 U.S. 483 (1964): A hotel clerk may not give valid consent to search a hotel room rented to a criminal suspect.

Bumper v. North Carolina, 391 U.S. 543 (1968): Consent obtained by police officers who obtain that consent by lying about the existence of a search warrant is not valid.

Schneckloth v. Bustamonte, 412 U.S. 218 (1973): Knowledge of the right to refuse consent is only one of the circumstances to be considered in determining whether a consent search is voluntary.

Florida v. Royer, 460 U.S. 491 (1983): Consent to search is not valid if it is obtained by the police during a seizure which was not based on probable cause.

Illinois v. Rodriguez, 497 U.S. 177 (1990): The police may enter a home without a warrant based upon the consent of a third party whom the police, at the time of entry, reasonably believe to possess common authority over the premises, but who in fact does not.

Florida v. Jimeno, 500 U.S. 248 (1991): Consent to search a car includes consent to search closed containers located within the car.

United States v. Drayton et al., 536 U.S. 194 (2002): The police may randomly approach individuals and ask for consent to search their luggage or personal belongings absent any indication that criminal activity is afoot.

Chapter Eleven: Plain View Searches

Texas v. Brown, 460 U.S. 730 (1983): It need not be immediately apparent that evidence is contraband for the plain view doctrine to apply; only probable cause is necessary.

Arizona v. Hicks, 480 U.S. 321 (1987): A plain view seizure requires probable cause that the item to be seized is contraband.

Horton v. California, 496 U.S. 128 (1990): Inadvertence is not a requirement of the plain view doctrine.

Chapter Twelve: Open Fields Searches

Oliver v. United States, 466 U.S. 170 (1984): The open fields doctrine applies outside the curtilage of a home, even when the property owner takes steps to exclude the public.

California v. Ciraolo, 476 U.S. 207 (1986): The Fourth Amendment is not violated by the naked-eye aerial observation of areas within the curtilage.

United States v. Dunn, 480 U.S. 294 (1987): A barn located fifty yards from a house and surrounded by a fence is not within the curtilage of the residence and is therefore not protected by the Fourth Amendment.

Chapter Thirteen: Vehicle Searches

Carroll v. United States, 267 U.S. 132 (1925): Police are authorized to undertake the warrantless roadside search of a vehicle if probable cause exists that evidence of criminal activity contained therein will be lost or destroyed if time is taken to secure a warrant.

Chambers v. Maroney, 399 U.S. 42 (1970): The warrantless search of a vehicle that has been trans-ported to a police station does not violate the Fourth Amendment so long as officers have probable cause to believe that it contains evidence of criminal activity.

Delaware v. Prouse, 440 U.S. 648 (1979): Except in situations where there is at least articulable and reasonable suspicion that a motorist is unlicensed or that a vehicle is unregistered, or that either the vehicle or occupants are subject to seizure for some violation of law, stopping a car solely for purposes of checking the driver's license and registration is unreasonable under the Fourth Amendment. In other words, the police may not make random traffic stops for purposes of checking a driver's license or vehicle registration in the absence of some violation of law.

New York v. Belton, 453 U.S. 454 (1981): Officers may search the passenger compartment of a vehicle and its contents incident to a lawful arrest. Not only may they look inside the glove compartment and other storage receptacles, but they may also examine any other closed containers even if there is a low probability that incriminating evidence will be discovered.

United States v. Cortez, 449 U.S. 411 (1981): When seeking to determine whether or not a particular investigative stop is justified, the totality of the circumstances must be considered. Within this context, the investigating officer must have an objective, particularized basis leading him or her to believe that criminal activity is afoot.

United States v. Ross, 456 U.S. 798 (1982): Officers may open closed containers found during the course of a warrantless vehicle search so long as they have probable cause to believe that contraband may be found therein.

Michigan v. Long, 463 U.S. 1032 (1983): A protective search of a vehicle's passenger compartment for weapons is reasonable under the principles articulated in *Terry v. Ohio*.

California v. Carney, 471 U.S. 386 (1985): A motor home that is being used on the public roadways in a manner other than as a residence or dwelling qualifies as an automobile for purposes of conducting a warrantless search under established Fourth Amendment standards.

Colorado v. Bertine, 479 U.S. 367 (1987): Evidence discovered within a closed container (i.e., purse, book bag, backpack, etc.) during the course of an inventory search incident to a lawful arrest is admissible under the Fourth Amendment.

Florida v. Wells, 495 U.S. 1 (1990): Evidence that is found within a closed container should be excluded in cases where the officer's discretion to look therein was not narrowly guided by agency policy.

California v. Acevedo, 500 U.S. 565 (1991): Police officers are authorized to search any container found within a vehicle without having to first secure a warrant so long as they have probable cause to believe that it holds contraband or other evidence of criminal activity.

Ohio v. Robinette, 519 U.S. 33 (1996): Police officers are not required under the Fourth Amendment to inform a motorist that he or she is free to leave before requesting consent to search a vehicle.

Pennsylvania v. Labron, 518 U.S. 938 (1996): The very fact that a vehicle is mobile creates an exigent circumstance precluding the need for officers to first obtain a warrant before searching a vehicle that has been lawfully stopped. In other words, officers are not required to secure a warrant before searching a vehicle so long as they have solid probable cause to believe that incriminating evidence may be found therein.

Whren v. United States, 517 U.S. 806 (1996): Petextual traffic stops are constitutional so long as an officer has probable cause to believe that a traffic violation or some other offense has occurred.

Maryland v. Wilson, 519 U.S. 408 (1997): Police officers may direct any and all passengers to exit and remain outside of a vehicle that has been lawfully stopped.

Knowles v. Iowa, 525 U.S. 113 (1998): The full search of a vehicle incident to a traffic stop in which the officer issues a citation rather than arresting the motorist violates the Fourth Amendment.

Wyoming v. Houghton, 526 U.S. 295 (1999): Where officers have probable cause to conduct a warrantless vehicle search, they are also authorized to search a passenger's personal belongings (i.e., purse, bag, or other such receptacle) where there exists the possibility that contraband may be contained therein.

Chapter Fourteen:
Regulatory Searches

South Dakota v. Opperman, 428 U.S. 364 (1976): A warrantless, suspicionless inventory search of an impounded vehicle does not violate the Fourth Amendment, but the search must follow standard operating procedures.

Illinois v. Lafayette, 462 U.S. 640 (1983): The police may search an arrestee, including his or her personal items, as part of a routine inventory incident to booking and jailing.

Camara v. Municipal Court, 387 U.S. 523 (1967): The Fourth Amendment bars prosecution of persons who refuse to permit warrantless code inspections of their personal residences.

Wyman v. James, 400 U.S. 309 (1971): Welfare caseworkers are permitted to make warrantless visits to the homes of welfare recipients.

Colonnade Catering Corp. v. United States, 397 U.S. 72 (1970): A statute permitting warrantless entries into liquor stores by government inspectors does not violate the Fourth Amendment.

United States v. Biswell, 406 U.S. 311 (1972): Warrantless inspections of federally licensed firearms dealerships do not violate the Fourth Amendment.

New York v. Burger, 482 U.S. 691 (1987): Inspections of vehicle junkyards fall within the "closely regulated business" exception to the Fourth Amendment's warrant requirement.

United States v. Martinez-Fuerte, 428 U.S. 543 (1976): Roadblocks near international borders for the purpose of detecting illegal aliens do not violate the Fourth Amendment.

Michigan Department of State Police v. Sitz, 496 U.S. 444 (1990): Warrantless, suspicionless highway sobriety checkpoints do not violate the Fourth Amendment.

City of Indianapolis v. Edmond, 531 U.S. 32 (2000): Suspicionless vehicle checkpoints for detecting illegal drugs violate the Fourth Amendment.

New Jersey v. T.L.O., 469 U.S. 325 (1985): School officials do not need a warrant or probable cause for a school disciplinary search.

O'Connor v. Ortega, 480 U.S. 709 (1987): Government employees enjoy Fourth Amendment protection in their offices.

Vernonia School District 47J v. Acton, 515 U.S. 646 (1995): Random, suspicionless drug tests of school athletes do not violate the Fourth Amendment.

Ferguson v. Charleston, 523 U.S. 67 (2001): The Fourth Amendment is violated when hospital personnel, working with the police, test pregnant mothers for drug use without their consent.

Board of Education of Independent School District v. Earls, 536 U.S. 822 (2002): Random, suspicionless drug tests of students who participate in extracurricular activities do not violate the Fourth Amendment.

Griffin v. Wisconsin, 483 U.S. 868 (1987): Probationers can be forced to submit to warrantless searches of their residences.

United States v. Knights, 534 U.S. 112 (2001): Evidence seized from the warrantless search of a probationer's apartment is admissible under the Fourth Amendment when the search is legally authorized by the terms of probation.

Chapter Fifteen: Electronic Surveillance

Olmstead v. United States, 277 U.S. 438 (1928): Electronic eavesdropping (i.e., wiretapping) does not constitute a search within the meaning of the Fourth Amendment unless a physical intrusion or trespass into a protected area occurs.

On Lee v. United States, 343 U.S. 747 (1952): The Fourth Amendment does not prohibit the use of an electronic eavesdropping device (i.e., a "wire") that is worn by the "friend" of a criminal suspect for purposes of gathering incriminating evidence.

Berger v. New York, 388 U.S. 41 (1967): Electronic eavesdropping constitutes a search, which in the absence of clearly limited guidelines regarding the information sought and how it is to be "returned," violates the Fourth Amendment prohibition against unreasonable searches and seizures.

Katz v. United States, 389 U.S. 347 (1967): Despite the fact that a telephone booth exists in public, individuals who make use of it possess a reasonable expectation of privacy. Thus, any electronic monitoring of the phone constitutes a search. No physical intrusion needs to occur in order for the Fourth Amendment to be triggered.

United States v. Karo, 468 U.S. 705 (1984): The warrantless monitoring of a homing device inside a private residence violates the Fourth Amendment.

Chapter Sixteen: Pretrial Identification Procedures

United States v. Wade, 388 U.S. 218 (1967): The Fifth Amendment does not prohibit the state from requiring a defendant to participate in a postindictment lineup conducted for identification purposes. However, the Sixth Amendment requires the presence of counsel during such procedures, given their critical nature. Any identification testimony derived from a post-indictment lineup procedure in which a defendant was denied the right to counsel violates the Sixth Amendment and is thus inadmissible at trial.

Foster v. California, 394 U.S. 440 (1969): Lineup procedures that are suggestive to the point that the resulting identification is all but inevitable violate the suspect's due process rights.

Kirby v. Illinois, 406 U.S. 682 (1972): The Sixth Amendment does not require that a suspect's attorney be present for any preindictment lineups conducted by the police for identification purposes.

United States v. Dionisio, 410 U.S. 1 (1973): The compelled production of a voice exemplar does not violate any portion of the Fourth Amendment. A grand jury subpoena does not constitute a "seizure." Consequently, a preliminary showing of reasonableness is not required when asking witnesses to provide voice and other noncommunicative exemplars. The compelled production of a voice exemplar does not violate the Fifth Amendment privilege against self-incrimination where such evidence is to be used for identification purposes and not for the testimonial or communicative content of the utterances.

Manson v. Brathwaite, 432 U.S. 98 (1977): The Fourteenth Amendment does not require the automatic exclusion of testimony based upon a police officer's identification of the defendant, even if it was obtained as the result of a procedure that may have been unnecessarily suggestive.

United States v. Crews, 445 U.S. 463 (1980): An in-court identification of a suspect by a witness is admissible even if the identification is the result of an illegal arrest when the witness's independent recollections of the suspect antedated the unlawful arrest.

Chapter Seventeen: Right to Counsel

Powell et al. v. Alabama, 287 U.S. 45 (1932): The denial of legal counsel in a capital case constitutes a violation of due process under the Fourteenth Amendment.

Gideon v. Wainwright, 372 U.S. 335 (1963): The Sixth Amendment requires the appointment of legal counsel to represent an indigent defendant facing prosecution on state felony charges.

Escobedo v. Illinois, 378 U.S. 478 (1964): The police must allow a suspect to speak with an attorney if one is requested during the course of a custodial interrogation.

Massiah v. United States, 377 U.S. 201 (1964): The Sixth Amendment prohibits the police from surreptitiously obtaining incriminating statements from a suspect who has previously been charged with a crime and retained an attorney.

United States v. Henry, 447 U.S. 264 (1980): The government cannot enlist the assistance of a jailhouse informant for purposes of gathering incriminating information from a criminal defendant.

Chapter Eighteen: The Development and Scope of the *Miranda* Warnings

Brown v. Mississippi, 297 U.S. 278 (1936): Confessions that are obtained by way of physical torture, coercion, or brutality on the part of law enforcement officials are not admissible at trial under the Fourteenth Amendment's due process clause.

Miranda v. Arizona, 384 U.S. 436 (1966): The police must inform a suspect of his or her constitutional right to legal representation and protection from self-incrimination during custodial interrogation. Any incriminating statements obtained in violation of these rights are inadmissible at trial.

Edwards v. Arizona, 451 U.S. 477 (1981): Officers may not reinitiate contact with a suspect who has previously invoked the right to remain silent and have the assistance of counsel during custodial interrogation. In other words, once a suspect states that he or she desires legal representation during the course of custodial interrogation, the questioning must stop immediately and may not resume until the request has been satisfied, even if only to inquire whether or not the individual has had a change of mind and wants to confess.

South Dakota v. Neville, 459 U.S. 553 (1983): Admission into evidence of a D.W.I. defendant's refusal to take a blood-alcohol test does not violate the Fifth Amendment right to avoid self-incrimination. The failure of an officer to inform a D.W.I. suspect that refusal to take a blood-alcohol test may be introduced at trial does not constitute a violation of due process.

Berkemer v. McCarty, 468 U.S. 420 (1984): The roadside questioning of a motorist who is detained pursuant to a lawful traffic stop does not constitute a custodial interrogation. Consequently, officers are not required to inform traffic violators of their *Miranda* rights.

New York v. Quarles, 467 U.S. 649 (1984): The concern for public safety clearly outweighs strict adherence to the principles of *Miranda.*

Oregon v. Elstad, 70 U.S. 298 (1985): A confession that is properly obtained subsequent to an unsolicited and unwarned statement is not automatically rendered inadmissible under the Fifth Amendment.

Michigan v. Jackson, 475 U.S. 625 (1986): The police may not interrogate a suspect who is in custody and has asked the court for assistance of counsel until he or she has had an opportunity to meet with an attorney. If officers initiate an interrogation, even without specific knowledge that a suspect has previously requested assistance of counsel during arraignment proceedings, any incriminating information obtained from such an encounter is inadmissible at trial.

Colorado v. Connelly, 479 U.S. 157 (1986): A suspect who is lacking a fully rational state of mind may validly waive his or her *Miranda* rights and, in the absence of any coercive police behavior, any incriminating statements are admissible under state rules of evidence.

Colorado v. Spring, 479 U.S. 564 (1987): The police are not required to provide suspects with advance notice of all possible topics of interrogation in order for a waiver of *Miranda* rights to be valid. In other words, the police do not have to tell a suspect which specific crime(s) they intend to ask questions about.

Connecticut v. Barrett, 79 U.S. 523 (1987): A suspect may validly waive portions of his or her *Miranda* rights and any statements (oral or written) may still be properly admitted into evidence at trial.

Patterson v. Illinois, 487 U.S. 285 (1988): A suspect who has been properly advised of his or her *Miranda* rights during postindictment questioning is deemed to have also been sufficiently informed of the accompanying Sixth Amendment right to counsel. A valid waiver of the *Miranda* rights simultaneously implicates both the Fifth Amendment right to remain silent as well as the Sixth Amendment right to counsel.

Arizona v. Roberson, 486 U.S. 675 (1988): The Supreme Court held that the previously established *Edwards* rule prohibits officers from initiating repeated interrogations of a suspect once he or she has invoked the Fifth Amendment right to counsel even if the subsequent interrogation focuses on an altogether separate offense.

Duckworth v. Eagan, 492 U.S. 195 (1989): It is not necessary for the *Miranda* warnings to be presented or recited exactly as they appeared in the original case.

Minnick v. Mississippi, 498 U.S. 146 (1990): When, during the course of custodial interrogation, a suspect asks for counsel, all questioning must immediately cease and may not resume until such time as counsel is present in the room.

Pennsylvania v. Muniz, 496 U.S. 582 (1990): Not only may the police ask routine questions of D.W.I. suspects during booking procedures, but they are also allowed to videotape the responses without having to first inform the arrestee of his or her *Miranda* rights.

Arizona v. Fulminante, 499 U.S. 279 (1991): The "harmless error" doctrine is applicable to cases involving the improper admission of an involuntary confession at trial.

McNeil v. Wisconsin, 501 U.S. 171 (1991): A request for assistance of counsel at a bail hearing does not constitute an invocation of the Fifth Amendment right to counsel under *Miranda* for other uncharged offenses.

Davis v. United States, 512 U.S. 452 (1994) Authorities may continue to question a suspect who has knowingly and voluntarily waived his or her *Miranda* rights until such time as he or she clearly asks for assistance of counsel.

Chapter Nineteen: What Constitutes Interrogation?

Brewer v. Williams, 430 U.S. 387 (1977): Officers are prohibited from appealing to a suspect's moral or religious beliefs for purposes of soliciting incriminating statements in the absence of legal representation.

Rhode Island v. Innis, 446 U.S. 291 (1980): The conversation between the two officers did not constitute an interrogation or its functional equivalent as the suspect was not directly involved in the exchange. Therefore, no Sixth Amendment right was either implicated or violated.

Arizona v. Mauro, 481 U.S. 520 (1987): The self-incrimination privilege of the Fifth Amendment does not forbid the introduction of incriminating statements made by a suspect to his or her spouse in the presence of a police officer, especially in instances where the suspect was not subjected to any compelling influences, psychological ploys, or direct questioning generally characteristic of custodial interrogation or its functional equivalent.

Chapter Twenty: Entrapment

Sherman v. United States, 356 U.S. 369 (1958): Entrapment occurs when the government induces a person to commit a crime that he or she would not have otherwise committed.

United States v. Russell, 411 U.S. 423 (1973): One cannot succeed with an entrapment defense if one was already predisposed to commit the crime in question.

Hampton v. United States, 425 U.S. 484 (1976): A person is not entrapped when, if he is predisposed to do so, he buys drugs from a government informant.

Mathews v. United States, 485 U.S. 58 (1988): A person can assert an entrapment defense even if he refuses to admit all elements of the crime in question.

Jacobson v. United States, 503 U.S. 540 (1992): Entrapment takes place when the government creates a person's disposition and then induces that person to commit the crime.

Chapter Twenty-One: Asset Forfeiture

United States v. Good, 510 U.S. 43 (1993): Unless exigent circumstances exist, the due process clause of the Fifth Amendment requires that the government provide notice to property owners and an opportunity to be heard before seizing real property.

United States v. Ursery, 518 U.S. 267 (1996): Civil forfeiture in addition to criminal prosecution does not violate the Fifth Amendment's double jeopardy clause.

Bennis v. Michigan, 516 U.S. 442 (1996): Civil forfeiture of property used for criminal activity can be constitutional even if the owner is not aware of its criminal use, provided that no innocent owner defense exists in state law.

United States v. Bajakajian, 524 U.S. 321 (1998): Forfeiture that is grossly disproportionate to the gravity of the offense is unconstitutional.

City of West Covina v. Perkins, 525 U.S. 234 (1999): The due process clause of the Fourteenth Amendment does not require the police to provide owners of seized property with notice about how to secure return of their property.

Florida v. White, 119 S.Ct. 1555 (1999): No warrant is necessary for the police to seize an automobile that is subject to forfeiture from a public place.

Chapter Twenty-Two: Civil Liability

Monroe v. Pape, 365 U.S. 167 (1961): 42 U.S.C. Section 1983 can serve as a cause of action against police officers who misuse their authority.

Monell v. Department of Social Services of New York, 436 U.S. 658 (1978): Local units of government can be held liable under 42 U.S.C. Section 1983 only when the constitutional violation is sanctioned by official municipal policy or custom.

Owen v. City of Independence, 445 U.S. 622 (1980): Municipalities can be held liable under 42 U.S.C. Section 1983 and cannot assert a good faith defense.

Briscoe v. LaHue, 460 U.S. 325 (1983): Police officers enjoy absolute immunity from civil liability when testifying, even if the testimony is perjured.

Malley v. Briggs, 475 U.S. 335 (1986): Individual police officers are only entitled to qualified immunity under Section 1983.

City of Canton v. Harris, 489 U.S. 378 (1989): Inadequate training can lead to municipal liability under Section 1983, but only if it amounts to deliberate indifference.

Will v. Michigan Department of State Police, 491 U.S. 58 (1989): Neither states nor state officials, acting in their official capacity, can be sued under Section 1983.

Hafer v. Melo, 502 U.S. 21 (1991): State officials who are sued in their individual capacity can be held liable under Section 1983.

Collins v. City of Harker Heights, 503 U.S. 115 (1992): A city's failure to warn its employees concerning hazards in the workplace cannot be held liable under Section 1983.

Board of the County Commissioners of Bryan County v. Brown, 520 U.S. 397 (1997): A county cannot be held liable under Section 1983 for a single hiring decision.

McMillian v. Monroe County, 520 U.S. 781 (1997): Whether a sheriff is a representative of the county or of the state is determined by the state's constitution, laws, or regulations.

County of Sacramento v. Lewis, 523 U.S. 833 (1998): A police officer will not be held liable for a substantive due process violation unless his or her conduct "shocks the conscience."

Saucier v. Katz, 533 U.S. 194 (2001): The questions of whether excessive force is used and whether qualified immunity should be granted are to be kept separate and are not fused into a single inquiry. ◆

Table of Cases

Introduction

The Supreme Court and the Police

All democratic societies question the level of authority over the individual citizen granted to the state. Social contract theory posits that, by choosing to live among others, individuals give up some of their liberty and permit the state to intervene in their lives. But how much? And in what manner? These questions are particularly relevant when the police, in the investigation of criminal activity, interfere with the liberty interests of citizens. While the criminal law sets forth the appropriate code of conduct for all citizens, criminal procedure comprises the rules governing the manner in which the state may go about depriving an individual of liberty. Criminal procedure includes when and in what manner law enforcement may detain, arrest, or search a person. It also includes when and how police may interrogate criminal suspects and conduct identification procedures.

Balancing the rights of the individual and the authority of the police is a difficult, but crucial, process. Packer (1964) asserts that there are two competing models of the criminal justice system: due process and crime control. The due process model is concerned primarily with protection of individual privacy. It emphasizes the importance of the formal legal process as a means of ensuring that mistakes are kept to a minimum and operates on the presumption of innocence. In contrast, the crime control model is primarily concerned with the reduction of crime and the protection of public order. It emphasizes the use of discretion and police power as a means of quickly and efficiently investigating and screening cases, and operates on the presumption of guilt. Criminal procedure law attempts to balance the differing goals of these two models, but it is a zero-sum game. Granting the police greater power to investigate crime means reducing individual liberty and privacy. Conversely, increasing individual rights may result in suspects who are factually guilty going free because the state is unable to prove legal guilt beyond a reasonable doubt, the burden of proof in criminal cases.

The United States Constitution, including the Bill of Rights and the Fourteenth Amendment, is the legal foundation for most criminal procedure decisions. The Bill of Rights sets forth 23 individual rights, and the Fourteenth Amendment guarantees of due process and equal protection have been interpreted by the United States Supreme Court to incorporate much of the Bill of Rights against state action. Originally, the Bill of Rights was conceived as applying only to the federal government, but during the twentieth century the Supreme Court has interpreted the due process clause of the Fourteenth Amendment to incorporate many of the individual rights contained in the Bill of Rights. Incorporation means that the individual right (such as the Fourth Amendment right to be free from unreasonable searches and seizures) is included in the Fourteenth Amendment's guarantees of due process and equal protection. Rights incorporated in the Fourteenth Amendment are those the Court has deemed "fundamental." These rights are applied against the states and include most of the criminal procedure-related provisions of the Fourth, Fifth, Sixth, and Eighth Amendments.

Other sources for criminal procedure law are state constitutions and federal and state statutes. States are free to provide more individual rights than the federal Constitution, but cannot abridge any federal constitutional rights. In the past, states were seen as somewhat less protective of the rights of criminal suspects. However, in recent years a number of state courts have interpreted their state constitutions as providing greater limitations on what the police may do. Consequently, criminal defendants may be accorded more rights and protections by state courts than by the United States Supreme Court.

As most criminal procedure law is derived from the provisions of the Bill of Rights, in particular the Fourth, Fifth, and Sixth Amendments, courts are frequently called upon to interpret the meaning of these Amendments and to apply them to current fact situations. For example, the Sixth Amendment prohibits compelling a person to testify against himself, but does requiring an individual to take a breathalyzer test or give a blood sample constitute testimony when the results may be used to prosecute him at trial? The Fourth Amendment prohibits the unreasonable seizure and search of persons, places and effects, but what is an "effect"? And what is "unreasonable"? Courts must answer these questions to determine when police officers have exceeded the scope of their authority, either intentionally or unintentionally. The United States Supreme Court has the final word on the constitutionality of any state action challenged as a violation of a constitutional right. Consequently, much of criminal procedure law is based on Supreme Court decisions. As courts decide only the case before them and do not issue policy directives, criminal procedure law has developed fitfully, on a case-by-case basis. Much of criminal procedure law has been written in the past 50 years since the Supreme Court began to apply the provisions of the Bill of Rights to the states, who conduct the bulk of criminal investigation and prosecution.

REFERENCES

Abrahamson, S.S. (1985). "Criminal Law and State Constitutions: The Emergence of State Constitutional Law." *Texas Law Review* 63: 1141.

Amar, A.R. (1994). "Fourth Amendment First Principles." *Harvard Law Review* 107: 757.

Caplan, G.M. (1985). "Questioning Miranda." *Vanderbilt Law Review* 38: 1417.

Cuddihy, W. (1990). "The Fourth Amendment: Origins and Original Meaning." Claremont, CA. Unpublished doctoral dissertation.

Grano, J.D. (1974). "Kirby, Biggers and Ash: Do Any Constitutional Safeguards Remain Against the Danger of Convicting the Innocent?" *Michigan Law Review* 72: 717.

Hemmens, C. (1997). "The Police, the Fourth Amendment, and Unannounced Entry: *Wilson v. Arkansas*." *Criminal Law Bulletin* 33(1): 29.

Hemmens, C., and J.R. Maahs. (1996). "Reason to Believe: When Does Detention End and a Consensual Encounter Begin? An Analysis of *Ohio v. Robinette*." *Ohio Northern Law Review* 23(2): 309.

Hemmens, C., R.V. del Carmen, and K.E. Scarborough. (1997). "Grave Doubts About 'Reasonable Doubt': Confusion in State and Federal Courts." *Journal of Criminal Justice* 25(3): 231.

LaFave, W.R. (1996). *Search and Seizure: A Treatise on the Fourth Amendment* (3rd edition). Minneapolis, MN: West.

Loewy, A.H. (1989). "Police-Obtained Evidence and the Constitution: Distinguishing Unconstitutionally Obtained Evidence from Unconstitutionally Used Evidence." *Michigan Law Review* 87: 907.

Mertens, W.J., and S. Wasserstrom. (1981). "The Good Faith Exception to the Exclusionary Rule: Deregulating the Police and Derailing the Law." *Georgetown Law Journal* 70: 365.

Packer, H. (1964). "Two Models of the Criminal Process." *University of Pennsylvania Law Review* 113: 1.

Schulhofer, S.J. (1987). "Reconsidering Miranda." *University of Chicago Law Review* 54: 435.

Slobogin, C., and J.E. Schumacher. (1993). "Reasonable Expectations of Privacy and Autonomy in Fourth Amendment Cases: An Empirical Look at 'Understandings Recognized and Permitted By Society.'" *Duke Law Journal* 42: 727.

Stuntz, W.J. (1992). "Implicit Bargains, Government Power, and the Fourth Amendment." *Stanford Law Review* 44: 553. ✦

Chapter One

The Exclusionary Rule

Introduction

The exclusionary rule provides that evidence obtained by law enforcement officers in violation of the Fourth Amendment guarantee against unreasonable searches and seizures is not admissible in a criminal trial to prove guilt. The primary purpose of the exclusionary rule is to deter police misconduct. While some proponents argue that the rule emanates from the Constitution, the Supreme Court has indicated that it is merely a judicially created remedy for violations of the Fourth Amendment.

The exclusionary rule is perhaps the most controversial legal issue in criminal justice. Application of the rule may lead to the exclusion of important evidence and the acquittal of persons who are factually, if not legally, guilty. Consequently, the exclusionary rule has been the subject of intense debate. Proponents argue it is the only effective means of protecting individual rights from police misconduct, while critics decry the exclusion from trial of relevant evidence. Despite calls for its abolition and shifts in the composition of the Supreme Court, the exclusionary rule remains entrenched in American jurisprudence. But while the rule has survived, it has not gone unscathed. Supreme Court decisions over the years have limited the scope of the rule, and created several exceptions.

The United States Supreme Court first addressed the issue of the admissibility of illegally obtained evidence in 1886, when it held in *Boyd v. United States*, 116 U.S. 616, that the forced disclosure of papers amounting to evidence of crimes violated the constitutional right of the defendant against unreasonable search and seizures, so such items were inadmissible in court proceedings. In 1914 the Supreme Court held in *Weeks v. United States*, that evidence illegally obtained by federal law enforcement officers was not admissible in a federal criminal trial. At the time the Fourth Amendment did not apply to the states, only the federal government. Because the Weeks decision applied only against the federal government, state law enforcement officers were still free to seize evidence illegally without fear of exclusion in state criminal proceedings. In addition, evidence seized illegally by state police could be turned over to federal law enforcement officers for use in federal prosecutions, as long as federal officers were not directly involved in the illegal seizure. This was known as the "silver platter" doctrine because illegally seized evidence could be turned over to federal law enforcement officers "as if on a silver platter" (LaFave and Israel 1992). In 1960, in *Elkins v. United States*, 364 U.S. 206, the Court put an end to this practice, prohibiting the introduction of illegally seized evidence in federal prosecutions regardless of whether the illegality was committed by state or federal agents.

In 1949, in *Wolf v. Colorado*, 338 U.S. 25, the Supreme Court applied the Fourth Amendment to the states, incorporating it into the due process clause of the Fourteenth Amendment. However, the Court refused to mandate the remedy of the exclusionary rule. Just three years later the Court modified its position somewhat, holding in *Rochin v. California* that evidence seized in a manner which "shocked the conscience" must be excluded as violative of due process. Exactly what type of conduct shocked the conscience was left to be determined on a case-by-case basis. The exclusionary rule thus became applicable to state criminal proceedings, but its application was uneven.

Finally, in 1961, in *Mapp v. Ohio*, the Court took the step it failed to in *Wolf* and explicitly applied the remedy of the exclusionary rule to the states. The Court did so because it acknowledged the states had failed to provide an adequate alternative remedy for violations of the Fourth Amendment. While there was language in *Mapp* that suggested the exclusionary rule originated from the Constitution and was not merely a judicially created remedy, subsequent decisions indicate the Court views the rule not as part of the Constitution, but rather a means of enforcing the Fourth Amendment prohibition against unreasonable searches and seizures.

The Supreme Court in *Mapp* stated that the exclusionary rule serves at least two purposes: the deterrence of police misconduct and the protection of judicial integrity. In recent years, however, the Court has focused almost entirely upon the deterrence of police misconduct, leading to the creation of several exceptions to the rule. Additionally, the Court has held that the exclusionary rule does not apply to a variety of proceedings other than the criminal trial.

In 1984 the Court held in *Massachusetts v. Sheppard* that evidence obtained by the police acting in good faith on a search warrant issued by a neutral and detached magistrate that is ultimately found to be invalid may nonetheless be admitted at trial. The Court stressed that the primary rationale for the exclusionary rule—deterrence of police misconduct—did not warrant exclusion of evidence obtained by police who act reasonably and in good-faith reliance upon the actions of a judge. By "good faith," the Court meant the police are unaware that the warrant is invalid.

The Court emphasized that the good-faith exception did not apply to errors made by the police, even if the errors were entirely inadvertent. The exception applies only to situations where the police relied on others who, it later turns out, made a mistake. Subsequent cases reiterated this point. In 1995, in *Arizona v. Evans,* the Court refused to apply the exclusionary rule to evidence seized by a police officer who acted in reliance on a computer entry, made by a court clerk, which was later found to be in error.

The Court has also established the "inevitable discovery" exception to the exclusionary rule. This exception, developed in *Nix v. Williams,* permits the use at trial of evidence illegally obtained by the police if they can demonstrate that they would have discovered the evidence anyway by legal means. The burden is on the police to prove they would in fact have discovered the evidence lawfully. Police have only infrequently been able to successfully establish this exception.

The Court has been reluctant to extend the reach of the exclusionary rule to proceedings other than criminal trials. The Court has consistently refused to apply the exclusionary rule to evidence seized by private parties, if they are not acting in concert with or at the behest of the police. The rule does not apply to evidence presented to the grand jury. An unlawful arrest does not bar prosecution of the arrestee, as the exclusionary rule is an evidentiary rule rather than a rule of jurisdictional limitation. The rule is inapplicable in both civil tax as-sessment proceedings and civil deportation proceedings. The exclusionary rule does not apply to parole revocation hearings.

The Court has also been reluctant to apply the exclusionary rule to aspects of the criminal trial which are not directly related to the determination of guilt. Thus, illegally obtained evidence may be used to impeach a defendant's testimony, or to determine the appropriate sentence for a convicted defendant.

REFERENCES

Amar, A.R. (1997). *The Constitution and Criminal Procedure.* New Haven, CT: Yale University Press.

Cole, D. (1999). *No Equal Justice.* New York: The New Press.

Decker, J.F. (1992). *Revolution to the Right: Criminal Procedure Jurisprudence During the Burger-Rehnquist Court Era.* New York: Garland.

LaFave, W.R., and J.H. Israel. (1992). *Criminal Procedure* (2nd edition). Minneapolis, MN: West Publishing. ✦

WEEKS V. UNITED STATES
232 U.S. 383 (1914)

FACTS

Weeks was arrested by a police officer without a warrant at the Union Station in Kansas City, Missouri, where he was employed by an express company. Other police officers had gone to the Weeks' house, and being told by a neighbor where the key was kept, found it and entered the house. They searched Weeks' room and took possession of various papers and articles found there, which were afterwards turned over to the United States Marshal. Later the same day police officers returned with the marshal, who thought he might find additional evidence, and, being admitted by someone in the house, probably a boarder, the marshal searched Weeks' room and carried away certain letters and envelopes found in the drawer of a chiffonier. Neither the marshal nor the police officer had a search warrant. Weeks was convicted of unlawful use of the mail, and the U.S. Supreme Court granted certiorari.

ISSUE

Is evidence that is illegally seized by the police admissible at trial?

HOLDING

No. The letters in question were taken from the house of the accused by an official of the United States, acting under color of his office, in direct violation of the constitutional rights of the defendant.

RATIONALE

"The right of the court to deal with papers and documents in the possession of the district attorney and other officers of the court, and subject to its authority, was recognized in an earlier case. That papers wrongfully seized should be turned over to the accused has been frequently recognized in the early as well as later decisions of the courts. In holding them and permitting their use upon the trial, we think prejudicial error was committed. As to the papers and property seized by the policemen, it does not appear that they acted under any claim of Federal authority such as would make the amendment applicable to such unauthorized seizures. . . . What remedies the defendant may have against them we need not inquire, as the Fourth Amendment is not directed to individual misconduct of such officials. Its limitations reach the Federal government and its agencies."

CASE SIGNIFICANCE

This case established the exclusionary rule, and applied it to the actions of federal law enforcement officers. The Supreme Court stopped short of applying the rule to state law enforcement officers, however, as the Court at this time had not yet incorporated the Fourth Amendment into the due process clause of the Fourteenth Amendment.

ROCHIN V. CALIFORNIA
342 U.S. 165 (1952)

FACTS

Having "some information" that Rochin was selling narcotics, three police officers entered his home and forced their way into the bedroom where Rochin and his wife were standing. When he was asked by the police about two capsules lying on the bedside table, Rochin put them in his mouth. After an unsuccessful struggle to extract them by force, the officers took Rochin to a hospital, where an emetic was forced into his stomach against his will. He vomited two capsules, which were found to contain morphine. These were admitted in evidence over his objection and he was convicted in a state court of violating a state law forbidding possession of morphine. The U.S. Supreme Court then granted certiorari.

ISSUE

Did the actions of the officers violate the limitations which the due process clause of the Fourteenth Amendment imposes on the conduct of criminal proceedings by the states?

HOLDING

Yes. The methods used by the police violated the due process clause of the Fourteenth Amendment.

RATIONALE

"The proceedings by which this conviction was obtained more than offends some fastidious squeamishness or private sentimentalism about combating crime too energetically. This is conduct that shocks the conscience. Illegally breaking into the privacy of the petitioner, the struggle to open his mouth and remove what was there, the forcible extraction of his stomach's contents—this course of proceeding by agents of government to obtain evidence is bound to offend even hardened sensibilities. They are methods too close to the rack and the screw to permit of constitutional differentiation. Due process of law, as a historic and generative principle, precludes defining, and thereby confining, these standards of conduct more precisely than to say that convictions cannot be brought about by methods that offend 'a sense of justice.' It would be a stultification of the responsibility which the course of constitutional history has cast upon this Court to hold that in order to convict a man the police cannot extract by force what is in his mind but can extract what is in his stomach. To attempt in this case to distinguish what lawyers call 'real evidence' from verbal evidence is to ignore the reasons for excluding coerced confessions. Use of involuntary verbal confessions in State criminal trials is constitutionally obnoxious not only because of their unreliability. They are inadmissible under the Due Process Clause even though statements contained in them may be independently established as true. Coerced confessions offend the community's sense of fair play and decency. So here, to sanction the brutal conduct which naturally enough was condemned by the court whose judgment is before us, would be to afford brutality the cloak of law. Nothing would be more calculated to discredit law and thereby to brutalize the temper of a society."

CASE SIGNIFICANCE

In this case the Supreme Court chose not to apply the federal exclusionary rule against the states (this was not done until *Mapp v. Ohio* in 1961), but to rely on the due process clause to overturn the conviction. The end result is the same. Today the evidence would be excluded through application of the exclusionary rule.

Mapp v. Ohio
367 U.S. 643 (1961)

Facts

Cleveland police officers arrived at Mapp's home and sought consent to search it for a bombing suspect. When she refused consent, officers showed Mapp a piece of paper that they claimed was a search warrant. Mapp took this piece of paper and placed it in her bosom. A struggle ensued in which the officers recovered the piece of paper and as a result of which they handcuffed appellant because she had been "belligerent" in resisting their official rescue of the "warrant" from her person. Mapp was then forcibly taken upstairs to her bedroom where the officers searched a dresser, a chest of drawers, a closet and some suitcases. They also looked into a photo album and through personal papers belonging to her. The search spread to the rest of the home. Police officers eventually found several drawings of nude individuals, and charged Mapp with possession of obscene materials. At the trial no search warrant was produced by the prosecution, nor was the failure to produce one explained or accounted for. Mapp was convicted of possession of obscene materials; she appealed, and the U.S. Supreme Court granted certiorari.

Issue

Should the evidence found in Mapp's home have been inadmissible at trial, thereby making the Fourth Amendment enforceable upon the states based on the due process clause of the Fourteenth Amendment?

Holding

Yes. All evidence obtained by searches and seizures in violation of the federal Constitution is inadmissible in a criminal trial in a state court.

Rationale

"Since the Fourth Amendment's right of privacy has been declared enforceable against the States through the Due Process Clause of the Fourteenth, it is enforceable against them by the same sanction of exclusion as is used against the Federal Government. Were it otherwise, then just as without the Weeks rule the assurance against unreasonable federal searches and seizures would be 'a form of words,' valueless and undeserving of mention in a perpetual charter of inestimable human liberties, so too, without that rule the freedom from state invasions of privacy would be so ephemeral and so neatly severed from its conceptual nexus with the freedom from all brutish means of coercing evi-dence as not to merit this Court's high regard as a freedom 'implicit in the concept of ordered liberty.'"

Case Significance

This ruling basically overturned the decision in *Wolf v. Colorado* (1949), which left a shortcut to conviction open to the state, which, according to the Court, "tends to destroy the entire system of constitutional restraints on which the liberties of the people rest." This ruling imposed the exclusionary rule (*Weeks v. United States*) upon the states.

Wong Sun v. United States
371 U.S. 471 (1963)

Facts

In a trial in a federal district court without a jury, petitioners were convicted of fraudulent and knowing transportation and concealment of illegally imported heroin, in violation of 21 U.S.C. 174. Although the court of appeals held that the arrests of both petitioners without warrants were illegal, because not based on "probable cause" within the meaning of the Fourth Amendment nor "reasonable grounds" within the meaning of the Narcotics Control Act of 1956, it affirmed their convictions, notwithstanding the admission in evidence over their timely objections of (1) statements made orally by petitioner Toy in his bedroom at the time of his arrest; (2) heroin surrendered to the agents by a third party as a result of those statements; and (3) unsigned statements made by each petitioner several days after his arrest, and after being lawfully arraigned and released on his own recognizance. The court of appeals held that these items were not the fruits of the illegal arrests, and, therefore, were properly admitted in evidence. The U.S. Supreme Court then granted certiorari.

Issue

Was the court of appeals incorrect in its holding that these items were not the fruits of illegal arrests, and, therefore, admissible in court?

Holding

Yes. The court of appeals was incorrect. Evidence obtained indirectly as a result of an unlawful arrest or search is not admissible.

Rationale

"There was neither reasonable grounds nor probable cause for Toy's arrest, since the information upon which it was based was too vague and came from too untested a source to accept it as probable cause for the issuance of an arrest warrant; and this defect was not cured by the fact that Toy fled when a supposed customer at his door early in the morning revealed that he was a narcotics agent. In view of the fact that, after his unlawful arrest, petitioner Wong Sun had been lawfully arraigned and released on his own recognizance and had returned voluntarily several days later when he made his unsigned statement, the connection between his unlawful arrest and the making of that statement was so attenuated that the unsigned statement was not the fruit of the unlawful arrest and, therefore, it was properly admitted in evidence. . . . The statements made by Toy in his bedroom at the time of his unlawful arrest were the fruits of the agents' unlawful action, and they should have been excluded from evidence. The narcotics taken from a third party as a result of statements made by Toy at the time of his arrest were likewise fruits of the unlawful arrest, and they should not have been admitted as evidence against Toy. . . . The seizure of the narcotics admitted in evidence invaded no right of privacy of person or premises, which would entitle Wong Sun to object to its use at his trial."

Case Significance

This case dealt with the "purged taint" exception to the exclusionary rule. Under the exclusionary rule, evidence which is seized in violation of the Fourth Amendment is excluded from evidence. Under the purged taint exception, however, if the prosecution can demonstrate that evidence was obtained in a manner unrelated to the illegal police activity, it may be admitted.

United States v. Crews
445 U.S. 463 (1980)

Facts

Immediately after being assaulted and robbed at gunpoint, the victim notified the police and gave them a full description of her assailant. Several days later, Crews, who matched the suspect's description, was seen by the police. Crews was taken into custody, ostensibly as a suspected truant from school, and was detained at police headquarters, where he was questioned, photographed, and then released. Thereafter, the victim identified Crews' photograph as that of her assailant. Crews was again taken into custody and at a court-ordered lineup was identified by the victim. Crews was then indicted for armed robbery and other offenses. On Crews' pretrial motion to suppress all identification testimony, the trial court found that his initial detention at the police station constituted an arrest without probable cause and accordingly ruled that the products of that arrest—the photographic and lineup identifications—could not be introduced at trial, but further held that the victim's ability to identify Crews in court was based upon independent recollection untainted by the intervening identifications and that therefore such testimony was admissible. At trial, the victim once more identified Crews as her assailant, and Crews was convicted of armed robbery. The District of Columbia Court of Appeals reversed, holding that the in-court identification testimony should have been excluded as a product of the violation of Crews' Fourth Amendment rights. The U.S. Supreme Court then granted certiorari.

Issue

Is the in-court identification of a suspect by a witness, when the identification is the result of an illegal arrest, admissible?

Holding

Yes. The in-court identification is admissible because the police's knowledge of Crews' identity and the victim's independent recollections of him both antedated the unlawful arrest and were thus untainted by the constitutional violation.

Rationale

"The victim's presence in the courtroom at Crews' trial was not the product of any police misconduct. Her identity was known long before there was any official misconduct, and her presence in court was thus not traceable to any Fourth Amendment violation. Nor did the illegal arrest infect the victim's ability to give accurate identification testimony. At trial, she merely retrieved her mnemonic representation of the assailant formed at the time of the crime, compared it to the figure of Crews in the courtroom, and positively identified him as the robber. Insofar as Crews challenges his own presence at trial, he cannot claim immunity from prosecution simply because his appearance in court was precipitated by an unlawful arrest. Crews is not himself a suppressible 'fruit,' and the illegality of his detention cannot deprive the Government of the opportunity to prove his guilt through the introduction of evidence wholly untainted by the police misconduct."

Case Significance

This case dealt with the "independent source" exception to the exclusionary rule. Under this exception, evidence related to an illegal police search may still be admitted at trial, if the prosecution can demonstrate that the evidence could have been obtained without the police misconduct.

NIX V. WILLIAMS
467 U.S. 431 (1984)

FACTS

Following the disappearance of a 10-year-old girl in Des Moines, Iowa, Williams was arrested and arraigned in Davenport, Iowa. The police informed Williams' counsel that they would drive Williams back to Des Moines without questioning him, but during the trip one of the officers began a conversation with Williams that ultimately resulted in his making incriminating statements and directing the officers to the child's body. A systematic search of the area that was being conducted with the aid of 200 volunteers and that had been initiated before Williams made the incriminating statements was terminated when Williams guided police to the body. Before trial in an Iowa state court for first-degree murder, the court denied Williams' motion to suppress evidence of the body and all related evidence, including the body's condition as shown by an autopsy, Williams having contended that such evidence was the fruit of his illegally obtained statements made during the automobile ride. Williams was convicted, and the Iowa Supreme Court affirmed, but later federal court habeas corpus proceedings ultimately resulted in the Supreme Court holding that the police had obtained Williams' incriminating statements through interrogation in violation of his Sixth Amendment right to counsel. However, it was noted that even though the statements could not be admitted at a second trial, evidence of the body's location and condition might be admissible on the theory that the body would have been discovered even if the incriminating statements had not been elicited from Williams. At Williams' second state court trial, his incriminating statements were not offered in evidence, nor did the prosecution seek to show that Williams had directed the police to the child's body. However, evidence concerning the body's location and condition was admitted, the court having concluded that the state had proved that if the search had continued the body would have been discovered within a short time in essentially the same condition as it was actually found. Williams was again convicted of first-degree murder, and the Iowa Supreme Court affirmed. In subsequent habeas corpus proceedings, the federal district court, denying relief, also concluded that the body inevitably would have been found. However, the court of appeals reversed, holding that—even assuming that there is an inevitable discovery exception to the exclusionary rule—the state had not met the exception's requirement that it be proved that the police did not act in bad faith. The U.S. Supreme Court then granted certiorari.

ISSUE

Was the body admissible at trial under the inevitable discovery exception to the exclusionary rule?

HOLDING

Yes. The evidence pertaining to the discovery and condition of the victim's body was properly admitted at Williams' second trial on the grounds that it would ultimately or inevitably have been discovered even if no violation of any constitutional provision had taken place.

RATIONALE

The core rationale for extending the exclusionary rule to evidence that is the fruit of unlawful police conduct is that such course is needed to deter police from violations of constitutional and statutory protections notwithstanding the high social cost of letting obviously guilty persons go unpunished. On this rationale, the prosecution is not to be put in a better position than it would have been in if no illegality had transpired. By contrast, the independent source doctrine—allowing admission of evidence that has been discovered by means wholly independent of any constitutional violation—rests on the rationale that society's interest in deterring unlawful police conduct and the public interest in having juries receive all probative evidence of a crime are properly balanced by putting the police in the same, not a worse, position that they would have been in if no police error or misconduct had occurred. Although the independent source doctrine does not apply here, its rationale is wholly consistent with and justifies adoption of the ultimate or inevitable discovery exception to the exclusionary rule. If the prosecution can establish by a preponderance of the evidence that the information ultimately or inevitably would have been discovered by lawful means—here the volunteers' search—then the deterrence rationale has so little basis that the evidence should be received. Under the inevitable discovery exception, the prosecution is not required to prove the absence of bad faith, since such a requirement would result in withholding from juries relevant and undoubted truth that would have been available to police absent any unlawful police activity. This would put the police in a worse position than they would have been in if no unlawful conduct had transpired, and would fail to take into account the enormous societal cost of excluding evidence in the search for truth in the administration of justice. Significant disincentives to obtaining evidence illegally—including the possibility of departmental discipline and civil liability—lessen the likelihood that the ultimate or inevitable discovery exception will promote police misconduct. The record here supports the finding that the search party ultimately or inevitably would have discovered the victim's body. The evidence clearly shows that the searchers were approaching the actual location of the body, that the search would have been resumed had Williams not led the police to the body, and that the body inevitably would have been found.

Case Significance

This case was an example of the "inevitable discovery" exception to the exclusionary rule. This exception is rarely used, as it is difficult to prove except in cases such as this one, where the police are searching for something at the time that the constitutional violation takes place.

United States v. Leon
468 U.S. 897 (1984)

Facts

Acting on the basis of information obtained from a confidential informant, officers of the Burbank (California) Police Department initiated a drug-trafficking investigation involving surveillance of Leon's activities. Based on an affidavit summarizing the police officers' observations, a search warrant for three residences and several automobiles was obtained. The search warrant application was reviewed by several deputy district attorneys and a judge. Ensuing searches produced large quantities of drugs and other evidence. Leon was indicted for several federal drug offenses, and filed motions to suppress the evidence seized pursuant to the warrant. The district court granted the motions in part, concluding that the affidavit was insufficient to establish probable cause. Although recognizing that the police had acted in good faith, the court rejected the government's suggestion that the Fourth Amendment exclusionary rule should not apply where evidence is seized in reasonable, good-faith reliance on a search warrant. The court of appeals affirmed, also refusing the government's invitation to recognize a good-faith exception to the exclusionary rule. The U.S. Supreme Court then granted certiorari.

Issue

Should the Fourth Amendment exclusionary rule be applied to evidence gathered by law enforcement officers acting in good faith on a warrant later deemed to be invalid?

Holding

No. The Fourth Amendment exclusionary rule should not be applied so as to bar the use in the prosecution's case in chief of evidence obtained by officers acting in reasonable reliance on a search warrant issued by a detached and neutral magistrate but ultimately found to be invalid.

Rationale

"An examination of the Fourth Amendment's origin and purposes makes clear that the use of fruits of a past unlawful search or seizure works no new Fourth Amendment wrong. The question whether the exclusionary sanction is appropriately imposed in a particular case as a judicially created remedy to safeguard Fourth Amendment rights through its deterrent effect, must be resolved by weighing the costs and benefits of preventing the use in the prosecution's case in chief of inherently trustworthy tangible evidence. Indiscriminate application of the exclusionary rule—impeding the criminal justice system's truth-finding function and allowing some guilty defendants to go free—may well generate disrespect for the law and the administration of justice. Application of the exclusionary rule should continue where a Fourth Amendment violation has been substantial and deliberate, but the balancing approach that has evolved in determining whether the rule should be applied in a variety of contexts—including criminal trials—suggests that the rule should be modified to permit the introduction of evidence obtained by officers reasonably relying on a warrant issued by a detached and neutral magistrate. The deference accorded to a magistrate's finding of probable cause for the issuance of a warrant does not preclude inquiry into the knowing or reckless falsity of the affidavit on which that determination was based, and the courts must also insist that the magistrate purport to perform his neutral and detached function and not serve merely as a rubber stamp for the police. Moreover, reviewing courts will not defer to a warrant based on an affidavit that does not provide the magistrate with a substantial basis for determining the existence of probable cause. However, the exclusionary rule is designed to deter police misconduct rather than to punish the errors of judges and magistrates. Admitting evidence obtained pursuant to a warrant while at the same time declaring that the warrant was somehow defective will not reduce judicial officers' professional incentives to comply with the Fourth Amendment, encourage them to repeat their mistakes, or lead to the granting of all colorable warrant requests. Even assuming that the exclusionary rule effectively deters some police misconduct and provides incentives for the law enforcement profession as a whole to conduct itself in accord with the Fourth Amendment, it cannot be expected, and should not be applied, to deter objectively reasonable law enforcement activity. In the ordinary case, an officer cannot be expected to question the magistrate's probable-cause determination or his judgment that the form of the warrant is technically sufficient. Once the warrant issues, there is literally nothing more the policeman can do in seeking to comply with the law, and penalizing the officer for the magistrate's error, rather than his own, cannot logically contribute to the deterrence of Fourth Amendment violations. A police officer's reliance on the magistrate's probable-cause determination and on the technical sufficiency of the warrant he issues must be objectively reasonable. Suppression remains an appropriate remedy if the magistrate or judge in issuing a warrant was misled by information in an affidavit that the affiant knew was false or would have known was false except for his reckless disregard of the truth, or if the issuing magistrate wholly abandoned his detached and neutral judicial role. Nor would an officer manifest objective good faith in relying on a warrant based on an affidavit so lacking in indicia of probable cause as to render official belief in its existence entirely unreasonable. Finally, depending on the circumstances of the particular case, a warrant may be so facially deficient—i.e., in failing to particularize the place to be searched or the things to be seized—that the executing officers cannot reasonably presume it to be valid."

CASE SIGNIFICANCE

This case, and *Massachusetts v. Sheppard,* decided the same day, are very important because they create the so-called "good-faith" exception to the exclusionary rule. This exception allows the introduction at trial of evidence that was seized in violation of the Fourth Amendment, so long as it can be shown that the police were unaware of the violation and relied in good faith on the actions of others—in this instance, a judge who issued the search warrant. It is important to recognize that the good-faith exception does not apply when the police knowingly or mistakenly violate the Fourth Amendment.

MASSACHUSETTS V. SHEPPARD
468 U.S. 981 (1984)

FACTS

On the basis of evidence gathered in the investigation of a homicide in the Roxbury section of Boston, a police detective drafted an affidavit to support an application for an arrest warrant and a search warrant authorizing the search of Sheppard's residence. The affidavit stated that the police wished to search for certain described items, including the victim's clothing and a blunt instrument that might have been used on the victim. The affidavit was reviewed and approved by the district attorney. Because it was Sunday, the local court was closed, and the police had a difficult time finding a warrant application form. The detective finally found a warrant form previously used in another district to search for controlled substances. After making some changes in the form, the detective presented it and the affidavit to a judge at his residence, informing him that the warrant form might need to be further changed. Concluding that the affidavit established probable cause to search Sheppard's residence and telling the detective that the necessary changes in the warrant form would be made, the judge made some changes, but did not change the substantive portion, which continued to authorize a search for controlled substances; nor did he alter the form so as to incorporate the affidavit. The judge then signed the warrant and returned it and the affidavit to the detective, informing him that the warrant was sufficient authority in form and content to carry out the requested search. The ensuing search of Sheppard's residence by the detective and other police officers was limited to the items listed in the affidavit, and several incriminating pieces of evidence were discovered. Thereafter, Sheppard was charged with first-degree murder. At a pretrial suppression hearing, the trial judge ruled that while the warrant was defective in that it did not particularly describe the items to be seized, the incriminating evidence could be admitted because the police had acted in good faith in executing what they reasonably thought was a valid warrant. At the subsequent trial, Sheppard was convicted. The Massachusetts Supreme Judicial Court held that the evidence should have been suppressed, and the U.S. Supreme Court granted certiorari.

ISSUE

Should evidence that is obtained based on a search warrant that is invalid because of a mistake made by a judge be excluded from trial?

HOLDING

No. Federal law does not require the exclusion of the disputed evidence when the police are not responsible for the error, and act in "good faith" in executing the warrant.

RATIONALE

"The exclusionary rule should not be applied when the officer conducting the search acted in objectively reasonable reliance on a warrant issued by a detached and neutral magistrate that subsequently is determined to be invalid. Here, there was an objectively reasonable basis for the officers' mistaken belief that the warrant authorized the search they conducted. The officers took every step that could reasonably be expected of them. At the point where the judge returned the affidavit and warrant to the detective, a reasonable police officer would have concluded, as the detective did, that the warrant authorized a search for the materials outlined in the affidavit. A police officer is not required to disbelieve a judge who has just advised him that the warrant he possesses authorizes him to conduct the search he has requested.

"An error of constitutional dimensions may have been committed with respect to the issuance of the warrant in this case, but it was the judge, not the police officer, who made the critical mistake. Suppressing evidence because the judge failed to make all the necessary clerical corrections despite his assurance that such changes would be made will not serve the deterrent function that the exclusionary rule was designed to achieve."

Case Significance

This case and *United States v. Leon*, decided the same day, were very important because they created the so-called "good-faith" exception to the exclusionary rule. This exception allows the introduction at trial of evidence that was seized in violation of the Fourth Amendment, so long as it can be shown that the police were unaware of the violation and relied in good faith on the actions of others—in this instance, a judge who issued the search warrant. It is important to recognize the good-faith exception does not apply when the police knowingly or mistakenly violate the Fourth Amendment.

Murray v. United States
487 U.S. 533 (1988)

Facts

While surveilling Murray and others suspected of illegal drug activities, federal agents observed Murray and a coconspirator driving vehicles into, and later out of, a warehouse, and upon the suspect's exit saw that the warehouse contained a tractor-trailer rig bearing a long container. Murray and his coconspirator later turned over their vehicles to other drivers, who were in turn followed and ultimately arrested, and the vehicles were lawfully seized and found to contain marijuana. After receiving this information, several agents forced their way into the warehouse without a search warrant and observed in plain view numerous burlap-wrapped bales. The agents left without disturbing the bales and did not return until they had obtained a warrant to search the warehouse. In applying for the warrant, they did not mention the prior entry or include any recitations of their observations made during that entry. Upon issuance of the warrant, they reentered the warehouse and seized 270 bales of marijuana and other evidence of crime. The district court denied petitioners' pretrial motion to suppress the evidence, rejecting their arguments that the warrant was invalid because the agents did not inform the magistrate about their prior warrantless entry, and that the warrant was tainted by that entry. The petitioners were subsequently convicted of conspiracy to possess and distribute illegal drugs. The court of appeals affirmed, assuming for purposes of its decision on the suppression question that the first entry into the warehouse was unlawful. The U.S. Supreme Court then granted certiorari.

Issue

Must evidence discovered by an illegal entry be suppressed, even if that same evidence is also discovered later pursuant to a valid warrant?

Holding

No. The Fourth Amendment does not require the suppression of evidence initially discovered during police officers' illegal entry of private premises, if that evidence is also discovered during a later search pursuant to a valid warrant that is wholly independent of the initial illegal entry.

Rationale

"The 'independent source' doctrine permits the introduction of evidence initially discovered during, or as a consequence of, an unlawful search, but later obtained independently from lawful activities untainted by the initial illegality. There is no merit to petitioners' contention that allowing the doctrine to apply to evidence initially discovered during an illegal search, rather than limiting it to evidence first obtained during a later lawful search, will encourage police routinely to enter premises without a warrant. Although the federal agents' knowledge that marijuana was in the warehouse was assuredly acquired at the time of the unlawful entry, it was also acquired at the time of entry pursuant to the warrant, and if that later acquisition was not the result of the earlier entry, the independent source doctrine allows the admission of testimony as to that knowledge. This same analysis applies to the tangible evidence, the bales of marijuana. The ultimate question is whether the search pursuant to warrant was in fact a genuinely independent source of the information and tangible evidence at issue. This would not have been the case if the agents' decision to seek the warrant was prompted by what they had seen during the initial entry or if information obtained during that entry was presented to the Magistrate and affected his decision to issue the warrant."

Case Significance

This case was an example of the "independent source" exception to the exclusionary rule. An illegal search would normally preclude the admission into evidence of any evidence discovered, but under this exception if the police can obtain a valid search warrant and go back and search again, then what they find may be admitted.

Minnesota v. Olson
495 U.S. 91 (1990)

Facts

Police suspected Olson of being the driver of the getaway car used in a robbery-murder. After recovering the murder weapon and arresting the suspected murderer, they surrounded the home of two women with whom they believed Olson had been staying, based on an anonymous tip. When police telephoned the home and told one of the women that Olson should come out, a male voice was heard saying, "Tell them I left." Without seeking permission and with weapons drawn, the officers entered the home, found Olson hiding in a closet, and arrested him. Shortly thereafter, he made an incriminating statement, which the trial court refused to suppress. He was convicted of murder, armed robbery, and assault. The Minnesota Supreme Court reversed, ruling that Olson had a sufficient interest in the women's home to challenge the legality of his warrantless arrest, that the arrest was illegal because there were no exigent circumstances to justify warrantless entry, and that his statement was tainted and should have been suppressed. The U.S. Supreme Court then granted certiorari.

Issue

May police officers lawfully make a warrantless, nonconsensual entry without an exigent circumstance?

Holding

No. The arrest violated Olson's Fourth Amendment rights. An overnight guest has a reasonable expectation of privacy.

Rationale

"Olson's status as an overnight guest is alone sufficient to show that he had an expectation of privacy in the home that society is prepared to recognize as reasonable. The distinctions relied on by the State between this case and *Jones*—that there the overnight guest was left alone and had a key to the premises with which he could come and go and admit and exclude others—are not legally determinative. All citizens share the expectation that hosts will more likely than not respect their guests' privacy interests even if the guests have no legal interest in the premises and do not have the legal authority to determine who may enter the household. There were no exigent circumstances justifying the warrantless entry: An entry may be justified by hot pursuit of a fleeing felon, the imminent destruction of evidence, the need to prevent a suspect's escape, or the risk of danger to the police or others; but, in the absence of hot pursuit, there must be at least probable cause to believe that one or more of the other factors was present and, in assessing the risk of danger, the gravity of the crime and likelihood that the suspect is armed should be considered."

Case Significance

This case clearly established that police officers may not enter the home of a third party to arrest a visitor unless they have consent to enter or there exists some exigent circumstance which justifies not obtaining a search warrant. An overnight guest is presumed to have a reasonable expectation of privacy while he or she is a guest in another's home.

Arizona v. Evans
514 U.S. 1 (1995)

Facts

Evans was arrested by Phoenix police during a routine traffic stop when a patrol car's computer indicated that there was an outstanding misdemeanor warrant for his arrest. A subsequent search of his car revealed a bag of marijuana, and he was charged with possession. Evans moved to suppress the marijuana as the fruit of an unlawful arrest, since the misdemeanor warrant had been quashed before his arrest. The trial court granted the motion, but the court of appeals reversed on the ground that the exclusionary rule's purpose would not be served by excluding evidence obtained because of an error by employees not directly associated with the arresting officers or their police department. In reversing, the Arizona Supreme Court rejected the distinction between clerical errors committed by law enforcement personnel and similar mistakes by court employees and predicted that the exclusionary rule's application would serve to improve the efficiency of criminal justice system record keepers. The U.S. Supreme Court then granted certiorari.

Issue

Must evidence which has been seized illegally but in good faith, based on a clerical error unknown to the arresting officer, be suppressed in accordance with the exclusionary rule?

Holding

No. The exclusionary rule does not require suppression of evidence seized in violation of the Fourth Amendment where the erroneous information resulted from clerical errors of court employees.

Rationale

"The exclusionary rule is a judicially created remedy designed to safeguard against future violations of Fourth Amendment rights through its deterrent effect. However, the issue of exclusion is separate from whether the Amendment has been violated. The Amendment does not expressly preclude the use of evidence obtained in violation of its commands, and exclusion is appropriate only where the rule's remedial objectives are thought most efficaciously served. The same framework that this Court used in *United States v. Leon* to determine that there was no sound reason to apply the exclusionary rule as a means of deterring misconduct on the part of judicial officers responsible for issuing search warrants applies in this case. The exclusionary rule was historically designed as a means of deterring police misconduct, not mistakes by court employees. In addition, Evans offers no evidence that court employees are inclined to ignore or subvert the Fourth Amendment or that lawlessness among these actors requires application of the extreme sanction of exclusion. In fact, the Justice Court Clerk testified that this type of error occurred only once every three or four years. Finally, there is no basis for believing that application of the exclusionary rule will have a significant effect on the court employees responsible for informing the police that a warrant has been quashed. Since they are not adjuncts to the law enforcement team engaged in ferreting out crime, they have no stake in the outcome of particular prosecutions. Application of the exclusionary rule also could not be expected to alter an arresting officer's behavior, since there is no indication that the officer here was not acting reasonably when he relied upon the computer record."

Case Significance

This case is important because it extends the "good-faith" exception to the exclusionary rule to cover errors by court employees. The Supreme Court has been unwilling to extend the exclusionary rule beyond its original parameters, instead creating exceptions for situations where a warrant is deemed invalid because of a mistake made by someone other than the police officer. ✦

Discussion Questions

1. What justification did the Supreme Court provide for imposing the exclusionary rule on the states in *Mapp v. Ohio*?

2. What is the primary purpose of the exclusionary rule, according to the Supreme Court?

3. What are some of the exceptions to the exclusionary rule?

4. Is the exclusionary rule based on a particular provision of the Constitution or Bill of Rights?

5. To what areas of criminal justice has the Supreme Court refused to apply the exclusionary rule? ✦

Chapter Two

What Constitutes Probable Cause?

Beck v. Ohio, 379 U.S. 89 (1964)

Draper v. United States, 358 U.S. 307 (1959)

Aguilar v. Texas, 378 U.S. 108 (1964)

Spinelli v. United States, 393 U.S. 410 (1969)

Illinois v. Gates, 462 U.S. 213 (1983)

INTRODUCTION

In principle, probable cause means the same thing regardless of the conduct in which the police engage. It has been defined by the Supreme Court as more than bare suspicion; it exists when "the facts and circumstances within [the officers'] knowledge and of which they [have] reasonably trustworthy information [are] sufficient to warrant a prudent man in believing that the [suspect] had committed or was committing an offense" (*Beck v. Ohio*).

These are legal definitions of little use to those on the front lines. A more practical definition of probable cause is more than 50 percent certainty. It lies somewhere below absolute certainty and proof beyond a reasonable doubt (the latter of which is necessary to obtain a criminal conviction), and somewhere above a hunch or reasonable suspicion (the latter of which is required to conduct a stop and frisk).

The notion of a "prudent man" means that courts consider what the average "person on the street" would believe, not what a person who has received special training in the identification and apprehension of law breakers (police officer, judge, etc.) would believe. This is not to say, however, that the experience of a police officer must take a back seat to the probable cause determination.

Probable cause is always required in the following scenarios: (1) arrests with warrants; (2) arrests without warrants; (3) searches and seizures of property with warrants; and (4) searches and seizures of property without warrants. When warrants are required, the probable cause determination is made by the magistrate charged with issuing the warrant; when warrants are not used, the police officer makes the probable

cause determination. Generally "probable cause can be obtained from police radio bulletins, tips from 'good citizen' informers who have happened by chance to see criminal activity, reports from victims, anonymous tips, and tips from 'habitual' informers who mingle with people in the underworld and who themselves may [even] be criminals. Probable cause can be based on various combinations of these sources" (Miles et al. 1988–89, 6:4).

When the police make *arrests,* the probable cause determination concerns whether an offense has been committed and whether the suspect did, in fact, commit the offense. In the case of a search, however, the probable cause issue concerns whether the items to be seized are connected with criminal activity and whether they can be found in the place to be searched. This means, then, that the courts sometimes treat the probable cause requirement different depending on the conduct the police engage in.

One point needs to be underscored: Probable cause to search does not necessarily create probable cause to arrest, and, alternatively, probable cause to arrest does not necessarily create probable cause to search. With regard to the latter point, consider this hypothetical: Police officers pursue a drug suspect into her residence and, based an a hot pursuit exigency, arrest her in her living room. Assuming probable cause was in place to pursue the suspect, the police do not possess unfettered latitude once in the house to search the place top to bottom. The courts have placed restrictions on what can be done in a situation such as this, that is, on how far the police can go with a search following (incident) to arrest. We will cover searches incident to arrest in a later chapter, but this example illustrates that the ingredients in the probable cause recipe are not always the same for arrests as they are for searches.

REFERENCE

Miles, J.G., Jr., D.B. Richardson, and A.E. Scudellari. (1988–1989). *The Law Officer's Pocket Manual.* Washington, D.C.: Bureau of National Affairs. ✦

BECK V. OHIO
379 U.S. 89 (1964)

FACTS

On the afternoon of November 10, 1961, William Beck was driving his car near East 115th Street and Beulah Avenue in Cleveland, Ohio. City police officers confronted him, identified themselves, and ordered him to pull over to the curb. The officers possessed neither an arrest warrant nor a search warrant. Placing him under arrest, they searched his car but found nothing of interest. They then took him to a nearby police station where they searched his person and found an envelope containing a number of clearing house slips. Beck was charged in the Cleveland Municipal Court with possession of clearing house slips in violation of a state criminal statute. He filed a motion to suppress the clearing house slips in question, arguing that the police had obtained them by means of an unreasonable search and seizure in violation of the Fourth and Fourteenth Amendments.

ISSUE

Were the arrest and subsequent search in violation of the Fourth Amendment?

HOLDING

Yes. Police have probable cause to arrest when they have reasonably trustworthy information that would warrant a person of "reasonable caution" to believe a crime is taking place or has taken place.

RATIONALE

"Whether an arrest without warrant is constitutionally valid depends upon whether, at the moment the arrest was made, the officer had probable cause to make it, that is, whether at that moment the facts and circumstances within his knowledge and of which he had reasonably trustworthy information were sufficient to warrant a prudent man in believing that the suspect had committed or was committing an offense."

CASE SIGNIFICANCE

This case is significant because the Court announced one of its most often cited definitions of probable cause, based on the "prudent man." *Beck* can be understood as requiring police officers to show probable cause based on what a reasonable person, not a single individual, would believe. While the officers in *Beck* may have thought, individually, that they had probable cause to stop the vehicle, the Court noted that a "prudent man," or reasonable person, would not have.

DRAPER V. UNITED STATES
358 U.S. 307 (1959)

FACTS

A federal narcotics agent was notified by a paid informer who had supplied reliable information in the past that Draper was selling drugs. The informant also notified the agent that Draper had gone to Chicago to obtain more drugs and that he would be returning on a train carrying a tan bag that would contain the narcotics. Finally, the informant described what clothes Draper would be wearing and mentioned that he would be walking quickly after exiting the train. The agent observed a man fitting the description given by the informant. Without a warrant, Draper was arrested. He was searched and drugs were found. Draper was convicted at trial despite his motion to suppress the evidence.

ISSUE

Can information provided by an informant that is later corroborated by a law enforcement officer establish probable cause to arrest?

HOLDING

Yes. So long as an informant's tip "is reasonably corroborated by other matters within the officer's knowledge," the tip can be considered credible for purposes of establishing probable cause to arrest.

RATIONALE

The informant had supplied reliable information in the past. Also, the agent took steps to verify the information supplied by the informant. When the information provided by the informant was found to be accurate, the officer had probable cause to arrest Draper.

CASE SIGNIFICANCE

Draper essentially permitted reliance on hearsay for purposes of establishing probable cause to arrest. Ordinarily hearsay is not admissible in a criminal trial. However, the Supreme Court appears not to have a problem with hearsay in the probable cause context, as long as law enforcement officers corroborate what was said. This case was also controversial because even though the informant supplied information that proved to be accurate, nothing the agent observed prior to Draper's arrest was itself incriminating. It is important to realize that *Draper* dealt with arrests, not searches, so it basically stands alone.

AGUILAR V. TEXAS
378 U.S. 108 (1964)

FACTS

A search warrant was issued on an affidavit from two police officers who swore that they had "received reliable information from a credible person and [did] believe" that illegal drugs were being stored in the place to be searched. Aguilar was convicted and appealed; the state supreme court denied his appeal, and the U.S. Supreme Court granted certiorari.

ISSUE

Must an affidavit for a search warrant based on a tip from an informant contain sufficient details about how the informant reached his or her conclusions and how he or she came by that knowledge?

HOLDING

Yes. An affidavit based on tips from an informant must clearly state (1) how the informant knows what he or she knows and (2) why the informant should be believed.

RATIONALE

A detailed statement about how the informant came to know of the criminal activity in question is important in assessing the informant's credibility, but it is not enough; the informant most prove to be reliable. Alternatively, an informant who has supplied reliable information in the past is more likely to be trusted than one who has not, but if the informant does not describe how he or she came to learn of the criminal activity in question, police may ultimately make an arrest based on less than probable cause. A detailed showing in both areas is necessary.

CASE SIGNIFICANCE

Aguilar is an important case because, unlike *Draper,* it dealt with a search. Also, it was more restrictive than *Draper;* that is, it required that police show how an informant knows what he or she knows and why he or she should be believed. These two prongs have come to be known as the "basis of knowledge" and "veracity" prongs, respectively. For nearly 20 years both prongs needed to be satisfied. Then in *Illinois v. Gates,* a case discussed shortly, the Court abandoned this two-pronged ruling.

SPINELLI V. UNITED STATES
393 U.S. 410 (1969)

FACTS

A search warrant was issued on the basis of an FBI agent's affidavit that alleged (1) that an informant had told the agent that Spinelli was taking illegal bets over the phone; (2) that surveillance had led the agent to conclude that Spinelli had gone to the apartment where the phone was located several times within a five-day period; and (3) Spinelli was a known gambler. Spinelli was convicted of traveling in interstate commerce with the intention of committing illegal gambling activities, and the U.S. Supreme Court granted certiorari.

ISSUE

Can a search warrant based on tips from an informant be issued when the affidavit on which it is based contains insufficient information concerning how the informant learned of the suspected criminal activity in question?

HOLDING

No. However, insufficient information with regard to *Aguilar*'s "basis of knowledge" claim can be overcome if the informant's tip describes the accused's criminal activity in enough detail that the magistrate knows that he or she is relying on more than a rumor.

RATIONALE

"We conclude, then, that in the present case the informant's tip—even when corroborated to the extent indicated—was not sufficient to provide the basis for a finding of probable cause. This is not to say that the tip was so insubstantial that it could not properly have counted in the magistrate's determination. Rather, it needed some further support. When we look to the other parts of the application, however, we find nothing alleged which would permit the suspicions engendered by the informant's report to ripen into a judgment that a crime was probably being committed."

CASE SIGNIFICANCE

Spinelli is important because it reaffirmed *Aguilar.* The Court concluded that the affidavit supplied by the FBI agent contained insufficient information concerning the "underlying circumstances" of the alleged gambling activity. That is, the affidavit failed to describe how the informant obtained his information. The Court concluded that Spinelli's past gambling activities were irrelevant to the probable cause determination, leaving the agent with the less than incriminating evidence that Spinelli repeatedly spoke on the phone. *Spinelli* was decided five years after *Aguilar.* Since both cases reinforced the same issues, they came to constitute what is now called the *Aguilar-Spinelli* test. In the next case, however, that test was all but abandoned.

ILLINOIS V. GATES
462 U.S. 213 (1983)

FACTS

In mid-1978, the Bloomingdale, Illinois Police Department received an anonymous letter informing them that Gates and his wife made a living selling drugs, that they bought most of their drugs in Florida, and that on a certain date Gates would be driving back from

Florida with a car full of drugs. A police officer obtained Gates' address and set forth to corroborate the various details (there were others) set forth in the anonymous letter. The officer found that Gates had flown down to Florida, stayed the night in a hotel, and driven north the next day in a car with Illinois license plates. The letter and the information resulting from the officer's investigation were set forth in an affidavit in support of a search warrant. A search warrant was issued. Officers serving the warrant found drugs in Gates' house and car. He was arrested and charged with violating state drug laws, and the U.S. Supreme Court granted certiorari.

ISSUE

Does an anonymous letter containing no information as to the informant's reliability and basis of knowledge coupled with corroboration by a police officer provide probable cause for obtaining a search warrant?

HOLDING

Yes. The two-pronged *Aguilar* test, requiring that police officers demonstrate informants' reliability and basis of knowledge, is abandoned in favor of a "totality of circumstances" analysis. A deficiency in one prong can be satisfied by a strong showing in the other.

RATIONALE

". . . [W]e conclude that it is wiser to abandon the 'two-pronged test' established by our decisions in *Aguilar* and *Spinelli*. In its place we reaffirm the totality-of-circumstances analysis that traditionally has informed probable cause determinations. . . . The task of the issuing magistrate is simply to make a practical, common-sense decision whether, given all the circumstances set forth in the affidavit before him, including the 'veracity' and 'basis of knowledge' of persons supplying hearsay information, there is a fair probability that contraband or evidence of a crime will be found in a particular place."

CASE SIGNIFICANCE

Gates is significant because it simplifies the probable cause analysis. If a police officer cannot adequately demonstrate an informant's reliability but can demonstrate the informant's basis of knowledge with a strong showing, then probable cause can be established. The reverse is also true; a weak showing in the "basis of knowledge" prong can be counteracted by a strong showing as to the informant's past reliability. ✦

DISCUSSION QUESTIONS

1. Discuss sources of information that would lead an officer to conclude that probable cause to *arrest* is present.

2. Discuss sources of information that would lead an officer to conclude that probable cause to *search* is present.

3. What does probable cause mean from a practical standpoint? That is, explain probable cause in simple, nonlegal terminology that could be understood by anyone.

4. What happens if probable cause to arrest or search is not present? Are the available remedies (e.g., exclusionary rule, civil liability) sufficient?

5. Our criminal justice system requires proof beyond a reasonable doubt for a finding of guilty in a criminal trial. Probable cause is a substantially lower standard. What explanations can you offer for this apparent discrepancy?

6. Was the Supreme Court's decision in *Illinois v. Gates* a smart one? Who most benefits most from the Court's decision in that case? ✦

Chapter Three

When Has a Seizure Occurred?

Schmerber v. California, 384 U.S. 757 (1966)

Cupp v. Murphy, 412 U.S. 291 (1973)

Michigan v. Chesternut, 486 U.S. 567 (1988)

Brower v. County of Inyo, 489 U.S. 593 (1989)

California v. Hodari D., 499 U.S. 621 (1991)

Florida v. Bostick, 501 U.S. 429 (1991)

Bond v. United States, 529 U.S. 334 (2000)

Kyllo v. United States, 533 U.S. 27 (2001)

Illinois v. McArthur, 531 U.S. 326 (2001)

Introduction

The Fourth Amendment is implicated when a search or seizure occurs. That is, whenever a person or piece of property is "seized," the Fourth Amendment applies. The definition of seizure has a very specific meaning in criminal procedure. Nothing has to be physically grasped for a seizure to take place. Indeed, even when police stop short of actually touching a person, their actions can still constitute a seizure. At the other extreme, though, there are certain things the police can do to inconvenience people without triggering the Fourth Amendment. It is important to distinguish between two types of seizures: (1) seizures of property and (2) seizures of persons.

As the Supreme Court declared in *United States v. Jacobsen,* 466 U.S. 109 (1984), a seizure of tangible property occurs "when there is some meaningful interference with an individual's possessory interest in that property." In determining if a piece of property is seized, courts often refer to people's "actual" or "constructive" possession. A piece of property is in a person's actual possession if the person is physically holding or grasping it. Constructive possession, by comparison, refers to possession of property without physical contact (e.g., a bag that is next to a person on the ground, but not in his or her hands). A piece of property is "seized," therefore, if the police remove it from a person's actual or constructive possession, such

as when they take a person's luggage at an airport and move it to another room to be searched.

Seizure of a person occurs when a police officer, by means of physical force or show of authority, intentionally restrains an individual's liberty in such a manner that a reasonable person would believe that he or she is not free to leave. Another way of understanding a Fourth Amendment seizure is by asking a question: Would a reasonable person believe that he or she is free to decline the officer's requests or otherwise terminate the encounter? In general, a "no" answer means a seizure has occurred. However, in a recent case, *Florida v. Bostick,* the Supreme Court stated that the appropriate test for determining whether a person—in that case, a person on a bus—is seized is whether a reasonable passenger would feel free to decline the officers' requests or otherwise terminate the encounter.

The seizure of a person does not have to be physical for the Fourth Amendment to be implicated. For example, a seizure can occur when a police officer simply questions a person. The Supreme Court stated in *Terry v. Ohio,* 392 U.S. 1 (1968) that "[N]ot all personal intercourse between policemen and citizens involves 'seizures' of persons" (p. 20, n. 16), but a seizure *does* occur when the officer's conduct in conjunction with questioning would convince a reasonable person that he or she is not free to leave.

A seizure can also occur in pursuit, even if the person sought by the police is never caught, although it is not always clear whether a pursuit constitutes a seizure. This is important because if the pursuit of a suspect is *not* a seizure, then the police may lawfully chase people without justification and, if the person discards anything during the chase, the police may lawfully seize the item because the Fourth Amendment does not apply. In fact, as the Supreme Court noted in *California v. Hodari D.,* when an officer chases a suspect but does not lay hands on him or her, a seizure does not occur until the suspect submits to police authority.

In *Hodari D.* a police officer chased a suspect on foot. The officer did not have justification to stop or arrest the suspect. The suspect discarded an item during the chase, which the officer stopped to pick up. The Supreme Court upheld the officer's action because the suspect was still in flight at the time the officer picked up the object. The Supreme Court did state in *Hodari D.,* however, that a seizure *does* occur the instant a police officer lays hands on a suspect during a chase, even if the suspect is able to break away from the officer's grasp.

The definitions of seizure offered thus far are general. The cases discussed throughout this chapter, however, offer some more specific definitions and address whether certain types of seizures can be considered constitutional. Concerning the definition of a seizure, the ruling from *Michigan v. Chesternut* states that following a person does not constitute a seizure within the meaning of the Fourth Amendment. Alternatively, the Supreme Court held in *Brower v. County of Inyo* that a roadblock used by the police to stop a fleeing felon constitutes a seizure within the meaning of the Fourth Amendment.

As to the appropriateness of certain seizures, we discuss the following cases. For example, in *Schmerber v. California,* the Supreme Court held that the warrantless "seizure" of blood is constitutional. In *Cupp v. Murphy* the Court ruled that the warrantless seizure of evidence that is likely to disappear does not violate the Fourth Amendment. In *Bond v. United States,* the Court held that it is a violation of the Fourth Amendment for police officers, without any suspicion, to physically manipulate bus passengers' luggage. Finally, in *Illinois v. McArthur,* the Court held that an officer's refusal to let a person into his or her residence, knowing that the person will destroy evidence therein, does not violate the Fourth Amendment. ✦

Schmerber v. California
384 U.S. 757 (1966)

Facts

Schmerber was arrested for driving under the influence of alcohol while he was in the hospital receiving treatment for injuries he suffered during an accident. A blood sample was taken by a doctor at the request of one of the police officers. The blood was drawn over Schmerber's protest, as well as his attorney's. The blood sample indicated intoxication and was admitted against Schmerber at trial. He was convicted of driving under the influence. He objected to admission of the evidence, arguing that the Fifth and Fourteenth Amendments had been violated when the blood sample was taken, and the U.S. Supreme Court granted certiorari.

Issue

Did the warrantless "seizure" of Schmerber's blood violate his constitutional rights?

Holding

No. Drawing blood from a criminal suspect without his or her consent does not violate the Constitution as long as it is done by trained medical professionals.

Rationale

"*Breithaupt* was also a case in which police officers caused blood to be withdrawn from the driver of an automobile involved in an accident, and in which there was ample justification for the officer's conclusion that the driver was under the influence of alcohol. There, as here, the extraction was made by a physician in a simple, medically acceptable manner in a hospital environment. There, however, the driver was unconscious at the time the blood was withdrawn and hence had no opportunity to object to the procedure. We affirmed the conviction there resulting from the use of the test in evidence, holding that under such circumstances the withdrawal did not offend 'that "sense of justice" of which we spoke in *Rochin v. California.*' *Breithaupt* thus requires the rejection of petitioner's due process argument, and nothing in the circumstances of this case or in supervening events persuades us that this aspect of *Breithaupt* should be overruled."

Case Significance

This case is significant not just because it permitted warrantless "seizures" of blood based on exigent circumstances (i.e., the fact that the alcohol in Schmerber's blood would "disappear" in time), but because it addressed several other important constitutional issues. The Court stated that seizure of blood, a type of real or physical evidence, does not violate the Fifth Amendment's self-incrimination clause because it is not testimonial evidence. Schmerber also argued that his right to counsel was denied, but the Court stated that because he wasn't yet charged with a crime, the Sixth Amendment did not apply. Finally, the Court held that Schmerber's due process rights were not violated because of the manner by which the blood was extracted.

Cupp v. Murphy
412 U.S. 291 (1973)

Facts

After being informed of his wife's death by strangulation, the defendant volunteered to come to the police station for questioning. Shortly after he arrived at the station, the police noticed a spot on the defendant's finger and asked if they could take some scrapings from underneath his fingernails. He refused and began rubbing his hands together and placing them in his pockets. At that point, the police forcibly, and without a warrant, took a scraping from the defendant's fingernails. The evidence from the scrapings was determined to have traces of skin, blood cells, and fabric from the victim's nightgown. The defendant was tried and convicted of second-degree murder. He appealed his conviction.

ISSUE

Does the warrantless seizure of evidence that is likely to disappear violate the Fourth Amendment?

HOLDING

No. Police may seize, without a warrant, evidence that is likely to disappear before a warrant can be obtained.

RATIONALE

"Where there is no formal arrest, as in the case before us, a person might [be] . . . less likely to take conspicuous, immediate steps to destroy incriminating evidence on his person." The limited intrusion, a stationhouse detention far short of an arrest, also justified the seizure.

CASE SIGNIFICANCE

This case addressed what is commonly referred to as "evanescent evidence," that is, evidence that is likely to disappear. Assuming the police have probable cause, *Cupp* stated that evanescent evidence can be seized without a warrant. In this case the seizure took place at a police station. However, if the police have probable cause that evidence is likely to disappear, or that the suspect may flee, or that harm may come to other individuals, then warrantless seizures can also be conducted in private residences. However, the seizures must be reasonable and not the result of exigencies that are police created.

MICHIGAN V. CHESTERNUT
486 U.S. 567 (1988)

FACTS

Four officers on patrol in a marked squad car observed a car pull over to the curb. A man emerged from the car and approached Chesternut, who was standing on the street corner. When Chesternut saw the patrol car nearing the corner where he stood, he turned and began to run away. The patrol car followed Chesternut, driving alongside him as he ran down the sidewalk. The officers observed Chesternut pull several packets out of his pocket and throw them away. Officers stopped to examine the items Chesternut had discarded and determined that they were codeine pills. Chesternut was arrested for possession of narcotics. At a preliminary hearing, he argued that the officer's conduct prior to disposal of the packets was a search and that the evidence should be excluded. The U.S. Supreme Court granted certiorari.

ISSUE

Does the act of following a person constitute a seizure within the meaning of the Fourth Amendment?

HOLDING

No. The appropriate test for determining whether a person is seized within the meaning of the Fourth Amendment is whether a reasonable person, viewing all the circumstances in their totality, would conclude that he or she is not free to leave.

RATIONALE

"The test provides that the police can be said to have seized an individual 'only if, in view of all the circumstances surrounding the incident, a reasonable person would have believed that he was not free to leave.' . . . Applying the Court's test to the facts of this case, we conclude that Chesternut was not seized by the police before he discarded the packets containing the controlled substance. Although Officer Peltier referred to the police conduct as a 'chase,' and the magistrate who originally dismissed the complaint was impressed by this description, the characterization is not enough, standing alone, to implicate Fourth Amendment protections. . . . [T]he police conduct involved here would not have communicated to the reasonable person an attempt to capture or otherwise intrude upon Chesternut's freedom of movement. The record does not reflect that the police activated a siren or flashers; or that they commanded Chesternut to halt, or displayed any weapons; or that they operated the car in an aggressive manner to block Chesternut's course or otherwise control the direction or speed of his movement."

CASE SIGNIFICANCE

This case is significant because it addressed the issue of when a person is considered "seized" by the police. The actions in this case are different from the typical stop and frisk or arrest situation because the police followed alongside Chesternut, and did not actually chase him. Since the police in this case did not block Chesternut's path or otherwise engage in actions that would suggest he was not free to leave, the Court concluded that a seizure did not take place. Accordingly, the Fourth Amendment was not implicated. You may be wondering about Chesternut's subsequent arrest. It was deemed constitutional because the police developed probable cause to arrest after stopping to pick up the packets and determining that they contained contraband. Had the police not stopped to pick up the packets and proceeded directly to the arrest stage, their actions would have been considered unconstitutional, because probable cause was developed only after determining what was in the packets.

BROWER V. COUNTY OF INYO
489 U.S. 593 (1989)

FACTS

Brower stole a car and eluded the police in a high-speed chase which took place over a 20-mile stretch. Accordingly, police parked an 18-wheeler truck and trailer across both lanes of the highway on which Brower was traveling, blocking his path. They also pointed the headlights of their police cars in Brower's direction, which was intended to blind him. Brower crashed into the roadblock and was killed. Brower's family and estate brought a Section 1983 civil lawsuit against the police, alleging that the roadblock violated Brower's Fourth Amendment right to be free from unreasonable seizures.

ISSUE

Is a roadblock used by the police to block a fleeing suspect considered a seizure within the meaning of the Fourth Amendment?

HOLDING

Yes. A Fourth Amendment seizure occurs where there is a "governmental termination of freedom of movement through means intentionally applied."

RATIONALE

"Consistent with the language, history, and judicial construction of the Fourth Amendment, a seizure occurs when governmental termination of a person's movement is effected through means intentionally applied. Because the complaint alleges that Brower was stopped by the instrumentality set in motion or put in place to stop him, it states a claim of Fourth Amendment 'seizure.'"

CASE SIGNIFICANCE

This case is important not because of the constitutionality of the police action, but because it addressed the definition of a seizure. The Court held that what the police did in Brower was "seize" him within the meaning of the Fourth Amendment. As such, constitutional protections applied. The Court remanded the case back to the court of appeals to determine whether the district court erred in concluding that the road block was reasonable. If the lower court decided that the road-block was reasonable, then the officers would not be held civilly liable. This case is an example of one of the many minute issues the Supreme Court considers. As far as criminal procedure goes, the Supreme Court is responsible for deciding constitutional questions, not questions of guilt, innocence, liability, and so forth. Those decisions are left to the lower courts.

CALIFORNIA V. HODARI D.
499 U.S. 621 (1991)

FACTS

Officers McColgin and Pertoso were on patrol in a high-crime area of Oakland, California. They wore street clothes but were also wearing jackets with the word "Police" across the front and back. When they turned around a corner, they observed approximately four youths surrounding a small red car parked near the curb. When the youths saw the officers approaching, they ran. Hodari and another youth ran west through an alley; the others fled south. The red car also headed south at high speed. The officers gave chase. Hodari emerged from the alley and, just as Officer Petoso almost caught up to him, he threw away what appeared to be a small rock. Shortly thereafter, Officer Petoso overtook Hodari, handcuffed him, and radioed for assistance. A search incident to arrest turned up $130 in cash. The "rock" that Hodari threw away turned out to be crack cocaine. Hodari argued that at the time of the chase he had been "seized," and that the cocaine was inadmissible because the officers lacked reasonable suspicion at that point.

ISSUE

Does a seizure occur when, while an officer is giving chase, a person tosses away contraband?

HOLDING

No. A seizure does not occur when a suspect flees from an officer and the officer applies no physical force. If a suspect submits to a police officer and/or the officer applies physical force, the suspect is seized within the meaning of the Fourth Amendment.

RATIONALE

"To say that an arrest is effected by the slightest application of physical force, despite the arrestee's escape, is not to say that for Fourth Amendment purposes there is a continuing arrest during the period of fugitivity. If, for example, Pertoso [the officer] had laid his hands upon Hodari to arrest him, but Hodari had broken away and had then cast away the cocaine, it would hardly be realistic to say that disclosure had been made during the course of an arrest. The present case, however, is even one step further removed. It does not involve the application of any physical force; Hodari was untouched by Officer Pertoso at the time he discarded the cocaine. His defense relies instead upon the proposition that a seizure occurs 'when the officer, by means of physical force or show of authority, has in some way restrained the liberty of a citizen.' Hodari contends that Pertoso's pursuit qualified as a 'show of authority' calling upon Hodari to halt. The narrow question before us is whether, with respect to a show of authority as with respect to application of physical force, a seizure occurs even though the subject does not yield. We hold that it does not."

CASE SIGNIFICANCE

This case considered yet another narrow area with regard to investigative stops and arrests. Hodari argued that prior to the point that he discarded the cocaine, a seizure had taken place, requiring at least reasonable suspicion. Had the Court ruled in Hodari's favor, then the police would not be able to chase suspicious individuals without justification. Fortunately for the law enforcement community, the Court held that it is permissible to chase suspicious individuals (who do not submit to police authority and where physical force is not used); however, for any subsequent intrusions such as a frisk or an arrest to be constitutional, appropriate justification must first be in place. Justification was present in this case because when Hodari discarded the contraband, the officer had probable cause to arrest, not to mention reasonable suspicion to stop. If Hodari successfully eluded the police and was not arrested, but the cocaine was nevertheless seized, it would be admissible against Hodari (assuming he was eventually found) under the abandonment doctrine.

FLORIDA V. BOSTICK
501 U.S. 429 (1991)

FACTS

Pursuant to a routine police drug interdiction effort intended to uncover drug trafficking, two police officers boarded a bus and questioned the passengers. Without any suspicion, they asked the defendant, Bostick, for his ticket and identification, then they asked to search his luggage, advising him of his right to refuse consent. Bostick consented to the search and cocaine was found in his luggage. He later sought suppression of the drugs, arguing that they had been improperly seized.

ISSUE

Did the Florida Supreme Court err in adopting a per se rule that every encounter on a bus is a seizure?

HOLDING

Yes. The appropriate test for determining when a seizure takes place is whether, taking into account all of the circumstances surrounding the encounter, a reasonable passenger would feel free to decline the officers' requests or terminate the encounter.

RATIONALE

"Our cases make it clear that a seizure does not occur simply because a police officer approaches an individual and asks a few questions. So long as a reasonable person would feel free 'to disregard the police and go about his business,' the encounter is consensual and no reasonable suspicion is required. The encounter will not trigger Fourth Amendment scrutiny unless it loses its consensual nature."

CASE SIGNIFICANCE

This case is important because it helped clarify the somewhat muddy definition of seizure. It led to a somewhat different test than that announced in *Chesternut*. In *Chesternut* the appropriate test for determining whether a seizure took place was whether a reasonable person would believe he or she was free to leave. Relying on this definition, Bostick argued that the he was not free to leave because the officers blocked his path and the bus was about to depart. The Florida Supreme Court agreed with this argument. However, the Supreme Court stated that the Florida court used the wrong test. Justice O'Connor, who wrote the Court's opinion, observed that Bostick would not have felt free to leave even if the police had not been there, given the imminent departure of the bus. Accordingly, the Supreme Court remanded the case back to the Florida court to determine whether, consistent with the new definition, a seizure actually took place.

BOND V. UNITED STATES
529 U.S. 334 (2000)

FACTS

Bond was a passenger on a Greyhound bus that left California bound for Little Rock, Arkansas. The bus stopped, as required, at the Border Patrol checkpoint at Sierra Blanca, Texas. Agent Cantu boarded the bus to check the immigration status of all the passengers. After he concluded that all of the passengers were lawfully in the United States, he walked toward the front of the bus.

On the way, he squeezed the soft luggage which passengers had placed in the overhead storage racks above the seats. As Cantu inspected the luggage above Bond's seat, he noticed that it contained a "brick-like" object. Bond claimed ownership of the bag and allowed Cantu to open it. Upon opening the bag, Cantu discovered a "brick" of methamphetamine. Bond was arrested, indicted, and convicted, despite his motion to exclude the drugs. The U.S. Supreme Court then granted certiorari.

ISSUE

Can a law enforcement officer engage in a suspicionless physical manipulation of a bus passenger's luggage?

HOLDING

No. It is a violation of the Fourth Amendment for law enforcement officials to, without suspicion, physically manipulate bus passengers' luggage.

RATIONALE

"Our Fourth Amendment analysis embraces two questions. First, we ask whether the individual, by his conduct, has exhibited an actual expectation of privacy; that is, whether he has shown that 'he [sought] to preserve [something] as private. . . .' Here, petitioner sought to preserve privacy by using an opaque bag and placing that bag directly above his seat. Second, we inquire whether the individual's expectation of privacy is 'one that society is prepared to recognize as reasonable. . . .' When a bus passenger places a bag in an overhead bin, he expects that other passengers or bus employees may move it for one reason or another. Thus, a bus passenger clearly expects that his bag may be handled. He does not expect that other passengers or bus employees will, as a matter of course, feel the bag in an exploratory manner. But this is exactly what the agent did here. We therefore hold that the agent's physical manipulation of petitioner's bag violated the Fourth Amendment."

CASE SIGNIFICANCE

This case straddled the line separating searches from frisks. Regardless, the Supreme Court has never permitted "physical manipulation" of luggage, people's clothing, or other items with anything less than probable cause. Here, the officer had no suspicion at all. The evidence was excluded. This case was a prime example of the exclusionary rule in operation. It was also a case that "fired up" critics of the exclusionary rule. Evidence belonging to a clearly guilty criminal was declared inadmissible, which probably means that Bond's conviction will be overturned.

KYLLO V. UNITED STATES
533 U.S. 27 (2001)

FACTS

In 1991, a special agent with the Department of Interior, Bureau of Land Management, began to suspect that Kyllo was cultivating marijuana in his Florence, Oregon triplex. In order to confirm his suspicions, the agent enlisted the help of the Oregon National Guard and used an Agema Termovision to scan the triplex. The scan was conducted from a vehicle parked on a public street and indicated that the roof of Kyllo's garage, as well as a side wall of his residence, were radiating more heat than neighboring homes. Based on the scan, tips from informants, evidence that Kyllo's wife had previously been arrested for drug offenses, and subpoenaed utility bills, a search warrant was issued. The warrant was executed and agents found 100 marijuana plants in Kyllo's home. Kyllo was indicted and then convicted in federal court following a plea agreement. Prior to his conviction, he argued that the thermal evidence should be excluded. The U.S. Supreme Court then granted certiorari.

ISSUE

Is it a violation of the Fourth Amendment for the government, without probable cause or a warrant, to use devices not in general public use to view details of a home?

HOLDING

Yes. It is a violation of the Fourth Amendment for the government, without a probable cause and a warrant, to use devices not in general public use to view details of a home.

RATIONALE

While the government argued that the thermal imager used in *Kyllo* did not result in "physical penetration" of the exterior walls and, as such, did not reveal any "intimate details" concerning what was happening in Kyllo's residence, the Court stated that the absence of physical intrusion could no longer "foreclose further Fourth Amendment inquiry." And, according to the Court, "in the home, our cases show, all details are intimate details, because the entire area is held safe from prying government eyes . . . how warm—or even how relatively warm—Kyllo was heating his residence" is an intimate detail.

CASE SIGNIFICANCE

This case is important because it placed significant restrictions on law enforcement's ability to rely on thermal imaging scans. Prior to *Kyllo*, in most jurisdictions the police could scan people's residences for excessive heat and then, with additional corroboration, use the information to obtain a search warrant. Now, in light of *Kyllo*, the police cannot legally use thermal imagers to scan people's homes without first obtaining a warrant based on probable cause. Thus, the Court in *Kyllo* was not directly concerned with the constitutionality of the thermal imaging scan, but rather with whether such a scan constitutes a search within the meaning of the Fourth Amendment. It held that thermal imaging scans are searches that must be supported by probable cause. To some critics, this decision seriously hampers law enforcement's ability to detect indoor marijuana growing operations.

ILLINOIS V. MCARTHUR
531 U.S. 326 (2001)

FACTS

Police officers accompanying a woman to the trailer where she lived were informed that her husband had a quantity of marijuana hidden therein. The officers asked the man for permission to search the trailer but were denied entry. While one of the officers left to secure a search warrant, the other officer refused to allow McArthur reentry into his residence. When the officer returned with a warrant, a search was initiated and a small quantity of marijuana was found. McArthur was arrested and charged with misdemeanor possession. The trial court accepted a motion to suppress based upon McArthur's claim that the evidence was the fruit of an unlawful seizure, namely the officers' refusal to let him reenter the trailer unaccompanied so that he could "have destroyed the marijuana." A state appellate court affirmed and the state supreme court denied the prosecution's request for leave to appeal; the U.S. Supreme Court then granted certiorari.

ISSUE

Did the refusal to allow McArthur reentry into his residence knowing that he would likely destroy evidence of criminal activity contained therein violate the Fourth Amendment seizure clause?

HOLDING

No. The brief seizure of McArthur's residence and the officer's refusal to allow him reentry did not violate the Fourth Amendment's seizure clause.

RATIONALE

The Fourth Amendment requires the issuance of a warrant based upon probable cause before a search and/or seizure may be undertaken. There are, however, a number and variety of judicially created exceptions to the warrant clause. One such exception is that of exigency. The Court has long held that suspects do not have a constitutional right to destroy evidence of their in-

volvement in criminal activity. Where time and circumstance preclude the police from obtaining a warrant, a narrowly limited search may be undertaken in the interest of preventing the imminent destruction of evidence. The facts of this case met such criteria. Had McArthur been allowed to reenter the residence, he would have surely destroyed the marijuana hidden therein before the police could return with a warrant. Knowing this, the police temporarily "seized" the residence from his possession. Because of the exigent circumstances and law enforcement interest at stake, combined with the brevity of the seizure, no Fourth Amendment violation was deemed to have occurred. The judgment of the Illinois Appellate Court was reversed and remanded.

CASE SIGNIFICANCE

This case gave the police authority to refuse an individual entry into a dwelling (or part of a dwelling) if there is reason to believe that once inside he or she will attempt to destroy evidence of criminal activity. In effect, the police are briefly "seizing" the dwelling (or part thereof, such as a room) until such time as a warrant can be secured. It is important to note, however, that the Court did not specify how long such a seizure may last. ✦

DISCUSSION QUESTIONS

1. Identify the various types of seizures that come under protection of the Fourth Amendment.

2. Was the Court's decision in *California v. Hodari D.* a reasonable one? In other words, was the Supreme Court correct in stating that seizures only occur when someone submits to police authority or is the target of some degree of physical force?

3. In *Brower v. County of Inyo* the Supreme Court declared that a police roadblock constitutes a seizure within the meaning of the Fourth Amendment. Should a person who is fleeing the police enjoy Fourth Amendment protection? Does the *Brower* decision in any way interfere with the police's ability to set up roadblocks to apprehend fleeing suspects?

4. In *Bond v. United States* the police searched a bus passenger's luggage and found contraband, but the evidence was ruled inadmissible. This case illustrates the controversy surrounding the exclusionary rule. Was it an appropriate decision to effectively let the defendant off because of police actions?

5. *Schmerber v. California* dealt with the warrantless "seizure" of the blood of a suspected drunk driver. To what extent is this decision relevant today, with the advent of breathalyzers and video cameras in police cars? ✦

Chapter Four

Arrest

Introduction

Students of criminal procedure often become confused when instructors toss around terms like "seizure," "stop," and "arrest" without elaborating on each term's distinct meaning. Think of *stops* and *arrests* as being different types of seizures. Additionally, think of both types of *seizures* as falling on a sliding scale of seriousness: an arrest is the most intrusive and a stop is the next most intrusive.

In one sense, distinguishing between an arrest and a lesser type of intrusion is easy. For example, when a suspect is handcuffed, placed in the back of a patrol car, and driven to the police station for booking, an arrest has clearly occurred. Alternatively, if a person is accosted by a single police officer and asked general questions about suspected involvement in a crime, an arrest has not occurred. However, there are many police-citizen encounters that fall between these two extremes. A stop can evolve into an arrest if the circumstances are just so. A seizure short of a formal arrest may be so intrusive as to constitute a *de facto* arrest, in which case probable cause, rather than reasonable suspicion, would be required to make the encounter constitutional.

Generally, the courts will weigh (1) the duration of a stop and (2) the degree of intrusion in assessing whether a stop evolves into an arrest. Sometimes the courts also refer to the officers' intentions and the manner in which the stop takes place. For example, in

Dunaway v. New York, the Supreme Court ruled that stationhouse detentions required probable cause. In that case, police officers took a man into custody during the course of a robbery/murder investigation. They read Dunaway his *Miranda* warnings and subjected him to questioning—without probable cause. The Supreme Court reversed Dunaway's subsequent conviction. Again, the Court did not decide on the arrest issue, but it did declare that custodial interrogation such as that in *Dunaway* must be supported by probable cause.

Notwithstanding the distinctions between arrests and lesser intrusions such as stops, it is also important to consider (1) the location where police make arrests and (2) whether warrants are required for doing so. For example, *United States v. Watson* instructs us that arrests made in public places do not require warrants. Even if the police attempt to arrest a person in a public place but that person subsequently flees into a private residence, a warrantless arrest can still be made. Such was the ruling in *United States v. Santana*. Even if the arrestable offense is not a serious one, the police can still make warrantless arrests in public. For example, in *Atwater v. City of Lago Vista*, the Supreme Court declared that the police can arrest people for seat belt violations and, by extension, other nonjailable offenses.

People enjoy substantial Fourth Amendment protection when the police effect arrests in private places. In particular, according to the Supreme Court's decision in *Payton v. New York*, it is unconstitutional for the police to make warrantless arrests of individuals in private places. Only if exigent (i.e., emergency) circumstances exist, such as the potential for the destruction of evidence, can the police make warrantless arrests in private places. In *Welsh v. Wisconsin*, the Court has also held that the police cannot enter people's homes without warrants to make arrests for nonjailable offenses. (Note that *Welsh* dealt with an arrest in a private place and is to be distinguished from *Atwater*).

Two important arrest cases deal with arrests made in other jurisdictions than that where the arrestee was to be tried. Specifically, *Frisbie v. Collins* dealt with the forcible apprehension of a defendant in another state. The defendant fled to another state to avoid apprehension, but was caught and forcibly brought back to the state where he was to stand trial. The Supreme Court upheld the abduction. Similarly, in *United States v. Alvarez-Machain*, the Court upheld the abduction of an individual from another country to be brought back to the United States for trial. A key qualifier to that decision, however, was that the abduction did not violate any extradition treaties. ✦

FRISBIE V. COLLINS
342 U.S. 519 (1952)

FACTS

Acting as his own attorney, Collins brought a *habeas corpus* action in federal court seeking release from a Michigan state prison, where he was serving a life sentence for murder. His petition alleged that while he was living in Illinois, Michigan officers forcibly seized him, handcuffed him, and took him back to Michigan. He claimed that trial under such circumstances violated the due process clause of the Fourteenth Amendment as well as the Federal Kidnapping Act, and that his conviction should have been nullified.

ISSUE

Does the forcible abduction of a defendant in a state other the state in which he or she is to stand trial deprive the court of authority to hear the case?

HOLDING

No. The power of a court to try a person for a crime is not impaired when the person is brought before the court by means of forcible abduction.

RATIONALE

"This Court has never departed from the rule announced in *Ker v. Illinois,* 119 U.S. 436, 444 (1886) that the power of a court to try a person for crime is not impaired by the fact that he had been brought within the court's jurisdiction by reason of a 'forcible abduction.' No persuasive reasons are now presented to justify overruling this line of cases. They rest on sound basis that due process of law is satisfied when one present in court is convicted of crime after having been fairly apprised of the charges against him and after a fair trial in accordance with constitutional procedural safeguards."

CASE SIGNIFICANCE

This case is significant because it permitted forcible abduction of criminal defendants so they can be brought to trial. This case did not, contrary to some interpretations, permit police to bring defendants to trial following an unlawful arrest. The arrest in this case was lawful in the sense that it was supported by probable cause. It was considered "wrongful," however, because the Michigan officers effectively violated the Federal Kidnapping Act by bringing Collins to trial. With regard to this latter issue the Court stated: "We think the [Federal Kidnapping] Act cannot fairly be construed so as to add to the list of sanctions detailed a sanction barring a state from prosecuting persons wrongfully brought to it by its officers." The Court was mainly concerned with whether forcible abduction crossing state lines violates the due process clause of the Fourteenth Amendment, and held that it does not.

UNITED STATES V. SANTANA
427 U.S. 38 (1976)

FACTS

In late 1974, Gilletti, an undercover narcotics officer, arranged to have McCafferty purchase heroin from Santana. McCafferty took marked money from the officer and went into Santana's house. McCafferty returned and provided Gilletti with several envelopes containing a brownish-white powder. Gilletti then arrested McCafferty. When Gilletti asked McCafferty where the money was, she stated that Santana had it. While McCafferty was being taken to the police station for booking, several other officers approached Santana's house and observed Santana standing in the doorway with a brown paper bag in her hand. They pulled to within 15 feet of Santana and got out of their van shouting "police" and displaying their identification. Santana retreated into the vestibule of her house, and the officers gave chase and caught her. During the scuffle, two bundles of heroin fell to the floor, which the police recovered. When Santana was told to empty her pockets, the marked money was found. Santana was charged with possession of heroin and intent to distribute. The U.S. Supreme Court granted certiorari.

ISSUE

Is a warrant required to arrest a person in a private residence when the arrest was set in motion in a public place?

HOLDING

No. A warrantless arrest that began in a public place is valid even when the suspect subsequently retreats into a private residence.

RATIONALE

"In *United States v. Watson* we held that the warrantless arrest of an individual in a public place upon probable cause did not violate the Fourth Amendment. Thus the first question we must decide is whether, when the police first sought to arrest Santana, she was in a public place. . . . While it may be true that under the common law of property the threshold of one's dwelling is 'private,' as is the yard surrounding the house, it is nonetheless clear that under the cases interpreting the Fourth Amendment Santana was in a 'public' place. She was not in an area where she had any expectation of privacy . . . she was not merely visible to the public but was as exposed to public view, speech, hearing, and touch as if she had been standing completely outside her house."

CASE SIGNIFICANCE

The Court permitted the officers to arrest based on the exigency of "hot pursuit." Because the arrest was set into motion in a public place, the police were justified in pursuing Santana into her residence. This case was somewhat strange in the sense that the Court decided the doorway to a person's residence is considered a public place. This ruling did not, at first glance, jibe with the notion of curtilage as applied to search cases. Students of criminal procedure are taught that people do have a reasonable expectation of privacy in the curtilage of their homes and, as such, the police must obtain a warrant to search in that area (assuming no exigent circumstances exist). The *Santana* decision was different, however, because it dealt with arrests, not searches. Had the facts in *Santana* dealt with a search instead of an arrest, the outcome would probably have been different.

UNITED STATES V. WATSON
423 U.S. 411 (1976)

FACTS

An informant, Khoury, phoned a postal inspector and informed him that Watson was in possession of a stolen credit card. On five to ten previous occasions Khoury had provided the inspector with reliable information on postal inspection matters, some involving Watson. Later the same day Khoury delivered the card to the inspector. On learning that Watson had agreed to furnish additional cards, the inspector asked Khoury to arrange to meet with Watson. Watson canceled that engagement, but on another day, Khoury met with Watson at a restaurant. Khoury had been instructed that if Watson had additional stolen credit cards, Khoury was to give a designated signal. The signal was given, the officers closed in, and Watson was arrested. A search incident to arrest revealed that Watson had no credit cards on his person, so the inspector asked if he could look inside Watson's car, which was standing within view. Watson said, "Go ahead," and repeated these words when the inspector cautioned that "[i]f I find anything, it is going to go against you." The inspector entered the car and found under the floor mat an envelope containing two credit cards in the names of other persons. These cards were the basis for two counts of a four-count indictment charging Watson with possessing stolen mail. The U.S. Supreme Court granted certiorari.

ISSUE

Is a warrantless arrest in a public place constitutional, so long as the police have probable cause?

HOLDING

Yes. Police officers may arrest people in public places, even if there is time to obtain a warrant, so long as probable cause is in place in advance.

RATIONALE

"The usual rule is that a police officer may arrest without a warrant one believed by the officer upon reasonable cause to have been guilty of a felony.... Just last term, while recognizing that maximum protection of individual rights could be assured by requiring a magistrate's review of the factual justification prior to any arrest, we stated that 'such a requirement would constitute an intolerable handicap for legitimate law enforcement' and noted that the Court 'has never invalidated an arrest supported by probable cause solely because the officers failed to secure a warrant.'"

CASE SIGNIFICANCE

The Supreme Court has repeatedly stated that warrantless arrests under exigent circumstances conform to Fourth Amendment requirements, so long as probable cause is in place *a priori*. An arrest in a public place is basically one of these exigencies; suspects would obviously flee if the police were required to first obtain a warrant before making the arrest. Even if there is time to obtain a warrant, the Court stated that officers need not obtain one. *Watson* therefore gave the police considerable latitude in terms of making arrests. Arrests in public places coupled with probable cause conform to the strictures of the Fourth Amendment.

DUNAWAY V. NEW YORK
442 U.S. 200 (1979)

FACTS

An informant stated that Dunaway was involved in the killing of a pizza restaurant owner. The informant was questioned, but the information he provided did not give the police probable cause for a warrant to arrest Dunaway. The police only had reasonable suspicion that Dunaway was involved in the killing. Detectives therefore asked patrol officers to pick up Dunaway and bring him to the stationhouse for questioning. Dunaway was taken into custody at a neighbor's house. He was then transported to the police station, placed in an interrogation room, and advised of his *Miranda* rights. He waived his right to counsel and made incriminating statements. The U.S. Supreme Court granted certiorari.

ISSUE

May a person be seized and transported to a police station for interrogation based only on reasonable suspicion?

HOLDING

No. Stationhouse detentions during which interrogation takes place must be supported by probable cause. Taking a person into custody against his or her will for the purpose of interrogation requires probable cause. Even if no formal arrest is made, the act of taking one into custody still requires probable cause.

RATIONALE

"The detention of petitioner was in important respects indistinguishable from a traditional arrest. Petitioner was not questioned briefly where he was found [as a *Terry* stop would permit]. Instead, he was taken from a neighbor's home to a police car, transported to a police station, and placed in an interrogation room. He was never informed that he was 'free to go'; indeed, he would have been physically restrained if he had refused to accompany the officer or had tried to escape their custody. The application of the Fourth Amendment's requirement of probable cause does not depend on whether an intrusion of this magnitude is termed an 'arrest' under state law. The mere facts that petitioner was not told he was under arrest, was not 'booked,' and would not have had an arrest recorded if the interrogation had proved fruitless, while not insignificant for all purposes, obviously do not make petitioner's seizure even roughly analogous to the narrowly defined intrusions involved in *Terry* and its progeny."

CASE SIGNIFICANCE

This case addressed the gray area between an investigative stop and a full-blown arrest. Had police simply accosted Dunaway and questioned him, then the Fourth Amendment probably would not have been violated. However, when they took Dunaway into custody, from within another person's dwelling, no less, they should have had probable cause. Probable cause was required even though Dunaway was never formally placed under arrest. The actions in this case amounted to a "*de facto* arrest," a seizure almost identical to a traditional arrest. It also does not matter that Dunaway was advised of his *Miranda* rights. His statements were considered "fruit of the poisonous tree" because they were arrived at via an unconstitutional seizure.

PAYTON V. NEW YORK
445 U.S. 573 (1980)

FACTS

Two days after the murder of a gas station attendant, New York detectives had assembled evidence sufficient to establish probable cause to believe that Payton had committed the murder. They broke into his apartment to arrest him without first obtaining a warrant. Payton was not there but was found later. While the officers were in the apartment, however, a shell casing, which was in plain view, was seized and used against Payton at his murder trial. The U.S. Supreme Court granted certiorari.

ISSUE

Absent exigent circumstances, is a warrantless entry for the purpose of making an arrest constitutional?

HOLDING

No. The constitutional protection granted to the individual's interest in the privacy of his own home applies equally to a warrantless entry for the purpose of arresting a resident of the house. Unless exigent circumstances are present, it is unconstitutional to make a warrantless entry into a private place for the purpose of effecting an arrest.

RATIONALE

"In terms that apply equally to seizures of property and to seizures of persons, the Fourth Amendment has drawn a firm line at the entrance to the house. Absent exigent circumstances, that threshold may not reasonably be crossed without a warrant."

CASE SIGNIFICANCE

This case reinforced the notion that people have a high expectation of privacy in their homes. The police must now obtain a warrant to arrest a person in a private place. Exceptions to this requirement exist, however. "Hot pursuit," an exigency, permits warrantless entry. Also, if there is probable cause to believe a suspect may pose a danger to other individuals, destroy evidence, or flee if not apprehended immediately, a warrantless entry is permissible.

WELSH V. WISCONSIN
466 U.S. 740 (1984)

FACTS

At about nine o'clock p.m. on a rainy night a person witnessed a car being driven erratically. After veering back and forth, the car swerved off the road and came to a stop in an open field. The car was not damaged and the driver was not injured. The witness pulled behind the car in order to prevent it from being driven on the road. The police were called, but the driver of the vehicle walked away prior to their arrival. A check of the vehicle's registration showed that Welsh, the owner, lived within a short distance of where the car had been abandoned. The police proceeded to Welsh's residence, entered it, and arrested him in his bedroom. At the time of this case Wisconsin law considered driving while intoxicated, the offense for which Welsh was arrested, a noncriminal violation punishable by a maximum fine of $200. The U.S. Supreme Court granted certiorari.

ISSUE

Does the Fourth Amendment permit the warrantless arrest of a suspect in a private dwelling, when the arrestable offense is not jailable?

HOLDING

No. The warrantless nighttime entry of a person's home to make an arrest for a nonjailable offense violates the Fourth Amendment.

RATIONALE

"It is axiomatic that 'the physical entry of the home is the chief evil against which the wording of the Fourth Amendment is directed.' . . . Consistently with these long-recognized principles, the Court decided in *Payton v. New York* that warrantless felony arrests in the home are prohibited by the Fourth Amendment, absent probable cause and exigent circumstances. . . . Our hesitation in finding exigent circumstances, especially when warrantless arrests in the home are at issue, is especially appropriate when the underlying offense for which there is probable cause to arrest is relatively minor. Before agents of the government may invade the sanctity of the home, the burden is on the government to demonstrate exigent circumstances that overcome the presumption of unreasonableness that attaches to all warrantless home entries. When the government's interest is only to arrest for a minor offense, that presumption of unreasonableness is difficult to rebut, and the government usually should be allowed to make such arrests only with a warrant issued upon probable cause by a neutral and detached magistrate. . . . We therefore conclude that the common-sense approach utilized by most lower courts is required by the Fourth Amendment prohibition on 'unreasonable searches and seizures,' and hold that an important factor to be considered when determining whether an exigency exists is the gravity of the underlying offense for which the arrest is being made."

CASE SIGNIFICANCE

Warrantless entry into the home is unconstitutional absent probable cause *and* exigent circumstances. The police had probable cause to enter Welsh's home, but the Supreme Court declared that minor offenses do not create a sufficient exigency such that warrantless entry should be sanctioned. Thus, not only should the police consider possible flight, destruction of evidence, or harm to others, but the seriousness of the underlying offense as well.

WINSTON V. LEE
470 U.S. 753 (1985)

FACTS

Following a robbery, the suspect, Lee, was shot in the leg. After he was hospitalized, the government sought a court order to have the bullet removed. The order was granted, but when it was discovered that the bullet was deeper than originally thought and that general anesthesia would be required, Lee sought another hearing in state court, which was denied. The issue went before the Supreme Court.

ISSUE

Does forcing a person to undergo surgery for the purpose of finding evidence violate the Fourth Amendment?

HOLDING

Yes. The seizure of evidence from inside a person's body by means of surgery violates the Fourth Amendment, unless the government can demonstrate a compelling need for the evidence.

RATIONALE

"A compelled surgical intrusion into an individual's body for evidence . . . implicates expectations of privacy and security of such magnitude that the intrusion may be 'unreasonable' even if likely to produce evidence of a crime. . . . The unreasonableness of surgical intrusions beneath the skin depends on a case-by-case approach, in which the individual's interests in privacy and security are weighed against society's interest in conducting the procedure. In a given case, the question whether the community's need for evidence outweighs the substantial privacy interest at stake is a delicate one admitting of few categorical answers."

CASE SIGNIFICANCE

This case is important because it illustrated that there are limits to what the government can do in searching for evidence. However, the Court did not say that the government can never engage in surgery to search for evidence. Three factors should first be considered: (1) the extent to which the procedure threatens the health or safety of the person; (2) the extent to which the intrusion impinges upon the person's "dignitary interests in personal privacy and bodily integrity"; and (3) the extent to which prohibiting the intrusion would affect the "community's interest in fairly and accurately determining guilt or innocence."

UNITED STATES V. ALVAREZ-MACHAIN
504 U.S. 655 (1992)

FACTS

Alvarez-Machain was a citizen and resident of Mexico. However, he was indicted in the U.S. for his participation in the kidnapping and murder of a Drug Enforcement Administration agent, Enrique Camarena-Salazar. Alvarez-Machain was abducted by U.S. authorities at his place of employment in Guadalajara, Mexico. He was then flown to El Paso, Texas, where he was arrested by DEA agents. He claimed at trial that the district court that was to try his case lacked jurisdiction because his abduction was in violation of an extradition treaty between the U.S. and Mexico.

ISSUE

Can a foreigner be forcibly abducted from his or her country of origin and brought to the U.S. for trial, provided the abduction does not violate any treaties?

HOLDING

Yes. The abduction of a foreigner that is not in violation of a treaty does not deprive a U.S. Court of jurisdiction over the foreigner's criminal trial, even if the abduction is over the other country's protest.

RATIONALE

"This Court has never departed from the rule announced in *Ker v. Illinois* . . . that the power of a court to try a person for crime is not impaired by the fact that he had been brought within the court's jurisdiction by reason of a 'forcible abduction.' No persuasive reasons are newly presented to justify overruling this line of cases. They rest on the sound basis that due process of law is satisfied when one present in court is convicted of [a] crime after having been fairly apprised of the charges against him and after a fair trial in accordance with constitutional procedural safeguards. There is nothing in the Constitution that requires a court to permit a guilty person rightfully convicted to escape justice because he was brought to trial against his will."

CASE SIGNIFICANCE

The Court stated that "[n]either the [extradition] treaty's language nor the history of negotiations and practice under it supports the proposition that it prohibits abductions outside its terms." This decision is therefore important because it permits authorities to forcibly abduct criminal defendants from other countries, assuming the abduction does not violate a treaty. This decision extended *Frisbie v. Collins* beyond the U.S. border.

ATWATER V. CITY OF LAGO VISTA
532 U.S. 318 (2001)

FACTS

A Texas police officer on traffic patrol observed Atwater and her two young children driving without their seatbelts. Failure to wear a seatbelt is a misdemeanor in Texas, punishable by a maximum $50 fine. Failure to wear a seatbelt is known as a citation-only offense, because it carries no possibility of incarceration. Nevertheless, the officer arrested Atwater. The officer's actions were authorized by Texas law, which holds that peace officers can arrest and cite for all offenses, even nonjailable ones. Atwater posted bail shortly after arrest and eventually pled no contest to the seat-belt violation. She then brought a Section 1983 lawsuit against the officer and his employer, alleging that the arrest violated her Fourth Amendment right to be free from unreasonable seizures.

ISSUE

Is it a violation of the Fourth Amendment to arrest a person for an offense that carries no jail term?

HOLDING

No. It is reasonable for a police officer with probable cause to believe a crime has been committed in his presence to make an arrest for a minor criminal offense. The Fourth Amendment permits arrest for offenses that carry no jail term.

RATIONALE

"Atwater has cited no particular evidence that those who framed and ratified the Fourth Amendment sought to limit peace officers' warrantless misdemeanor arrest authority to instances of actual breach of the peace, and the Court's review of framing-era documentary history has likewise failed to reveal any such design. Nor is there in any of the modern historical accounts of the Fourth Amendment's adoption any substantial indication that the Framers intended such a restriction.

Indeed, to the extent the modern histories address the issue, their conclusions are to the contrary. The evidence of actual practice also counsels against Atwater's position. During the period leading up to and surrounding the framing of the Bill of Rights, colonial and state legislatures, like Parliament before them, regularly authorized local officers to make warrantless misdemeanor arrests without a breach of the peace condition. That the Fourth Amendment did not originally apply to the States does not make state practice irrelevant in unearthing the Amendment's original meaning. A number of state constitutional search-and-seizure provisions served as models for the Fourth Amendment, and the fact that many of the original States with such constitutional limitations continued to grant their officers broad warrantless misdemeanor arrest authority undermines Atwater's position."

CASE SIGNIFICANCE

In many ways this case is both significant and insignificant. It is significant because it granted wide latitude to law enforcement in terms of making arrests for minor offenses. On the other hand, it is doubtful that many police officers will now decide to start arresting people for minor, nonjailable offenses. Importantly, the offense in *Atwater,* even though fairly minor, was criminal. The Supreme Court did not address the constitutionality of arrests for noncriminal offenses; for example, in most states exceeding the posted speed limit (within reason) is not a criminal offense, but rather a violation. ✦

DISCUSSION QUESTIONS

1. *Atwater* gave police the authority to arrest people for seatbelt violations and other nonjailable offenses. Is this decision likely to affect the police profession in a noticeable way? That is, are police officers now more likely to arrest people for seatbelt violations?

2. Discuss examples of exigent circumstances that would permit police to make warrantless arrests in private places.

3. What factors help the courts distinguish between an arrest and a lesser intrusion such as a *Terry* stop?

4. What is the requisite justification for a constitutionally valid arrest? What happens if that justification is not present? (At least two remedies are conceivable.)

5. Based on your assessment of the cases covered in this chapter, has the Supreme Court been more "friendly" to the police or to criminals? That is, which group (police or criminals) has had the largest number of cases decided in its favor? ✦

Chapter Five
Standards for the Use of Force

Tennessee v. Garner, 471 U.S. 1 (1985)

Graham v. Connor, 490 U.S. 396 (1989)

INTRODUCTION

Almost every state has a law or regulation concerning police use of force. The American Law Institute adopted just one such regulation which resembles many others in place around the country. Section 120.7 states that a police officer "may use such force as is reasonably necessary to effect the arrest, to enter premises to effect the arrest, or to prevent the escape from custody of an arrested person." Further, deadly force is authorized when the crime in question is a felony and when such force "creates no substantial risk to innocent persons" and the officer "reasonably believes" that there is a "substantial risk" that the fleeing felon will inflict harm on other people or police officers.

In *Tennessee v. Garner,* the Supreme Court adopted a rule similar to the American Law Institute's formulation. *Garner* involved the shooting death of a young, unarmed fleeing felon. The result was the leading Supreme Court precedent concerning the use of deadly force to apprehend fleeing felons. The *Garner* decision declared unconstitutional a Tennessee statute that authorized police officers who give notice of the intent to arrest to "use all the necessary means to effect the arrest" if the suspect flees or resists.

The Court ruled that deadly force may be used when: (1) it is necessary to prevent the suspect's escape and (2) the officer has probable cause to believe the suspect poses a serious threat of death or serious physical injury to other people or police officers. One would think that the Supreme Court would be unanimous in a decision such as this, but three justices dissented, noting that the statute struck down by the majority "assist[s] the police in apprehending suspected perpetrators of serious crimes and provide[s] notice that a lawful police order to stop and submit to arrest may not be ignored with impunity."

Four years after *Garner,* the Supreme Court decided the landmark case of *Graham v. Connor,* which set the standard for nondeadly force. The Court declared emphatically that all claims involving allegations of excessive force against police officers must be analyzed under the Fourth Amendment's reasonableness requirement. Further, the Court adopted an "objective reasonableness" test to decide when excessive force is used. This requires focusing on what a *reasonable* police officer would do "without regard to [the officer's] underlying intent or motivation." In helping to decide what a reasonable police officer would do, the Court looked to three factors: (1) the severity of the crime; (2) whether the suspect poses a threat; and (3) whether the suspect is resisting and/or attempting to flee the scene. Courts must, in focusing on these three factors, allow ". . . for the fact that police officers are often forced to make split-second judgments—about the amount of force that is necessary in a particular situation." Generally, then, if the crime in question is a serious one and the suspect is dangerous and resists arrest, the suspect will have difficulty succeeding with an excessive force claim.

Incidentally, both the *Garner* and *Graham* decisions resulted from Section 1983 lawsuits. Garner's surviving family members and Graham himself both sued on the grounds that their constitutional rights had been violated. Unlike many of the cases this book focuses on, which involve evidence of crimes (weapons, drugs, confessions, etc.), *Garner* and *Graham* did not focus on how evidence was obtained, because there was none. The only remedy available to Garner's family and Graham was civil litigation. ✦

TENNESSEE V. GARNER
471 U.S. 1 (1985)

FACTS

Memphis police officers responded to a prowler call. When they arrived at the scene, a woman was standing on her porch pointing toward the adjacent house. She said "they" were breaking in next door. One officer went behind the adjacent house. He heard a door slam and observed Garner, 15, running across the back yard. He stopped at a six-foot high chain-link fence located at the edge of the yard. The officer's flashlight illuminated Garner's face and hands. There was no sign of a weapon. The officer yelled, "Police, halt," and took steps toward Garner as he was beginning to climb the fence. The officer was convinced that Garner would escape if he made it over the fence. As such, the officer shot Garner. He died from a gunshot wound to the back of the head. The officer was acting under Tennessee state law, which stated that "if, after notice of the intention to arrest the defendant, he either flee[s] or forcibly resist[s], the officer may use all the necessary means to effect the arrest." Garner's family brought a Section 1983 lawsuit, alleging that Garner's seizure violated the Fourth Amendment.

ISSUE

Is it a violation of the Fourth Amendment for police to use deadly force to apprehend a fleeing felon who poses no apparent threat to others?

HOLDING

Yes. It is a violation of the Fourth Amendment for police to use deadly force on a nonviolent fleeing felon, unless there is probable cause to believe that the suspect poses a significant threat of death or serious injury to the officer or others.

RATIONALE

"The use of deadly force to prevent the escape of all felony suspects, whatever the circumstances, is constitutionally unreasonable. It is not better that all felony suspects die than that they escape. Where the suspect poses no immediate threat to the officer and no threat to others, the harm resulting from failing to apprehend him does not justify the use of deadly force to do so. It is no doubt unfortunate when a suspect who is in sight escapes, but the fact that the police arrive a little late or are a little slower of foot does not always justify killing the suspect. A police officer may not seize an unarmed, nondangerous suspect by shooting him dead. The Tennessee statute is unconstitutional insofar as it authorizes the use of deadly force against such fleeing suspect."

CASE SIGNIFICANCE

This is the most significant Supreme Court case addressing deadly force to date, as it placed restrictions on when the police can use deadly force to apprehend fleeing felons. Deadly force is now permissible only when, after warning the suspect, the officer has probable cause that serious harm or injury will befall other individuals. It is worth mentioning that *Garner* probably did not alter police practice in all jurisdictions around the country. At issue in the case was the constitutionality of Tennessee's statute. Other states maintained, and continue to maintain, restrictive statutes governing the use of deadly force. The same applies to police departments around the country; many adopted restrictive deadly force policies well before the Court's decision in *Garner*.

GRAHAM V. CONNOR
490 U.S. 396 (1989)

FACTS

Graham, a diabetic, asked a friend to drive him to a nearby convenience store so he could purchase some orange juice to counteract an insulin reaction. There were too many people in line at the store, so he left and asked to be driven to his friend's house. Officer Connor of the Charlotte (NC) Police Department became suspicious in light of Graham's quick entry into and exit from the convenience store. The officer followed the car and stopped it. The driver explained that Graham was having an insulin reaction, but the officer ordered both men out of the car while he determined what happened in the store. Other officers arrived and handcuffed Graham. They ignored his attempts to explain what happened. Graham sustained several injuries during the encounter, but was eventually released. He brought a Section 1983 lawsuit (based on 42 U.S.C. 1983) against the police, alleging that the officers applied excessive force.

ISSUE

Can police officers be held liable under the Fourth Amendment for excessive force and, if so, what standard should be used?

HOLDING

Yes. The appropriate standard is objective reasonableness under the Fourth Amendment.

RATIONALE

"The 'reasonableness' of a particular use of force must be judged from the perspective of a reasonable officer on the scene, rather than with the 20/20 vision of hindsight. The Fourth Amendment is not violated by an arrest based on probable cause, even though the wrong person is arrested, nor by the mistaken execution of a valid search warrant on the wrong premises. With respect to a claim of excessive force, the same standard of reasonableness at the moment applies: 'Not every push or shove, even if it may later seem unnecessary in the peace of a judge's chamber,' violates the Fourth Amendment. The calculus of reasonableness must embody allowance for the fact that police officers are often forced to make split-second judgments—in circumstances that are tense, uncertain, and rapidly evolving—about the amount of force that is necessary in a particular situation."

CASE SIGNIFICANCE

Graham is the leading Supreme Court case dealing with excessive force. It cleared up any past ambiguities as to the appropriate constitutional standard by which to judge excessive force claims. Now, when a plaintiff alleges that a police officer violated his or her Fourth Amendment rights, he or she must show that the officer acted in an objectively unreasonable fashion, that is, "without regard to [the officer's] underlying intent or motivation." ✦

DISCUSSION QUESTIONS

1. *Garner* and *Graham* set fairly strict standards for the use of deadly and nondeadly force. To what extent do these standards directly affect law enforcement officers?

2. Besides *Garner* and *Graham,* what other documents, cases, laws, and standards govern the use of force in the law enforcement profession?

3. Why do you suppose the Supreme Court chose the Fourth Amendment's reasonableness standard as the appropriate one for evaluating claims of unconstitutional force by the police?

4. *Graham* applies to the police, not corrections officers. The Supreme Court has announced that that Eighth Amendment should be used to judge claims of unconstitutional force by corrections officers. Moreover, the Court has declared that corrections officers cannot be held liable for Eighth Amendment violations unless their conduct is malicious and sadistic (see *Hudson v. McMillian,* 503 U.S. 1 [1992]). Why do you suppose a higher standard has been adopted for corrections officers?

5. What can be done to combat excessive force?

6. Is excessive force as much of a problem today as it has been in the past? ✦

Chapter Six

Searches With Warrants

INTRODUCTION

Search warrants require three essential components. First, they are required to be issued by a neutral and detached magistrate. Second, probable cause is required. Finally, warrants need to conform to the Fourth Amendment's particularity requirement. Some attention also needs to be given to the procedures for serving search warrants as well as to when search warrants are required and how they are to be issued. Each of these topics is addressed in the paragraphs that follow.

Most judges are considered neutral and detached. Even so, the Supreme Court has focused, in a number of cases, on this first critical warrant requirement. For example, in *Coolidge v. New Hampshire,* the Court declared that a state attorney general cannot issue a search warrant. State attorneys general are chief prosecutors and thus inclined to side with law enforcement officers.

There have even been some cases where the Court has focused on the extent to which judges can be viewed as neutral and detached. For example, in *Lo-Ji Sales, Inc. v. New York,* 442 U.S. 319 (1979), a magistrate issued a warrant for two "obscene" items, but he also authorized the police to seize any other items that he might find obscene upon examination of the location to be searched. The magistrate then accompanied the officers on the search, discovered items which he deemed to be obscene, and added them to the initial warrant. The items were then admitted into evidence against the defendants. The Supreme Court declared that the mag-

istrate was not acting in a neutral and detached capacity: ". . . he was not acting as a judicial officer but as an adjunct law-enforcement officer." Also, if a magistrate has a financial interest in the issuance of warrants, he or she cannot be considered neutral and detached.

Probable cause was discussed in Chapter Two, and we do not need to revisit its definition here. However, it is important to point out that, as a component of a valid search warrant, probable cause is required. The probable cause showing in a search warrant is twofold. First, the officer applying for the search warrant most show probable cause that the items to be seized are connected with criminal activity. Second, the officer must show probable cause that the items to be seized are in the location to be searched.

The particularity requirement for search warrants is twofold. First, the warrant must specify the place to be searched. Next, the warrant must specify the items to be seized. The reason for this particularity requirement stems from the framers' concerns with so-called "general warrants." General warrants, which were issued by the English Crown, permitted basically limitless searches for evidence of treason.

Contrary to popular belief, search warrants do not need to state with absolute precision the place to be searched. It "is enough if the description is such that the officer with a search warrant can, with reasonable effort, ascertain and identify the place intended" (*Steele v. United States,* 267 U.S. 498 [1925]). However, the items mentioned in the warrant should be described with sufficient specificity that a reasonable officer would know where to look for them.

In situations where the warrant incorrectly specifies the place to be searched, the courts will focus on the reasonableness of the officers' mistake. For example, in *Maryland v. Garrison,,* police officers obtained a warrant to search the person of Lawrence McWebb and the premises known as 2036 Park Avenue third floor apartment. They believed that McWebb's apartment occupied the entire third floor when, in fact, there were two apartments on that floor—one of which belonged to Garrison. The Court held that the warrant was valid because it was based on information by a trusted informant and because the police inquired with the local utility company and were given the impression that there was only one apartment on the third floor. As for the items to be seized, the warrant must clearly specify what the police wish to seize.

Next, there are several important requirements concerning the service of search warrants. One of these requirements, known as the knock and announce rule, is discussed in Chapter Seven. Aside from the knock and announce rule, two cases are important. First, the police may also detain people as needed while serving a search warrant (*Michigan v. Summers*). According to the Court, "a warrant to search for contraband founded on probable cause implicitly carries with it the limited authority to detain the occupants of the premises while a proper search is conducted." Second, in *Steagald v. United States,* the Supreme Court responded to Justice Marshall's concern that while an arrest warrant may protect a person "from an unreasonable seizure, it [does] absolutely nothing to protect [a third party's] privacy interest in being free from an unreasonable invasion and search of his home." Accordingly, the Court decided that in such situations the police must obtain not only an arrest warrant for the person they seek, but a *separate* warrant to search a third-party residence for the arrestee.

Finally, two additional cases that we consider in this chapter deal with the issuance of search warrants. First, in *Zurcher v. Stanford Daily,* the Supreme Court held that a warrant can be issued for the search of premises controlled by an innocent third party, provided that probable cause is present. Next, in *Mincey v. Arizona,* the Court held that if no exigent circumstances exist, a warrant must be obtained to search the scene of a homicide. ✦

COOLIDGE V. NEW HAMPSHIRE
403 U.S. 443 (1971)

FACTS

Pamela Mason, a 14-year-old girl, left her home in Manchester, New Hampshire, during a bad snow storm, apparently because she was called away for a babysitting job. Her body was found several days later near a busy highway. She had been murdered. Coolidge was questioned and asked to take a lie detector test. Detectives also interviewed Coolidge's wife while her husband was at the police station taking the lie detector test. The wife produced four guns and clothing that she thought her husband was wearing on the night of the murder. Coolidge was held in a jail cell overnight on an unrelated charge, then released the next day. Two weeks later the attorney general, who was also a justice of the peace, issued a warrant to the police to search Coolidge's car. Incriminating evidence was found in the trunk. The U.S. Supreme Court later granted certiorari.

ISSUE

Can a warrant be issued by a member of the executive branch of government?

HOLDING

No. The warrant issued by the attorney general, the state's chief investigator and prosecutor, was invalid because it was not issued by a neutral and detached magistrate.

RATIONALE

"The classic statement of the policy underlying the warrant requirement of the Fourth Amendment is that of Mr. Justice Jackson, writing for the Court in *Johnson v. United States,* 333 U.S. 10: 'The point of the Fourth Amendment, which often is not grasped by zealous officers, is not that it denies law enforcement the support of the usual inferences which reasonable men draw from evidence. Its protection consists in requiring that those inferences be drawn by a neutral and detached magistrate instead of being judged by the officer engaged in the often competitive enterprise of ferreting out crime. Any assumption that evidence sufficient to support a magistrate's disinterested determination to issue a search warrant will justify the officer in making a search without a warrant would reduce the Amendment to a nullity and leave the people's homes secure only in the discretion of police officers.'"

CASE SIGNIFICANCE

The Fourth Amendment expressly requires that warrants be issued by a neutral and detached magistrate. For some years, however, the Supreme Court did not decide who is to be considered neutral and detached. This case resolved the issue; attorneys general and other employees of the executive branch of government are not considered neutral and detached for purposes of the Fourth Amendment. Even members of the judicial branch can be considered not neutral and detached. If, for example, a judge receives a fee for each warrant issued, the warrant will be invalid under the Fourth Amendment (see *Connally v. Georgia,* 429 U.S. 245 [1977]).

ZURCHER V. STANFORD DAILY
436 U.S. 547 (1978)

FACTS

On Friday, April 9, 1971, officers of the Palo Alto Police Department and the Santa Clara County Sheriff's Department responded to a call from the director of the Stanford University Hospital requesting the removal of several demonstrators who had seized control of the hospital's offices and occupied them for nearly 24 hours. Several officers were injured while attempting to interrupt the demonstration. The next day, the Sunday edition of the *Stanford Daily* printed several pictures of the violent confrontation. The day after that, the district attorney secured a warrant to search the *Stanford Daily*'s offices for the pictures in question, so that the police could identify the people responsible for injuring police officers during the confrontation. The *Stanford Daily* was an innocent third party, as the warrant did not implicate the newspaper. A thorough search took place but no evidence other than the published photos was found. The paper brought a lawsuit against the police, arguing that a subpoena should have been used instead of a search, and the U.S. Supreme Court granted certiorari.

ISSUE

Can a search warrant be issued to search premises controlled by innocent third parties for evidence?

HOLDING

Yes. Searches with warrants of property belonging to third parties are permissible, so long as probable cause is in place and the evidence is subject to seizure.

RATIONALE

"The critical element in a reasonable search is not that the owner of the property is suspected of crime but that there is reasonable cause to believe that the specific 'things' to be searched for and seized are located on the property in which entry is sought. . . . Aware of the long struggle between Crown and press and desiring to curb unjustified official intrusions, the Framers took the enormously important step of subjecting searches to the test of reasonableness and to the general rule requiring search warrants issued by neutral magistrates. They nevertheless did not forbid warrants where the press was involved, did not require special showings that subpoenas would be impractical, and did not insist that the owner of the place to be searched, if connected with the press, must be shown to be implicated in the offense being investigated. Further, the prior cases do no more than insist that the courts apply the warrant requirement with particular exactitude when First Amendment interest would be endangered by the search. As we see it, no more than this is required where the warrant requested is for the seizure of criminal evidence reasonably believed to be on the premises occupied by a newspaper. Properly administered, the preconditions for a warrant—probable cause, specificity with respect to the place to be searched and the things to be seized, and overall reasonableness—should afford sufficient protection against the harms that are assertedly threatened by warrants for searching newspaper offices."

CASE SIGNIFICANCE

This case is significant because it expanded the authority of law enforcement officials to search for evidence. A search need not be addressed at a particular person's dwelling. Instead, the focus now is on where the evidence to be seized is located. If such evidence is located in a third-party dwelling, the Fourth Amendment does not prohibit a search in such a location, so long as probable cause and a warrant are in place prior to the search. In most circumstances, though, searches of the type described in *Zurcher* should be limited to contraband, the fruits of crime, or the instrumentalities of crime.

MINCEY V. ARIZONA
437 U.S. 385 (1978)

FACTS

Undercover police officer Headricks purchased heroin from Mincey in his apartment. Later that day, Headricks returned with several other plainclothes police officers and a deputy district attorney. The door was opened by Hodgman, a friend of Mincey. Headricks slipped inside and then went into the bedroom. Hodgman unsuccessfully attempted to shut the door before any of the other officers could gain entry. Meanwhile, shots were fired in the bedroom. Officer Headricks emerged from the bedroom and collapsed on the floor. When officers entered the bedroom, they found Mincey on the floor, wounded and barely conscious. A young woman was also found in the bedroom closet. Homicide detectives learned of the incident and responded to the house 10 minutes after the shooting. They took charge of the crime scene and began to collect evidence. The search lasted four days and included an exhaustive search of the apartment. More than 200 objects were seized. Headricks died later in the hospital. The U.S. Supreme Court later granted certiorari.

ISSUE

Is a search warrant required to search the scene of a homicide?

HOLDING

Yes. If no exigent circumstances exist, a warrant must be obtained to search a murder scene.

RATIONALE

"The Fourth Amendment proscribes all unreasonable searches and seizures, and it is a cardinal principle that 'searches conducted outside judicial process, without prior approval by judge or magistrate, are per se unreasonable under the Fourth Amendment—subject only to a few specifically established and well-delineated exceptions.' The Arizona Supreme Court did not hold that the search of the petitioner's apartment fell within any of the exceptions to the warrant requirement previously recognized by this Court, but rather that the search of a homicide scene should be recognized as an additional exception."

CASE SIGNIFICANCE

This case is important because, according to the Court, "the seriousness of the offense under investigation did not itself create exigent circumstances of the kind that under the Fourth Amendment justify a warrantless search, where there is no indication that evidence would be lost, destroyed, or removed during the time required to obtain a search warrant and there is no suggestion that a warrant could not easily and conveniently have been obtained." In other words, murder scenes do not create "exigent circumstances," which generally permit warrantless searches.

STEAGALD V. UNITED STATES
451 U.S. 204 (1981)

FACTS

An informant provided the Drug Enforcement Administration with the phone number where Lyons, a federal fugitive, could be reached over the next 24 hours. An address that corresponded to the number was obtained from the phone company. Two days later, two DEA agents drove to the address to search for Lyons. Lyons had an outstanding arrest warrant. Gaultney and Steagald were observed outside the house. Officers approached them with guns drawn, frisked them, and demanded identification. When agents went to the front door, Gaultney's wife answered the door and told the agents that she was alone in the house. She was detained by one agent while another searched the house. Lyons was not found but a substance that appeared to be cocaine was observed in plain view. The agent in charge sent someone to obtain a search warrant. Meanwhile, the search continued and additional incriminating evidence was found. When a search warrant was issued and served, 43 pounds of cocaine was discovered. The case later came before the U.S. Supreme Court.

ISSUE

Without a separate search warrant, can police officers search the home of a third party for a person for whom they have an arrest warrant?

HOLDING

No. An arrest warrant is valid only for an arrest in a suspect's place of residence or in a public place, not in a third-party dwelling. A separate search warrant must also be obtained before arrest warrants can be served in third-party dwellings.

RATIONALE

". . . [W]hether the arrest warrant issued in this case adequately safeguarded the interests protected by the Fourth Amendment depends upon what the warrant authorized the agents to do. To be sure, the warrant embodied a judicial finding that there was probable cause to believe that Ricky Lyons had committed a felony, and the warrant therefore authorized the officers to seize Lyons. However, the agents sought to do more than use the warrant to arrest Lyons in a public place or in his home; instead, they relied on the warrant as legal authority to enter the home of a third person based on their belief that Ricky Lyons might be a guest there. Regardless of how reasonable this belief might have been, it was never subjected to the detached scrutiny of a judicial officer. Thus, while the warrant in this case may have protected Lyons from an unreasonable seizure, it did absolutely nothing to protect petitioner's privacy interest in being free from an unreasonable invasion and search of his home. Instead, petitioner's only protection from an illegal entry and search was the agent's personal determination of probable cause. In the absence of exigent circumstances, we have consistently held that such judicially untested determinations are not reliable enough to justify an entry into a person's home to arrest him without a warrant, or a search of a home for objects in the absence of a search warrant. We see no reason to depart from this settled course when the search of a home is for a person rather than an object."

CASE SIGNIFICANCE

This case is significant because it placed restrictions on the service of arrest warrants. Arrest warrants can only be served in one of two places: (1) public areas and (2) the suspect's place of residence. Since *Steagald,* when suspects are sought in third-party dwellings, a separate search warrant must also be obtained. This assumes, however, that no exigent circumstances are present. Had the police in *Steagald* been able to show that Lyons would have escaped had they waited for a search warrant, the search would have been upheld.

MICHIGAN V. SUMMERS
452 U.S. 692 (1981)

FACTS

Summers descended the front stairs of his house and was confronted by Detroit police officers who were there to execute a search warrant to look for narcotics. The officers requested Summers' assistance in gaining entry and detained him while the search was conducted. Narcotics were found in the basement and Summers was arrested. A search incident to arrest also revealed that narcotics were in his coat pocket. The case later came before the U.S. Supreme Court.

ISSUE

Do police have authority to detain residents of a house that is to be searched pursuant to a valid warrant?

HOLDING

Yes. A warrant carries with it the authority to detain residents of houses to be searched pursuant to a valid warrant.

RATIONALE

"If the evidence that a citizen's residence is harboring contraband is sufficient to persuade a judicial officer that an invasion of the citizen's privacy is justified, it is constitutionally reasonable to require that citizen to remain while the officers of the law execute a valid warrant to search his home. Thus, for Fourth Amendment purposes, we hold that a warrant to search for contraband founded on probable cause implicitly carries with it the limited authority to detain the occupants of the premises while a proper search is conducted. . . . Because it was lawful to require Summers to re-enter and to remain in the house until evidence establishing probable cause to arrest him was found, his arrest and the search incident thereto was constitutionally permissible."

CASE SIGNIFICANCE

This case is significant because it enhanced the authority police possess by virtue of obtaining a search warrant. However, the key to this case is that it dealt with the detention of the person whose residence was to be searched. With regard to the detention of third parties who may be at the scene, the Supreme Court has been much more restrictive. In *Ybarra v. Illinois*, 444 U.S. 85 (1979), the Court refused to sanction the pat-down search of a patron of a bar that was about to be searched pursuant to valid warrant. The Court did not sanction the pat down because the state was unable to provide any articulable suspicion that Ybarra, a patron of the bar, was a threat to the officers who were there to serve the search warrant.

MARYLAND V. GARRISON
480 U.S. 79 (1987)

FACTS

Baltimore police officers obtained and executed a warrant to search the person of Lawrence McWebb and the "premises known as 2036 Park Avenue third floor apartment." The police reasonably believed that there was only one apartment on the third floor, but in fact there were two. The warrant was mistakenly served in Garrison's apartment. Police found heroin, and Garrison was convicted for possession of a controlled substance. The case later came before the U.S. Supreme Court.

ISSUE

Is evidence admissible when officers mistakenly and in good faith execute a search warrant at a location not authorized in the warrant?

HOLDING

Yes. A warrant that lacks particularity with regard to the place to be searched is valid if it is served in good faith.

RATIONALE

"Plainly, if the officers had known, or even if they should have known, that there were two separate dwelling units on the third floor of 2036 Park Avenue, they would have been obligated to exclude Garrison's apartment from the scope of the requested warrant. But we must judge the constitutionality of their conduct in light of the information available to them at the time they acted. Those items of evidence that emerge after the warrant is issued have no bearing on whether or not a warrant was validly issued. Just as the discovery of contraband cannot validate a warrant invalid when issued, so is it equally clear that the discovery of facts demonstrating that a valid warrant was unnecessarily broad does not retroactively invalidate the warrant. The validity of the warrant must be assessed on the basis of the information that the officers disclosed, or had a duty to discover and to disclose, to the issuing magistrate. On the basis of that information, we agree with the conclusion of all three Maryland courts that the warrant, insofar as it authorized a search that turned out to be ambiguous in scope, was valid when it issued."

CASE SIGNIFICANCE

The Fourth Amendment requires that no warrants shall issue without, among other things, describing the place to be searched and the persons or things to be seized. This is known as the "particularity requirement." Search warrants satisfy the particularity requirement with a valid address and a description of the items to be seized. The warrant in *Garrison* was deficient in terms of the place to be searched; that is, the address was incomplete. Nevertheless, the Supreme Court applied the good faith doctrine. In its reasoning, the Court stated that there was a reasonable effort on the part of the officers to determine the address of the location to be searched. Had they not taken these steps and, instead, sought a "general warrant" to search multiple dwellings, the evidence would not have been admissible.

CALIFORNIA V. GREENWOOD
486 U.S. 35 (1988)

FACTS

In early 1984, Investigator Stracner of the Laguna Beach Police Department learned that a suspect had informed a federal drug-enforcement agent that a truck filled with illegal narcotics was going to Greenwood's residence. A neighbor had also complained that many vehicles had stopped at Greenwood's house for short periods of time during the night. Stracner placed Greenwood's house under surveillance and confirmed that several vehicles came and went late at night. She asked the neighborhood's trash collector to pick up the garbage bags in front of Greenwood's house and turn them over to her. A search of the garbage bags revealed evidence of narcotics use. Information from the garbage search was used in an affidavit for a search warrant. A warrant was issued, served, and drugs were found. Greenwood was arrested and posted bail. More complaints came in about narcotics use at his house. The garbage was searched for a second time and, again, evidence of narcotics use was found. Greenwood was arrested again, and the case came before the U.S. Supreme Court.

ISSUE

Can items placed in the trash for collection on a public street be searched without a warrant or probable cause?

HOLDING

Yes. Trash left for collection in an area open to the public is considered abandoned. No expectation of privacy exists in garbage left in opaque bags outside the curtilage of a home.

RATIONALE

"The warrantless search and seizure of the garbage bags left at the Greenwood house would violate the Fourth Amendment only if the Greenwoods manifested a subjective expectation of privacy in their garbage that society accepts as objectively reasonable. . . . It may well be that the Greenwoods did not expect that the contents of their garbage bags would become known to the police or other members of the public. An expectation of privacy does not give rise to Fourth Amendment protection, however, unless society is prepared to accept that expectation as objectively reasonable. . . . Here we conclude that the Greenwoods exposed their garbage to the public sufficiently to defeat their claim to Fourth Amendment protection. It is common knowledge that plastic garbage bags left on or at the side of a public street are readily accessible to animals, children, scavengers, snoops, and other members of the public."

CASE SIGNIFICANCE

This case is significant because it reinforced the distinction between looking for evidence of a crime and engaging in "searches" within the meaning of the Fourth Amendment. In this case, the Court said that a search did not take place because there is no expectation of privacy in garbage placed on a public street for removal. The Court effectively said that garbage left for removal is "abandoned." Nothing prohibits law enforcement officials from examining, even without any justification, property considered abandoned.

MINNESOTA V. CARTER
525 U.S. 83 (1998)

FACTS

Based on information supplied by an informant, a police officer went to an apartment where narcotics violations were presumably taking place. The officer observed through the ground floor window people putting white powder into bags. When Carter and an accomplice, Johns, left the apartment, they were stopped by the police in their car. Officers observed a handgun in the car and arrested both men. A search of the automobile incident to arrest revealed drugs and drug paraphernalia. The officers then obtained an arrest warrant and returned to the apartment to arrest Thompson, the lessee. A search of the apartment revealed additional drugs. The officers later learned that Carter and Johns visited Thompson's apartment from another city and that they were only there for a short time for the purpose of packaging drugs. The case later came before the U.S. Supreme Court.

ISSUE

Does a person who is in another's apartment with consent and for the purpose of doing business enjoy an expectation of privacy?

HOLDING

No. A person who is in another's dwelling with consent and is there to do business does not enjoy a reasonable expectation of privacy.

RATIONALE

"Respondents here were obviously not overnight guests, but were essentially present for a business transaction and were only in the home for a matter of hours. There is no suggestion that they had a previous relationship with Thompson, or that there was any other purpose to their visit. Nor was there anything similar to the overnight guest relationship in *Olson* to suggest a degree of acceptance into the household. While the apartment was a dwelling for Thompson, it was for these respondents simply a place to do business."

CASE SIGNIFICANCE

The Supreme Court has stated that overnight guests enjoy an expectation of privacy in third-party dwellings. In this case, however, the guests were there for a short time and only to do business. The Court held that they did not enjoy an expectation of privacy. This decision is important because the defendants argued that the officers' actions were unconstitutional because they engaged in an unjustified search, thereby violating their Fourth Amendment rights. The Court stated that the Fourth Amendment was never implicated because even though the officers were government actors (one requirement for a Fourth Amendment search to take place), the defendants did not enjoy an expectation of privacy in the apartment (the second requirement for a search). ✦

DISCUSSION QUESTIONS

1. Identify several officials who cannot be considered neutral and detached for purposes of the Fourth Amendment.

2. Is it possible for the police to manipulate the Fourth Amendment's particularity requirement to their benefit?

3. The Fourth Amendment clearly lists the requirements for a valid warrant, yet the Supreme Court has authorized several varieties of warrantless searches and seizures. Why do you suppose this is? ✦

Chapter Seven

The Knock and Announce Rule

Wilson v. Arkansas, 514 U.S. 927 (1995)

Richards v. Wisconsin, 520 U.S. 385 (1997)

United States v. Ramirez, 523 U.S. 65 (1998)

INTRODUCTION

At common law, the police were entitled to break into a house to make an arrest after announcing their presence as well as the reason for being there. Nowadays, the method of entry the police can use to serve warrants (arrest and search) is usually set forth in legislation. With regard to federal law enforcement, for example, 18 U.S.C. Section 3109 states that an officer "may break open any outer or inner door or window of a house . . . to execute a search warrant, if, after notice of his authority and purpose, he is refused admittance."

Almost without exception the law requires that police officers announce their presence and state their authority (e.g., "Police officers, search warrant!"). There are several reasons for this: (1) it helps avoid needless destruction of property; (2) it helps prevent violence resulting from unnecessary surprise; and (3) it helps preserve people's dignity and privacy. Of course, there are certain situations where these reasons for a "knock and announce" requirement do not serve their intended purposes. The second reason can work against its intention; requiring police to announce their presence may increase the possibility of violence rather than reducing it. What, then, are the criteria for determining when a knock and announce is not required? It is useful to turn to Supreme Court precedent to answer this question.

One of the first cases where the Court addressed the constitutionality of the common law knock and announce requirement was *Wilson v. Arkansas*. The Supreme Court ruled that the officers *were* required to follow the knock and announce requirement when serving warrants.

The Supreme Court later clarified its position in the case of *Richards v. Wisconsin*. There, the Court held that police can dispense with the knock and announce requirement if they have *reasonable suspicion* that such a requirement "would be dangerous or futile, or that it would inhibit the effective investigation of the crime by, for example, allowing the destruction of evidence." Basically, then, if the police have reasonable suspicion to believe that exigent circumstances are present, it is not always necessary that they knock on the door and announce their presence.

We conclude this chapter with some attention to the Supreme Court's decision in *United States v. Ramirez*. There, the Court confronted the issue of whether the Fourth Amendment requires that the police show more than reasonable suspicion for the purpose of dispensing with the knock and announce requirement when the service of a warrant will result in the destruction of property (note that probable cause is still necessary in order to secure a warrant). It held that the Fourth Amendment does *not* require a higher standard, but it did note that "[e]xcessive or unnecessary destruction of property in the course of a search may violate the Fourth Amendment, even though the entry itself is lawful and the fruits of the search not subject to suppression" (*United States v. Ramirez*). ◆

WILSON V. ARKANSAS
514 U.S. 927 (1995)

FACTS

Wilson engaged in several narcotics transactions with a police informant over a period of several months. Based on these transactions, police officers obtained an arrest warrant for Wilson and a search warrant for her home. Once they arrived at Wilson's residence, the officers identified themselves and stated that they had a warrant as they entered the home through an unlocked door. The officers found several incriminating items. Wilson sought suppression of the evidence on the grounds that the officers did not follow the common law practice of knocking and announcing their presence.

ISSUE

In the absence of exigent circumstances, does the Fourth Amendment's reasonableness clause require that officers "knock and announce" their presence during the service of warrants?

HOLDING

Yes. Unless exigent circumstances exist, the Fourth Amendment's reasonableness clause requires that officers knock and announce their presence when serving search or arrest warrants.

RATIONALE

"An examination of the common law of search and seizure . . . leaves no doubt that the reasonableness of a search of a dwelling may depend in part on whether law enforcement officers announce their presence and authority prior to entering. . . . Our own cases have acknowledged that the common-law principle of announcement is embedded in Anglo-American law, but we have never squarely held that this principle is an element of the reasonableness inquiry under the Fourth Amendment. We now so hold."

CASE SIGNIFICANCE

This case was intended to restrict law enforcement officers from forcibly entering people's residences to serve warrants when doing so is not necessary. It also reinforced the importance of privacy interests in the home. However, if the threat of physical violence exists, if evidence is likely to be destroyed, or if the suspect is likely to escape, then announcement is not necessary. It would be unreasonable to require officers to place their lives in danger, or risk losing evidence or the suspect, by always announcing their presence during the service of warrants.

RICHARDS V. WISCONSIN
520 U.S. 385 (1997)

FACTS

Officers obtained a warrant to search Richards' hotel room for drugs and drug paraphernalia. The officers' request for a no-knock warrant was denied by the judge. When attempting to serve the warrant, one officer knocked on Richards' door and identified himself as a maintenance worker. Richards then saw one of the uniformed officers and slammed the door. At that point, the officers identified themselves and forcibly entered the unit. A search revealed incriminating evidence. An officer later justified the no-knock entry on the grounds that "police officers are never required to knock and announce when executing a search warrant in a felony drug investigation because of the special circumstances of today's drug culture." The case later came before the U.S. Supreme Court.

ISSUE

Does the Fourth Amendment permit a blanket exception to the common law knock and announce requirement for felony drug warrants?

HOLDING

No. The Fourth Amendment does not permit a blanket exception to the knock and announce requirement for felony drug warrants. Instead, the police must have reasonable suspicion—determined on a case-by-case basis—that knocking and announcing their presence "would be dangerous or futile, or that it would inhibit the effective investigation of the crime by, for example, allowing the destruction of evidence."

RATIONALE

". . . [T]he fact that felony drug investigations may frequently present circumstances warranting a no-knock entry cannot remove from the neutral scrutiny of a reviewing court the reasonableness of the police decision not to knock and announce in a particular case. Instead, in each case, it is the duty of a court confronted with the question to determine whether the facts and circumstances of the particular entry justified dispensing with the knock-and-announce requirement. . . . In order to justify a 'no knock' entry, the police must have reasonable suspicion that knocking and announcing their presence, under the particular circumstances, would be dangerous or futile, or that it would inhibit the effective investigation of the crime by, for example, allowing the destruction of evidence."

CASE SIGNIFICANCE

This case offered some clarification to the Court's decision in *Wilson v. Arkansas. Wilson* held that the police are required to knock and announce their presence when serving warrants, but that there are numerous exceptions to the rule. In *Richards,* the Court emphatically stated that there are no *blanket* exceptions, and that each situation must be viewed individually. However, Justice Brennan's dissent in *Ker v. California,* 374 U.S. 23 (1963), a case decided some years earlier, offered some useful guidelines that, arguably, are still in place today: "[T]he Fourth Amendment is violated by an unannounced police intrusion into a private home, with or without an arrest warrant, except (1) where the persons within already know of the officers' authority and purpose, or (2) where the officers are justified in the belief that persons within are in imminent peril of bodily harm, or (3) where those within, made aware of the presence of someone outside (because, for example, there has been a knock at the door), are then engaged in activity which justifies the officers in their belief that an escape or the destruction of evidence is being attempted."

UNITED STATES V. RAMIREZ
523 U.S. 65 (1998)

FACTS

With probable cause that a dangerous fugitive was staying at Ramirez's residence, federal agents obtained a no-knock warrant. Early in the morning, the agents announced their presence over a loudspeaker and simultaneously broke a window in the garage and pointed a gun through the opening to prevent anyone from obtaining weapons that an informant stated were being kept there. Ramirez awoke to the noise, assumed he was being burglarized, and grabbed a pistol and shot it through the ceiling of the garage. The police returned fire and Ramirez surrendered. The fugitive was never found, but Ramirez was charged with felony possession of a firearm. The U.S. Supreme Court granted certiorari.

ISSUE

Does the Fourth Amendment require a heightened showing of "more specific inferences of exigency" before any no-knock entry that will cause destruction of property?

HOLDING

No. The Fourth Amendment does not hold officers to a higher standard than reasonable suspicion where a no-knock warrant results in destruction of property.

RATIONALE

"Under *Richards,* a no-knock entry is justified if police have a 'reasonable suspicion' that knocking and announcing would be dangerous, futile, or destructive to the purposes of the investigation. Whether such a 'reasonable suspicion' exists depends in no way on whether police must destroy property in order to enter."

CASE SIGNIFICANCE

This case flowed directly from *Wilson v. Arkansas* and *Richards v. Wisconsin.* The question before the Court in this case was whether police need a high degree of certainty with regard to the presence of exigent circumstances when serving warrants that result in destruction of property, in this case the breaking of a window. The Court held that reasonable suspicion, not a high standard, is all that is required. This decision is sensible because the police may not necessarily know in advance whether property may need to be destroyed in order to serve the warrant. This decision effectively wiped out several Ninth Circuit decisions that "a more compelling showing of an exigency to justify a destructive no-knock entry than when a no-knock entry was effected without property damage." ✦

DISCUSSION QUESTIONS

1. Is the knock and announce rule too rigid?

2. Should the police be able to dispense with the knock and announce rule on more occasions?

3. Identify circumstances when it is not practical to knock and announce.

4. Identify circumstances when a knock and announce requirement is critical.

5. What are the possible consequences of either sticking with or dispensing with the knock and announce requirement? ✦

Chapter Eight
Stop and Frisk

INTRODUCTION

As we have seen, probable cause is required to justify a search or seizure within the meaning of the Fourth Amendment. But much police activity does not reach the level of intrusion that occurs when a search or seizure is carried out. For example, the police routinely have to confront people on the street or pull over automobiles in order to question them or enforce traffic laws. If probable cause were required under such circumstances, there would be very little the police could do in terms of investigating suspicious activity.

Recognizing how essential these "lesser intrusions" are to the police mission, the Supreme Court in *Terry v. Ohio* established a different level of justification for such activities. The standard the Court created was "reasonable suspicion," something below probable cause, but above a hunch. *Terry* dealt with so-called "stop and frisk" activities, but reasonable suspicion as a standard of justification also permeates other arenas of criminal procedure (traffic stops, for example).

In *Terry* an officer's attention was drawn to two men on a street corner who appeared to the officer to be "casing" a store for a robbery. The officer approached the men and asked them to identify themselves. The officer then proceeded to pat the men down and found a gun on each man. The men were placed under arrest. They tried to suppress the guns, but the Supreme Court eventually held the officer's actions valid in the interest of "effective crime prevention and detection." Bal-ancing an intrusion that was arguably less serious than a search with the interests of society in apprehending law breakers, the Court held that a lower standard than probable cause was required because "street encounters between citizens and police officers are incredibly rich in diversity."

There is no clear definition of "reasonable suspicion," just as there is no clear definition of probable cause. As a level of justification lying below probable cause, then, reasonable suspicion is "considerably less than proof of wrongdoing by a preponderance of evidence" (*United States v. Sokolow*), but more than an unparticularized hunch. Recently, the Supreme Court held that the appropriate standard for determining whether reasonable suspicion exists is one that focuses on the totality of circumstances (*United States v. Arvizu*). Also, the Supreme Court agrees that substantial deference should be given to trained police officers in deciding when reasonable suspicion is present (see *United States v. Cortez*).

Like probable cause, reasonable suspicion can be based on a number of different sources, including informants. But because the reasonable suspicion standard falls below probable cause on the justification scale, less information is required. In *Adams v. Williams,* for example, the Supreme Court held that reasonable suspicion may be based on an anonymous telephone tip so long as the police are able to corroborate certain details released by the informant. In a similar case, *Alabama v. White,* the Supreme Court observed: "Reasonable suspicion is a less demanding standard than probable cause not only in the sense that reasonable suspicion can be established with information that is different but also in the sense that reasonable suspicion can arise from information that is less reliable than that required to show probable cause." But anonymous tips alone are insufficient for establishing reasonable suspicion (*Florida v. J. L.*).

In *United States v. Hensley,* the Supreme Court unanimously held that the reasonable suspicion standard is satisfied when the police rely on "wanted" flyers, even flyers from other jurisdictions. A restriction on this ruling was that the flyer, regardless of its place of origin, be based on articulable facts which connect the suspect to criminal activity. The Court in *Hensley* also had to decide if a stop based on reasonable suspicion of *prior* criminal activity was permissible under the Fourth Amendment's reasonableness standard. All decisions up to that point dealt with suspected criminal activity immediately before the officer's arrival or criminal activity likely to have occurred but for the officer's arrival. In *Hensley* the police stopped a man 12 days after the commission of a robbery for which he was suspected. The Court upheld the police's action and stated that it "would not only hinder the investigation, but might also enable the suspect to flee in the interim and to remain at large."

One of the Supreme Court's most recent decisions concerning reasonable suspicion is *Illinois v. Wardlow*. In that case Chicago police officers were patrolling an area known for narcotics traffic. Upon seeing the officers, Wardlow ran and was chased down by the police. He was caught and patted down. The officers found a Colt .38 pistol and arrested him. Wardlow appealed his conviction, arguing that the stop and frisk were illegal because the officers did not have reasonable suspicion. The Court disagreed with his arguing, noting that "a location's characteristics are relevant in determining whether the circumstances are sufficiently suspicious to warrant further investigation." In addition, the Court noted that "it was Wardlow's unprovoked flight that aroused the officers' suspicion" and that "nervous, evasive behavior is another pertinent factor in determining reasonable suspicion, and headlong flight is the consummate act of evasion." Thus, in the Court's view, the officers did have reasonable suspicion to stop and frisk Wardlow.

So far we have focused almost exclusively on the definition of reasonable suspicion. Other Supreme Court cases, however, deal with restrictions concerning stops and frisks themselves. These restrictions focus (1) on how far the police can "go" in terms of frisking someone and (2) how long stops can take. Concerning the first of these restrictions, *Minnesota v. Dickerson* informs us that the police may seize contraband detected through the sense of touch during a protective pat-down search only if the contraband is immediately apparent and no manipulation takes place. Thus, frisks are truly limited to "pat downs." As for the time involved in a stop, the Supreme Court's decision in *United States v. Sharpe* was that a 40-minute detention for the purpose of a limited investigation does not violate the Fourth Amendment, provided that reasonable suspicion is present. In fact, the Court has upheld stops that last substantially longer, even as much as several hours. ✦

Terry v. Ohio
392 U.S. 1 (1968)

Facts

A Cleveland detective (McFadden) on a downtown beat which he had been patrolling for many years observed two strangers (Terry and another man, Chilton) on a street corner. He saw them proceed alternately back and forth along an identical route, pausing to stare in the same store window, which they did for a total of about 24 times. Each completion of the route was followed by a conference between the two on a corner, at one of which they were joined by a third man (Katz), who left swiftly. Suspecting the two men of "casing a job, a stick-up," the officer followed them and saw them rejoin the third man a couple of blocks away in front of a store. The officer approached the three, identified himself as a policeman, and asked their names. The men "mumbled something," whereupon McFadden spun petitioner around, patted down his outside clothing, and found in his overcoat pocket, but was unable to remove, a pistol. The officer ordered the three into the store. He removed petitioner's overcoat, took out a revolver, and ordered the three to face the wall with their hands raised. He patted down the outer clothing of Chilton and Katz and seized a revolver from Chilton's outside overcoat pocket. He did not put his hands under the outer garments of Katz (since he discovered nothing in his pat down which might have been a weapon), or under petitioner's or Chilton's outer garments, until he felt the guns. The three were taken to the police station. Petitioner and Chilton were charged with carrying concealed weapons. The defense moved to suppress the weapons. The court denied the motion to suppress and admitted the weapons into evidence. The court distinguished between an investigatory "stop" and an arrest, and between a "frisk" of the outer clothing for weapons and a full-blown search for evidence of crime. Terry and Chilton were found guilty, an intermediate appellate court affirmed, and the state supreme court dismissed the appeal on the ground that "no substantial constitutional question" was involved. The U.S. Supreme Court then granted certiorari.

Issue

May a police officer conduct a stop and frisk based on reasonable suspicion?

Holding

Yes. A police officer who has "reasonable suspicion" of criminal activity may briefly stop an individual and question him, and if the officer fears for his safety, he may conduct a pat-down search of the outer clothing of the suspect.

Rationale

"Where a reasonably prudent officer is warranted in the circumstances of a given case in believing that his safety or that of others is endangered, he may make a reasonable search for weapons of the person believed by him to be armed and dangerous regardless of whether he has probable cause to arrest that individual for a crime or the absolute certainty that the individual is armed. Though the police must whenever practicable secure a warrant to make a search and seizure, that procedure cannot be followed where swift action based upon on-the-spot observations of the officer on the beat is required. The reasonableness of any particular search and seizure must be assessed in light of the particular circumstances against the standard of whether a man of reasonable caution is warranted in believing that the action taken was appropriate. The officer here was performing a legitimate function of investigating suspicious conduct when he decided to approach petitioner and his companions. An officer justified in believing that an individual whose suspicious behavior he is investigating at close range is armed may, to neutralize the threat of physical harm, take necessary measures to determine whether that person is carrying a weapon. A search for weapons in the absence of probable cause to arrest must be strictly circumscribed by the exigencies of the situation. An officer may make an intrusion short of arrest where he has reasonable apprehension of danger before being possessed of information justifying arrest. The officer's protective seizure of petitioner and his companions, and the limited search which he made, were reasonable, both at their inception and as conducted. The actions of petitioner and his companions were consistent with the officer's hypothesis that they were contemplating a daylight robbery and were armed. The officer's search was confined to what was minimally necessary to determine whether the men were armed, and the intrusion, which was made for the sole purpose of protecting himself and others nearby, was confined to ascertaining the presence of weapons."

CASE SIGNIFICANCE

This case is very important, for it authorized police to conduct a "stop and frisk," or investigative detention. This may be done on less than probable cause—all the police need is "reasonable suspicion." While a stop is a seizure, and a frisk is a search, both may be conducted with less evidence than that required for an arrest or a full search. This decision, handed down by the often vilified "liberal" Warren Court, was actually a major victory for police officers, as it gives them tremendous authority to investigate possible criminal activity.

ADAMS V. WILLIAMS
407 U.S. 143 (1972)

FACTS

Acting on a tip supplied moments earlier by a reliable informant known to him, a police officer asked Adams to open his car door. Adams responded by instead rolling down the car window, at which point the officer reached into the car and found a loaded handgun (which had not been visible from the outside) in Adams' waistband, precisely where the informant had said it would be. Adams was arrested for unlawful possession of a handgun. A search incident to the arrest disclosed heroin on Adams' person (as the informant had also reported), as well as other weapons in the car. Adams was convicted and sentenced to prison. His petition for federal habeas corpus relief was denied by the district court. The court of appeals reversed, holding that the evidence that had been used in the trial resulting in Williams' conviction had been obtained by an unlawful search. The U.S. Supreme Court then granted certiorari.

ISSUE

May a police officer conduct a stop and frisk based on information provided by a reliable informant?

HOLDING

Yes. As *Terry v. Ohio* recognizes, a policeman making a reasonable investigatory stop may conduct a limited protective search for concealed weapons when he has reason to believe that the suspect is armed and dangerous. Additionally, a stop and frisk based on information not personally observed by a police officer is reasonable under the Fourth Amendment.

RATIONALE

The Supreme Court "rejects Williams' argument that reasonable cause for a stop and frisk can only be based on the officer's personal observation, rather than on information supplied by another person. Informant's tips, like all other clues and evidence coming to a policeman on the scene, may vary greatly in their value and reliability. One simple rule will not cover every situation. Some tips, completely lacking in indicia of reliability, would either warrant no police response or require further investigation before a forcible stop of a suspect would be authorized. But in some situations—for example, when the victim of a street crime seeks immediate police aid and gives a description of his assailant, or when a credible informant warns of a specific impending crime— the subtleties of the hearsay rule should not thwart an appropriate police response."

CASE SIGNIFICANCE

This case extended the availability of the stop and frisk procedure to situations where a police officer obtains information from an informant rather than from personal observation (as was the case in *Terry v. Ohio*). This was a logical extension of the stop and frisk doctrine, since an arrest, which requires probable cause, may also be made based on information obtained from a reliable informant.

UNITED STATES V. CORTEZ
449 U.S. 411 (1981)

FACTS

After discovering several sets of distinctive footprints in the same area of the Arizona desert, border patrol officers concluded that the same person was illegally guiding groups of persons into the United States. Two border patrol agents chose a clear Sunday night to monitor a segment of the highway east of the point where the illegal aliens were to be picked up. After observing only one vehicle of the kind that the guide would likely use to carry aliens pass them, the agents stopped the vehicle. After observing that the person sitting in the passenger's seat was wearing shoes with soles matching the distinctive prints, the officers identified themselves and told the driver that they were conducting an immigration check and asked if he was carrying any passengers in the vehicle. The driver told the agents that he had picked up some hitchhikers. The officers then searched the vehicle, found the people, and arrested the driver and the guide. Cortez was convicted of several federal offenses, and appealed to the Supreme Court.

ISSUE

Did the facts and circumstances justify an investigative stop of the vehicle?

HOLDING

Yes. The objective facts and circumstantial evidence justified an investigative stop of the vehicle.

RATIONALE

"In determining what cause is sufficient to authorize police to stop a person, the totality of the circumstances—the whole picture—must be taken into account. Based upon that whole picture the detaining officers must have a particularized and objective basis for suspecting the particular person stopped of criminal activity. The process of assessing all of the circumstances does not deal with hard certainties, but with probabilities, and the evidence collected must be weighed as understood by those versed in the field of law enforcement. Also, the process must raise a suspicion that the particular individual being stopped is engaged in wrongdoing."

CASE SIGNIFICANCE

This case is significant because it clarified the *Terry* decision. It suggested that a fair degree of deference should be given to law enforcement officers in deciding whether reasonable suspicion to stop is in place. The case also gave reference to officers' training and suggested that courts should respect the deductive processes of trained police officers—once they have accumulated as much information about the suspect's behavior as possible.

UNITED STATES V. SHARPE
470 U.S. 675 (1984)

FACTS

A Drug Enforcement Administration (DEA) agent on patrol in an area under surveillance for suspected drug trafficking noticed an overloaded pickup truck with an attached camper traveling in tandem with a Pontiac. Savage was driving the truck, and Sharpe was driving the Pontiac. After following the two vehicles for about twenty miles, the agent decided to make an "investigative stop" and radioed the South Carolina State Highway Patrol for assistance. An officer responded, and he and the DEA agent continued to follow the two vehicles. When they attempted to stop the vehicles, the Pontiac driven by Sharpe pulled over to the side of the road, but the truck driven by Savage continued on, pursued by the state officer. After identifying himself and obtaining identification from Sharpe, the DEA agent attempted to radio the highway patrol officer. The DEA agent was unable to contact the state officer to see if he had stopped the truck, so he radioed the local police for help. In the meantime, the state officer had stopped the truck, questioned Savage, and told him that he would be held until the DEA agent arrived. The agent, who had left the local police with the Pontiac, arrived at the scene approximately 15 minutes after the truck had been stopped. After confirming his suspicion that the truck was overloaded and upon smelling marijuana, the agent opened the rear of the camper without Savage's permission and observed a number of burlap-wrapped bales resembling bales of marijuana that the agent had seen in previous investigations. The agent then placed Savage under arrest and, returning to the Pontiac, also arrested Sharpe. Chemical tests later showed that the bales contained marijuana. Both men were charged with federal drug offenses, and, after the district court denied their motion to suppress the contraband, were convicted. The court of appeals reversed, holding that because the investigative stops failed to meet the Fourth Amendment's requirement of brevity governing detentions on less than probable cause, the marijuana should have been suppressed as the fruit of unlawful seizures. The U.S. Supreme Court then granted certiorari.

ISSUE

Was the detention of Savage for a period of time necessary to conduct a limited investigation reasonable for the purposes of the Fourth Amendment?

HOLDING

Yes. The detention of Savage clearly met the Fourth Amendment's standard of reasonableness.

RATIONALE

"In evaluating the reasonableness of an investigative stop, this Court examines whether the officer's action was justified at its inception, and whether it was reasonably related in scope to the circumstances which justified the interference in the first place. As to the first part of the inquiry, the officers had an articulable and reasonable suspicion that respondents were engaged in marijuana trafficking, and the record abundantly supports that assumption, given the circumstances when the officers attempted to stop the Pontiac and the truck. As to the second part of the inquiry, while the brevity of an investigative detention is an important factor in determining whether the detention is unreasonable, courts must also consider the purposes to be served by the stop as well as the time reasonably needed to effectuate those purposes. The Court of Appeals' decision would effectively establish a per se rule that a 20-minute detention is too long to be justified under the *Terry* doctrine. Such a result is clearly and fundamentally at odds with this Court's approach in this area. In assessing whether a detention is too long in duration to be justified as an investigative stop, it is appropriate to examine whether the police diligently pursued a means of investigation that was likely to confirm or dispel their suspicions quickly, during which time it was necessary to detain the defendant. Here, the DEA agent diligently pursued his investigation, and clearly no delay unnecessary to the investigation was involved."

CASE SIGNIFICANCE

This case makes clear that there is no set time limit for an investigative stop. The length of time permitted depends upon the purpose of the stop and the time needed to carry out that purpose. In this case, the Court said 20 minutes was reasonable—in other cases, that time period might be more or less, depending on the circumstances.

UNITED STATES V. HENSLEY
469 U.S. 221 (1985)

FACTS

Following an armed robbery in the Cincinnati suburb of St. Bernard, Ohio, a St. Bernard police officer, on the basis of information obtained from an informant that Hensley had driven the getaway car during the robbery, issued a "wanted flyer" to other police departments in the area. The flyer stated that Hensley was wanted for investigation of the robbery, described him and the date and location of the robbery, and asked the other departments to pick him up and hold him for the St. Bernard police. Subsequently, on the basis of the flyer and after inquiring without success as to whether a warrant was outstanding for Hensley's arrest, police officers from Covington, Kentucky, another Cincinnati suburb, stopped an automobile that Hensley was seen driving. One of the officers recognized a passenger in the car as a convicted felon and, upon observing a revolver butt protruding from underneath that passenger's seat, arrested him. After a search of the car uncovered other handguns, Hensley was also arrested. Hensley was then indicted on the federal charge of being a convicted felon in possession of firearms. He moved to suppress the handguns from evidence on the grounds that the Covington police had stopped him in violation of the Fourth Amendment. The federal district court denied Hensley's motion, and he was convicted. The court of appeals reversed, holding that the stop of Hensley's car was improper because the crime being investigated was not imminent or ongoing, but rather was already completed, that the "wanted" flyer was insufficient to create a reasonable suspicion that Hensley had committed a crime, and that therefore his conviction rested on evidence obtained through an illegal arrest. The U.S. Supreme Court then granted certiorari.

ISSUE

May the police conduct an investigative stop of an individual who is the subject of a "wanted" flyer?

HOLDING

Yes. The ability to briefly stop that person, ask questions, or check identification in the absence of probable cause promotes the strong government interest in solving crimes and bringing offenders to justice.

RATIONALE

"Restraining police action until after probable cause is obtained would not only hinder the investigation but might also enable the suspect to flee and remain at large. The law enforcement interests at stake in these circumstances outweigh the individual's interest to be free of a stop and detention that is no more extensive than permissible in the investigation of imminent or ongoing crimes. When police have a reasonable suspicion, grounded in specific and articulable facts, that a person they encounter was involved in or is wanted in connection with a completed felony, then a *Terry* stop may be made to investigate that suspicion. If a "wanted flyer" has been issued on the basis of articulable facts supporting a reasonable suspicion that the person wanted has committed an offense, then reliance on that flyer justifies a stop to check identification, to pose questions, or to detain the person briefly while attempting to obtain further information. It is the objective reading of the flyer that determines whether police officers from a department other than the one that issued the flyer can defensibly act in reliance on it. Assuming that the police make a *Terry* stop in objective reliance on a flyer, the evidence uncovered in the course of the stop is admissible if the police who issued the flyer possessed a reasonable suspicion justifying the stop, and if the stop that occurred was not significantly more intrusive than would have been permitted the issuing department. Under the above principles, the investigatory stop of Hensley was reasonable under the Fourth Amendment, and therefore the evidence discovered during the stop was admissible. The justification for a stop did not evaporate when the armed robbery was completed. Hensley was reasonably suspected of involvement in a felony and was at large from the time the suspicion arose until the stop by the Covington police. A brief stop and detention at the earliest opportunity after the suspicion arose was fully consistent with Fourth Amendment principles. The flyer issued by the St. Bernard police, objectively read and supported by a reasonable suspicion on the part of the issuing department, justified the length and intrusiveness of the stop and detention that occurred."

CASE SIGNIFICANCE

This case extended the reach of the stop and frisk procedure to situations where a police officer has not observed suspicious conduct, but has it on good authority that an individual is a criminal suspect. *Terry* allowed a stop and frisk on reasonable suspicion; in this case the Supreme Court allowed a police officer to treat a "wanted" flyer or bulletin as sufficient information to create "reasonable suspicion."

UNITED STATES V. SOKOLOW
490 U.S. 1 (1989)

FACTS

Sokolow was stopped in Honolulu International Airport by Drug Enforcement Administration agents. There were several reasons why the agents stopped Sokolow: (1) he paid $2,100 for two plane tickets from a roll of $20 bills; (2) he traveled under a name that did not match the name under which his telephone number was listed; (3) his destination was Miami, a city known for its illegal drug traffic; (4) he stayed in Miami for only 48 hours, despite the fact that a round-trip flight from Miami to Honolulu takes approximately 20 hours; (5) he appeared nervous while moving about the terminal; and (6) he did not check any luggage. The agents found 1,063 grams of cocaine in his carry-on luggage and Sokolow was convicted of drug possession. The case later came before the U.S. Supreme Court.

ISSUE

Was there reasonable suspicion to stop Sokolow based on a "drug-courier profile"?

HOLDING

Yes. The circumstances in this case established reasonable suspicion that Sokolow was transporting illegal drugs. Accordingly, the stop was justified based on the *Terry* exception to the Fourth Amendment's probable cause requirement.

RATIONALE

"Any one of these factors is not by itself proof of any illegal conduct and is quite consistent with innocent travel. But we think taken together they amount to reasonable suspicion. . . . A court sitting to determine the existence of reasonable suspicion must require the agent to articulate the factors leading to that conclusion, but the fact that these factors may be set forth in a 'profile' does not somehow detract from their evidentiary significance as seen by a trained agent. . . . The reasonableness of the officer's decision to stop a suspect does not turn on the availability of less intrusive investigatory techniques."

CASE SIGNIFICANCE

Sokolow is significant because it addressed whether "drug-courier profiles" can be used to establish reasonable suspicion to conduct a *Terry* stop. It is important to understand, however, that the Court did not decide on the constitutionality of drug-courier profiling. Instead, it was concerned with whether the facts as set forth in this case created reasonable suspicion to stop. As indicated in the Court's reasoning, it did not matter whether Sokolow's actions fit a "profile," only that the actions provided sufficient justification to conduct a stop.

ALABAMA V. WHITE
496 U.S. 325 (1990)

FACTS

Police received an anonymous telephone tip that White would be leaving a particular apartment at a particular time in a particular vehicle, that she would be going to a particular motel, and that she would be in possession of cocaine. They immediately proceeded to the apartment building, saw a vehicle matching the caller's description, observed White as she left the building and entered the vehicle, and followed her along the most direct route to the motel, stopping her vehicle just short of the motel. A consensual search of the vehicle revealed marijuana and, after White was arrested, cocaine was found in her purse. The Court of Criminal Appeals of Alabama reversed her conviction on possession charges, holding that the trial court should have suppressed the marijuana and cocaine because the officers did not have the reasonable suspicion necessary under *Terry v. Ohio* to justify the investigatory stop of the vehicle. The U.S. Supreme Court then granted certiorari.

ISSUE

Does an anonymous tip, corroborated by the police, create "reasonable suspicion" to justify a stop and frisk?

HOLDING

Yes. The anonymous tip, as corroborated by independent police work, exhibited sufficient indicia of reliability to provide reasonable suspicion to make the investigatory stop.

RATIONALE

"Under *Adams v. Williams,* an informant's tip may carry sufficient 'indicia of reliability' to justify a *Terry* stop even though it may be insufficient to support an arrest or search warrant. Moreover, *Illinois v. Gates* adopted a 'totality-of-the-circumstances' approach to determining whether an informant's tip establishes probable cause, whereby the informant's veracity, reliability, and basis of knowledge are highly relevant. These factors are also relevant in the reasonable-suspicion context, although allowance must be made in applying them for the lesser showing required to meet that standard. Standing alone, the tip here is completely lacking in the necessary indicia of reliability, since it provides virtually nothing from which one might conclude that the caller is honest or his information reliable and gives no indication of the basis for his predictions regarding White's criminal activities. However, although it is a close question, the totality of the circumstances demonstrates that significant aspects of the informant's story were sufficiently corroborated by the police to furnish reasonable suspicion. Although not every detail mentioned by the tipster was verified—e.g., the name of the woman leaving the apartment building or the precise apartment from which she left—the officers did corroborate that a woman left the building and got into the described vehicle. Given the fact that they proceeded to the building immediately after the call and that White emerged not too long thereafter, it also appears that her departure was within the time frame predicted by the caller. Moreover, since her four-mile route was the most direct way to the motel, but nevertheless involved several turns, the caller's prediction of her destination was significantly corroborated even though she was stopped before she reached the motel. Furthermore, the fact that the caller was able to predict her future behavior demonstrates a special familiarity with her affairs. Thus, there was reason to believe that the caller was honest and well informed, and to impart some degree of reliability to his allegation that White was engaged in criminal activity."

CASE SIGNIFICANCE

This case stood for the proposition that the amount and quality of information necessary to establish "reasonable suspicion" is not as high as that required for "probable cause."

MINNESOTA V. DICKERSON
508 U.S. 366 (1993)

FACTS

Based upon Dickerson's seemingly evasive actions when approached by police officers and the fact that he had just left a building known for cocaine traffic, the officers decided to investigate further. They stopped and frisked Dickerson. The pat-down search revealed no weapons, but the officer conducting it testified that he felt a small lump in Dickerson's jacket pocket that he believed to be a lump of crack cocaine upon examining it with his fingers, whereupon he reached into the pocket and retrieved a small bag of cocaine. The state trial court denied Dickerson's motion to suppress the cocaine, and he was found guilty of possession of a controlled substance. The Minnesota Court of Appeals reversed. In affirming, the state supreme court held that both the stop and the frisk of Dickerson were valid under *Terry v. Ohio*, but found the seizure of the cocaine to be unconstitutional. Refusing to enlarge the "plain-view" exception to the Fourth Amendment's warrant requirement, the court appeared to adopt a categorical rule barring the seizure of any contraband detected by an officer through the sense of touch during a pat-down search. The U.S. Supreme Court then granted certiorari.

ISSUE

Was the officer's manipulation of the crack cocaine in the suspect's pocket permissible under *Terry*?

HOLDING

No. The police may seize contraband detected through the sense of touch during a protective pat-down search only if the contraband is immediately apparent and no manipulation takes place.

RATIONALE

"*Terry* permits a brief stop of a person whose suspicious conduct leads an officer to conclude, in light of his experience, that criminal activity may be afoot, and a pat-down search of the person for weapons when the officer is justified in believing that the person may be armed and presently dangerous. This protective search—permitted without a warrant and on the basis of reasonable suspicion less than probable cause—is not meant to discover evidence of crime, but must be strictly limited to that which is necessary for the discovery of weapons, which might be used to harm the officer or others. If the protective search goes beyond what is necessary to determine if the suspect is armed, it is no longer valid under *Terry,* and its fruits will be suppressed. In *Michigan v. Long,* the seizure of contraband other than weapons during a lawful *Terry* search was justified by reference to the Court's cases under the 'plain view' doctrine. That doctrine—which permits police to seize an object without a warrant if they are lawfully in a position to view it, if its incriminating character is immediately apparent, and if they have a lawful right of access to it—has an obvious application by analogy to cases in which an officer discovers contraband through the sense of touch during an otherwise lawful search. Thus, if an officer lawfully pats down a suspect's outer clothing and feels an object whose contour or mass makes its identity immediately apparent, there has been no invasion of the suspect's privacy beyond that already authorized by the officer's search for weapons. The officer who conducted the search was not acting within the lawful bounds marked by *Terry* at the time he gained probable cause to believe that the lump in Dickerson's jacket was contraband. The officer never

thought that the lump was a weapon, but did not immediately recognize it as cocaine. Rather, he determined that it was contraband only after he squeezed, slid, and otherwise manipulated the pocket's contents. While *Terry* entitled him to place his hands on Dickerson's jacket and to feel the lump in the pocket, his continued exploration of the pocket after he concluded that it contained no weapon was unrelated to the sole justification for the search under *Terry*. Because this further search was constitutionally invalid, the seizure of the cocaine that followed is likewise unconstitutional."

CASE SIGNIFICANCE

This case is significant because it made clear the limitations of the frisk portion of the stop and frisk procedure. The frisk is permitted only for officer safety, and officers are barred from removing items they feel during the frisk that they know are not weapons. The Court does leave the door slightly open, however—if an officer can demonstrate that he felt an item which he knew immediately, without any additional manipulation, was contraband, then he could seize it. Some lower courts have allowed such seizures, while others have not.

FLORIDA V. J.L
529 U.S. 266 (2000)

FACTS

Miami-Dade police received an anonymous tip that a young black man wearing a plaid shirt standing at a particular bus stop was carrying a gun. Upon arriving at the specified location, officers observed an individual matching the description provided by the caller. A frisk was conducted and a weapon was recovered from the pocket of "J.L.," who was then arrested on charges of carrying a concealed firearm without a permit as well as underage possession of a firearm. The trial court granted J.L.'s motion to suppress but an intermediate appellate court reversed. The Florida Supreme Court held that the search was unlawful and the U.S. Supreme Court granted certiorari.

ISSUE

Does the Fourth Amendment authorize police to undertake a warrantless frisk based solely upon an anonymous tip?

HOLDING

No. An anonymous tip that a person is carrying a gun is insufficient to justify a warrantless stop and frisk in the absence of further information that criminal activity is afoot.

Rationale

"In *Terry v. Ohio* (1968), the Supreme Court granted police officers authority under the Fourth Amendment to conduct limited warrantless frisks in situations where there exists reason to believe that criminal activity may be afoot and that an individual is armed and dangerous. This authority is limited insofar as the officer must be acting upon information or suspicious behavior that has been observed firsthand. In the present case the officers themselves did not observe any suspicious behavior but, instead, relied upon information provided by an anonymous caller whose reputation for giving reliable information was unverifiable. Although the tipster accurately described J.L.'s appearance and whereabouts, the Court nonetheless rejected the State's request for a broader interpretation and application of the *Terry* standard. In essence, the Court reasoned that although an anonymous tip may accurately describe an individual's appearance and location, this limited information does not adequately justify a warrantless stop and frisk of that person."

Case Significance

This case is important because it established the rule of law that police officers cannot conduct a *Terry* stop and frisk based solely on anonymous information that a particular individual may be armed with a weapon. When the police receive information of this type it must first be corroborated by their own observation and experience before being acted upon. Although responding officers will understandably be anxious to act upon such tips, it is instead suggested that they take a moment to observe the suspect firsthand in order to: (1) establish whether or not criminal activity is afoot; and (2) determine the reasonable likelihood that the individual is actually armed and dangerous. In the event that officers act immediately upon uncorroborated information provided by an anonymous tipster, the resulting stop and frisk will be deemed violative of the Fourth Amendment and any incriminating evidence that is seized will be rendered inadmissible. Just because a tipster has accurately described an individual's location and physical characteristics (e.g., race, height, weight, clothing, etc.), this information does not constitute prima facie evidence that criminal activity is afoot or that the person is actually armed and dangerous. Instead, officers are required by the ruling in this case to independently verify such information through visual observation buttressed by their past experiences in similar situations.

Illinois v. Wardlow
528 U.S. 119 (2000)

Facts

Chicago police officers converged upon a neighborhood with a reputation for high crime and open-air drug transactions. Two officers observed Wardlow immediately flee the area on foot and, upon catching up to him, seized a firearm unlawfully in his possession. A motion to suppress was denied and Wardlow was convicted on charges of unlawful use of a weapon by a felon. A state appellate court reversed on grounds that the arresting officer lacked reasonable suspicion for the detention as required by *Terry v. Ohio*. The state supreme court affirmed on the basis that Wardlow's flight from the area was, in and of itself, not enough to justify the ensuing stop and frisk. The U.S. Supreme Court then granted certiorari.

Issue

Does an individual's sudden flight from a high-crime area create reasonable suspicion justifying a *Terry* stop and frisk?

Holding

Yes. An individual's unprovoked flight from a high-crime area, taken in combination with other factors such as characteristics of the location and nervous or evasive behavior, are enough to create reasonable suspicion authorizing the police to undertake a *Terry* stop and frisk.

Rationale

In this particular case the Supreme Court ruled that there was no violation of Wardlow's Fourth Amendment rights. Cases such as this are governed by the rule established in *Terry v. Ohio* requiring officers to first develop reasonable suspicion that criminal activity is afoot and that an individual may be armed and dangerous before initiating a stop and frisk. "The fact that Wardlow immediately fled the area upon becoming aware of a police presence does not in and of itself satisfy this standard. However, when taken in conjunction with other factors such as an individual's nervous/evasive behavior and the neighborhood's reputation for drug-related activity, a brief detention such as that which Wardlow experienced may be justified. Once stopped, officers are authorized to conduct a limited frisk of the individual to ensure their own safety as well as that of others." In other words, while immediate flight from an area does not in and of itself indicate that criminal activity is afoot, officers are reasonably justified in the detention on an individual for purposes of making such a determination. If no evidence of unlawful behavior is discovered, then the individual must be allowed to go on his or her way.

CASE SIGNIFICANCE

This case addressed the long-standing question of whether or not officers are authorized to stop an individual who has done nothing more than flee the area upon becoming aware of their presence. While flight alone does not automatically justify detention, an individual may be lawfully stopped when such evasive activity occurs in light of an officer's firsthand knowledge about criminal activity patterns within a given neighborhood. Thus, if an officer knows that a given area has a history of open-air drug transactions (or other forms of criminal activity) and an individual is observed fleeing the vicinity upon becoming aware of a police presence, the officer is justified in making an investigative *Terry* stop for purposes of determining whether or not criminal activity is afoot. During the course of this stop a limited frisk of the individual may also be undertaken for purposes of ensuring officer safety. If no weapons or evidence of criminal activity are discovered, then the individual must immediately be released and allowed to go on his or her way.

UNITED STATES V. ARVIZU
534 U.S. 266 (2002)

FACTS

A border patrol agent working in the Arizona desert received notification from a monitoring center that sensors had detected motion in a remote geographic location. From this information, combined with experience, the agent surmised that the alarm was most likely triggered by an alien smuggler trying to avoid detection during a shift change when few border patrol personnel were available. Arriving in the vicinity of the alarm, only a single vehicle was observed in the area. Based upon timing, the agent concluded that the vehicle he observed was the one responsible for tripping the sensor. As the vehicle passed his location, the agent observed that it was occupied by a large number of individuals and that the driver avoided making eye contact although they were the only two vehicles within miles of one another. Deciding to stop and investigate further, the agent asked for and received consent from the driver (Arvizu) to search the vehicle. Discovered within was a cache of marijuana exceeding 100 pounds resulting in Arvizu being charged with possession with intent to distribute. At trial in federal district court, Arvizu's motion to suppress on grounds that the agent lacked reasonable suspicion for the stop

was denied and he was convicted. The Ninth Circuit Court of Appeals reversed on grounds that each of the factors used as a basis for justifying the stop was, when considered independently of one another, equally consistent with innocent behavior. The U.S Supreme Court then granted certiorari.

ISSUE

Is a "factor-by-factor" examination of the grounds for making an investigative stop the appropriate Fourth Amendment standard?

HOLDING

No. The appropriate Fourth Amendment standard for assessing the legality of an investigative stop is not one of a "factor-by-factor" nature but, rather, one that takes into consideration a totality of the circumstances.

RATIONALE

The Supreme Court granted certiorari because the question at hand posed important implications for the future enforcement of federal drug and immigration laws. Specifically, the Ninth Circuit Court of Appeals reversed Arvizu's conviction on grounds that the factors giving rise to the investigative stop, when considered independently of one another, were equally consistent with otherwise innocent behavior. Rejecting this "factor-by-factor" approach, the Court reiterated its historical reliance on a "totality of the circumstances" standard for determining whether or not the detaining officer has developed a particularized and objective basis for suspecting that criminal activity is afoot. Applying these standards to the present case led the Supreme Court to conclude that although many of the factors used to justify the stop of Arvizu's vehicle were equally consistent with otherwise innocent behavior, the totality of the circumstances formed a particularized and objective basis for making the stop. The decision of the Ninth Circuit Court of Appeals was reversed and remanded.

CASE SIGNIFICANCE

This decision is important because it reinforced the judicial principle that cases such as this are to be judged not on a "factor-by-factor" basis but, instead, on a totality of the circumstances. The Supreme Court again gave considerable deference to an officer's observations made at the scene combined with his or her specialized training and unique experiences. Quite simply, the Court prefers to avoid "second-guessing" an officer's well-reasoned judgment where there does not appear to exist any blatant abuses of discretionary power on his or her part. In terms of practical significance, it becomes vitally important for officers who encounter such situations to carefully articulate the various behaviors, circumstances, experiences, training, and factors contributing to their particularized and objective belief that criminal activity was afoot. Otherwise, the basis for making an investigative stop as well as the potential exclusion of critical evidence will surely be at issue. ✦

DISCUSSION QUESTIONS

1. Do you agree with the Supreme Court's decision in *Terry*?

2. Presumably, a person who is not "stopped" is free to leave. If a person is confronted by a police officer, and not technically stopped, is that person truly free to leave?

3. Has the Supreme Court expanded on or chipped away at *Terry*? How so?

4. Do you agree with the practice of drug-courier profiling? Why or why not?

5. Identify as many factors as you can that would give a police officer reasonable suspicion to conduct a stop. ✦

Chapter Nine

Search Incident to Arrest

INTRODUCTION

Imagine a situation where a police officer with probable cause arrests a suspect, who then reaches into his pocket. Imagine further what would go through the police officer's mind as he or she observes this behavior. Such is the reasoning behind the "search incident to arrest" exception to the Fourth Amendment's warrant requirement. The logic for permitting police officers to engage in a search of a suspect incident to arrest (i.e., following an arrest) is that it would be impractical—even dangerous—to wait for a warrant.

The leading case in the area of incident searches is *Chimel v. California.* As the Supreme Court stated, a search incident to arrest is permitted "to remove any weapons that the [arrestee] might seek to use in order to resist arrest or effect his escape" and to "seize any evidence on the arrestee's person in order to prevent its concealment or destruction."

The most basic requirement concerning searches incident to arrest—one that often goes overlooked—is that the arrest must be lawful. When the arrest itself is not lawful, i.e., when it is not based on probable cause, any search that follows is unlawful. Another important threshold issue with regard to searches incident to arrest concerns the nature of the offense. Courts have grappled with whether a search should be permitted when the offense on which the arrest is based is not serious. Because the rationale of the exception is officer safety, then is officer safety likely to be compromised when a minor as opposed to a serious offense justifies the arrest?

Two important Supreme Court cases have sought to answer these questions. First, in *United States v. Robinson,* the Court reversed a lower court's decision that only a pat down of the suspect's outer clothing was permissible following an arrest for driving with a revoked license. And in a companion case to *Robinson, Gustafson v. Florida,* 414 U.S. 260 (1973), the Court upheld the search of a suspect after his arrest for failure to have his driver's license.

The Supreme Court offered two reasons for its opinions in *Robinson* and *Gustafson.* First, according to Chief Justice Rehnquist, "[i]t is scarcely open to doubt that the danger to an officer is far greater in the case of the extended exposure which follows the taking of a suspect into custody and transporting him to the police station than in the case of the relatively fleeting contact resulting from the typical *Terry* stop." Second, the Court believed a bright-line rule was in order given the stakes involved: "A police officer's determination as to how and where to search the person of a suspect whom he has arrested is necessarily a quick *ad hoc* judgment which the Fourth Amendment does not require to be broken down in each instance into an analysis of each step in the search" (*United States v. Robinson*).

Generally, a search incident to arrest should take place close in time to the arrest. However, in *United States v. Edwards,* the Supreme Court—in a 5–4 decision—upheld the warrantless search and seizure of an arrestee's clothing ten hours after his arrest, while he was in jail. The Court noted that "searches and seizures that could be made on the spot at the time of arrest may legally be conducted later when the accused arrives at the place of detention." The Court did point out, however, that the taking of Edwards' clothing at the time of the arrest would have been impractical because it "was late at night[,] no substitute clothing was then available for Edwards to wear, and it would certainly have been unreasonable for the police to have stripped respondent of his clothing and left him exposed in his cell throughout the night." Thus, the *Edwards* decision established the rule that noncontemporaneous searches incident to arrest are permissible when (1) an immediate search is nearly impossible and (2) the exigency still exists at the time of the later search.

The Supreme Court has also restricted the scope of searches incident to arrest. Returning to *Chimel v. California,* the Supreme Court created the so-called "arm-span rule." In the Court's words, a search incident to arrest is limited to the area "within [the] immediate control" of the person arrested, that is, "the area from within which he might have obtained either a weapon or something that could have been used as evidence against him." This includes shoulder bags and other permissible items, as was decided in *Illinois v. Lafayette* (462 U.S. 640 [1983]). However, the search incident to arrest exception does not permit warrantless searches of moveable containers at a point in time *after* a lawful arrest. This decision was reached in *United States v. Chadwick*, a case also briefed in this chapter.

The cases discussed thus far have focused narrowly on the scope of the incident search exception with reference to the arrestee. What if another person *besides* the arrestee poses a threat to the police? This concern has led to several exceptions to the arm-span rule, to which we now turn.

First, in *Maryland v. Buie*, the Supreme Court expanded the scope of the incident search in two ways. It held that the police may, as part of a search incident to arrest, look in areas immediately adjoining the place of arrest for other persons who might attack the officers; no justification is required. The key, however, is that such a search occurs incident to arrest. Next, the Court held that at any point up to the time the arrest is completed, the police may engage in a "protective sweep" (i.e., "a cursory visual inspection of those places in which a person might be hiding"), but reasonable suspicion must exist for such a sweep to be justified. Thus, no justification is required *after* arrest, but reasonable suspicion is required to engage in a sweep up to the point of the arrest.

Aside from the possible danger to police officers from "confederates" is the potential for such third parties to engage in the destruction of evidence. Only one Supreme Court case appears to address this issue: *Vale v. Louisiana.* In that case, police had warrants authorizing the arrest of the defendant. While engaged in surveillance of the house, the officers observed the defendant come out of the house and engage in what appeared to be a drug sale. They arrested the defendant outside the home, but then went back inside the house and searched it, according to the officers because two of the defendant's relatives had arrived at the house in the meantime and could have destroyed evidence. *Vale* was actually a case concerning exigent circumstances, and the Court reversed the Louisiana Supreme Court's decision that upheld the search, but the Court's opinion was not particularly instructive. It stated in relevant part that "no reason, so far as anything before us appears, to suppose that it was impracticable for [the officers] to obtain a search warrant as well," but did not expressly state that related searches would always be unconstitutional. ✦

WARDEN V. HAYDEN
387 U.S. 294 (1967)

FACTS

The police were informed that an armed robbery had occurred and that the suspect, Hayden, had thereafter entered a certain house. Minutes later they arrived there and were told by Hayden's wife that she had no objection to their searching the house. Certain officers arrested Hayden in an upstairs bedroom when it became clear he was the only man in the house. Others simultaneously searched the first floor and cellar. One found weapons in a flush tank; another, looking "for a man or the money," found in a washing machine clothing of the type the suspect was said to have worn. Ammunition was also found. These items were admitted into evidence without objection at Hayden's trial, which resulted in his conviction. After unsuccessful state court proceedings Hayden sought and was denied habeas corpus relief in district court. The court of appeals found the search lawful, but reversed on the ground that the clothing seized during the search was immune from seizure, being of "evidential value only." The U.S Supreme Court then granted certiorari.

ISSUE

Is there, under the Fourth Amendment, a distinction between merely evidentiary materials—which may not be seized either under the authority of a search warrant or during the course of a search incident to arrest—and those objects which may validly be seized including the instrumentalities and means by which a crime is committed, the fruits of crime such as stolen property, weapons by which escape of the person arrested might be effected, and property the possession of which is a crime?

HOLDING

No. The distinction prohibiting seizure of items of only evidential value and allowing seizure of instrumentalities, fruits, or contraband is no longer accepted as being required by the Fourth Amendment.

RATIONALE

"There is no rational distinction between a search for 'mere evidence' and one for an 'instrumentality' in terms of the privacy which is safeguarded by the Fourth Amendment; nor does the language of the Amendment itself make such a distinction. The clothing items involved here are not 'testimonial' or 'communicative' and their introduction did not compel Hayden to become a witness against himself in violation of the Fifth Amendment. The premise that property interests control government's search and seizure rights, on which *Gouled v. United States* partly rested, is no longer controlling as the Fourth Amendment's principal object is the protection of privacy, not property. The related premise of *Gouled* that government may not seize evidence for the purpose of proving crime has also been discredited. The Fourth Amendment does not bar a search for that purpose provided that there is probable cause, as there was here, for the belief that the evidence sought will aid in a particular apprehension or conviction. The remedy of suppression, with its limited, functional consequence, has made possible the rejection of both the related *Gouled* premises. Just as the suppression of evidence does not require the return of such items as contraband, the introduction of 'mere evidence' does not entitle the State to its retention if it is being wrongfully withheld. The numerous and confusing exceptions to the 'mere evidence' limitation make it questionable whether it affords any meaningful protection."

CASE SIGNIFICANCE

This case stood for two propositions: (1) that a warrant is not required if probable cause and exigent circumstances exist; and (2) that there is no distinction between types of evidence.

CHIMEL V. CALIFORNIA
395 U.S. 752 (1969)

FACTS

Police officers armed with an arrest warrant, but not a search warrant, were admitted to Chimel's home by his wife, where they awaited his arrival. When he entered he was arrested. Although he denied the officers' request to "look around," they nonetheless conducted a search of the entire house "on the basis of the lawful arrest." At Chimel's trial on burglary charges, items taken from his home were admitted over objection that they had been unconstitutionally seized. His conviction was affirmed by the California appellate courts, which held that the search was justified as incident to a valid arrest. The U.S Supreme Court then granted certiorari.

ISSUE

May police officers search the area surrounding an arrestee incident to a lawful arrest?

HOLDING

Yes. Police may search the area within the immediate control of an arrestee, in order to discover any weapons or to prevent the destruction of evidence.

RATIONALE

An arresting officer may search the arrestee's person to discover and remove weapons and to seize evidence to prevent its concealment or destruction, and may search the area "within the immediate control" of the person arrested, meaning the area from which he might gain possession of a weapon or destructible evidence. For the routine search of rooms other than that in which an arrest occurs, or for searching desk drawers or other closed or concealed areas in that room itself, absent well-recognized exceptions, a search warrant is required. While the reasonableness of a search incident to arrest depends upon "the facts and circumstances—the total atmosphere of the case," those facts and circumstances must be viewed in the light of established Fourth Amendment principles, and the only reasoned distinction is one between: (1) a search of the person arrested and the area within his reach, and (2) more extensive searches. The scope of the search here was unreasonable under the Fourth and Fourteenth Amendments, as it went beyond petitioner's person and the area from within which he might have obtained a weapon or something that could have been used as evidence against him, and there was no constitutional justification, in the absence of a search warrant, for extending the search beyond that area.

CASE SIGNIFICANCE

This case made it clear that the police may not only search a person when making and arrest, but may also search an area surrounding the arrestee—what the court termed the "area of immediate control," and which other courts have described as the "lunge area." This extension of the search incident exception is based on the same rationale—to allow officers to protect themselves from harm and to prevent the possible destruction of evidence.

VALE V. LOUISIANA
399 U.S. 30 (1970)

FACTS

Police officers, possessing warrants for Vale's arrest, were watching the house where he resided. They observed what they suspected was an exchange of narcotics between a known addict and Vale outside the house, after Vale had gone into the house and brought something out to the addict. They arrested Vale at the front steps and announced that they would then search his house incident to his arrest. A search of the then-unoccupied house disclosed narcotics in a bedroom. The Louisiana Supreme Court, affirming Vale's conviction for possessing heroin, held that the search did not violate the Fourth Amendment, as it occurred "in the immediate vicinity of the arrest" and was "substantially contemporaneous therewith." The U.S Supreme Court then granted certiorari.

ISSUE

May the police conduct a warrantless search of a suspect's home when the suspect is arrested outside the home and there are no exigent circumstances present?

HOLDING

No. The warrantless search of appellant's house violated the Fourth Amendment.

RATIONALE

"Even under *Chimel v. California*, holding that the warrantless search of a house can be justified as incident to a lawful arrest, there is no precedent of this Court to sustain the validity of this search. If a search of a house is to be upheld as incident to an arrest, the arrest must take place inside the house. A warrantless search of a dwelling is constitutionally valid only in 'a few specifically established and well-delineated exceptions,' and the search cannot be justified solely because narcotics, which are easily destroyed, are involved."

CASE SIGNIFICANCE

This case limited the "search incident to arrest" exception somewhat. Police may not use the exception to conduct a search of a residence if the suspect is arrested outside the residence.

UNITED STATES V. ROBINSON
414 U.S. 218 (1973)

FACTS

Robinson was arrested for driving while his license was revoked. In accordance with prescribed procedures, the arresting officer made a search of Robinson's person, in the course of which he found in a coat pocket a cigarette package containing heroin. Robinson was charged and convicted of drug possession. The court of appeals reversed on the ground that the heroin had been obtained as a result of a search in violation of the Fourth Amendment, and the U.S Supreme Court granted certiorari.

ISSUE

May a police officer conduct a full search of an arrestee, even though he does not fear for his safety?

HOLDING

Yes. In the case of a lawful custodial arrest a full search of the person is not only an exception to the warrant requirement of the Fourth Amendment, but is also a "reasonable" search under that Amendment.

RATIONALE

"A search incident to a valid arrest is not limited to a frisk of the suspect's outer clothing and removal of such weapons as the arresting officer may, as a result of such frisk, reasonably believe and ascertain that the suspect has in his possession, and the absence of probable fruits or further evidence of the particular crime for which the arrest is made does not narrow the standards applicable to such a search. A custodial arrest of a suspect based on probable cause is a reasonable intrusion under the Fourth Amendment and a search incident to the arrest requires no additional justification, such as the probability in a particular arrest situation that weapons or evidence would in fact be found upon the suspect's person; and whether or not there was present one of the reasons supporting the authority for a search of the person incident to a lawful arrest need not be litigated in each case. Since the custodial arrest here gave rise to the authority to search, it is immaterial that the arresting officer did not fear Robinson or suspect that he was armed."

CASE SIGNIFICANCE

This case stands for the proposition that the police may always conduct a full body search when making an arrest. Prior to this decision, many lower courts allowed a full search only if the police officer feared for his safety. Now, any time a police officer takes a person into custody, for any offense, the officer may conduct a full body search.

UNITED STATES V. EDWARDS
415 U.S. 800 (1974)

FACTS

Edwards was arrested shortly after 11 p.m. and taken to jail. The next morning, a warrantless seizure was made of his clothing and over his objection at his later trial, which resulted in conviction, was used as evidence. The court of appeals reversed, holding that the court held that the warrantless seizure of Edwards' clothing "after the administrative process and the mechanics of the arrest [had] come to a halt" was unconstitutional. The U.S Supreme Court then granted certiorari.

ISSUE

Did the warrantless search of Edwards' clothing several hours after his seizure and while he was in custody violate the Fourth Amendment?

HOLDING

No. The search and seizure of Edwards' clothing did not violate the Fourth Amendment.

RATIONALE

"At the time Edwards was placed in his cell, the normal processes incident to arrest and custody had not been completed, and the delay in seizing the clothing was not unreasonable, since at that late hour no substitute clothing was available, and when the next morning the police were able to supply substitute clothing and took Edwards' clothing for laboratory analysis, they did no more than they were entitled to do incident to the usual arrest and incarceration. Once an accused has been lawfully arrested and is in custody, the effects in his possession at the place of detention that were subject to search at the time and place of arrest may lawfully be searched and seized without a warrant even after a substantial time lapse between the arrest and later administrative processing, on the one hand, and the taking of the property for use as evidence, on the other."

CASE SIGNIFICANCE

This case is important because it gave police the authority to conduct a search incident to arrest at some point after the arrest—there is no requirement that the search be "contemporaneous" with the arrest. This was a significant expansion of the search incident exception, which was originally created to protect officers making an arrest. Extending the time period for the search seems to run counter to the rationale for the exception, but relieves police officers from having to do the search right away or not at all.

UNITED STATES V. CHADWICK
430 U.S. 1 (1977)

FACTS

Railroad employees observed three men loading a heavy container, which was leaking talcum powder (often used to mask the smell of marijuana), onto a train. The employees notified federal agents as to this suspicious activity, so the agents waited for the men in Boston, their destination. The agents did not obtain a search warrant. Instead, they allowed a trained narcotics dog to sniff the container carried by the men just before it was loaded into the trunk of a car. The dog was alerted to the smell of marijuana and the three men were arrested. The men were searched following the arrest and keys to the container were taken from one of the men. All three men as well as the container were taken to the local federal building. Over an hour later, and without a warrant or consent, agents used the keys obtained from one of the men to open the container. Marijuana was found inside. The men were charged with and convicted of possession with intent to distribute, and the case came before the U.S Supreme Court.

ISSUE

May police, with probable cause but no warrant or consent, and if no exigent circumstances are present, search a moveable container?

HOLDING

No. The warrantless search of a moveable container is unconstitutional so long as exigent circumstances do not exist.

RATIONALE

"The factors which diminish the privacy aspects of an automobile do not apply to Chadwick's footlocker. . . . Unlike an automobile, whose primary function is transportation, luggage is intended as a repository of personal effects . . . [and] a person's expectations of privacy in personal luggage are substantially greater than in an automobile. . . . Nor does the container's mobility justify dispensing with the added protections of the Warrant Clause."

CASE SIGNIFICANCE

This case is important because it dealt with a fairly rare law enforcement activity—searches of containers not found in a house or an automobile. The decision treated searches of moveable containers (not found in an automobile) like searches of homes. That is, not just probable cause but also a warrant must be in place before authorities can engage in such searches. However, if exigent circumstances exist, officers can dispense with the warrant requirement. Also, had the search been of a container found in the car (as opposed to being loaded into a car), and the search fell under the well-known automobile exception to the Fourth Amendment's warrant requirement, then the police's actions would have been considered constitutional.

ILLINOIS V. LAFAYETTE
462 U.S. 640 (1983)

FACTS

After LaFayette was arrested for disturbing the peace, he was taken to the police station. There, without obtaining a warrant and in the process of booking him and inventorying his possessions, the police removed the contents of a shoulder bag LaFayette had been carrying and found amphetamine pills. LaFayette was subsequently charged with violating the Illinois Controlled Substances Act, and at a pretrial hearing the trial court ordered suppression of the pills. The Illinois Appellate Court affirmed, holding that the shoulder bag search did not constitute a valid search incident to a lawful arrest or a valid inventory search of LaFayette's belongings. The U.S Supreme Court then granted certiorari.

ISSUE

Did the shoulder bag search constitute a valid search incident to a lawful arrest?

HOLDING

Yes. The search of LaFayette's shoulder bag was a valid inventory search.

RATIONALE

"Consistent with the Fourth Amendment, it is reasonable for police to search the personal effects of a person under lawful arrest as part of the routine administrative procedure at a police station incident to booking and jailing the suspect. The justification for such searches does not rest on probable cause, and hence the absence of a warrant is immaterial to the reasonableness of the search. Here, every consideration of orderly police administration—protection of a suspect's property, deterrence of false claims of theft against the police, security, and identification of the suspect—benefiting both the police and the public points toward the appropriateness of the examination of LaFayette's shoulder bag. The fact that the protection of the public and of LaFayette's property might have been achieved by less intrusive means does not, in itself, render the search unreasonable. Even if some less intrusive means existed, it would be unreasonable to expect police officers in the everyday course of business to make fine and subtle distinctions in deciding which containers or items may be searched, and which must be sealed without examination as a unit."

CASE SIGNIFICANCE

This case stands for the proposition that inventory searches are per se reasonable, so long as they are not used as a pretext for investigation. This decision allows the police great discretion to conduct inventory searches, so long as there exists a standardized procedure for the inventory.

MARYLAND V. BUIE
494 U.S. 325 (1990)

FACTS

Following an armed robbery by two men, one of whom was wearing a red running suit, several police officers obtained arrest warrants for Buie and his suspected accomplice and executed the arrest warrant for Buie at his house. After Buie was arrested upon emerging from the basement, one of the officers entered the basement "in case there was someone else" there and seized a red running suit lying in plain view. The trial court denied Buie's motion to suppress the running suit, the suit was introduced into evidence, and Buie was convicted of armed robbery and a weapons offense. The intermediate appellate court affirmed the denial of the suppression motion, but the state supreme court reversed, ruling that the running suit was inadmissible because the officer who conducted the "protective sweep" of the basement did not have probable cause to believe that a serious and demonstrable potentiality for danger existed when he searched the basement. The U.S Supreme Court then granted certiorari.

ISSUE

May a police officer conduct a warrantless "protective sweep" of the area where a suspect is arrested?

HOLDING

Yes. The Fourth Amendment permits a limited protective sweep in conjunction with an in-home arrest when the searching officer possesses a reasonable belief based on specific and articulable facts that the area to be swept harbors an individual posing a danger to those present during the arrest.

RATIONALE

"In holding that, respectively, an on-the-street 'frisk' and a roadside search of an automobile's passenger compartment were reasonable despite the absence of a warrant or probable cause, *Terry v. Ohio* and *Michigan v. Long* balanced the Fourth Amendment interests of the persons with whom they were dealing against the immediate interests of the police in protecting themselves from the danger posed by hidden weapons. Here, the police had an analogous interest in taking steps to assure themselves that Buie's house was not harboring other persons who were dangerous and who could unexpectedly launch an attack, and the fact that Buie had an expectation of privacy in rooms that were not examined by the police prior to the arrest does not mean that such rooms were immune from entry. No warrant was required, and as an incident to the arrest the officers could, as a precautionary matter and without probable cause or reasonable suspicion, look in closets and other spaces immediately adjoining the place of arrest from which an attack could be launched. Beyond that, however, just as in *Terry* and *Long,* there must be articulable facts which, taken together with the rational inferences from those facts, would warrant a reasonably prudent officer in believing that the area to be swept harbors an individual posing a danger. Such a protective sweep is not a full search of the premises, but may extend only to a cursory inspection of those spaces where a person may be found. The sweep lasts no longer than is necessary to dispel the reasonable suspicion of danger and in any event no longer than it takes to complete the arrest and depart the premises."

CASE SIGNIFICANCE

This case allowed police officers to conduct a limited protective sweep of the premises when they make an arrest, but only if they can articulate the facts which indicate they may be in danger. In addition, searches are limited to possible hiding spots, and must be of short duration. ✦

DISCUSSION QUESTIONS

1. How large should an arrestee's "grabbing area" be?

2. Is it possible that the police could manipulate a protective sweep to their advantage?

3. While this chapter does not cover automobile searches, it is true that the police can search an entire automobile incident to arrest, even if the arrestee is handcuffed and out of the car. Do you agree with this practice? Why or why not?

4. Identify reasons for the search incident to arrest exception to the Fourth Amendment's warrant requirement.

5. Provide an example of an unconstitutional search incident to arrest. ✦

Chapter Ten
Consent Searches

Stoner v. California, 376 U.S. 483 (1964)

Bumper v. North Carolina, 391 U.S. 543 (1968)

Schneckloth v. Bustamonte,
   412 U.S. 218 (1973)

Florida v. Royer, 460 U.S. 491 (1983)

Illinois v. Rodriguez, 497 U.S. 177 (1990)

Florida v. Jimeno, 500 U.S. 248 (1991)

United States v. Drayton et al.,
   536 U.S. 194 (2002)

INTRODUCTION

There is one clear-cut situation where absolutely no justification is required in order for the police to engage in a search. This situation is consent. When a person consents to a search, neither probable cause nor reasonable suspicion are necessary. Consent searches are still bound by the Fourth Amendment, but they begin following someone's waiver of his or her Fourth Amendment rights.

Cases involving consensual searches can be placed into three categories. Consensual searches must be voluntary, so several cases have focused on the meaning of this term. Other cases have defined the scope of consent searches and still others have focused on exactly whether third party individuals can give consent in order to subject another person's private effects to a search.

The general rule is that validly obtained consent justifies a warrantless search with or without probable cause. However, for consent to be valid it must be voluntary. If consent is the result of duress or coercion, then any evidence obtained as a result will be inadmissible. When does duress or coercion take place? There is no clear answer to this question. Instead, the Court has opted for a "totality of circumstances" test. The Court did state, however, that by looking at the "surrounding circumstances" of the consent, including whether a show of force was made, whether the person's age, mental condition, or intellectual capacities inhibit understanding, whether the person is or was in custody, and/or whether consent was granted "only after the official

conducting the search has asserted that he possesses a warrant" (*Bumper v. North Carolina*).

Importantly, consent to search may be valid even if the consenting party is unaware of the fact that he or she can refuse consent (*Schneckloth v. Bustamonte*). As the Court stated in *Ohio v. Robinette*, "just as it 'would be thoroughly impractical to impose on the normal consent search the detailed requirements of an effective warning,' so too would it be unrealistic to require police officers to always inform detainees that they are free to go before a consent to search may be deemed involuntary." Likewise, nothing prohibits authorities from randomly approaching individuals and asking for consent to search, even without suspicion that criminal activity is afoot (*United States v. Drayton et al.*). Consent must be voluntary, however.

Importantly, while a consent search need not be based on probable cause or any other standard of justification, if consent is obtained following an unlawful seizure, then it will not be considered valid. Such was the decision reached in *Florida v. Royer*. There, the Supreme Court held that because Royer ". . . was being illegally detained when he consented to the search of his luggage, . . . the consent was tainted by the illegality and was ineffective to justify the search."

The scope of a consent search is limited to the terms of the consent. In other words, the person giving consent "calls the shots." This was the decision reached in the case of *Florida v. Jimeno*. For example, if a person says "you may look around" does not necessarily mean the police can look *anywhere* for evidence of criminal activity.

A handful of Supreme Court cases have focused on whether third parties can give consent to have another person's property searched (e.g., a landlord consenting to have a tenant's apartment searched; parents consenting to have their child's room searched, etc.). As far as the immediate family is concerned, the general rule is that wives and husbands can give consent to have their partners' property searched and parents can give consent to have their children's property searched, but children cannot give consent to have their parent's property searched. The reason children cannot give consent is that they are considered "incompetent" to give voluntary consent, given their age. By contrast, landlords cannot give consent to search property rented to another person (*Stoner v. California*).

More confusing is the situation of a roommate, former girlfriend, friend, or extended family member. Two important Supreme Court cases are relevant here. First, third-party consent can be given if (1) the third-party individual possesses "common authority" over the area to be searched and (2) the nonconsenting party (e.g., the roommate) is not present (*United States v. Matlock*, 415 U.S. 164 [1974]). According to the Court, "common authority" rests on "mutual use of the property by persons generally having joint access or control for most purposes." Thus, a third party could give consent to have a shared bathroom searched but not to have her roommate's bedroom searched. What happens, however, if the nonconsenting party is present and affirmatively objects to the search? The courts are divided on this issue.

There are some cut-and-dried situations where two people possess common authority over a particular area, but what happens when it is not clear to officers at the scene whether common authority exists? In response to this question, the Supreme Court has held that warrantless entry of private premises by police officers is valid if based on the "apparent authority" doctrine. In other words, a warrantless entry of a residence is valid if it is based on the consent of a person whom the police reasonably believe has authority to grant consent, even if their beliefs are erroneous (*Illinois v. Rodriguez*). The test for reasonableness in this situation, according to the Court, is: "[W]ould the facts available to the officer at the moment [of the entry] . . . warrant a man of reasonable caution in the belief that the consenting party had authority over the premises?" *Rodriguez* involved consent given by a former girlfriend who possessed apparent authority to grant consent because she still had a key to her ex-boyfriend's apartment. ✦

STONER V. CALIFORNIA
376 U.S. 483 (1964)

FACTS

Police investigating the armed robbery of a grocery store found several items which led them to suspect Stoner was the robber. They tracked him to a hotel where, without a search or arrest warrant, they entered and searched Stoner's room in his absence, having been given access to and consent to search by a hotel clerk. There they found evidence associated with the crime. Stoner was arrested two days later in another state, and following a trial in which the articles were used as evidence, was convicted. He appealed, and the U.S. Supreme Court granted certiorari.

ISSUE

May a hotel clerk give valid consent to search a hotel room rented to a criminal suspect?

HOLDING

No. A hotel guest is entitled to the constitutional protection against unreasonable searches and seizures. The hotel clerk had no authority to permit the room search and the police had no basis to believe that petitioner had authorized the clerk to permit the search.

RATIONALE

"It is true that when a person engages a hotel room he undoubtedly gives 'implied or express permission' to 'such persons as maids, janitors or repairmen' to enter his room 'in the performance of their duties.' But the conduct of the night clerk and the police in the present case was of an entirely different order."

CASE SIGNIFICANCE

This case made it clear that a hotel guest has a reasonable expectation of privacy in his or her hotel room, even though he or she does not own it and hotel staff may enter it for purposes related to the operation of the hotel. Consent to allow hotel staff into the room does not eliminate the reasonable expectation of privacy.

BUMPER V. NORTH CAROLINA
391 U.S. 543 (1968)

FACTS

Four police officers appeared at Bumper's home, announced that they had a search warrant, and were told by the owner, Bumper's grandmother, to "go ahead." In fact, the officers did not have a search warrant. The search turned up evidence implicating Bumper in a rape. At the hearing on a motion to suppress, which was denied, the prosecutor stated that he did not rely on a warrant to justify the search, but on the consent of the grandmother. Bumper was convicted, and the state supreme court affirmed. The U.S. Supreme Court then granted certiorari.

ISSUE

Is consent obtained by police officers who lie about the existence of a search warrant valid?

HOLDING

No. A search cannot be justified as lawful on the basis of consent when that "consent" has been given only after the official conducting the search has asserted that he possesses a warrant; such consent is not voluntary, and consent must be voluntary.

RATIONALE

"When a prosecutor seeks to rely upon consent to justify the lawfulness of a search, he has the burden of proving that the consent was, in fact, freely and voluntarily given. This burden cannot be discharged by showing no more than acquiescence to a claim of lawful authority. A search conducted in reliance upon a warrant cannot later be justified on the basis of consent if it turns out that the warrant was invalid. The result can be no different when it turns out that the State does not even attempt to rely upon the validity of the warrant, or fails to show that there was, in fact, any warrant at all. When a law enforcement officer claims authority to search a home under a warrant, he announces in effect that the occupant has no right to resist the search. The situation is instinct with coercion—albeit colorably lawful coercion. Where there is coercion there cannot be consent."

CASE SIGNIFICANCE

This case established the requirement that police officers not mislead suspects about the existence of a search warrant in an attempt to gain consent to search. Consent obtained in such a fashion is deemed involuntary, and thus invalid. Left unanswered by the Supreme Court in this case was whether consent obtained by an officer who merely threatens to obtain a search warrant is valid. Lower courts are split on this issue.

SCHNECKLOTH V. BUSTAMONTE
412 U.S. 218 (1973)

FACTS

A police officer on routine patrol stopped a car with Bustamonte and five others in it for having a headlight and license plate light out. During the course of a consent search of a car that had been stopped by officers for traffic violations, evidence was discovered that was used to convict Bustamonte of unlawfully possessing a check. In a habeas corpus proceeding, the court of appeals, reversing the district court, held that the prosecution had failed to prove that consent to the search had been made with the understanding that it could freely be withheld. The U.S. Supreme Court then granted certiorari.

ISSUE

Must the state prove that the individual giving consent to a search knows he or she has the right to withhold consent?

HOLDING

No. When the subject of a search is not in custody and the state would justify a search on the basis of his consent, the Fourth and Fourteenth Amendments require that it demonstrate that the consent was in fact voluntary; voluntariness is to be determined from the totality of the surrounding circumstances. While knowledge of a right to refuse consent is a factor to be taken into account, the state need not prove that whoever gave permission to search knew that he or she had a right to withhold his or her consent.

RATIONALE

"In determining whether a defendant's will was overborne in a particular case, the Court has assessed the totality of all the surrounding circumstances—both the characteristics of the accused and the details of the interrogation. Some of the factors taken into account have included the youth of the accused, his lack of education, or his low intelligence, the lack of any advice to the accused of his constitutional rights, the length of detention, the repeated and prolonged nature of the questioning, and the use of physical punishment such as the deprivation of food or sleep. The Court determined the factual circumstances surrounding the confession, assessed the psychological impact on the accused, and evaluated the legal significance of how the accused reacted.

"The significant fact of all of the Court's past decisions on this subject is that none of them turned on the presence or absence of a single controlling criterion; each reflected a careful scrutiny of all the surrounding circumstances. In none of them did the Court rule that the Due Process Clause required the prosecution to prove as part of its initial burden that the defendant knew he had a right to refuse to answer the questions that were put. While the state of the accused's mind, and the failure of the police to advise the accused of his rights, were certainly factors to be evaluated in assessing the 'voluntariness' of an accused's responses, they were not in and of themselves determinative."

CASE SIGNIFICANCE

This case clarified the requirements for obtaining consent to conduct a search. Where the Supreme Court requires, under *Miranda v. Arizona,* that a suspect in custody be advised of his right to remain silent before the police may lawfully interrogate him, there is no such requirement that police advise a suspect of his right to refuse consent to a search when seeking such consent. Thus the Court has created a hierarchy of protection of individual rights—a suspect must be informed of his Fifth and Sixth Amendment rights before police may proceed with a custodial interrogation, but a suspect need not be informed of his Fourth Amendment rights before police seek a waiver of those rights.

FLORIDA V. ROYER
460 U.S. 491 (1983)

FACTS

After purchasing a one-way airline ticket to New York City at Miami International Airport under an assumed name and checking his two suitcases bearing identification tags with the same assumed name, Royer went to the concourse leading to the airline boarding area. He was approached by two detectives, who previously had observed him and believed that his characteristics fit a "drug-courier profile." Upon request, but without oral consent, Royer produced his airline ticket and driver's license, which carried his correct name. When the detectives asked about the discrepancy in names, Royer explained that a friend had made the ticket reservation in the assumed name. The detectives then informed Royer that they were narcotics investigators and that they had reason to suspect him of transporting narcotics, and, without returning his airline ticket or driver's license, asked him to accompany them to a small room adjacent to the concourse. Without Royer's consent, one of the detectives retrieved his luggage from the airline and brought it to the room. While he did not respond orally to the detectives' request that he consent to a search of the luggage, Royer produced a key and unlocked one of the suitcases in which marijuana was found. When Royer said he did not know the combination to the lock on the second suitcase but did not object to its being opened, the officers pried it open and found more marijuana. Royer was then arrested. Following the Florida trial court's denial of his pretrial motion to suppress the evidence obtained in the search of the suitcases, Royer was convicted of felony possession of marijuana. The Florida Court of Appeals reversed, holding that Royer had been involuntarily confined without probable cause, that at the time his consent to search was obtained, the involuntary detention had exceeded the limited restraint permitted by *Terry v. Ohio*, and that such consent was therefore invalid because tainted by the unlawful confinement. The U.S. Supreme Court then granted certiorari.

ISSUE

Is consent to search valid if it is obtained by the police during a seizure which was not based on probable cause?

HOLDING

No. Royer's consent was not valid because it was tainted by the illegal seizure.

RATIONALE

"Detective Johnson testified at the suppression hearing and the Florida District Court of Appeal held that there was no probable cause to arrest until Royer's bags were opened. Clearly, then, probable cause to arrest Royer did not exist at the time he consented to the search of his luggage. The facts are that a nervous young man with two American Tourister bags paid cash for an airline ticket to a 'target city.' These facts led to inquiry, which in turn revealed that the ticket had been bought under an assumed name. The proffered explanation did not satisfy the officers. We cannot agree with the state that every nervous young man paying cash for a ticket to New York City under an assumed name and carrying two heavy American Tourister bags may be arrested and held to answer for a serious felony charge. Because we affirm the Florida District Court of Appeals' conclusion that Royer was being illegally detained when he consented to the search of his luggage, we agree that the consent was tainted by the illegality and was ineffective to justify the search. The judgment of the Florida District Court of Appeal is accordingly affirmed."

CASE SIGNIFICANCE

This case stands for the proposition that consent obtained by the police during an illegal seizure is not valid. This means the police must make sure that they do not exceed their authority to detain a suspect before seeking consent. Once a seizure is deemed to have occurred, the full protections of the Fourth Amendment apply.

ILLINOIS V. RODRIGUEZ
497 U.S. 177 (1990)

FACTS

Rodriguez was arrested in his apartment and charged with possession of illegal drugs, which the police had observed in plain view and seized. The officers did not have an arrest or search warrant, but gained entry to the apartment with the assistance of Gail Fischer, who represented that the apartment was "ours" and that she had clothes and furniture there, unlocked the door with her key, and gave the officers permission to enter. The trial court granted Rodriguez's motion to suppress the seized evidence, holding that at the time Fischer consented to the entry she did not have common authority because she had moved out of the apartment. The Appellate Court of Illinois affirmed, and the U.S. Supreme Court granted certiorari.

ISSUE

May the police enter without a warrant based upon the consent of a third party whom the police, at the time of entry, believe to possess common authority over the premises, but who in fact does not?

HOLDING

Yes. A warrantless entry is valid when based upon the consent of a third party whom the police, at the time of the entry, reasonably believe to possess common authority over the premises, but who in fact does not.

RATIONALE

"What Rodriguez is assured by the Fourth Amendment is not that no government search of his house will occur unless he consents; but that no such search will occur that is unreasonable. As with the many other factual determinations that must regularly be made by government agents in the Fourth Amendment context, the reasonableness of a police determination of consent to enter must be judged not by whether the police were correct in their assessment, but by the objective standard of whether the facts available at the moment would warrant a person of reasonable caution in the belief that the consenting party had authority over the premises. If not, then warrantless entry without further inquiry is unlawful unless authority actually exists. But if so, the search is valid."

CASE SIGNIFICANCE

This case stands for the proposition that police may enter a building based on the consent of a person who lives there or has the authority to exclude others. The police need not ask if the person in fact has such authority; rather, they may make that assumption based on their observation of the situation. So long as the conclusion is reasonable, the consent will be upheld by the courts. This is known as the "apparent authority" rule. It means that at times police may be better off not asking if the person giving consent to a search has the authority to give such consent.

FLORIDA V. JIMENO
500 U.S. 248 (1991)

FACTS

Having stopped Jimeno's car for a traffic infraction, Officer Trujillo, who had been following the car after overhearing Jimeno arranging what appeared to be a drug transaction, declared that he had reason to believe that Jimeno was carrying narcotics in the car, and asked permission to search it. Jimeno consented, and Trujillo found cocaine inside a folded paper bag on the car's floorboard. Jimeno was charged with possession with intent to distribute cocaine in violation of Florida law, but the state trial court granted his motion to suppress the cocaine on the ground that his consent to search the car did not carry with it specific consent to open the bag and examine its contents. The Florida District Court of Appeals and Florida Supreme Court affirmed, and the U.S. Supreme Court granted certiorari.

ISSUE

Does consent to search a car include consent to search closed containers located within a car?

HOLDING

Yes. A criminal suspect's Fourth Amendment right to be free from unreasonable searches is not violated when, after he gives police permission to search his car, they open a closed container found within the car that might reasonably hold the object of the search.

RATIONALE

"The Amendment is satisfied when, under the circumstances, it is objectively reasonable for the police to believe that the scope of the suspect's consent permitted them to open the particular container. Here, the authorization to search extended beyond the car's interior surfaces to the bag, since Jimeno did not place any explicit limitation on the scope of the search, and was aware that Trujillo would be looking for narcotics in the car, and since a reasonable person may be expected to know that narcotics are generally carried in some form of container. There is no basis for adding to the Fourth Amendment's basic test of objective reasonableness a requirement that, if police wish to search closed containers within a car, they must separately request permission to search each container."

CASE SIGNIFICANCE

This case clarified the scope of consent to search an automobile. Prior Supreme Court cases were in conflict whether such consent extended to containers within the car. One case held that it did, while another case held that the police could seize, but not search, containers within the car. This case made it clear that consent to search a car extends to all containers within the car.

UNITED STATES V. DRAYTON ET AL.
536 U.S. 194 (2002)

FACTS

Drayton and a friend traveling together on a bus in Florida were approached during a bus sweep and asked for consent to search their luggage for drugs or weapons. Finding nothing in their carry-on baggage, the officer then asked the men for consent to search their persons. A pat down of the first subject (Brown) revealed packages of drugs taped to both thighs underneath his clothing. A consensual pat down of the second subject (Drayton) revealed the same. Both men were arrested and charged with conspiracy to distribute cocaine. At trial in federal district court, Drayton moved to suppress the evidence on grounds of coercive police conduct. Finding none, the district court denied the motion whereupon Drayton was convicted. The Eleventh Circuit Court of Appeals reversed and remanded with instructions to grant the motion to suppress, and the U.S. Supreme Court granted certiorari.

ISSUE

May the police randomly approach individuals and ask for consent to search their luggage (or personal belongings, person, etc.) absent any indication that criminal activity is afoot?

HOLDING

Yes. The police are authorized to approach individuals, even when they have no basis for suspecting that criminal activity is afoot, and ask for consent to search their luggage (or personal belongings, person, etc.) so long as compliance is not induced by coercive means.

RATIONALE

The Court has long held that the police do not violate the Fourth Amendment by simply approaching an individual and asking questions even when there is no evidence that criminal activity is afoot. If, however, an individual refuses to speak with the police he or she must be allowed to go on his or her way unfettered. Furthermore, refusal to engage the police in conversation or consent to a search cannot be used as a basis for detention. Finally, officers are prohibited from using coercive or intimidating tactics in order to gain consent for a search. These principles, traceable to the Court's earlier ruling in the similar case of *Florida v. Bostick* (1991), are again reinforced by this decision. Where the individual is free to leave and go about his or her business, no seizure has occurred under the Fourth Amendment. Having determined that respondents in the present case were not coerced but, instead, consented freely to

the search at issue, no Fourth Amendment violation was deemed to have occurred.

CASE SIGNIFICANCE

The decision in this case reaffirmed the Court's earlier ruling in *Florida v. Bostick*. Both cases authorized the police to approach individuals in public and not only ask questions, but also ask them for consent to search even in situations where there is no evidence that criminal activity is underway. If the individual refuses to talk and the officer lacks reasonable suspicion to believe that something is amiss, he or she must be allowed to leave unfettered. The fact that an individual refuses to answer an officer's otherwise groundless questions or refuses to give consent for a search cannot be used as a basis for detention. In other words, just because someone refuses to talk to the police does not automatically justify a detention of that individual. In reality, it is not at all difficult for an officer to develop reasonable suspicion that an individual who refuses to answer questions or consent to a search may actually be trying to conceal involvement in some form of unlawful activity. Once the officer has developed reasonable suspicion to believe that criminal activity is afoot, he or she has a legally justifiable basis to detain the individual. ✦

DISCUSSION QUESTIONS

1. What is your opinion of consent searches? Who do they favor, suspects or law enforcement officials?

2. The police are not required to advise people of their right to refuse consent. Do you agree with this? Why or why not?

3. Should parents be allowed to give consent to have police search the rooms of their children? What if the children are over eighteen and pay rent?

4. Should a person who consents to a search be able to define the scope of the consent given? If so, what possible problems could this pose?

5. If the police confront a person in an airport and ask consent to search the person's bag, and the person refuses, what is the likely consequence of this action? ✦

Chapter Eleven
Plain View Searches

Texas v. Brown, 460 U.S. 730 (1983)

Arizona v. Hicks, 480 U.S. 321 (1987)

Horton v. California, 496 U.S. 128 (1990)

INTRODUCTION

Untrained observers frequently suggest that "plain view" applies in situations where evidence can be seen without having to "search" for it. While this may be a *literal* interpretation of what it means for something to be in plain view, it is not the interpretation the courts use. Plain view has a very specific meaning in criminal procedure, and the doctrine only applies in certain situations.

The plain view doctrine first emerged in the Supreme Court's decision in *Coolidge v. New Hampshire,* 403 U.S. 443 (1971). The issue in *Coolidge* was whether evidence seized during a search of cars belonging to Coolidge was admissible. The police had a warrant to search the cars, but it was later deemed invalid, so the state argued that the evidence should still be admissible because the cars were in "plain view" from a public street and from the house in which Coolidge was arrested. The Court did not buy this argument, pointing out that just because the police could *see* the cars from where they were was not enough to permit seizure of the evidence in question. However, the Court did point out that had the police been *in* an area such as a car and house, evidence that is "immediately apparent as such" and is discovered "inadvertently" would be admissible. In other words, part of the reason the evidence was not admissible in *Coolidge* was that the police officers were not lawfully "in" the cars when the evidence was seized.

To summarize, the Court decided in *Coolidge* that a plain view *seizure* is authorized when: (1) the police are lawfully *in* the area where the evidence is located; (2) the items are "immediately apparent" as subject to seizure; and (3) the discovery of the evidence is "inadvertent." The first prong of the *Coolidge* ruling—the lawful access prong—has remained relatively stable over time. The second and third prongs, however, have undergone

significant interpretation in recent years. We now consider each prong separately.

First, for the plain view doctrine to apply, the police must have lawful access to the object to be seized. Consider what the Supreme Court had to say in *Coolidge*:

> [P]lain view *alone* is never enough to justify the warrantless seizure of evidence. This is simply a corollary of the familiar principle . . . that no amount of probable cause can justify a warrantless search or seizure absent "exigent circumstances." Incontrovertible testimony of the senses that an incriminating object is on premises belonging to a criminal suspect may establish the fullest possible measure of probable cause. But even where the object is contraband, this Court has repeatedly stated and enforced the basic rule that the police may not enter and make a warrantless seizure.

This excerpt from the Court's opinion in *Coolidge* reinforces the requirement that just because the police may *see* contraband does not necessarily mean they can seize it. If, for example, evidence is seen laying in a vacant lot or other public place, it may be seized. In such a situation, a search has not occurred. However, evidence that may be viewed from a public place but is in fact on private property cannot be seized unless a warrant is obtained or exigent circumstances are present. So, if a police officer on foot patrol observes a marijuana plant in the window of a private citizen, he or she may not enter the premises and seize the plant, even though such observation establishes "the fullest possible measure of probable cause."

What is meant by *lawful vantage point*? There are four specific situations where police officers can be found in a lawful vantage point for purposes of the plain view doctrine. The first is during a warranted search. For example, if an officer comes upon an article during the execution of a valid search warrant, the plain view doctrine may apply, subject to further restrictions described below. Second, officers are in a lawful vantage point during a valid arrest. This includes warrantless arrests in public, warrantless arrests based on exigent circumstances, and arrests with warrants. Third, when a warrantless search is conducted, the police officer is in a lawful vantage point, assuming of course that the warrantless search is based on probable cause. Finally, as illustrated in the previous paragraph, officers are always in a lawful vantage point during "nonsearches."

In addition to the requirement that the police have lawful access to an object for the plain view doctrine to apply, it must also be "immediately apparent" that the object is subject to seizure. "Immediately apparent" means that the officer has probable cause to seize the object. This was the decision reached in *Arizona v. Hicks.* In that case, the police entered the defendant's apartment without a warrant because a bullet had been fired through his floor into an apartment below, injuring a person. The warrantless entry was based on the exigency of looking for the shooter, for other potential victims, and for the weapon used in the incident. Once inside the apartment, the officer observed new stereo equipment that seemed out of place given the surroundings. The officer suspected the stereo equipment was stolen, but did not have probable cause to believe as such, so he picked up a turntable so that he could obtain its serial number. He then called in the information and confirmed that it was stolen. The Court held that this warrantless action did not satisfy the plain view doctrine. It was not immediately apparent to the officer that the stereo equipment was stolen.

Keep in mind that probable cause to seize and "immediately apparent" are one and the same. Officers do not need to be absolutely certain that the object is subject to seizure for the plain view doctrine to apply. This was the decision reached in *Texas v. Brown.* In that case, Brown was stopped late at night at a routine driver's license checkpoint. Brown opened the glove box in order to look for his license, at which point an opaque balloon, knotted at the opening, fell from his hand onto the floor of the passenger side of the vehicle. The officer observed what he perceived to be drug paraphernalia in the glove compartment and ultimately seized the balloon and its contents. The balloon was later proved to contain heroin, and Brown was convicted of narcotics offenses. The Texas Court of Criminal Appeals reversed Brown's conviction, pointing that the plain view doctrine did not apply because the officer did not *know* incriminatory evidence was before him when he seized the balloon. A unanimous Supreme Court reversed, stating: "The fact that [the officer] could not see through the opaque fabric of the balloon is all but irrelevant; the distinctive character of the balloon itself spoke volumes as to its contents—particularly to the trained eye of the officer."

The role of inadvertency in the plain view determination has received considerable attention. The original position of the Supreme Court in *Coolidge v. New Hampshire* was that objects seized under the plain view doctrine must not have been "anticipated" by the police. For example, assume that a police officer obtains a warrant to search a suspect's home for the proceeds from a robbery. Assume further that the officer *expects* to find guns in the house, but does not state in the warrant that guns will be sought. If, during the search, the officer finds guns, under the Supreme Court's old rul-

ing, the guns would not be admissible because the officers expected to find them. This restriction on the plain view doctrine came to be known as the *inadvertency requirement.* The rationale for this restriction was that an officer who anticipates discovering evidence of a crime should seek prior judicial authorization (i.e., a warrant). Further, the Fourth Amendment's particularity requirement would be compromised if "general" searches were permitted.

In *Horton v. California,* the Court declared that inadvertency, although a "characteristic of most legitimate 'plain view' seizures, . . . is not a necessary condition" of the doctrine. The Court offered two reasons for abandoning the inadvertency requirement imposed in *Coolidge.* First, according to *Horton,* as long as a warrant particularly describes the places to be searched and the objects to be seized, the officer cannot expand the area of the search once the evidence is found. In other words, it is unlikely that once officers find the evidence listed in the warrant they will go on "fishing expeditions," looking for evidence not listed in the warrant. According to the Court, the particularity requirement itself ensures that people's privacy is protected.

Second, the Court noted that "[E]venhanded law enforcement is best achieved by the application of objective standards of conduct, rather than standards that depend upon the subjective stated of mind of the officer." An inadvertency requirement would force the courts to dwell on police officers' subjective motivations, which would be both time consuming and distracting. The Court went on to note that "[t]he fact that an officer is interested in an item of evidence and fully expects to find it in the course of a search should not invalidate its seizure if the search is confined in area and duration by the terms of the warrant or a valid exception to the warrant requirement." ✦

Texas v. Brown
460 U.S. 730 (1983)

Facts

A Fort Worth, Texas, police officer stopped Brown's automobile at night at a routine driver's license checkpoint. While asking Brown for his license, the police officer shined his flashlight into the car and saw an opaque, green balloon, knotted near the tip, fall from Brown's hand to the seat beside him. Based on his experience, the officer was aware that narcotics were frequently packaged in such balloons, and while Brown was looking in the glove compartment for his license, the officer shifted his position to obtain a better view of the interior of the automobile. He then noticed small plastic vials, loose white powder, and an open bag of balloons in the glove compartment. After Brown said that he had no driver's license in his possession and complied with the officer's request to get out of the car, the officer picked up the green balloon, which contained a powdery substance within its tied-off portion. Brown was then advised that he was under arrest, an on-the-scene inventory search of the car was conducted, and other items were seized. At a suppression hearing, a police department chemist testified that heroin was contained in the balloon seized by the officer and that narcotics frequently were so packaged. Brown was subsequently convicted. The Texas Court of Criminal Appeals reversed, holding that the evidence should have been suppressed. Rejecting the state's contention that the so-called "plain view" doctrine justified the seizure, the court concluded that for that doctrine to apply, not only must the officer be legitimately in a position to view the object, but also it must be "immediately apparent" to the police that they have evidence before them. The U.S. Supreme Court then granted certiorari.

ISSUE

For the plain view exception to apply, must it be "immediately apparent" that the items seen by the officer are contraband?

HOLDING

No. there is no such requirement for the plain view exception.

RATIONALE

The plain view doctrine provides grounds for a warrantless seizure of a suspicious item when the officer's access to the item has some prior justification under the Fourth Amendment. This rule merely reflects an application of the Fourth Amendment's central requirement of reasonableness to the law governing seizures of property. Here, the officer's initial stop of Brown's vehicle was valid, and his actions in shining his flashlight into the car and changing his position to see what was inside did not violate any Fourth Amendment rights. The "immediately apparent" language in *Coolidge* does not establish a requirement that a police officer "know" that certain items are contraband or evidence of a crime. "The seizure of property in plain view involves no invasion of privacy and is presumptively reasonable, assuming that there is probable cause to associate the property with criminal activity." Probable cause is a flexible, common-sense standard, merely requiring that the facts available to the officer would warrant a man of reasonable caution to believe that certain items may be contraband or stolen property or useful as

evidence of a crime; it does not demand any showing that such a belief be correct or more likely true than false. In view of the police officer's testimony here, corroborated by that of the police department chemist, as to the common use of balloons in packaging narcotics, the officer had probable cause to believe that the balloon contained an illicit substance. Moreover, the requirement of the plain view doctrine under *Coolidge* that the officer must discover incriminating evidence "inadvertently," without knowing in advance the location of the particular evidence and intending to seize it by use of the doctrine as a pretext, was no bar to the seizure here.

CASE SIGNIFICANCE

This case clarifies the holding in *Coolidge v. New Hampshire,* in which the Supreme Court created the "plain view" exception to the search warrant requirement. There is no requirement that a police officer know with absolute certainty that an item he or she sees in plain view is contraband. In addition, officers may adjust their position and use items such as flashlights to improve their vision; so long as they are lawfully present the plain view exception still applies.

ARIZONA V. HICKS
480 U.S. 321 (1987)

FACTS

A bullet fired through the floor of Hicks' apartment injured a man on the floor below. Police entered Hicks' apartment to search for the shooter, for other victims, and for weapons, and there seized three weapons and discovered a stocking-cap mask. While there, one of the policemen noticed two sets of expensive stereo components and, suspecting that they were stolen, read and recorded their serial numbers—moving some of them, including a turntable, to do so—and phoned in the numbers to headquarters. Upon learning that the turntable had been taken in an armed robbery, the officer seized it immediately. Hicks was subsequently indicted for the robbery, but the state trial court granted his motion to suppress the evidence that had been seized, and the Arizona Court of Appeals affirmed. Relying upon a statement in *Mincey v. Arizona* that a warrantless search must be "strictly circumscribed by the exigencies which justify its initiation," the court of appeals held that the policeman's obtaining the serial numbers violated the Fourth Amendment because it was unrelated to the shooting, the exigent circumstance that justified the initial entry and search. Both state courts rejected the contention that the policeman's actions were justified under the "plain view" doctrine. The U.S. Supreme Court then granted certiorari.

Issue

Is a "plain view" search exempt from the requirement for probable cause?

Holding

No. The policeman's actions come within the purview of the Fourth Amendment. The mere recording of the serial numbers did not constitute a "seizure" since it did not meaningfully interfere with Hicks' possessory interest in either the numbers or the stereo equipment. However, the moving of the equipment was a "search" separate and apart from the search that was the lawful objective of entering the apartment.

Rationale

The fact that the search uncovered nothing of great personal value to Hicks is irrelevant. The plain view doctrine does not render the search "reasonable" under the Fourth Amendment. The policeman's action directed to the stereo equipment was not ipso facto unreasonable simply because it was unrelated to the justification for entering the apartment. That lack of relationship always exists when the "plain view" doctrine applies. However, the search was invalid because the policeman had only a "reasonable suspicion"—i.e., less than probable cause to believe—that the stereo equipment was stolen. Probable cause is required to invoke the "plain view" doctrine as it applies to seizures. It would be illogical to hold that an object is seizable on lesser grounds, during an unrelated search and seizure, than would have been needed to obtain a warrant for it if it had been known to be on the premises. Probable cause to believe the equipment was stolen was also necessary to support the search here, whether legal authority to move the equipment could be found only as the inevitable concomitant of the authority to seize it, or also as a consequence of some independent power to search objects in plain view. The policeman's action cannot be upheld on the ground that it was not a "full-blown search" but was only a "cursory inspection" that could be justified by reasonable suspicion instead of probable cause. A truly cursory inspection—one that involves merely looking at what is already exposed to view, without disturbing it—is not a "search" for Fourth Amendment purposes, and therefore does not even require reasonable suspicion. Merely inspecting those parts of the turntable that came into view during the latter search would not have constituted an independent search, because it would have produced no additional invasion of Hicks' privacy interest. But taking action, unrelated to the objectives of the authorized intrusion, which exposed to view concealed portions of the apartment, or its contents, did produce a new invasion of respondent's privacy unjustified by the exigent circumstance that validated the entry. This is why the distinction between looking at a suspicious object in plain view and moving it even a few inches is much more than trivial for purposes of the Fourth Amendment. It matters not that the search uncovered nothing of any great personal value to Hicks—serial numbers rather than (what might conceivably have been hidden behind or under the equipment) letters or photographs. A search is a search, even if it happens to disclose nothing but the bottom of a turntable.

Case Significance

This case made clear that the plain view doctrine does not allow police officers to seize, on less than probable cause, any item they happen to see that is in "plain view." In addition, the officers must have reason to believe the item is seizable—that it is contraband.

Horton v. California
496 U.S. 128 (1990)

Facts

A California policeman determined that there was probable cause to search Horton's home for the proceeds of a robbery and the robbers' weapons. His search warrant affidavit referred to police reports that described both the weapons and the proceeds, but the warrant issued by the magistrate only authorized a search for the proceeds. Upon executing the warrant, the officer did not find the stolen property but did find the weapons in plain view and seized them. The trial court refused to suppress the seized evidence, and Horton was convicted of armed robbery. The California Court of Appeals affirmed. Since the officer had testified that while he was searching Horton's home for the stolen property he was also interested in finding other evidence connecting Horton to the robbery, the seized evidence was not discovered "inadvertently." However, in rejecting Horton's argument that *Coolidge v. New Hampshire* required suppression of that evidence, the court of appeals relied on a state supreme court decision holding that *Coolidge*'s discussion of the inadvertence limitation on the "plain view" doctrine was not binding because it was contained in a four-justice plurality opinion. The U.S. Supreme Court then granted certiorari.

ISSUE

Is inadvertence a requirement of the "plain view" doctrine?

HOLDING

No. The Fourth Amendment does not prohibit the warrantless seizure of evidence in plain view even though the discovery of the evidence was not inadvertent. Although inadvertence is a characteristic of most legitimate plain view seizures, it is not a necessary condition.

RATIONALE

Coolidge is a binding precedent. However, the second of the *Coolidge* plurality's two limitations on the plain view doctrine—that the discovery of evidence in plain view must be inadvertent—was not essential to the Court's rejection of the State's plain view argument in that case. Rather, the first limitation—that plain view alone is never enough to justify a warrantless seizure—adequately supports the Court's holding that gunpowder found in vacuum sweepings from one of the automobiles seized in plain view on the defendant's driveway in the course of his arrest could not be introduced against him because the warrantless seizures violated the Fourth Amendment. In order for a warrantless seizure of an object in plain view to be valid, two conditions must be satisfied in addition to the essential predicate that the officer did not violate the Fourth Amendment in arriving at the place from which the object could be plainly viewed. First, the object's incriminating character must be "immediately apparent." Although the cars in *Coolidge* were obviously in plain view, their probative value remained uncertain until after their interiors were swept and examined microscopically. Second, the officer must have a lawful right of access to the object itself. Justice Harlan, who concurred in the *Coolidge* judgment but did not join the plurality's plain view discussion, may well have rested his vote on the fact that the cars' seizure was accomplished by means of a warrantless trespass on the defendant's property. There are two flaws in the *Coolidge* plurality's conclusion that the inadvertence requirement was necessary to avoid a violation of the Fourth Amendment's mandate that a valid warrant "particularly describ[e] ... [the] ... things to be seized." First, evenhanded law enforcement is best achieved by applying objective standards of conduct, rather than standards that de-pend upon the officer's subjective state of mind. The fact that an officer is interested in an item and fully expects to find it should not invalidate its seizure if the search is confined in area and duration by a warrant's terms or by a valid exception to the warrant requirement. Second, the suggestion that the inadvertence requirement is necessary to prevent the police from conducting general searches, or from converting specific warrants into general warrants, is not persuasive because that interest is already served by the requirements that an unparticularized warrant not be issued and that a warrantless search be circumscribed by the exigencies which justify its initiation. Here, the search's scope was not enlarged by the warrant's omission of reference to the weapons; indeed, no search for the weapons could have taken place if the named items had been found or surrendered at the outset. The prohibition against general searches and warrants is based on privacy concerns, which are not implicated when an officer with a lawful right of access to an item in plain view seizes it without a warrant.

CASE SIGNIFICANCE

This case made clear that there is no requirement that the discovery of evidence be inadvertent, or accidental, for the plain view doctrine to apply. Consequently, so long as a police officer is lawfully present, if he or she observes something which he or she knows is contraband, he or she may seize it. ✦

DISCUSSION QUESTIONS

1. How is "plain view" used differently in the legal sense compared to everyday use?

2. The Supreme Court has dispensed with the inadvertency requirement with respect to plain view seizures. Do you agree with this decision?

3. Pursuant to the plain view doctrine, it must be immediately apparent to the police that an item is subject to seizure. Do you agree with this requirement? Why or why not?

4. Describe how the plain view doctrine might be used to the advantage of law enforcement officials.

5. Does the plain view doctrine favor suspects or the police? List several reasons for your answer. ✦

Chapter Twelve

Open Fields Searches

Oliver v. United States, 466 U.S. 170 (1984)

California v. Ciraolo, 476 U.S. 207 (1986)

United States v. Dunn, 480 U.S. 294 (1987)

INTRODUCTION

The physical setting in which police activity takes place is also important in determining whether the Fourth Amendment applies. Clearly, the inside of a residence is protected by the Fourth Amendment, but what about the outside? If the outside is protected, how far beyond the residence can the strictures of the Fourth Amendment be expected to apply? In answer to these questions, courts refer to the term "curtilage." Curtilage has been defined, according to the Supreme Court, as the "area to which extends the intimate activity associated with the sanctity of a man's home and the privacies of life." This definition should be contrasted with the definition of an "open field." An open field is any unoccupied or undeveloped real property falling outside the curtilage of a home (*Oliver v. United States*).

Open fields do not enjoy Fourth Amendment protection, but homes and curtilage do. Note, however, that open fields need not be "open" or "fields" to fall beyond the reach of the Fourth Amendment. If a barn that is located 50 yards from a house is not used for "intimate activities," it *can* be considered an open field, even though it is located on private property (see *United States v. Dunn*). This is because "Open fields do not provide the setting for those intimate activities that the [Fourth] Amendment is intended to shelter from government interference or surveillance" (*Oliver v. United States*).

In *Oliver*, the Court went on to observe that "there is no societal interest in protecting the privacy of those activities, such as the cultivation of crops, that occur in open fields. Moreover, as a practical matter, these lands usually are accessible to the public and the police in ways that a home, office or commercial structure would not be. It is not generally true that fences or [No Tres-

passing] signs effectively bar the public from viewing open fields in rural areas."

The courts consider four different factors when distinguishing between open fields and curtilage: (1) the proximity of the area to the house; (2) whether the area is included within fences or other enclosures surrounding the house; (3) the nature of the use to which the land/property is being put; and (4) the steps taken by the resident to protect the area from observation (*United States v. Dunn*). These four issues were considered by the Court in *United States v. Dunn*. In that case police entered the defendant's property without a warrant, climbed over several fences, and peered inside his barn. They eventually obtained a warrant to search the barn, but the Court ruled that their earlier activity was a search within the meaning of the Fourth Amendment.

A twist on the aforementioned scenarios occurs when the police perform so-called "flyovers," that is, when they perform aerial surveillance from fixed-wing aircraft and/or helicopters. In *California v. Ciraolo*, the Supreme Court ruled that naked-eye observation of a fenced-in backyard from a height of 1000 feet did not constitute a search. The logic offered by the Court was that in "an age where private and commercial flight in the public airways is routine, it is unreasonable for respondent to expect that his marijuana plants were constitutionally protected" from such observation.

Similarly, in *Florida v. Riley*, 488 U.S. 445 (1989), the Court held that the Fourth Amendment was not implicated when the police flew a helicopter at an altitude of 400 feet over the defendant's partially covered greenhouse, which was found to contain marijuana. "Riley no doubt intended and expected that his greenhouse would not be open to public inspection, and the precautions he took [, including placing a wire fence around the greenhouse and a Do Not Enter sign,] protected against ground-level observation," but the fact that any person could position him or herself over the greenhouse in a helicopter was not enough to amount to a Fourth Amendment violation. The Court supported its position in this matter by noting that the helicopter's altitude was within legal parameters and Federal Aviation Administration guidelines. ✦

OLIVER V. UNITED STATES
466 U.S. 170 (1984)

FACTS

Acting on reports that marijuana was being raised on Oliver's farm, narcotics agents of the Kentucky State Police went to the farm to investigate. Arriving at the farm, they drove past Oliver's house to a locked gate with a

"No Trespassing" sign, but with a footpath around one side. The agents then walked around the gate and along the road and found a field of marijuana over a mile from Oliver's house. Oliver was arrested and indicted for manufacturing a controlled substance in violation of a federal statute. After a pretrial hearing, the district court suppressed evidence of the discovery of the marijuana field, applying *Katz v. United States,* and holding that petitioner had a reasonable expectation that the field would remain private and that it was not an "open" field that invited casual intrusion. The court of appeals reversed, holding that *Katz* had not impaired the vitality of the open fields doctrine of *Hester v. United States,* which permits police officers to enter and search a field without a warrant. The U.S. Supreme Court then granted certiorari.

Issue

Does the "open fields doctrine" apply when a property owner attempts to create a "reasonable expectation of privacy" by excluding others from the property?

Holding

Yes. The open fields doctrine should be applied in both cases to determine whether the discovery or seizure of the marijuana in question was valid. There is no expectation of privacy, despite the property owner's attempts to exclude the public.

Rationale

The open fields doctrine was founded upon the explicit language of the Fourth Amendment, whose special protection accorded to persons, houses, papers, and effects does not extend to the open fields. Open fields are not "effects" within the meaning of the Amendment, the term "effects" being less inclusive than "property" and not encompassing open fields. The government's intrusion upon open fields is not one of those "unreasonable searches" proscribed by the Amendment. Because open fields are accessible to the public and the police in ways that a home, office, or commercial structure would not be, and because fences or "No Trespassing" signs do not effectively bar the public from viewing open fields, the asserted expectation of privacy in open fields is not one that society recognizes as reasonable. Moreover, the common law, by implying that only the land immediately surrounding and associated with the home warrants the Fourth Amendment protections that attach to the home, conversely implies that no expectation of privacy legitimately attaches to open fields. Steps taken to protect privacy, such as planting the marijuana on secluded land and erecting fences and "No Trespassing" signs around the property,

do not establish that expectations of privacy in an open field are legitimate in the sense required by the Fourth Amendment.

Case Significance

This case is important because it made clear that "open fields" are not protected by the Fourth Amendment, even under a "reasonable expectation of privacy" analysis. This gives police the authority to ignore fences and "No Trespassing" signs and seize evidence which may be used against a criminal suspect, even though the police violated criminal law in obtaining it.

California v. Ciraolo
476 U.S. 207 (1986)

Facts

Santa Clara, California, police received an anonymous telephone tip that marijuana was growing in Ciraolo's backyard, which was enclosed by two fences and shielded from view at ground level. Officers who were trained in marijuana identification secured a private airplane, flew over Ciraolo's house at an altitude of 1,000 feet, and readily identified marijuana plants growing in the backyard. A search warrant was later obtained on the basis of one of the officer's naked-eye observations and an aerial photograph of the backyard. The search warrant was executed, and numerous marijuana plants were seized. After the trial court denied Ciraolo's motion to suppress the evidence of the search, he pled guilty to a charge of cultivation of marijuana. The California Supreme Court reversed on the ground that the warrantless aerial observation of Ciraolo's yard violated the Fourth Amendment, and the U.S. Supreme Court granted certiorari.

Issue

Does a warrantless aerial observation of the curtilage violate the Fourth Amendment?

Holding

No. The Fourth Amendment is not violated by the naked-eye aerial observation of areas within the curtilage.

Rationale

"The touchstone of Fourth Amendment analysis is whether a person has a constitutionally protected reasonable expectation of privacy, which involves the two inquiries of whether the individual manifested a subjective expectation of privacy in the object of the challenged search, and whether society is willing to recognize that expectation as reasonable. In pursuing the second inquiry, the test of legitimacy is not whether the individual chooses to conceal assertedly 'private activity,' but whether the government's intrusion infringes upon the personal and societal values protected by the Fourth Amendment. On the record here, Ciraolo's expectation of privacy from all observations of his backyard was unreasonable. That the backyard and its crop were within the 'curtilage' of Ciraolo's home did not itself bar all police observation. The mere fact that an individual has taken measures to restrict some views of his activities does not preclude an officer's observation from a public vantage point where he has a right to be and which renders the activities clearly visible. The police observations here took place within public navigable airspace, in a physically nonintrusive manner. The police were able to observe the plants readily discernible to the naked eye as marijuana, and it was irrelevant that the observation from the airplane was directed at identifying the plants and that the officers were trained to recognize marijuana. Any member of the public flying in this airspace who cared to glance down could have seen everything that the officers observed. The Fourth Amendment simply does not require police traveling in the public airways at 1,000 feet to obtain a warrant in order to observe what is visible to the naked eye."

CASE SIGNIFICANCE

This case limited the protection afforded by the curtilage. At common law, the curtilage was considered the grounds and buildings closely surrounding a dwelling. Other Supreme Court decisions have extended the protections afforded the home to the curtilage. If something is in the open fields, the Fourth Amendment simply does not apply. If an area is within the curtilage, the Fourth Amendment does apply. This case, however, limits such protection. So long as police make their observation of the curtilage from the air, and have a legal right to be in the airspace, no search warrant is required.

UNITED STATES V. DUNN
480 U.S. 294 (1987)

FACTS

Drug Enforcement Administration agents, having discovered that Carpenter had bought large quantities of chemicals and equipment used to make controlled substances, placed tracking "beepers" in some of the equipment and one of the chemical containers, which, when transported in Carpenter's truck, led the agents to Dunn's ranch. Aerial photographs of the ranch showed the truck backed up to a barn behind the ranch house. The ranch was completely encircled by a perimeter fence, and contained several interior barbed wire fences, including one around the house approximately 50 yards from the barn, and a wooden fence enclosing the front of the barn, which had an open overhang and locked, waist-high gates. Without a search warrant, agents crossed the perimeter fence, several of the barbed wire fences, and the wooden fence in front of the barn. They were led there by the smell of chemicals. They did not enter the barn but stopped at the locked gate and shined a flashlight inside, observing what they took to be a drug laboratory. They then left the ranch, but entered it twice the next day to confirm the laboratory's presence. They then obtained a search warrant and executed it, arresting Dunn and seizing chemicals and equipment, as well as bags of amphetamines they discovered in the house. After the district court denied Dunn's motion to suppress all evidence seized pursuant to the warrant, Dunn was convicted of conspiracy to manufacture controlled substances and related offenses. However, the court of appeals reversed, holding that the barn was within the residence's curtilage and therefore within the Fourth Amendment's protective ambit. The U.S. Supreme Court then granted certiorari.

ISSUE

Was the barn located 50 yards from the house and surrounded by a fence within the curtilage of the residence, and therefore protected by the Fourth Amendment?

HOLDING

No. The area near the barn was not within the curtilage of the house for Fourth Amendment purposes.

RATIONALE

Extent-of-curtilage questions should be resolved with particular reference to the following four factors, at least to the extent that they bear upon whether the area claimed to be curtilage is so intimately tied to the home itself that it should be placed under the home's "umbrella" of protection: (1) the proximity of the area to the home; (2) whether the area is within an enclosure surrounding the home; (3) the nature and uses to which the area is put; and (4) the steps taken by the resident to protect the area from observation by passersby. Applying the first factor to the instant case, the barn's substantial distance from the fence surrounding the house (50 yards) and from the house itself (60 yards) supports no inference that it should be treated as an adjunct of the house. Second, the barn did not lie within the fence surrounding the house, which plainly demarks the area that is part and parcel of the house, but stands out as a distinct and separate portion of the ranch. Third, it is especially significant that the officers possessed objective data indicating that the barn was not being used as part of Dunn's home, in that the aerial photographs showed that Carpenter's truck was backed up to the barn, apparently to unload its contents, which included the chemical container, and the officers detected strong chemical odors coming from, and heard a motor running in, the barn. Fourth, Dunn did little to protect the barn area from observation by those standing outside, the ranch's fences being of the type used to corral livestock, not to ensure privacy. Dunn's contention that, because the barn is essential to his business, he possessed an expectation of privacy in it and its contents independent from his home's curtilage, is without merit. Even assuming that the barn could not be entered lawfully without a warrant, Dunn's argument ignores the fact that, prior to obtaining the warrant, the officers never entered the barn but conducted their observations from the surrounding open fields after crossing over Dunn's ranch-style fences. The Court's prior decisions have established that the government's intrusion upon open fields is not an unreasonable search; that the erection of fences on an open field—at least of the type involved here—does not create a constitutionally protected privacy interest; that warrantless naked-eye observation of an area protected by the Fourth Amendment is not unconstitutional; and that shining a flashlight into a protected area, without probable cause to search the area, is permissible.

CASE SIGNIFICANCE

This case sets out the Court's definition of curtilage. This is important, because if an item is within the curtilage, the Fourth Amendment applies and police officers are limited in their ability to conduct warrantless searches. If an item is determined to be outside the curtilage, then it is by definition considered within the "open fields," which are not covered by the protections of the Fourth Amendment. Police are not barred by the Constitution from conducting warrantless searches in the open fields. ✦

DISCUSSION QUESTIONS

1. According to the Supreme Court, it is possible for someone to have an "open field" on his or her private property. Do you agree with this decision? Why or why not?

2. What steps must a property owner take in order to ensure that some part of his or her land falls within the curtilage of a home?

3. Clearly, there are no bright-line Supreme Court decisions concerning the definition of curtilage. Should there be?

4. The Supreme Court has permitted aerial surveillance of people's private property. Do you agree with this decision?

5. Do the Supreme Court's open fields decisions favor law enforcement or criminal suspects? Offer several reasons for your answer. ✦

Chapter Thirteen
Vehicle Searches

INTRODUCTION

Although the Fourth Amendment generally requires the issuance of a warrant based upon probable cause before a search can be undertaken, there exist a number and variety of judicially created exceptions to this rule. One such exception is that pertaining to vehicle searches. This chapter outlines the principal Supreme Court cases that guide the authority of law enforcement officers to conduct warrantless vehicle searches where there exists probable cause to believe that a crime has been or is being committed. Because this line of cases forms a basis for many of today's drug trafficking arrests made on the nation's roadways, it is imperative that officers understand the constitutional limits of their authority in this continuously evolving area of the law.

The authority of law enforcement officers to undertake a warrantless roadside search of a motor vehicle dates back to the 1920s (*Carroll v. United States*), when Prohibition agents stopped two brothers and seized the alcohol they were bootlegging. On appeal, the Supreme Court ruled that the warrantless search was permissible based upon the agents' articulable belief that criminal activity was afoot. Furthermore, the Court recognized that if the agents had taken time to secure a warrant, the vehicle would have likely fled the scene before they could return. Thus was born the vehicle search exception to the Fourth Amendment's warrant requirement.

In the decades since this initial decision, the Supreme Court has greatly expanded the authority of officers to undertake warrantless vehicle searches so that they may now inspect an entire vehicle as well as any closed containers (purses, luggage, etc.) found therein so long as there exists articulable probable cause to believe that evidence of criminal activity will be discovered (e.g., *Wyoming v. Houghton*). However, this is not to suggest that police behavior has gone totally unchecked or unrestrained in this area of the law. Although it is true that the Supreme Court condoned the practice of pretextual traffic stops in the case of *Whren v. United States*, it has in other instances condemned police behavior such as the detention of motorists without probable cause. Combine these seemingly contradictory holdings with the dozen or so other landmark decisions in this area, and it becomes quickly apparent why this body of law is of such relevance to the daily activities of all law enforcement personnel.

In sum, the cases that follow outline the general authority of officers to conduct warrantless vehicle searches where there exists probable cause to believe that evidence of criminal activity will be discovered therein. While many cases serve to strengthen the crime-fighting ability of police, others stand as examples of officer behavior that border or fall beyond the boundaries of reasonableness, and thereby violate the Fourth Amendment. ✦

CARROLL V. UNITED STATES
267 U.S. 132 (1925)

FACTS

Prohibition agents engaged in routine patrol along the highways leading into and out of Detroit observed the "Carroll boys" en route to Grand Rapids. Based upon knowledge that the boys were bootleggers in Grand Rapids and, having been previously unable to catch them in the act of transporting then-illegal alcoholic beverages, the federal agents stopped the pair and conducted a search of the vehicle resulting in discovery of the expected incriminating evidence. The evidence was admitted at trial and the pair was convicted of violating the National Prohibition Act. The U.S. Supreme Court granted certiorari to determine if the roadside search of the vehicle violated the Fourth Amendment's warrant requirement.

ISSUE

Does the Fourth Amendment prohibit officers from conducting the warrantless roadside search of a vehicle where there exists probable cause to believe that evidence of criminal activity will be found therein?

HOLDING

No. Police are authorized to undertake the warrantless roadside search of a vehicle if there exists probable cause to believe that evidence of criminal activity contained therein will be lost or destroyed if time is taken to secure a warrant.

RATIONALE

To determine if the roadside search of petitioner's vehicle violated the Fourth Amendment, the Court first traced the legislative history of the National Prohibition Act passed by Congress for purposes of enforcing the Eighteenth Amendment. Specific attention was given to the scope of search and seizure powers granted to officials responsible for enforcing the Act's statutory provisions. In a portion of the Act known as the Stanley Amendment, Congress provided for the punishment of officers who searched a private dwelling or building without a warrant or in a manner that was malicious and lacked probable cause. A strict reading of this section led the Justices to observe that Congress had not specifically prohibited agents from searching automobiles or vehicles of transportation without a warrant. Noting that the language of the Fourth Amendment did not prohibit all searches and seizures but only those of an "unreasonable" nature, the Court concluded that the Act was not inconsistent with these constitutional principles. Finally, and most importantly, the Court acknowledged the fact that if the agents had taken time to secure a warrant before undertaking their roadside search, there was a high likelihood that both the suspect vehicle and the evidence contained therein would have been lost or destroyed. Given the situation where there exists probable cause to believe that a car contains evidence of criminal activity accentuated by the risk that evidence will be lost or destroyed if time is taken to secure judicial authorization, the Court excepted roadside vehicle searches from the Fourth Amendment's warrant requirement.

CASE SIGNIFICANCE

This landmark case established the principle of law that officers are constitutionally authorized to undertake the warrantless roadside search of a vehicle where there exists probable cause to believe that it contains ev-

idence of criminal activity. This authority is premised upon the knowledge that if time is taken to secure judicial authorization before undertaking a search, the vehicle and its occupants as well as the evidence concealed therein will likely be "long gone" when the officers return. This case not only established what is known as the "automobile exception" to the Fourth Amendment's warrant requirement but, in doing so, serves as a fundamental basis for many of the ancillary roadside authorities exercised by law enforcement personnel today.

CHAMBERS V. MARONEY
399 U.S. 42 (1970)

FACTS

Chambers was arrested along with three other men when the vehicle they were traveling in was stopped by police following the reported armed robbery of a gas station. The vehicle was driven to a nearby police station where a warrantless search revealed two revolvers, several "dumdum" bullets, money taken from the gas station attendant, and cards bearing the name of another station attendant who reported being robbed a week earlier. In a warrant-authorized search of Chambers' home conducted the following morning, officers seized additional "dumdum" bullets similar to those recovered from the vehicle. This evidence was introduced, but Chambers' first trial ended in a mistrial. Chambers was represented by a different court-appointed attorney and convicted of committing both robberies upon retrial. Chambers filed unsuccessful *habeas corpus* appeals in both the Pennsylvania Supreme Court and federal district court. The Court of Appeals for the Third Circuit affirmed, and the U.S. Supreme Court granted certiorari.

ISSUE

Does the Fourth Amendment prohibit the warrantless search of a vehicle that has been moved from the original location where it was stopped to a police station?

HOLDING

No. The warrantless search of a vehicle that has been transported to a police station does not violate the Fourth Amendment so long as officers have probable cause to believe that it contains evidence of criminal activity.

RATIONALE

In deciding this case, the Supreme Court noted that although the search in question was not justifiable under the "incident to a lawful arrest" exception, it was permissible on grounds of exigency. More specifically, the Court referred to its prior ruling in *Carroll v. United States,* which established the principle of law that a warrantless vehicle search may be undertaken where the police have probable cause to believe that evidence of criminal activity will be found therein but there exists no time to secure a warrant. With regard to the facts of the present case, the Court saw no constitutional difference between seizing the suspect vehicle and then awaiting judicial authorization as compared to immediately undertaking a warrantless search. In either instance, the outcome would have been the same. Thus, so long as there exists probable cause to believe that a vehicle contains evidence of criminal activity, the police are constitutionally authorized to undertake an immediate search of that vehicle even in situations where time permits them to obtain a warrant before doing so.

Case Significance

This case is important insofar as it eliminated the requirement that officers delay a vehicle search where there exists time for them to first obtain a warrant. This decision clearly expanded the standard definition of an exigent circumstance previously relied upon by lower courts hearing similar cases. Prior to this decision, officers were required to first obtain a warrant unless there existed a risk that the vehicle might flee the scene or that evidence of a crime might somehow be destroyed. Today, this requirement no longer applies. Thus, if the police make an arrest and for some reason are unable to immediately undertake a search of the vehicle at the scene, they may indefinitely delay doing so where there exists probable cause to believe that evidence of criminal activity will be found therein. Of course, the safest method to ensure that any evidence seized during a vehicle search will be admitted at trial is to secure a properly authorized warrant where time permits.

Delaware v. Prouse
440 U.S. 648 (1979)

Facts

A Delaware patrol officer stopped a vehicle and, upon making his approach, observed within plain view a quantity of marijuana of the floorboard. Prouse, a passenger in the vehicle, was arrested and subsequently indicted for possession of a controlled substance. Prior to trial, Prouse entered a motion to suppress the evidence as the result of an unlawful traffic stop. The patrol officer testified at the hearing that he had not observed any violations or suspicious activity. Rather, he admitted to having made the stop solely for purposes of checking the driver's license and registration. The officer was not acting pursuant to any established standards, guidelines, or procedures promulgated by his agency or the state for purposes of conducting such spot checks. The trial court granted Prouse's motion to suppress on grounds that the stop and detention were capricious and thus violative of the Fourth Amendment. The Delaware Supreme Court affirmed, noting that a random stop of a motorist in the absence of specific articulable facts which justify the stop by indicating a reasonable suspicion that a violation of the law has occurred is constitutionally impermissible and violative of the Fourth and Fourteenth Amendments to the United States Constitution. The Supreme Court granted certiorari to resolve an apparent conflict between this decision, which had been embraced by five other jurisdictions, and a contrary determination adopted by six others that the Fourth Amendment does not prohibit such groundless stops.

Issue

Does the Fourth Amendment prohibit officers from stopping a vehicle being operated on a public roadway for purposes of checking the driver's license and vehicle registration in the absence of probable cause or some violation of law?

Holding

Yes. Except in situations where there is at least articulable and reasonable suspicion that a motorist is unlicensed or that a vehicle is unregistered, or that either the vehicle or occupants are subject to seizure for some violation of law, stopping a car solely for purposes of checking the driver's license and registration is unreasonable under the Fourth Amendment. In other words, the police may not make random traffic stops for purposes of checking a driver's license or vehicle registration in the absence of some violation of law.

Rationale

Both the Fourth and Fourteenth Amendments were triggered in this case due to the fact that stopping a vehicle and detaining its occupants, even if only for a brief period of time, constitutes a seizure. During a traffic stop, motorists are required to pull to the side of the road generally as the result of an officer's unsettling show of authority. Not only does the ensuing detention interfere with the motorist's freedom of physical movement, but is also inconvenient and can cause a substantial amount of psychological anxiety. Given these eventualities, the question becomes one of balancing the interests of the state against those of the individual. In its defense, the State of Delaware argued that it had a vested interest in keeping unsafe drivers and vehicles off the public roadways and, although the officer was not acting pursuant to any established standards or procedures, such spot checks were an essential element in its comprehensive traffic safety program. The Court rejected this assertion, however, on the grounds that the state presented no empirical evidence to demonstrate that the spot checks were an effective deterrent. With regard to individual interests, the Court noted that just as an individual does not lose all protections of the Fourth Amendment when stepping from his home onto the sidewalk, neither should these protections be lost when an individual steps from the sidewalk into a car. In the end, the Court remained unconvinced that the incremental contribution to highway safety of the random spot checks justifies the practice under the Fourth Amendment. The decision of the Delaware Supreme Court that the traffic stop had been illegal was thus affirmed.

CASE SIGNIFICANCE

This case is significant in several regards. First, it is interesting to note that it was not until this decision was rendered in 1979 that traffic stops lacking the element of probable cause or at least reasonable, articulable suspicion were held unconstitutional under the Fourth Amendment as a general rule of law. Second, the case clearly required that officers develop, at a minimum, reasonable, articulable suspicion that a violation of law has occurred before making a traffic stop. In simple terms, this case stands for the principle of law that officers must develop some violation of the law, moving or otherwise, before making a traffic stop. In the absence of some lawful basis, the traffic stop will be deemed unconstitutional and any derived evidence will most likely be ruled inadmissible. Third, the Court noted that the Fourth Amendment prohibited random spot checks, but not necessarily full-scale roadblocks where every passing motorist is stopped. This caveat, along with the Court's fixation on the absence of any policy or standards for guiding officer behavior, has implications for the manner in which state legislatures frame their roadway safety programs. Thus, the Court seems to suggest that if states develop detailed standards for conducting blanket roadside checks of driver's licenses, such procedures may pass constitutional muster.

NEW YORK V. BELTON
453 U.S. 454 (1981)

FACTS

Belton was the passenger of a vehicle stopped for speeding by a New York state police officer. Upon making contact the officer not only sensed an odor of burnt marijuana, but also spotted an envelope believed to contain an additional quantity of the substance. Everyone was told to exit the vehicle, whereupon each was arrested for possession. While searching the vehicle's interior incident to arrest, the officer found within a coat belonging to Belton a quantity of cocaine. At trial, Belton entered a motion to suppress on grounds that the evidence had been improperly seized. When this motion was denied, Belton pled guilty to a lesser-included offense while still preserving his claim that the seizure had been unwarranted. The Appellate Division of the New York Supreme Court upheld the search and seizure based upon the rationale that once a suspect has been lawfully arrested, an officer has authority to search the immediate area for additional contraband. However, this ruling was overturned by the New York Court of Appeals on the grounds that "[a] warrantless search of the zippered pockets of an inaccessible jacket may not be upheld as a search incident to a lawful arrest where there is no longer any danger that the arrestee or a confederate might gain access to the article." The U.S. Supreme Court then granted certiorari.

ISSUE

Do officers have authority to search the passenger compartment of a vehicle and its contents incident to a lawful arrest?

HOLDING

Yes. Officers may search the passenger compartment of a vehicle and its contents incident to a lawful arrest. Not only may they may look inside the glove compartment and other storage receptacles, but they may also examine any other closed containers even if there is a low probability that incriminating evidence will be discovered.

RATIONALE

Chimel v. California, 395 U.S. 752 (1969) established the general rule of law that officers are authorized to search an individual and his or her immediate surroundings incident to a lawful arrest in order to prevent escape or the destruction of evidence. While this principle seemed straightforward enough at the time, there continued to exist considerable ambiguity among lower courts in defining the scope of an arrestee's immediate surroundings. In the interest of establishing more specific parameters for the meaning of this phrase, the Court concluded that the relatively limited space of a vehicle's passenger compartment constituted an area "into which an arrestee might reach in order to grab a weapon or evidentiary item." With little additional elaboration it was thus established that "when a policeman has made a lawful custodial arrest of the occupant of an automobile, he may, as a contemporaneous incident of that arrest, search the passenger compartment of that automobile." Furthermore, it was determined that officers are free to examine the contents of any containers—open or closed—given the relative ease with which one can reach almost anywhere inside a passenger compartment. Lastly, the Court noted that containers within the passenger compartment are subject to search even if there is a low probability that they will yield evidence related to the original offense for which the individual has been arrested.

Case Significance

Prior to this decision, officers were restricted to searching the "wingspan" within an arrestee's immediate control. This case, however, expanded the permissible scope of a vehicle search incident to lawful arrest. In particular, it not only allowed officers to search the entire passenger compartment, but also any open or closed containers found therein. Perhaps not surprisingly, members of the criminal element will attempt to conceal evidence of their illegal activity inside the otherwise "innocent looking" containers one might naturally expect to find inside a car—cigarette packages, purses, glove boxes, cassette cases, ashtrays, cosmetic bags, etc. Officers are now authorized to search these articles for evidence and weapons, even after an arrestee has been physically removed from the vehicle and no longer has access to them. Furthermore, officers are empowered to look inside such containers even when there is a low probability of discovering evidence related to the initial offense for which the subject was arrested. For example, if an officer arrests a motorist on traffic warrants, s/he may search the entire passenger compartment and all containers therein even in the absence of any belief that evidence or weapons will be found. In other words, officers who have made a lawful arrest are not required to articulate any belief or suspicion in order to search the interior of a vehicle. In turn, it is no longer valid for an individual to claim that arresting officers lacked an articulable reason for searching the interior of a vehicle in which they were traveling. Finally, it is important to point out that the Supreme Court did not address within the context of this case whether the same rules applied to the search of a vehicle's trunk. Rather, this issue would later be addressed in a separate case (*United States v. Ross*).

United States v. Cortez
449 U.S. 411 (1981)

Facts

Border patrol agents discovered a distinctive "chevron-shaped" set of shoeprints in the desert sand at a crossing location frequented by illegal immigrants and alien smugglers. The evidence suggested that groups of aliens were being transported on clear nights by a vehicle that approached from the east and returned in the same direction. Believing that they might be able to catch "chevron" in the act of smuggling illegal aliens, the agents took up a roadside position from which they were able to observe a solitary vehicle that traveled in the anticipated directions. The agents stopped the vehicle—a pickup truck with a camper shell—at which time they came into contact with Cortez and another passenger (Hernandez-Loera) who was wearing shoes with the distinctive "chevron" print. Cortez freely opened the camper shell, revealing to the agents a number of aliens who were being transported illegally into the country. Prior to trial, Cortez moved to suppress the evidence against him on grounds that the agents lacked adequate justification for making their investigative stop. The federal district court that initially heard the case denied the motion, resulting in conviction. The Ninth Circuit Court of Appeals reversed on grounds that the agents lacked sufficient justification for making the stop, and thus violated Cortez's Fourth Amendment rights. The U.S. Supreme Court then granted certiorari.

Issue

Does circumstantial evidence supported by objective facts suggesting that a particular vehicle is involved in criminal activity provide a sufficient basis for an initiating an investigative stop?

Holding

Yes. When seeking to determine whether or not a particular investigative stop is justified, the totality of the circumstances must be considered. Within this context, the investigating officer must have an objective, particularized basis leading him or her to believe that criminal activity is afoot.

Rationale

A unanimous Supreme Court ruled that the objective facts and circumstantial evidence justified an investigative stop of the vehicle operated by Cortez. Before reaching this conclusion the Court had to first determine the appropriate level of "cause" necessary to justify such stops. On this point, it was reasoned that the "totality of the circumstances" was the standard to be relied upon. In other words, after looking at the "whole picture," detaining officers must possess a particularized and objective basis for suspecting that criminal activity is afoot. The Court also noted that trained officers are more capable of drawing inferences from such situations than are members of the general public. Finally, it was reasoned that the intrusion upon the privacy of Cortez was adequately limited in both its scope and reasonableness to be justified under the Fourth Amendment.

CASE SIGNIFICANCE

This case affirmed the long-standing principle that in order to lawfully stop a vehicle the detaining officer must possess a particularized and objective belief that criminal activity is afoot. While this burden may sound difficult to satisfy, officers actually have considerable latitude in making such determinations. This latitude stems from the Court's recognition of the fact that behavior that might appear innocent to the average observer may be altogether differently interpreted as suspicious or criminal activity by a trained officer. Thus, an officer's specialized training or past experiences may be taken into account when assessing whether or not adequate cause was present to justify a stop. This ruling also instructed lower courts to consider not only the immediate facts giving rise to a stop, but also the totality of the circumstances, or "whole picture," in determining whether or not detention was justified.

UNITED STATES V. ROSS
456 U.S. 798 (1982)

FACTS

Washington, D.C. police, acting upon information that an individual was selling drugs kept in the trunk of a vehicle, proceeded to the location, stopped the car, and arrested the driver. One of the officers opened the vehicle's trunk and looked inside a closed brown paper bag to discover several glassine bags containing a white powdery substance that later tested positive as heroin. The officer drove the vehicle to a police station where another warrantless search was undertaken. This time a zippered leather pouch containing cash was recovered. The evidence was admitted at trial over objection and Ross was convicted of possession with intent to distribute. A federal court of appeals reversed on grounds that although the officers had a legal basis for stopping and searching the entire car, including its trunk, they did not have a justifiable basis to open the paper bag or leather pouch without a warrant. The U.S. Supreme Court then granted certiorari.

ISSUE

Does the Fourth Amendment prohibit officers from opening closed containers during the course of conducting a warrantless vehicle search?

HOLDING

No. Officers may open closed containers found during the course of a warrantless vehicle search so long as they have probable cause to believe that contraband may be found therein.

RATIONALE

In reaching this decision, the Supreme Court first noted that warrantless vehicle searches are authorized in situations where an officer has probable cause to believe that contraband may be found therein. Moreover, the scope of this search is not limited by the nature of a container that may be used to conceal the object of the search. Instead, the scope of a search is more appropriately defined by the object being sought and the types of places in which it may be concealed. Thus, the smaller an object the broader the permissible scope of a search becomes.

CASE SIGNIFICANCE

This case is important insofar at it broadens the authority of officers to conduct warrantless vehicle searches. As long as an officer has probable cause to believe that a vehicle contains contraband or evidence of illegal activity, he or she may undertake a warrantless search for such evidence. If the object of that search is large in size, then the permissible scope of a search for that object must be limited to places where it might reasonably be secreted. Thus, one cannot look for a long-barreled rifle in a book bag or purse. If, on the other hand, one is looking for narcotic evidence which can be hidden almost anywhere, then the permissible scope of a search becomes much broader and could very well extend to a book bag or an even smaller receptacle. Accordingly, officers must tailor the scope of a search to only those places where the object of interest might reasonably be concealed.

MICHIGAN V. LONG
463 U.S. 1032 (1983)

FACTS

Two officers observed Long drive his vehicle into a ditch. Stopping to investigate, they also observed Long exit the vehicle in a manner suggesting that he was intoxicated. When the officers asked Long to produce his license and registration he turned and began walking back to his vehicle. The officers followed and observed a hunting knife on the driver's side floorboard of the vehicle. The officers conducted a pat-down search of Long's person but did not find any weapons. One of the officers then observed something protruding from under a front seat armrest and, upon lifting its cover, discovered a baggie of marijuana. Long was placed under arrest for possession of marijuana. An inventory search of the vehicle revealed an additional quantity of marijuana in the trunk. Long's objection to introduction of the evidence at trial was denied and he was convicted. An appeals court affirmed, ruling that the protective search of the vehicle's passenger compartment was valid under *Terry v. Ohio* and that the inventory search of the trunk was also valid under *South Dakota v. Opperman*. The Michigan Supreme Court reversed on grounds that *Terry* did not justify the passenger compartment search and that the marijuana found in the trunk was therefore the fruit of an illegal search. The U.S. Supreme Court then granted certiorari.

ISSUE

Are the police authorized under the principles of *Terry v. Ohio* to conduct a limited protective search of a vehicle's passenger compartment for weapons?

HOLDING

Yes. A protective search of a vehicle's passenger compartment for weapons is reasonable under the principles articulated in *Terry v. Ohio*.

RATIONALE

In *Terry v. Ohio*, the Court ruled that police are authorized to conduct limited protective pat-down searches for weapons that may endanger their safety or that of others. The language of that decision did not restrict protective searches to the person. In the interest of officer and public safety, the scope of a protective search may be expanded beyond the immediate person to include the passenger compartment of a vehicle in instances where the officer has reasonable and articulable suspicion that the suspect is armed and dangerous.

CASE SIGNIFICANCE

This case is important because it extended the *Terry* "stop and frisk" doctrine beyond the person to also include vehicles. This means that a limited protective search of a vehicle's passenger compartment is authorized in situations where an officer possesses reasonable belief that the suspect is dangerous and might gain control of a weapon. The decision does not allow officers to conduct an exhaustive search of the vehicle; rather, it authorizes them to undertake a cursory overview of the passenger compartment to see if any weapons are readily accessible. Officers may only take a "quick peek" in open areas such as between or underneath the seats and on the floorboards. The decision does not allow officers to look inside the glove box, trunk or closed containers—only those areas where a suspect might gain immediate control of a weapon. Finally, it is important to note that even though a suspect may be under a state of control—such as being in handcuffs—officers are still authorized to undertake a limited search of the vehicle's passenger compartment for weapons that might be used to harm them.

CALIFORNIA V. CARNEY
471 U.S. 386 (1985)

FACTS

A federal drug enforcement agent developed information that Carney was using his motor home located in a downtown San Diego parking lot as a location to exchange marijuana for sex. After observing individuals enter and leave the motor home, the agent stopped a youth who confirmed that he had in fact been given a quantity of marijuana in return for sex. The agent convinced the young man to return to the motor home and lure Carney outside. As Carney answered the door and stepped out, an accompanying agent entered the motor home and confirmed the presence of marijuana. The motor home was impounded and taken to a nearby police station, where closer inspection revealed additional marijuana. Carney was charged with possession of marijuana for sale, his motion to suppress was denied, and he was convicted. A state court of appeals affirmed, but the California Supreme Court later reversed on grounds that the motor vehicle exception to the Fourth Amendment did not apply insofar as Carney's expectation of privacy was equivalent to that which applies to dwellings. The U.S. Supreme Court then granted certiorari.

ISSUE

Does the motor vehicle exception to the Fourth Amendment's warrant requirement apply to motor homes?

HOLDING

Yes. A motor home that is being used on the public roadways in a manner other than as a residence or dwelling qualifies as an automobile for purposes of conducting a warrantless search under established Fourth Amendment standards.

RATIONALE

A six-justice majority reversed the California Supreme Court's ruling that Carney's motor home constituted a residence/dwelling for purposes of Fourth

Amendment analysis. More specifically, the Court reasoned that two well-established exceptions to the Fourth Amendment's warrant requirement apply where motor homes are being used on public roadways—first, the vehicle is readily mobile and, second, pervasive governmental regulation of vehicles creates a diminished expectation of privacy for the occupants. In making this finding, the Court avoided creating confusion on such matters by eliminating the need for lower courts to consider factors such as a given motor home's size and "quality of its appointments" in order to determine whether it should be regarded as more of a vehicle or dwelling. Finally, the Court also noted that excluding motor homes from the already well-established automobile exception to the Fourth Amendment would obviously ignore the fact that they could easily be used for purposes of trafficking drugs and/or concealing other forms of illegal activity.

CASE SIGNIFICANCE

This case is important for law enforcement purposes insofar as it settled the question of whether or not a motor home constitutes a "residence" within the meaning of the Fourth Amendment. More specifically, the Court ruled that a motor home that is used on the public roadways in a manner other than as a residence or dwelling qualifies as an "automobile" for purposes of conducting warrantless searches. This decision authorizes officers to search motor homes traveling on the open roadways or situated in locations not regularly used for residential purposes (i.e., a parking lot) on the basis of exigency so long as there exists probable cause to believe that evidence of criminal activity will be found therein. It is important to note, however, that the decision failed to address the question of whether or not officers are authorized to search motor homes located in an area that is commonly used for residential purposes (i.e., a camping facility). In these types of situations officers are advised to treat the motor home as a "residence" requiring the issuance of a warrant before undertaking a search of its contents.

COLORADO V. BERTINE
479 U.S. 367 (1987)

FACTS

Bertine was arrested for DUI, and, pursuant to agency policy, his vehicle was inventoried before being impounded. During the course of this inventory a backpack containing drugs and related paraphernalia was discovered. Prior to trial Bertine's motion to suppress was granted on grounds that it violated the state's constitution. The Colorado Supreme Court affirmed and the U.S. Supreme Court granted certiorari.

ISSUE

Is evidence discovered inside a closed container (i.e., a backpack, purse, etc.) during a warrantless inventory search incident to a lawful arrest admissible under the Fourth Amendment?

HOLDING

Yes. Evidence discovered within a closed container during the course of an inventory search incident to a lawful arrest is admissible under the Fourth Amendment.

RATIONALE

The Fourth Amendment does not prohibit the introduction of evidence discovered within a closed container during a vehicle inventory search conducted incident to a lawful arrest. This decision was guided in large part by the Court's earlier rulings in *South Dakota v. Opperman,* 428 U.S. 364 (1976, inventory searches of automobiles consistent with the Fourth Amendment) and *Illinois v. Lafayette,* 462 U.S. 640 (1983, inventory searches of personal effects at the police station consistent with the Fourth Amendment). Furthermore, the Court reasoned, inventory searches serve the governmental interests of: (1) protecting an owner's property while it is in police custody; (2) insuring against claims of lost, stolen, or vandalized property; and (3) guarding the police from danger. Before undertaking an inventory search, the police are not required to weigh the individual's privacy interest on the one hand and the likelihood that the container might reveal dangerous or valuable items on the other. Finally, the majority rejected the contention that the inventory search of Bertine's vehicle was unconstitutional because its undertaking was a matter of officer discretion.

CASE SIGNIFICANCE

This case is important for law enforcement purposes because it allowed the police to conduct warrantless searches of vehicles as well as any closed containers found therein incident to a lawful arrest. Prior to this decision, the Court had not specifically answered the question of whether or not the police could open closed containers discovered during such situations. It is important, however, for officers to avoid using the authority extended by this decision as a ruse for undertaking purely investigative searches. Thus, if closed containers must be opened during the course of an inventory search and contraband is discovered therein, the officer should clearly articulate that his or her motivation for undertaking the search was justified on one of the three grounds noted above.

FLORIDA V. WELLS
495 U.S. 1 (1990)

FACTS

Wells, who had been arrested for driving under the influence, gave a Florida state trooper permission to open the trunk of his vehicle for purposes of conducting an inventory search. Two marijuana cigarette butts were found in the ashtray, along with a locked suitcase inside the trunk. The trooper directed two employees of the impound lot to forcibly open the suitcase, revealing a large quantity of marijuana. At trial, Wells' motion to suppress the marijuana found in the suitcase was denied. He pleaded no contest to possession of a controlled substance but retained his right to appeal the motion to suppress. An intermediate appeals court held that the trial court erred in denying the motion to suppress. The Florida Supreme Court affirmed this ruling. Specifically, the Florida Supreme Court relied upon language in *Colorado v. Bertine* requiring departments to adopt policies carefully circumscribing officer discretion during inventory searches. The U.S. Supreme Court granted certiorari to determine if its opinion in Bertine had been correctly applied to the facts in Wells' case.

ISSUE

Should trial courts exclude evidence discovered within a closed container during a vehicle search in which the officer's discretion to look therein was not narrowly guided by policy?

HOLDING

Yes. Evidence that is found within a closed container should be excluded in cases where the officer's discretion to look therein was not narrowly guided by agency policy.

RATIONALE

In *Colorado v. Bertine*, the U.S. Supreme Court held that law enforcement agencies must adopt policies narrowly limiting officer discretion during vehicle inventory searches. In seeking to resolve the evidentiary question presented by Wells' case, the Florida appellate judiciary strictly interpreted this as an "either-or" proposition—either officers are to be given complete liberty in opening closed containers found during vehicle searches, or they are to be absolutely prohibited from doing so. In other words, a decision that had traditionally been left to officer discretion (whether or not to open a closed container and look therein) was now to be replaced by a generalized *a priori* policy stating how such situations were to be routinely handled. In revisiting this issue as it applied to the present case, the U. S. Supreme Court expressed concern with the Florida judiciary's "all-or-nothing" approach. On one hand the majority noted that giving officers too much discretion could easily turn an inventory search into "a ruse for a general rummaging in order to discover incriminating evidence." On the other hand, it admitted seeing no reason for reducing inventory searches into purely mechanical operations. In the end, the Court struck a balance between the two extremes by stating: "A police officer must be allowed sufficient latitude to determine whether a particular container should or should not be opened in light of the nature of the search and characteristics of the container itself." Thus, where the contents of a particular container are not readily discernible from exterior examination, officers should retain the discretion to probe further in the interest of protecting the owner's property. This finding did not, however, dispense with the existing requirement under *Bertine* that officer behavior during inventory searches be at least generally guided by agency policy. Because the Florida Highway Patrol did not have any policy whatsoever, the evidence against Wells should have been excluded at trial.

CASE SIGNIFICANCE

The primary significance of this case is to be found in the fact that it clarified the Court's position on the previous matter of *Colorado v. Bertine*. In particular, it steered lower courts away from the same type of "all-or-nothing" approach applied by the Florida appellate judiciary. Had this early trend not been corrected, law enforcement might eventually have found itself in a situation where officer discretion was altogether eliminated, or at least severely restrained, during vehicle inventory searches. Some observers might argue that the element of officer discretion should never enter into such matters and that behavior in these situations should be closely controlled by standardized policies in order to avoid potential abuse. Others observers might assert that even in the most routine inventory searches there frequently arise unique circumstances or considerations that defy generalized rules and procedures. Apparently, the majority tried to pacify both positions by stating that, consistent with its earlier holding in *Bertine*, agencies must adopt policies which "reign in" officer behavior during inventory searches while at the same time allowing for limited latitude in situations that defy generalized treatment.

CALIFORNIA V. ACEVEDO
500 U.S. 565 (1991)

FACTS

California police officers received information from a federal DEA agent regarding a shipment of drugs being sent via Federal Express to one Jamie Daza within their jurisdiction. Officers observed Daza claim the package and proceed with it to his residence. Shortly thereafter they observed an individual enter and then leave the apartment with a half-full knapsack. Officers stopped the vehicle in which this individual was traveling, searched the knapsack, and seized 1.5 pounds of marijuana that was contained therein. Later still, the officers observed Acevedo enter the residence and leave carrying a brown paper bag they knew to be consistent with the packaging of the initial shipment. Acevedo placed the bag in the trunk of his vehicle and drove off, whereupon officers in an unmarked vehicle who feared imminent destruction of the evidence stopped him. The officers opened the trunk of his vehicle, looked inside the bag and discovered a quantity of marijuana. Acevedo was arrested and charged with violation of state drug laws. At trial, Acevedo pled guilty after his motion to suppress was denied. A reconsideration of the motion prevailed when an appellate court concluded that although the officers had probable cause to believe that the bag contained marijuana, they were not authorized to open it without a search warrant. The California Supreme Court denied the prosecution's petition for review, and the U.S. Supreme Court granted certiorari.

ISSUE

Does the Fourth Amendment prohibit officers from opening a container suspected of holding contraband during the course of conducting a warrantless vehicle search?

HOLDING

No. Police officers are authorized to search any container found within a vehicle without having to first secure a warrant so long as they have probable cause to believe that it holds contraband or other evidence of criminal activity.

RATIONALE

In this particular case the Court was asked to clarify whether or not the police may lawfully search a container believed to hold contraband during the course of conducting a warrantless vehicle search. Following an examination of the relevant case law, a six-justice majority decided that the doctrine established in 1925 by *Carroll v. United States* controls all automobile searches. This means that the police may search a vehicle as well as any containers so long as there exists probable cause to believe that contraband or evidence of illegal behavior will be found therein.

CASE SIGNIFICANCE

The decision in this case not only served to reinforce the authority of officers to conduct warrantless vehicle searches but, in fact, greatly extended it. In the past, officers had been prohibited from opening any closed containers (i.e., luggage, purses, etc.) found inside a vehicle on grounds that the owner possessed a heightened expectation of privacy. This restriction was lifted, however, by the Court's decision in *United States v. Ross*, which held that the warrantless search of a vehicle included any closed containers found therein so long as there exists probable cause to search the vehicle. The immediate decision expanded upon this ruling to authorize police to search closed containers found within a vehicle so long as there exists probable cause to believe that the container—as opposed to the vehicle itself—will reveal evidence of criminal activity. In simple terms, there is no requirement that the police have probable cause to search the vehicle—all that is needed is probable cause to search the container itself.

OHIO V. ROBINETTE
519 U.S. 33 (1996)

FACTS

Robinette, who had been stopped for speeding and given a verbal warning, was asked before being released from the scene if his vehicle contained any contraband. Answering in the negative, he gave permission for the car to be searched. Discovered therein was a small amount of marijuana and a pill that later tested positive for methamphetamine. Robinette was arrested and charged with possession of a controlled substance. The trial court rejected a motion to suppress whereupon Robinette pleaded no contest and was convicted. The Ohio Court of Appeals reversed the conviction and the Ohio Supreme Court affirmed on grounds that the continued detention constituted an illegal seizure. Specifically, it stated that officers must inform motorists that they are free to leave before asking for consent to search. The U.S. Supreme Court then granted certiorari.

ISSUE

Does an officer have to specifically inform a motorist that he or she is free to leave the scene before requesting consent to search the vehicle?

HOLDING

No. Police officers are not required under the Fourth Amendment to inform a motorist that he or she is free to leave before requesting consent to search a vehicle.

RATIONALE

An eight-justice majority reversed the Ohio Supreme Court's ruling that officers must inform a motorist that he or she is "free to go" prior to asking for consent to search his or her vehicle. In particular, it was reasoned that in assessing the validity of a given consent search, the element of voluntariness is the most important factor to be considered. However, it is not necessary for the state to establish that an individual possesses the specific knowledge that he or she has the right to refuse a consent search in order for one to be valid. Finally, the Court concluded that it would be unrealistic to require that police officers always inform motorists that they are free to go in order for a given consent search to be considered both voluntary and valid.

CASE SIGNIFICANCE

The decision in this case was one that clearly favored and facilitated the law enforcement endeavor. By refusing to require that police officers specifically inform motorists that they are free to leave before requesting permission to search a vehicle, the Court emphasized that the determination of whether or not a particular consent to search is voluntary should not turn on a single statement. Rather, this determination should be based on a totality of the circumstances. While the Court has decreed that officers do not have to inform a motorist that he or she is free to leave, this does not absolve officers of the responsibility to ensure that the totality of the circumstances surrounding the stop remain as noncoercive as is reasonably possible. In sum, a court that is asked to determine whether or not a particular consent to search was voluntarily given or coerced is going to put greater emphasis on evaluating the full range of circumstances under which consent was given than it will on some brief disclaimer made by the officer. Finally, states may choose to provide citizens with increased protection beyond the minimal standards required by the Constitution. Thus, some jurisdictions may require officers to provide such a warning before seeking consent, but this will vary from state to state.

PENNSYLVANIA V. LABRON
518 U.S. 938 (1996)

FACTS

Police officers observed Labron participate in a number of street-corner drug transactions that subsequently led to his arrest. A search of the vehicle involved in these transactions yielded a quantity of cocaine that was submitted for consideration as evidence at trial. The trial court, however, suppressed this evidence and the state supreme court affirmed. In essence, the Pennsylvania Supreme Court concluded from its reading of previous U.S. Supreme Court opinions on warrantless vehicle searches that the exception applied only in instances where there existed both probable cause and some exigent circumstance. Because the circumstances surrounding Labron's arrest did not present any apparent form of exigency, the state supreme court ultimately held that the evidence had been improperly seized and had thus been properly excluded at trial. The U.S. Supreme Court granted certiorari to determine if the language in its prior decisions had been properly interpreted and applied.

ISSUE

Where time clearly permits, does the Fourth Amendment require that officers first obtain a warrant before searching a vehicle that has been lawfully stopped?

HOLDING

No. The very fact that a vehicle is mobile creates an exigent circumstance precluding the need for officers to first obtain a warrant before searching a vehicle that has been lawfully stopped. In other words, officers are not required to secure a warrant before searching a vehicle so long as they have solid probable cause to believe that incriminating evidence may be found therein.

RATIONALE

In a per curiam opinion, the U.S. Supreme Court reversed the lower court's conclusion that the evidence against Labron had been improperly introduced at trial. More specifically, a seven-justice majority held that the search in question fell squarely within the automobile exception to the Fourth Amendment. Thus, it was reasoned that although the officers may have had time to secure a warrant, the search of Labron's vehicle was nonetheless justified on two grounds. Primary among these justifications was the vehicle's mobility. Secondly, the officers had probable cause to believe that the vehicle contained evidence of criminal activity. The fact that these two justifications were present thereby precludes the need for officers to obtain a warrant prior to undertaking searches of this type. However, had these two justifications (mobility and probable cause) been lacking, the search would have violated the Fourth Amendment.

CASE SIGNIFICANCE

The Court's decision in this case clearly weighed in favor of law enforcement. Specifically, the case expanded the authority of police to conduct warrantless vehicle searches even where there is time to obtain a warrant. Recall that the Court first sanctioned warrantless vehicle searches due to exigency in the case of *Carroll v. United States.* In that case, it was decided that Prohibition agents were authorized to search the Carroll vehicle because they did not have time to obtain a warrant—had they taken the time to do so, the vehicle would have either left the scene or the occupants would have destroyed the evidence in question. In the years that have elapsed since the *Carroll* decision, lower courts have not allowed the police to conduct warrantless vehicle searches where there was adequate time to obtain a judicial order. The decision in the present case altogether dispensed with the requirement that officers obtain a warrant where there exists time or opportunity to do so. Thus, even if an officer has time to get a warrant before searching a car, he or she is no longer required to do so.

WHREN V. UNITED STATES
517 U.S. 806 (1996)

FACTS

Plainclothes officers working an area known for its high prevalence of drug transactions observed a truck waiting at a stop sign for an uncharacteristically long period of time. Abruptly, the truck turned the corner and departed at a high rate of speed. The officers gave chase, eventually stopping the truck for the observed traffic violations. Upon approaching the vehicle, officers saw several baggies of crack cocaine in Whren's hands, resulting in his and the driver's arrest. Prior to trial on federal drug charges, Whren moved to suppress the evidence on grounds that not only did the officers lack probable cause to believe that drug-related activity had occurred, but that the stop itself was purely pretextual in nature. The motion to suppress was denied, Whren was convicted, and the court of appeals affirmed. The U.S. Supreme Court then granted certiorari.

ISSUE

Do pretextual traffic stops—those made for no other reason than to identify vehicle occupants—violate the Fourth Amendment?

HOLDING

No. Petextual traffic stops are constitutional so long as an officer has probable cause to believe that a traffic violation or some other offense has occurred.

RATIONALE

A unanimous Supreme Court affirmed Whren's conviction holding that officers need only possess probable cause to believe that a crime has been committed in order to make a traffic stop. In reaching this conclusion, the Court denied Whren's request to replace this standard with one limiting officers to only those stops that are reasonable. Acknowledging that the prevailing standard lends itself to potential abuse by officers who might make stops based upon impermissible factors such as a motorist's race, the Court nonetheless remained unpersuaded that a change in standards was necessary. More specifically, the Court reasoned that the standard proposed by *Whren* would make the Fourth Amendment's protection turn on trivialities concerning police enforcement practices that would no doubt vary considerably from place to place and time to time.

CASE SIGNIFICANCE

This case is important for day-to-day law enforcement purposes insofar as it affirmed the authority of officers to make traffic stops so long as there exists probable cause to believe that an offense has been committed. In particular, the decision endorses a practice known as "pretextual stops" in which an officer detains a motorist on one or more traffic violations although the true motivation for making the stop may lie in identifying the vehicle's occupants and probing for further evidence of criminal activity. Clearly, as the Court duly acknowledged, the inherent danger in affirming this authority is to be found in its potential for abuse. To be sure, pretextual stops are at the core of today's heated debate concerning racial profiling.

MARYLAND V. WILSON
519 U.S. 408 (1997)

FACTS

A Maryland state trooper observed a speeding vehicle with registration violations. While attempting to stop the car the trooper noticed that two of the three passengers repeatedly ducked out of view as if trying to hide something. When the vehicle finally yielded and the trooper made contact with the driver, he also noticed that the front seat passenger appeared to be extremely nervous. While the driver searched for the vehicle's rental paperwork, the trooper directed the front seat passenger—Wilson—to step out and speak with him. Upon doing so, a small quantity of crack cocaine fell to the ground, resulting in his arrest for possession with intent to distribute. Prior to trial Wilson entered a motion to suppress on grounds that the trooper's order to exit the vehicle constituted an unreasonable seizure under the Fourth Amendment. The Circuit Court for Baltimore County granted Wilson's motion which was in turn unsuccessfully challenged by prosecutors before a court of special appeals. The U.S. Supreme Court then granted certiorari.

ISSUE

Does the Fourth Amendment prohibit police officers from requiring passengers to exit the vehicle during a lawful traffic stop?

HOLDING

No. Police officers may direct any and all passengers to exit and remain outside of a vehicle that has been lawfully stopped.

RATIONALE

In reaching the determination that officers can require any and all passengers to exit a vehicle that has been lawfully stopped, a seven-justice majority balanced the public interests at stake against those of the individual. On the public interest side, it was noted that the risk to officer safety during a traffic stop remains high regardless of whether an individual is the driver or a passenger. It was further noted that the danger to officer safety during a traffic stop is likely to be greater when a vehicle contains multiple occupants in addition to the driver. In examining the personal liberty interests at stake, the Court first noted that by ordering a passenger to exit the vehicle all that has changed in terms of the inconvenience imposed is the individual's physical location. In other words, he or she has already been detained as a result the initial traffic stop, so requiring him or her to also exit the vehicle does not require any further inconvenience than that which has already been imposed. Additionally, the Court noted that by requiring a passenger to exit the vehicle, he or she would be denied access to any possible weapon that might be concealed therein. Given the minimal inconvenience imposed upon the passengers, the Court ruled in favor of the officer safety interests at stake, thereby reversing the lower court's judgment.

CASE SIGNIFICANCE

This case clarified an officer's authority to lawfully order any and all passengers out of the vehicle during a traffic stop. The authority to lawfully order the driver out of a vehicle was previously established by the *Mimms* decision in 1977. However, the opinion in that case failed to specify whether or not this authority extended to all occupants of the vehicle. The decision in the immediate case put this issue to rest. Here again, the Court ruled in favor of the state out of concern for officer safety over the slight inconvenience imposed upon a passenger who is required to briefly exit the vehicle. In terms of day-to-day law enforcement practice, an officer's directive that all passengers exit the vehicle during a traffic stop can sometimes lead to roadside disagreements, especially where passengers take issue with whether or not the officer can lawfully require them to do so. Thus, the decision in this case can be a dual-edged sword, to the extent that although it is intended to ensure officer safety, it also has the potential to jeopardize officer safety by inadvertently escalating the tempers of traffic violators and their passengers.

KNOWLES V. IOWA
525 U.S. 113 (1998)

FACTS

Iowa law authorized police officers to either cite or arrest traffic violators. Knowles, who had been stopped for speeding, was issued a citation by the attending officer who then proceeded to conduct a full search of the vehicle before releasing him. During the course of this search the officer found a quantity of marijuana and narcotic paraphernalia resulting in Knowles' arrest. Prior to trial Knowles entered a motion to suppress the evidence on grounds that since he had received a citation and not arrested the search did not qualify under the "incident to arrest" exception created in *United States v. Robinson.* The trial court rejected this claim, finding Knowles guilty. The Iowa Supreme Court affirmed by creating a "search incident to citation" exception to the Fourth Amendment. In essence, the court reasoned that so long as an officer has probable cause, an actual arrest is not necessary in order for the search to be constitutionally permissible. The U.S. Supreme Court then granted certiorari.

ISSUE

Does the Fourth Amendment prohibit officers from undertaking a full vehicle search in situations where the traffic violator is issued a citation instead of being placed under arrest?

HOLDING

Yes. The full search of a vehicle incident to a traffic stop in which the officer issues a citation rather than arresting the motorist violates the Fourth Amendment.

RATIONALE

In a unanimous opinion, the U.S. Supreme Court reversed the Iowa Supreme Court's decision creating a "search incident to citation" exception to the Fourth Amendment. This ruling was based on the fact that neither of the two historical rationales for allowing officers to conduct such searches (i.e., mobility and/or the need to disarm a dangerous suspect) was present to justify the search of Knowles' vehicle. The Court further reasoned that the risk to officer safety while issuing a traffic citation is "a good deal less" than when making a custodial arrest. Lastly, it was noted that officers have other bases for conducting a vehicle search without having to create a new "incident to citation" exception.

CASE SIGNIFICANCE

Many states allow officers the discretion to issue a citation in lieu of making a full custodial arrest for certain types of traffic violations. This option does not, however, give the officer authority to conduct a search incident to a citation. In situations where an officer decides to let a violator leave the scene after issuing a summons, the only acceptable basis for conducting a search of the vehicle is by developing probable cause or obtaining informed consent. In the absence of one of these two grounds, officers are prohibited under the *Knowles* decision from searching a vehicle based solely on the issuance of a citation.

WYOMING V. HOUGHTON
526 U.S. 295 (1999)

FACTS

A Wyoming state trooper stopped a vehicle in which Houghton and two others were traveling. The trooper inquired about the trio's use of illegal drugs after noticing a syringe in the driver's shirt pocket. The driver confirmed that he in fact used drugs, whereupon the trooper initiated a search of the vehicle's passenger compartment. Laying in the back seat was a purse that Houghton, who had lied to the trooper about her true identity, admitted to owning. Looking inside the purse, presumably for some form of identification, the trooper found a quantity of methamphetamine and related narcotic paraphernalia. Houghton was arrested and convicted for possession of a controlled substance despite arguing at trial that the evidence should have been suppressed under the Fourth Amendment. The

Wyoming Supreme Court reversed the conviction on grounds that the officer had no justifiable basis for searching the purse. The U.S. Supreme Court then granted certiorari.

ISSUE

Does the Fourth Amendment prohibit officers from searching a passenger's personal belongings (i.e., purse, bag, or other such receptacle) during the course of a warrantless vehicle search?

HOLDING

No. Where officers have probable cause to conduct a warrantless vehicle search, they are also authorized to search a passenger's personal belongings where there exists the possibility that contraband may be contained therein.

RATIONALE

The U.S. Supreme Court reversed the ruling of the Wyoming Supreme Court. More specifically, the search of Houghton's purse was found not to have violated the Fourth Amendment on the grounds that neither the Court's earlier decision in *United States v. Ross* nor the historical evidence relied upon in that case raised a distinction among packages or containers based upon ownership. In simple terms, the Court clarified that under the *Ross* decision, all receptacles—regardless of whom they belong to—were subject to search where officers have probable cause to believe that the vehicle may contain contraband. Thus, it does not matter whom the purse, bag, or container belongs to—if it is found within a vehicle that is being searched by the police, it may be opened for purposes of determining whether or not it contains contraband. Finally, the Court noted two additional reasons for allowing officers to search any and all containers found within a vehicle despite ownership. Among these was the fact that not only is a passenger's expectation of privacy considerably diminished while traveling in a vehicle, but that the governmental interests in preventing the loss or intentional destruction of evidence are substantial.

CASE SIGNIFICANCE

The practical significance of this case for law enforcement lies in the fact that it allows officers to search the personal belongings of all passengers in a vehicle so long as the vehicle has been lawfully stopped and there is probable cause to believe that the search will reveal evidence of criminal activity. Thus, where an officer makes a traffic stop and then develops probable cause to believe that the vehicle contains contraband or other evidence of criminal activity, he or she may undertake a search not only of the vehicle, but of any personal belongings of the passengers as well. This means that officers no longer have to obtain the consent of the passenger whose belongings are to be searched. ✦

Discussion Questions

1. Why does the Supreme Court allow police officers to search motor vehicles without a warrant?

2. If police officers have information that criminal activity is taking place inside a motor home that is parked at a campground, must they first obtain a warrant in order to conduct a search?

3. Are police officers at liberty to completely disassemble a motor vehicle on the side of the road? Why or why not?

4. Why is it important for police departments to develop specific policies guiding officer behavior during inventory searches?

5. What should police officers do if they encounter a locked briefcase in the trunk of a vehicle that has already been seized in conjunction with a drug trafficking offense?

6. Are officers required to immediately conduct a motor vehicle inventory search at the time of arrest or can they wait until a more convenient opportunity? Why or why not?

7. Are officers required to conduct a motor vehicle inventory search at the scene where an arrest is made, or can they first transport the car to an alternate location? Why or why not?

8. How have dash-mounted video cameras in police cars affected the ability of officers to conduct warrantless roadside vehicle searches? ✦

Chapter Fourteen

Regulatory Searches

Introduction

The Supreme Court has authorized numerous varieties of searches under the administrative justification exception to the Fourth Amendment's probable cause and warrant requirements. Sometimes they are described as "special needs beyond law enforcement" searches. Other times they are called "regulatory" searches. To avoid confusion, this book calls them regulatory searches. The types of searches considered in this chapter are: (1) inventory searches; (2) inspections; (3) checkpoints; (4) school disciplinary searches; (5) gov-

ernment employee searches; (6) drug and alcohol testing; and (7) probation supervision searches.

Inventories can be of vehicles and/or of a person's personal items. Usually, a search occurs under the automobile exception (in the case of an automobile) or a search incident to arrest (when a person is involved), and an inventory is taken after the fact for the purpose of developing a record of items in custody.

Vehicle inventories occur under a number of situations, usually after a car has been impounded for traffic or parking violations. In *South Dakota v. Opperman,* the Supreme Court held that warrantless inventories are permissible on administrative/regulatory grounds; however, they must (1) follow a *lawful* impoundment; (2) be of a routine nature, following standard operating procedures; and (3) not be a "pretext concealing an investigatory police motive." Thus, even though an inventory search can be perceived as a fallback measure which permits a search when probable cause is lacking, it cannot be used in lieu of a "regular" search requiring probable cause.

The inventory search exception to the Fourth Amendment's warrant requirement applies in the case of person inventories as well. Such searches are often called "arrest inventories." The general rule is that the police may search an arrestee and his/her personal items, including containers found in his/her possession, as part of a routine inventory incident to the booking and jailing procedure. Neither a search warrant nor probable cause is required (*Illinois v. Lafayette*).

Concerning home inspections, in *Camara v. Municipal Court* the Court noted that nonconsensual administrative searches of private residences amount to a significant intrusion upon the interests protected by the Fourth Amendment. Nowadays, then, warrants are required for authorities to engage in home inspections. However, the meaning of "probable cause" in such warrants differs from that discussed earlier. The Court has stated that if an area "as a whole" needs inspection, based on factors such as the time, age, and condition of the building, then the probable cause requirement will be satisfied. The key is that probable cause in the inspection context is not "individualized" as in the typical warrant. That is to say, inspections of this sort are geared toward buildings, not persons.

A second type of home inspection is a welfare inspection. In *Wyman v. James,* the Supreme Court upheld the constitutionality of a statute that allowed welfare caseworkers to make warrantless visits to the homes of welfare recipients. The reason for such inspections is to ensure that welfare recipients are conforming with applicable guidelines and rules. The Court declared that welfare inspections are not searches within the meaning of the Fourth Amendment, which means they can be conducted without a warrant *or* probable cause. Of course, such inspections should be based on neutral criteria, nor should they mask intentions to look for evidence of criminal activity.

With respect to business inspections, in *Colonnade Catering Corp. v. United States* the Supreme Court upheld a statute criminalizing refusal to allow warrantless entries of liquor stores by government inspectors.

Similarly, in *United States v. Biswell* the Court upheld the warrantless inspection of a firearms dealership. In *Biswell* the Court observed that "[w]hen a dealer chooses to engage in this pervasively regulated business and to accept a federal license, he does so with the knowledge that his business records, firearms and ammunition will be subject to effective inspection." A key restriction on this ruling, however, is that authorities cannot use "unauthorized force" for the purpose of gaining entrance.

In a later case, *Donovan v. Dewey*, 452 U.S. 494 (1981), the Court modified the "closely regulated business" exception. The Court decided that it is not enough that an industry is "pervasively regulated" for the business inspection exception to apply. Three additional criteria must be met: (1) the government must have a "substantial" interest in the activity at stake; (2) warrantless searches must be necessary to the effective enforcement of the law; and (3) the inspection protocol must provide "a constitutionally adequate substitute for a warrant."

The Court clarified the *Dewey* criteria in *New York v. Burger*. In that case, the Court upheld the warrantless inspection of a vehicle junkyard for the purpose of identifying "vehicle dismantlers." Justice Blackman noted that *Dewey*'s first criterion was satisfied because vehicle theft was a serious problem in New York. The second criterion was satisfied because "surprise" inspections were necessary if stolen vehicles and parts were to be identified, and the third criterion—adequate substitute—was satisfied because junkyard operators were notified that inspections would be unannounced and conducted during normal business hours.

Now we turn our attention to checkpoints. In *United States v. Martinez-Fuerte* the Court upheld the Immigration and Naturalization Service's (INS) decision to establish roadblocks near the Mexican border designed to discover illegal aliens. The Court offered a number of reasons for its decision. First, "[t]he degree of intrusion upon privacy that may be occasioned by a search of a house hardly can be compared with the minor interference with privacy resulting from the mere stop for questioning as to residence." Second, motorists could

avoid the checkpoint if they so desired. Third, the Court noted that the traffic flow near the border was heavy, so individualized suspicion was not possible. Fourth, the location of the roadblock was not decided by the officers in the field "but by officials responsible for making overall decisions." Finally, a requirement that such stops be based on probable cause "would largely eliminate any deterrent to the conduct of well-disguised smuggling operations, even though smugglers are known to use these highways regularly."

In *Michigan Department of State Police v. Sitz* the Court upheld warrantless, suspicionless checkpoints designed to detect evidence of drunk driving. In that case, police checkpoints were set up at which all drivers were stopped and briefly (approximately 25 seconds) observed for signs of intoxication. If such signs were found, the driver would be detained for sobriety testing and, if the indication was that the driver was intoxicated, an arrest would be made. The Court weighed the magnitude of the governmental interest in eradicating the drunk driving problem against the slight intrusion to motorists stopped briefly at such checkpoints. Key to the constitutionality of Michigan's checkpoint were two additional factors: (1) evenhandedness was ensured because the locations of the checkpoints were chosen pursuant to written guidelines and every driver was stopped; and (2) the officers themselves were not given discretion to decide whom to stop. Significantly, the checkpoint was deemed constitutional even though motorists were *not* notified of the upcoming checkpoint *or* given an opportunity to turn around and go the other way.

The regulatory search rationale is *not* acceptable, by comparison, to detect evidence of criminal activity. This was the decision reached in the recent Supreme Court case *City of Indianapolis v. Edmond*. There the Court decided whether a city's suspicionless checkpoints for detecting illegal drugs were constitutional.

With respect to disciplinary searches, public school administrators and teachers may search students without a warrant if they possess reasonable suspicion that the search will yield evidence that the student has violated the law or is violating the law or rules of the school. However, such school disciplinary searches must not be "excessively intrusive in light of the age and sex of the students and the nature of the infraction." This was the decision reached in *New Jersey v. T.L.O.* In *T.L.O.*, a high school student was caught smoking in a school bathroom (in violation of school policy) and was sent to the assistant vice-principal. The assistant vice-principal searched the student's purse for cigarettes, and found evidence implicating the student in the sale of marijuana. The Court held that the evidence was admissible because the administrator had sufficient justification to search the purse for evidence concerning the school's anti-smoking policy.

In a case very similar to *T.L.O.*, although not involving a public school student, the Court held that neither a warrant nor probable cause was needed to search a government employee's office, but the search must be "a noninvestigatory work-related intrusion or an investigatory search for evidence of suspected work-related employee misfeasance" (*O'Connor v. Ortega*). Justice O'Connor summarized the Court's reasoning: "[T]he delay in correcting the employee misconduct caused by the need for probable cause rather than reasonable suspicion will be translated into tangible and often irreparable damage to the agency's work, and ultimately to the public interest."

It is important to note, however, that the Court was limiting its decision strictly to work-related matters: "[W]e do not address the appropriate standard when an employee is being investigated for criminal misconduct or breaches of other nonwork-related statutory or regulatory standards."

Concerning drug testing, in a recent case, *Ferguson v. Charleston*, the Supreme Court addressed the constitutionality of drug testing of hospital patients. The question before the Supreme Court was, is the Fourth Amendment violated when hospital personnel, working with the police, test pregnant mothers for drug use without their consent? Not surprisingly, the Court answered yes.

The Supreme Court has recently extended its drug testing decisions to include public school students. Specifically, in *Vernonia School District 47J v. Acton* the Court upheld a random drug testing program for school athletes. The program had been instituted because the district had been experiencing significant student drug use. Under the program, all students who wished to play sports were required to be tested at the beginning of the season and then to be retested randomly later in the season. The Court noted that athletes enjoy a lesser expectation of privacy given the semi-public nature of locker rooms where the testing took place. Also, athletes are often subject to other intrusions, including physical exams, so drug testing involved "negligible" privacy intrusions according to the Court.

Even more recently, the Supreme Court affirmed *Vernonia School District* in *Board of Education of Independent School District v. Earls*. However, the Supreme Court held that random, suspicionless drug testing of students who participate in extracurricular activities

". . . is a reasonable means of furthering the School District's important interest in preventing and deterring drug use among its schoolchildren and does not violate the Fourth Amendment."

Finally, it has been established that people on probation enjoy a lesser expectation of privacy than the typical citizen. In *Griffin v. Wisconsin* the Court held that a state law or agency rule permitting probation officers to search probationers' homes without a warrant and based on reasonable grounds is not unconstitutional. The majority (of only five justices) concluded that probation supervision "is a 'special need' of the State permitting a degree of impingement upon privacy that would not be constitutional if applied to the public at large." The same almost certainly applies to parolees, but the Supreme Court has not addressed this issue.

Recently, in *United States v. Knights,* the Supreme Court held that warrantless searches of probationers are permissible not only for probation-related purposes (e.g., to ensure that probation conditions are being conformed with), but for investigative purposes. In that case, a probationer was suspected of vandalizing utility company facilities. A police detective searched the probationer's residence and found incriminating evidence. The Supreme Court held that "[t]he warrantless search of Knights, supported by reasonable suspicion and authorized by a probation condition, satisfied the Fourth Amendment." ✦

South Dakota v. Opperman
428 U.S. 364 (1976)

Facts

Opperman's car had been impounded on several occasions for parking violations. Police finally impounded Opperman's car and, following standard department procedures, they inventoried the contents of the car. In doing so they discovered marijuana in the glove compartment. Opperman was arrested and charged with narcotics offenses. He sought suppression of the evidence and the U.S. Supreme Court granted certiorari.

Issue

Do police inventory searches of impounded vehicles violate the Fourth Amendment?

Holding

No. A warrantless, suspicionless inventory search of an impounded vehicle does not violate the Fourth Amendment. However, the impoundment must be lawful, the search should follow "standard operating procedures," and the search should not be used as a pretext concealing a motive to obtain incriminating evidence.

RATIONALE

"The police procedures followed in this case did not involve an 'unreasonable' search in violation of the Fourth Amendment. The expectation of privacy in one's automobile is significantly less than that relating to one's home or office. . . . When vehicles are impounded, police routinely follow caretaking procedures by securing and inventorying the cars' contents. These procedures have been widely sustained as reasonable under the Fourth Amendment. This standard practice was followed here, and there is no suggestion of any investigatory motive on the part of the police."

CASE SIGNIFICANCE

This case is important because it was the first to constitutionally sanction police inventory searches. The Court permitted regulatory searches of this nature on less than probable cause for several reasons, such as the needs to protect the owner's property while an impounded vehicle is in possession of the police, protect against claims of lost or stolen property, and protect the public from dangerous items (such as weapons) which might be concealed in the car. Even though the Court stated that inventory searches should not be relied upon to obtain incriminating evidence, it is clear that, if the police do not have probable cause to engage in a conventional search, inventories can act as something of a fallback measure. In a recent decision, *Whren v. United States,* 517 U.S. 806 (1996), the Supreme Court basically sanctioned pretextual searches, so the Court's admonition in *Opperman* against using inventory searches for more than just inventorying can probably be taken with a grain of salt.

ILLINOIS V. LAFAYETTE
462 U.S. 640 (1983)

FACTS

Lafayette was arrested for disturbing the peace and was taken to the police station. Lafayette's shoulder bag was subjected to a warrantless search as part of the process of booking him. The search was done for the purpose of inventorying his possessions, but also turned up amphetamine pills. Lafayette was charged with drug possession, but prior to trial sought suppression of the drugs on the grounds that they were obtained via an unconstitutional search. The trial court suppressed the drugs and the U.S. Supreme Court granted certiorari.

ISSUE

May the police search an arrestee, including his or her personal items, as part of a routine inventory incident to booking and jailing?

HOLDING

Yes. The police may search a person, including his or her personal effects, as part of a routine inventory incidence to the booking and jailing procedure. However, the arrest leading to booking and jailing must be lawful.

RATIONALE

"Consistent with the Fourth Amendment, it is reasonable for police to search the personal effects of a person under lawful arrest as part of the routine administrative procedure at a police station incident to booking and jailing the suspect. The justification for such searches does not rest on probable cause, and hence the absence of a warrant is immaterial to the reasonableness of the search. Here, every consideration of orderly police administration—protection of a suspect's property, deterrence of false claims of theft against the police, security, and identification of the suspect—benefiting both the police and the public points toward the appropriateness of the examination of Lafayette's shoulder bag."

CASE SIGNIFICANCE

This case permitted an inventory of an arrestee's personal items as part of the booking procedure. This is an important and logical part of the booking process. Allowing such searches preserves police and suspect safety, according to the Supreme Court.

CAMARA V. MUNICIPAL COURT
387 U.S. 523 (1967)

FACTS

Camara was charged with violating the San Francisco Housing Code for refusing to allow housing inspectors engage in a warrantless inspection of the apartment where he resided. While awaiting trial, Camara claimed that the inspection ordinance was unconstitutional because it permitted searches without warrants or any suspicion, in violation of the Fourth Amendment. The U.S. Supreme Court granted certiorari.

ISSUE

Does the Fourth Amendment bar prosecution of persons who refuse to permit warrantless code inspections of their personal residences?

HOLDING

Yes. Nonconsensual administrative searches of private residences violate the Fourth Amendment. Under the Fourth Amendment, people have a constitutional right to insist that code inspectors obtain a warrant to search their private residences.

RATIONALE

"Under the present system, when the inspector demands entry, the occupant has no way of knowing whether enforcement of the municipal code involved requires inspection of his premises, no way of knowing the lawful limits of the inspector's power to search, and no way of knowing whether the inspector himself is acting under proper authorization. These are questions which may be reviewed by a neutral magistrate without any reassessment of the basic agency decision to canvass an area. Yet, only by refusing entry and risking a criminal conviction can the occupant at present challenge the inspector's decision to search. And even if the occupant possesses sufficient fortitude to take this risk, as appellant did here, he may never learn any more about the reason for the inspection than that the law generally allows housing inspectors to gain entry. The practical effect of this system is to leave the occupant subject to the discretion of the official in the field. This is precisely the discretion to invade private property which we have consistently circumscribed by a requirement that a disinterested party warrant the need to search. . . . We simply cannot say that the protections provided by the warrant procedure are not needed in this context; broad statutory safeguards are no substitute for individualized review, particularly when those safeguards may only be invoked at the risk of a criminal penalty."

CASE SIGNIFICANCE

This case is important because it prohibited warrantless, nonconsensual "inspections" of private residences. The decision reinforced the Supreme Court's interest in preserving the privacy of people in their homes. Code inspections of the nature discussed in *Camara* are still permissible, but authorities are now required to obtain a warrant to "inspect" beforehand. The only time government officials are permitted to enter a residence without a warrant is either with valid consent or exigent circumstances. Neither was present in this case.

WYMAN V. JAMES
400 U.S. 309 (1971)

FACTS

James, who was a recipient of Aid to Families with Dependent Children (AFDC), was served with notice that her home would be visited by a caseworker. She offered to supply information concerning her need for public assistance, but she refused to permit the caseworker to visit her home. Pursuant to a state statute, her AFDC benefits were revoked because she refused to let the caseworker in her home. The U.S. District Court for the Southern District of New York held that James' refusal to grant the caseworker entry should not be grounds for termination of her AFDC benefits. The U.S. Supreme Court then granted certiorari.

ISSUE

Are welfare caseworkers constitutionally permitted to make warrantless visits to the homes of welfare recipients?

HOLDING

Yes. Welfare caseworkers who make warrantless visits to the homes of welfare recipients do not violate the Fourth Amendment.

RATIONALE

"There are a number of factors that compel us to conclude that the home visit proposed for Mrs. James is not unreasonable: 1. The public's interest in this particular segment of the area of assistance to the unfortunate is protection and aid for the dependent child whose family requires aid for that child. The focus is on the child and, further it is on the child who is dependent. There is no more worthy object of the public's concern. . . . 2. The agency, with tax funds provided from federal as well as from state sources, is fulfilling a public trust. The State, working through its qualified welfare agency, has appropriate and paramount interest and concern in seeing and assuring that the intended and proper objects of that tax-produced assistance are the ones who benefit from the aid it dispenses. . . . 3. One who dispenses purely private charity naturally has an interest in and expects to know how his charitable funds are utilized and put to work. . . . 4. The emphasis of the New York statutes and regulations is upon the home, upon 'close contact' with the beneficiary, upon restoring the aid recipient 'to a condition of self-support,' and upon the relief of his distress . . . [and] 5. The home visit, it is true, is not required by federal statute or regulation. But it has been noted that the visit is 'the heart of welfare administration'; that it affords 'a personal, rehabilitative orientation, unlike that of most federal programs'; and that the 'more pronounced service orientation' effected by Congress with the 1956 amendments to the Social Security Act 'gave redoubled importance to the practice of home visiting.'"

CASE SIGNIFICANCE

This is another example of a regulatory search case. It stands in something of a contrast to the previous case because it permits warrantless entries by welfare caseworkers. The Court saw fit to permit such visits because they are not technically searches, or even "inspections" per se. It is not the home that is searched or inspected. Rather, the caseworker visits to ensure that the intended recipients of public assistance are receiving it and to help the recipient(s) become self-sufficient. The five reasons announced by the Court in support of its decision suggest that the public interest in proper welfare administration is more important than the individual recipient's interest in being free from warrantless home visitations.

COLONNADE CATERING CORP. V. UNITED STATES
397 U.S. 72 (1970)

FACTS

Federal agents, acting without a warrant, inspected the catering establishment of a licensed New York liquor dealer for possible liquor law violations. When the owner refused to open the door to his locked storeroom, the agents broke the lock, entered, and seized several bottles of liquor. The owner was prosecuted with violating liquor laws and sought suppression of the seized liquor on the grounds that it was obtained in violation of the Fourth Amendment. The U.S. Supreme Court granted certiorari.

ISSUE

Are government inspectors permitted to enter liquor stores without a warrant?

HOLDING

Yes. The statute permitting warrantless entries into liquor stores by government inspectors does not violate the Fourth Amendment.

RATIONALE

"We agree that Congress has broad power to design such powers of inspection under the liquor laws as it deems necessary to meet the evils at hand. The general rule laid down in *See v. City of Seattle* . . .—'that administrative entry, without consent, upon the portions of commercial premises which are not open to the public may only be compelled through prosecution or physical force within the framework of a warrant procedure'—is therefore not applicable here. In *See*, we reserved decision on the problems of 'licensing programs' requiring inspections, saying they can be resolved 'on a case-by-case basis under the general Fourth Amendment standard of reasonableness." . . . What we said in *See* reflects this Nation's traditions that are strongly opposed to using force without definite authority to break down doors. We deal here with the liquor industry, long subject to close supervision and inspection. As respects that industry, and its various branches including retailers, Congress has broad authority to fashion standards of reasonableness for searches and seizures. . . ."

CASE SIGNIFICANCE

The Court's opinion in this case was esoteric and a bit brief, but it is still important because it gave permission for authorities to engage in warrantless inspections of licensed liquor-selling establishments. Indeed, it is necessary to read between the lines when deciphering this case. The Court agreed with the district court's decision to suppress the evidence, but held that Colonnade Catering could nevertheless be fined for refusing to grant entry to the inspectors. In other words, it upheld the New York statute penalizing refusal to grant entry to inspectors. More importantly, this case tempered a previous decision, *See v. City of Seattle*, 387 U.S. 541 (1967), a companion case to *Camara*. In *See*, the Court refused to sanction a citywide inspection program geared toward detecting fire code violations. But the present case created what is now known as the "closely regulated businesses" exception to *Camara* and *See:* The Court held for the first time that certain closely regulated businesses can be inspected without a warrant. Liquor-selling establishments are considered closely regulated, and so are firearms dealerships and vehicle junkyards, as the following cases, *Biswell* and *Burger*, attest.

UNITED STATES V. BISWELL
406 U.S. 311 (1972)

FACTS

Biswell owned and operated a pawn shop and possessed a federal license to sell firearms. A treasury agent visited his store, identified himself, and then inspected Biswell's books and requested entry into a locked gun storage room. Biswell asked whether the agent had a search warrant. The agent said he did not, but that his inspection was authorized by federal law. The agent gave Biswell a copy of the law and he relented. Biswell opened the storage room. The agent then seized two sawed-off rifles for which Biswell had not paid a special tax. Biswell appealed his subsequent conviction, and the U.S. Supreme Court granted certiorari.

ISSUE

Are warrantless inspections of federally licensed firearms dealerships permissible under the Fourth Amendment?

HOLDING

Yes. Warrantless inspections of firearms dealerships do not violate the Fourth Amendment. The warrantless search of a locked storage room during business hours as part of an inspection authorized by federal law does not violate the Fourth Amendment.

RATIONALE

"Federal regulation of the interstate traffic in firearms is not as deeply rooted in history as is governmental control of the liquor industry, but close scrutiny of this traffic is undeniably of central importance to federal efforts to prevent violent crime and to assist the States in regulating the firearms traffic within their borders. . . . Large interests are at stake, and inspection is a crucial part of the regulatory scheme, since it assures that weapons are distributed through regular channels and in a traceable manner and makes possible the prevention of sales to undesirable customers and the detection of the origin of particular firearms."

CASE SIGNIFICANCE

This case is important in that it opened the constitutional door to another type of inspection, that of a firearms dealership. The Court said that "[w]hen a dealer chooses to engage in this pervasively regulated business and to accept a federal license, he does so with the knowledge that his business records, firearms, and ammunition will be subject to effective inspection." In other words, inspections are to be expected as no more than a price to pay for selling closely regulated products such as firearms.

NEW YORK V. BURGER
482 U.S. 691 (1987)

FACTS

Burger owned a junkyard at which automobiles were dismantled and their parts sold. Pursuant to a New York statute authorizing warrantless inspections of automobile junkyards, police officers entered Burger's junkyard and asked to see his license as well as records describing the automobiles and parts on the premises.

Burger stated that he did not have such documents, which are required by law. The officers announced their intentions to "inspect" the junkyard. They found stolen vehicles and parts. Burger was charged with possession of stolen property and another offense. He sought suppression of the evidence, arguing that the statute permitting the inspections was unconstitutional, and the U.S. Supreme Court granted certiorari.

ISSUE

Do inspections of vehicle junkyards fall within the "closely regulated business" exception to the Fourth Amendment's warrant requirement?

HOLDING

Yes. Warrantless inspections of vehicle junkyards for the purpose of identifying vehicle dismantlers do not violate the Fourth Amendment.

RATIONALE

"The New York regulatory scheme satisfies the three criteria necessary to make reasonable warrantless inspections pursuant to [the statute in question]. First, the State has a substantial interest in regulating the vehicle-dismantling and automobile-junkyard industry because motor vehicle theft has increased in the State and because the problem of theft is associated with this industry. . . . Second, regulation of the vehicle-dismantling industry reasonably serves the State's substantial interest in eradicating automobile theft . . . [and third, the statute] provides a 'constitutionally adequate substitute for a warrant. . . . The statute informs the operator of a vehicle dismantling business that inspections will be made on a regular basis. . . . Thus, the vehicle dismantler knows that the inspections to which he is subject do not constitute discretionary acts by a government official but are conducted pursuant to the statute.'"

CASE SIGNIFICANCE

This case is important for two reasons. First, the Court recognized that automobile junkyards are closely regulated businesses, which permits warrantless inspections. This case is also important because in it the Court clearly announced the three requirements for an inspection of the type considered here to be constitutionally valid. First, there must be a "substantial" government interest in improving the health and safety of the public. Second, the inspections must be necessary to further the regulatory scheme. Finally, the statute authorizing the inspection must serve as a constitutionally adequate substitute for a warrant, providing the owner with notice that search is being made pursuant to the law and has a limited scope and limiting the discretion of the officers who engage in the search. The Court felt all three conditions were satisfied in this case.

UNITED STATES V. MARTINEZ-FUERTE
428 U.S. 543 (1976)

FACTS

Martinez-Fuerte and others, traveling by vehicle from Mexico to the U.S., were arrested at the permanent immigration checkpoint operated by the U.S. Border Patrol away from the international border with Mexico. Each sought suppression of certain evidence based on the ground that the immigration checkpoint violated the Fourth Amendment's proscription against unreasonable searches and seizures and the U.S. Supreme Court granted certiorari.

ISSUE

Do roadblocks near the Mexican border designed to discover illegal aliens violate the Fourth Amendment?

HOLDING

No. Roadblocks near international borders for the purpose of detecting illegal aliens do not need to be authorized in advance by a judicial warrant.

RATIONALE

"To require that such stops always be based on reasonable suspicion would be impractical because the flow of traffic tends to be too heavy to allow the particularized study of a given car necessary to identify it as a possible carrier of illegal aliens. Such a requirement also would largely eliminate any deterrent to the conduct of well-disguised smuggling operations, even though smugglers are known to use these highways regularly. . . . [Further, w]hile the need to make routine checkpoint stops is great, the consequent intrusion on Fourth Amendment interests is quite limited, the interference with legitimate traffic being minimal and checkpoint operations involving less discretionary enforcement activity than roving-patrol stops. . . . Under the circumstances of these checkpoint stops, which do not involve searches, the Government or public interest in making such stops outweighs the constitutionally protected interest of the private citizen."

CASE SIGNIFICANCE

The checkpoint considered in this case was one operated by the Border Patrol several miles inside the U.S. border, near the convergence of two main roads and in an area that restricts vehicle passage around the checkpoint. The Court sanctioned the stops because they were brief and done with the sole purpose of detecting illegal aliens. Most drivers are simply waved on by, and only a handful of motorists are ordered to pull over into a holding area where citizenship is determined. In the Court's words, "Neither the vehicle nor its occupants are searched, and visual inspection of the vehicle is limited to what can be seen without a search." Had the agents been given vast discretion to search the whole of people's cars, the checkpoint probably would not have been lawful.

MICHIGAN DEPARTMENT OF STATE POLICE V. SITZ
496 U.S. 444 (1990)

FACTS

The Michigan Department of State Police instituted a sobriety checkpoint program under guidelines set forth by an advisory committee. The guidelines described how the checkpoints were to be operated, where they were to be set up, and how public notice was to be provided. The guidelines further provided that checkpoints would be set up along certain state roads and that all vehicles passing through would be stopped and their drivers briefly examined for signs of intoxication. If signs of intoxication were detected, the driver would be directed out of the flow of traffic and subjected to a field sobriety test. The checkpoint at issue in this case was one that was in operation for about 75 minutes during which time 126 vehicles passed through. The average delay per car was 25 seconds. Two drivers were detained for sobriety testing; one was arrested. Another person drove through the checkpoint without stopping but was followed and stopped a short time thereafter. One day before the checkpoint went into operation, a group of drivers filed a complaint in the Circuit Court of Wayne County, Michigan, claiming that the checkpoints were unconstitutional, and the U.S. Supreme Court granted certiorari.

ISSUE

Do warrantless, suspicionless highway sobriety checkpoints violate the Fourth Amendment?

HOLDING

No. Warrantless, suspicionless highway sobriety checkpoints are consistent with the Fourth Amendment.

RATIONALE

"No one can seriously dispute the magnitude of the drunken driving problem or the States' interest in eradicating it. Media reports of alcohol-related death and mutilation on the Nation's roads are legion. The anecdotal is confirmed by the statistical. . . . For decades, this Court has 'repeatedly lamented the tragedy.' . . . Conversely, the weight bearing on the other scale—the measure of the intrusion on motorists stopped briefly at sobriety checkpoints—is slight. . . . In sum, the balance of the State's interest in preventing drunken driving, the extent to which this system can reasonably be said to advance that interest, and the degree of intrusion upon individual motorists who are briefly stopped, weighs in favor of the state program. We therefore hold that it is consistent with the Fourth Amendment."

CASE SIGNIFICANCE

This case is important because it upheld warrantless, suspicionless sobriety checkpoints. The Court held that such checkpoints do not violate the Fourth Amendment, but it suggested that part of the reason for this was that the checkpoints were operated pursuant to clearly defined policies, every vehicle was stopped, and there was little discretion (in terms of who would be stopped) accorded to each individual officer. Also, the detentions were, on average, very brief, so the Court looked favorably on the checkpoints, even though they technically amounted to "seizures" within the meaning of the Fourth Amendment.

CITY OF INDIANAPOLIS V. EDMOND
531 U.S. 32 (2000)

FACTS

The city of Indianapolis operated a checkpoint program under which officers, without any suspicion, would stop certain vehicles at roadblocks throughout the city for the purpose of discovering unlawful narcotics. Once a vehicle was stopped, at least one officer would approach the car, advise the driver that he or she was stopped at a narcotics checkpoint, ask the driver for his or her license and registration, look for signs of impairment, conduct an open-view examination of the vehicle from the outside, and allow a trained drug dog to walk around the outside of the car. Two people stopped at the checkpoints filed suit in the U.S. District Court for the Southern District of Indiana, asserting that the checkpoints violated the Fourth Amendment. The U.S. Supreme Court granted certiorari.

ISSUE

Do suspicionless vehicle checkpoints for detecting illegal drugs violate the Fourth Amendment?

HOLDING

Yes. Because suspicionless vehicle checkpoints for detecting illegal drugs are "indistinguishable from the general interest in crime control," the checkpoints violate the Fourth Amendment.

RATIONALE

"We have never approved a checkpoint program whose primary purpose was to detect evidence of ordinary criminal wrongdoing. Rather, our checkpoint cases have recognized only limited exceptions to the general rule that a seizure must be accompanied by some measure of individualized suspicion. We suggested in *Prouse* that we would not credit the 'general interest in crime control' as justification for a regime of suspicionless stops. . . . Consistent with this suggestion, each of the checkpoint programs that we have approved was designed primarily to serve purposes closely related to the problems of policing the border or the necessity of ensuring roadway safety. Because the primary purpose of the Indianapolis narcotics checkpoint program is to uncover evidence of ordinary criminal wrongdoing, the program contravenes the Fourth Amendment."

CASE SIGNIFICANCE

This case is important because it addressed checkpoints that were markedly different from those discussed in the previous cases. The checkpoints operated in Indianapolis were different because their sole purpose was to detect evidence of criminal activity. In the other checkpoint cases already discussed the focus was on patrolling the borders and/or ensuring roadway safety. The Court held that because Indianapolis's checkpoint program served little more than a general crime control function—instead of being concerned with broader issues of safety—it violated the Fourth Amendment's proscription against unreasonable searches and seizures.

NEW JERSEY V. T.L.O.
469 U.S. 325 (1985)

FACTS

A high-school teacher caught a 14-year-old freshman smoking in the restroom, in violation of a school rule. The student was brought to the principal's office and was questioned by the assistant vice-principal. The student denied that she had been smoking. The assistant vice-principal then demanded to see her purse, opened the purse, and found a pack of cigarettes. The assistant vice-principal also noticed a pack of rolling papers, which are often used to roll marijuana. A more thorough search of the student's purse revealed a small amount of marijuana, a pipe, several empty plastic bags, cash, and other incriminating information. The evidence was admitted against the student in a New Jersey juvenile court proceeding. The New Jersey court held that school officials can search a student if the official has reasonable suspicion or reasonable cause to believe a search is necessary to enforce a school policy. The U.S. Supreme Court then granted certiorari.

ISSUE

Is probable cause necessary for a school disciplinary search?

HOLDING

No. School officials do not need a warrant or probable cause for a school disciplinary search. Instead, the search should be judged on its reasonableness and premised on "reasonable grounds" that it will turn up the evidence sought.

RATIONALE

"Schoolchildren have legitimate expectations of privacy. They may find it necessary to carry with them a variety of legitimate, noncontraband items, and there is no reason to conclude that they have necessarily waived all rights to privacy in such items by bringing them onto school grounds. But striking a balance between schoolchildren's legitimate expectations of privacy and the school's equally legitimate need to maintain an environment in which learning can take place requires some easing of the restrictions to which searches by public authorities are ordinarily subject. Thus, school officials need not obtain a warrant before searching a student who is under their authority. Moreover, school officials need not be held subject to the requirement that searches be based on probable cause to believe that the subject of the search has violated or is violating the law. Rather, the legality of a search of a student should depend simply on the reasonableness, under all the circumstances, of the search. Determining the reasonableness of any search involves a determination of whether the search was justified at its inception and whether, as conducted, it was reasonably related in scope to the circumstances that justified the interference in the first place. Under ordinary circumstances the search of a student by a school official will be justified at its inception where there are reasonable grounds for suspecting that the search will turn up evidence that the student has violated or is violating either the law or the rules of the school."

CASE SIGNIFICANCE

The case serves as a prime example of the Court's balancing approach used in judging the constitutionality of so-called regulatory searches. The Court felt that even though a search of T.L.O. took place, the school's interest in maintaining an environment conducive to learning was more important. Even so, the Court did require that "reasonable grounds" be in place before disciplinary searches can commence. This way, public school students cannot be searched on a whim. Note that this case dealt with grades K–12; the story is markedly different for college students. The courts have generally held that college students enjoy Fourth Amendment protection and cannot be searched and/or seized on less than probable cause.

O'CONNOR V. ORTEGA
480 U.S. 709 (1987)

FACTS

Dr. Ortega was Chief of Professional Education at Napa State Hospital for 17 years. His primary duty was to train young physicians in psychiatric residency programs. In July 1981, hospital officials began to suspect Ortega of possible job-related malfeasance. Allegations surfaced that Ortega coerced subordinates to contribute funds for the purchase of a computer and that he had sexually harassed and inappropriately disciplined several residents. While he was on administrative leave, hospital officials searched his office. State property and several personal items were seized, which were then used against Ortega in a dismissal hearing. He brought a Section 1983 suit (see Chapter Twenty-two), alleging that his Fourth Amendment rights were violated. The U.S. Supreme Court granted certiorari.

ISSUE

Do government employees enjoy Fourth Amendment protection in their offices?

HOLDING

Yes. Neither a warrant nor probable cause is necessary to search a government employee's office, but the search must be noninvestigative and intended to discover evidence of work-related malfeasance. Searches and seizures by government employers of their employees are subject to the restrictions of the Fourth Amendment. However, probable cause is not necessary for searches and seizures that are noninvestigative and work-related. The search and seizure must be judged in terms of its "reasonableness."

RATIONALE

"Searches and seizures by government employers or supervisors of the private property of their employees . . . are subject to the restraints of the Fourth Amendment. . . . The workplace includes those areas and items that are related to work and are generally within the employer's control. At a hospital, for example, the hallways, cafeteria, offices, desks, and file cabinets, among other areas, are all part of the workplace. These areas remain part of the workplace context even if the employee has placed personal items in them, such as a photograph placed in a desk or a letter posted on an employee bulletin board. . . . We hold, therefore, that public employer intrusions on the constitutionally protected privacy interests of government employees for noninvestigatory, work-related purposes, as well as for investigations of work-related misconduct, should be judged by the standard of reasonableness under all the circumstances. Under this reasonableness standard, both the inception and the scope of the intrusion must be reasonable."

CASE SIGNIFICANCE

This case is important because it provided that government employees enjoy Fourth Amendment protection in the workplace. However, even though the Court said government employees enjoy this protection, it did not require that probable cause, or even reasonable suspicion, be in place to search and seize property. Instead, as in *T.L.O.*, the search and seizure should be judged in terms of their reasonableness. Note that this decision does not apply to searches of private employees offices by private employers. Private employers are not bound by the strictures of the Fourth Amendment.

VERNONIA SCHOOL DISTRICT 47J v. ACTON
515 U.S. 646 (1995)

FACTS

Officials in an Oregon public school district noticed an increase in student drug use. The officials became particularly concerned that the increase in drug use could increase the risk of sports-related injuries. A parent "input night" was held during which the parents in attendance gave unanimous support for a policy of drug testing, through urinalysis, of student athletes. The policy that was adopted provided that all students who wished to participate in athletics had to sign a form consenting to drug testing, that all athletes were tested near the beginning of the season, and that 10 percent of the athletes would be randomly tested at weekly intervals after that. A seventh-grade student was not allowed to participate in sports because he and his parents refused to sign the consent form. The student and his parents filed a lawsuit, claiming that the drug testing procedure violated the Fourth Amendment, and the U.S. Supreme Court granted certiorari.

ISSUE

Are random, suspicionless drug tests of school athletes permissible under the Fourth Amendment?

HOLDING

Yes. Random, suspicionless drug tests of school athletes do not violate the Fourth Amendment. The decreased expectation of privacy of students who participate in school sports coupled with the relative unobtrusiveness of the search and the need to promote student safety all combine to mean that the Oregon public school district's policy did not violate the Fourth Amendment.

RATIONALE

"State-compelled collection and testing of urine constitutes a 'search' under the Fourth Amendment. . . . [T]he 'reasonableness' of [such] a search is judged by balancing the intrusion on the individual's Fourth Amendment interests against the promotion of legitimate governmental interests. . . . The first factor to be considered in determining reasonableness is the nature of the privacy interests on which the search intrudes. Here, the subject of the policy are children who have been committed to the temporary custody of the State as schoolmaster; in that capacity, the State may exercise a degree of supervision and control greater than it could exercise over free adults. The requirements that public school children submit to physical examinations and be vaccinated indicated that they have a lesser privacy expectation with regard to medical examinations and procedure than the general population. Student athletes have even less of a legitimate privacy expectation, for an element of communal undress is inherent in athletic participation, and athletes are subject to preseason physical exams and rules regulating their conduct. Finally, the privacy interests compromised by the process of obtaining urine samples under the Policy are negligible, since the conditions of collection are nearly identical to those typically encountered in public restrooms. In addition, the tests look only for standard drugs, not medical conditions, and the results are released to a limited group."

CASE SIGNIFICANCE

This case was the first to uphold random, suspicionless drug tests of students seeking to participate in school athletics. The Court adopted a balancing approach, weighing the privacy interests of each individual student with the school district's interest of promoting safety during sports-related activities. The Court felt that the district's interest was more important than each individual student's privacy rights. So, even though the drug tests are considered "searches," the Court held that no justification is necessary for officials to conduct them.

FERGUSON V. CHARLESTON
523 U.S. 67 (2001)

FACTS

In the fall of 1988, staff at the Charleston, South Carolina, public hospital became concerned over the apparent increase in the use of cocaine by patients who received prenatal treatment. Staff at the hospital approached the city and agreed to cooperate in prosecuting pregnant mothers who tested positive for drugs. A task force was set up consisting of hospital personnel, police, and other local officials. The task force formulated a policy for how to conduct the tests, preserve the evidence, and use it to prosecute those who tested positive. Ferguson and several other women tested positive for cocaine, and the case came before the U.S. Supreme Court.

ISSUE

Is the Fourth Amendment violated when hospital personnel, working with the police, test pregnant mothers for drug use without their consent?

HOLDING

Yes. Hospital personnel who test patients without their consent for drug use and then turn the evidence over to the police violate the Fourth Amendment.

RATIONALE

"Because the hospital seeks to justify its authority to conduct drug tests and to turn the results over to police without the patients' knowledge or consent, this case differs from the four previous cases in which the Court considered whether comparable drug tests fit within the closely guarded category of constitutionally permissible suspicionless searches. . . . Those cases employed a balancing test weighing the intrusion on the individual's privacy interest against the 'special needs' that supported the program. The invasion of privacy here is far more substantial than in those cases. In previous cases, there was no misunderstanding about the purpose of the test or the potential use of the test results, and there were protections against the dissemination of the results to third parties. Moreover, those cases

involved disqualification from eligibility for particular benefits, not the unauthorized dissemination of test results. The critical difference, however, lies in the nature of the 'special needs' asserted. In each of the prior cases, the 'special need' was divorced from the State's general law enforcement interest. Here, the policy's central and indispensable feature from its inception was the use of law enforcement to coerce patients into substance abuse treatment."

CASE SIGNIFICANCE

This case is important because it placed restrictions on the so-called regulatory or suspicionless search doctrine. The Court reaffirmed the requirement that regulatory searches be conducted without special law enforcement interests in mind. Instead, the benefit to public safety must outweigh individual privacy interests for suspicionless searches to be constitutionally valid. The Court felt that the public interest in capturing pregnant women who abused drugs was not as significant as the women's privacy interests.

BOARD OF EDUCATION OF INDEPENDENT SCHOOL DISTRICT V. EARLS
536 U.S. 822 (2002)

FACTS

The Student Activities Drug Testing Policy implemented by the Board of Education of Independent School District No. 92 of Pottawatomie County required students participating in extracurricular activities to submit to random, suspicionless urine tests intended to detect the use of illegal drugs. Together with their parents, two students, Lindsay Earls and Daniel James, brought a Section 1983 lawsuit against the school district, alleging that the drug testing policy violated the Fourth Amendment as incorporated to the states through the due process clause of the Fourteenth Amendment. The district court found in favor of the school district, but the Tenth Circuit reversed, holding that the policy violated the Fourth Amendment. It concluded that random, suspicionless drug tests would only be permissible were there some identifiable drug abuse problem. The U.S. Supreme Court then granted certiorari.

ISSUE

Do random, suspicionless drug tests of students who participate in extracurricular activities violate the Fourth Amendment?

HOLDING

No. Suspicionless drug tests of students participating in extracurricular activities do not violate the Fourth Amendment.

RATIONALE

". . . [T]he Court concludes that the invasion of students' privacy is not significant, given the minimally intrusive nature of the sample collection and the limited uses to which the test results are put. The degree of intrusion caused by collecting a urine sample depends upon the manner in which production of the sample is monitored. Under the Policy, a faculty monitor waits outside the closed restroom stall for the student to produce a sample and must listen for the normal sounds of urination to guard against tampered specimens and ensure an accurate chain of custody. This procedure is virtually identical to the 'negligible' intrusion approved in *Vernonia School District 47J v. Acton.* . . . The Policy clearly requires that test results be kept in confidential files separate from a student's other records and released to school personnel only on a 'need to know' basis. Moreover, the test results are not turned over to any law enforcement authority. Nor do the test results lead to the imposition of discipline or have any academic consequences. Rather, the only consequences of a failed drug test is to limit the student's privilege of participating in extracurricular activities."

CASE SIGNIFICANCE

This case is easily reconciled with *Ferguson.* There, the urine tests were handed over to law enforcement personnel. Here, the tests were only used to determine whether a student should be allowed to participate in extracurricular activities. The Court concluded that the policy in question here served the school district's interest in protecting the health and safety of its students, so the minimal intrusions did not violate the Fourth Amendment. This case is therefore important because it carefully outlines the requirements of a constitutional regulatory drug testing program.

GRIFFIN V. WISCONSIN
483 U.S. 868 (1987)

FACTS

In September 1980, Griffin was convicted on charges of resisting arrest, disorderly conduct, and obstructing an officer. He was placed on probation. One of the conditions of his probation was that he allow any probation officer to search his home without a warrant as long as the probation officer's supervisor approved and that

here were "reasonable grounds" to believe contraband would be found. On April 5, 1983, a detective on the Beloit Police Department informed Lew, Griffin's probation officer's supervisor, that there might be guns at Griffin's apartment. Lew, who was accompanied by another probation officer and three plainclothes police officers, went to Griffin's apartment. Griffin answered the door and Lew told him that they were there to search his apartment. A handgun was found during the search. Griffin was convicted of possession of a firearm by a felon. The U.S. Supreme Court then granted certiorari.

ISSUE

Can a probationer be forced to submit to warrantless searches of his or her residence?

HOLDING

Yes. Probationers can be forced to submit to warrantless searches of their residences. However, "reasonable grounds" that contraband will be found is the necessary level of justification.

RATIONALE

"A State's operation of a probation system, like its operation of a school, government office or prison, or its supervision of a regulated industry, likewise presents 'special needs' beyond normal law enforcement that may justify departures from the usual warrant and probable cause requirements. . . . To a greater or lesser degree, it is always true of probationers (as we have said it to be true of parolees) that they do not enjoy 'the absolute liberty to which every citizen is entitled, but only . . . conditional liberty properly dependent on observance of special [probation] restrictions. . . . A warrant requirement would interfere to an appreciable degree with the probation system, setting up a magistrate rather than the probation officer as the judge of how close a supervision the probationer requires. Moreover, the delay inherent in obtaining a warrant would make it more difficult for probation officials to respond quickly to evidence of misconduct, and would reduce the deterrent effect that the possibility of expeditious searches would otherwise create."

CASE SIGNIFICANCE

This case is important because it treats probationers differently from ordinary citizens. The Court sanctioned warrantless searches of probationers' residences because, it argued, they enjoy a lesser expectation of privacy as part of being placed on probation. The Court has sanctioned similar searches of parolees' homes as well. The same logic applies. In this case the Court focused more on "special needs" of law enforcement than a balancing approach, weighing the individual's privacy interests with the state's interest in promoting public safety.

UNITED STATES V. KNIGHTS
534 U.S. 112 (2001)

FACTS

As a condition of his probation on drug charges, Knights was required to submit to searches conducted by any probation or law enforcement officer even in the absence of a warrant or probable cause. Knights was convicted on drug charges and given probation. Three days into probation, Knights became the primary suspect in an arson case. A sheriff's deputy investigating the case drove by Knights' residence and noticed in the bed of a pickup truck several potentially incriminating items, not the least of which was a Molotov cocktail and various explosive materials. Knowing the terms of Knights' probation, the deputy undertook a search of the apartment resulting in the discovery of additional incriminating evidence. Knights was arrested and indicted by a federal grand jury. A motion to suppress the evidence found in his apartment was accepted on grounds that the purpose of the search was more investigatory than probationary in nature. The Ninth Circuit Court of Appeals affirmed on grounds that the terms of Knights' probation were limited to probationary searches and not investigatory searches. The U.S. Supreme Court then granted certiorari.

ISSUE

Is evidence seized from a warrantless search of a probationer's apartment admissible under the Fourth Amendment when the search is legally authorized by the terms of probation?

HOLDING

Yes. The warrantless search of Knights' apartment resulting in the discovery of incriminating criminal evidence did not violate the Fourth Amendment because Knights' probation conditions required that he submit to warrantless searches.

RATIONALE

"The Fourth Amendment's touchstone is reasonableness, and a search's reasonableness is determined by assessing, on the one hand, the degree to which it intrudes upon an individual's privacy and, on the other, the degree to which it is needed to promote legitimate government interests. . . . Knights' status as a probationer subject to a search condition informs both sides

of that balance. The sentencing judge reasonably concluded that the search condition would further the two primary goals of probation—rehabilitation and protecting society from future criminal violations. Knights was unambiguously informed of the search condition. Thus, Knights' reasonable expectation of privacy was significantly diminished. In assessing the governmental interest, it must be remembered that the very assumption of probation is that the probationer is more likely than others to violate the law. . . . The State's interest in apprehending criminal law violators, thereby protecting potential victims, may justifiably focus on probationers in a way that it does not on the ordinary citizen. On balance, no more than reasonable suspicion was required to search this probationer's house. The degree of individualized suspicion required is a determination that a sufficiently high probability of criminal conduct makes the intrusion on the individual's privacy interest reasonable. Although the Fourth Amendment ordinarily requires probable cause, a lesser degree satisfies the Constitution when the balance of governmental and private interests makes such a standard reasonable."

CASE SIGNIFICANCE

This case gave the police authority to conduct investigatory searches where required by the terms of an individual's probation. In other words, if the terms of an individual's probation require submission to a warrantless search, any incriminating evidence discovered as a result should be ruled admissible under the Fourth Amendment. Caution must be exercised, however, to ensure that searches of an investigatory nature are not excluded from the terms of the probationary contract. To the extent that investigatory searches are excluded, officers will be limited in their authority to initiate such warrantless intrusions. Where such searches are not specifically excluded from the terms of probation, this ruling serves to greatly expand the authority of officers conducting investigations focusing upon previously adjudicated and therefore known offenders. ✦

DISCUSSION QUESTIONS

1. Regulatory searches require no justification, yet they are still searches. What is your assessment of regulatory searches?

2. Which types of regulatory searches are more invasive than others? Why?

3. As of this writing, the Supreme Court is hearing a case on whether the police should be able to insti-

tute checkpoints to ask people whether they have information about a crime, and then arrest drunk drivers and people with contraband in plain view. How should the Court rule?

4. A controversial practice with respect to probation searches is the emerging practice of police-probation partnerships. This practice teams police offi-cers with probationers to conduct spot checks of certain probationers once they come on proba-tion. What is your opinion of this practice?

5. Identify examples of closely regulated businesses that would fall under the regulatory searches ex-ception to the Fourth Amendment. ✦

Chapter Fifteen

Electronic Surveillance

Olmstead v. United States, 277 U.S. 438 (1928)

On Lee v. United States, 343 U.S. 747 (1952)

Berger v. New York, 388 U.S. 41 (1967)

Katz v. United States, 389 U.S. 347 (1967)

United States v. Karo, 468 U.S. 705 (1984)

INTRODUCTION

Law enforcement has historically been constrained in the collection of evidence by electronic means on at least two grounds. Primary among these has been the Supreme Court ruling that electronic eavesdropping constitutes a search under the Fourth Amendment (*Katz v. United States*). Secondly, there has long existed a general lack of technological resources and competence within law enforcement circles. While it is difficult to accurately predict what the future holds, it seems relatively safe to assert that both of these constraints are rapidly evaporating as the result of recent terrorist attacks against U.S. interests. In other words, the events of September 11, 2001, have placed an unprecedented emphasis on the use of various technologies to detect, prevent, and prosecute criminal activities both before and after the fact. Changes in this area of the law are likely to be very dramatic as the "War on Terror" escalates and continues into the indefinite future.

Although the cases included here stem from less dramatic events, each contributes to a comprehensive understanding of the constitutional principles guiding the collection of evidence by electronic means. Upon close review of these cases, two important points bear mention. First, it should be noted that there exist only a limited number of cases in this particular area of the law. Additionally, there exist even fewer cases dealing with the countless new forms of technology and the varieties of crime that they often breed (generally through the use of computers, etc.). Finally, the cases within this area are rather "dated" insofar as they do not remain abreast of the current public safety interests that are at stake (again, referring to the risk of terrorist attacks). When these three facts are taken in conjunction with one another, it becomes readily apparent how and why this area of the law is so fertile for future growth.

Be that as it may, the cases briefed within this chapter deal not only with wiretapping (e.g., *Olmstead* and *Katz*), but with other forms of electronic eavesdropping as well. These include the wearing of concealed recording devices or "wires" (*On Lee v. United States*) as well as the use of homing devices to track the movement of people, packages or objects (*United States v. Karo*). While these cases are indeed narrowly focused, numerically few, and historically dated, they nonetheless continue to guide the manner in which law enforcement utilizes such investigative resources. ✦

OLMSTEAD V. UNITED STATES
277 U.S. 438 (1928)

FACTS

Olmstead was convicted in federal court for violation of the National Prohibition Act. In essence, he was the principal actor in a large-scale alcohol smuggling operation. The evidence used to convict Olmstead was obtained by prohibition agents who electronically eavesdropped on a number of telephone conversations. More specifically, the bugging devices were placed on phone lines outside the location from where the calls were both made and received. The Ninth Circuit Court of Appeals affirmed Olmstead's conviction, and the U.S. Supreme Court granted certiorari.

ISSUE

Does electronic eavesdropping (i.e., wiretapping) constitute a search within the meaning of the Fourth Amendment where there occurs no physical trespass or intrusion into a protected area?

HOLDING

No. Electronic eavesdropping does not constitute a search within the meaning of the Fourth Amendment unless there occurs a physical intrusion or trespass into a protected area.

RATIONALE

In reaching the conclusion that electronic eavesdropping does not constitute a search unless there occurs a physical intrusion or trespass into a protected area, the Supreme Court gave a very strict interpretation of the Fourth Amendment's language. Specifically, the Court observed: "The Amendment does not forbid what was done here. There was no searching. There was no seizure. The evidence was secured by the use of the sense of hearing and that only. There was no entry of the houses or the offices of the defendants." The majority further reasoned that: "[O]ne who installs in his house a telephone instrument with connecting wires intends to project his voice to those quite outside, and that the wires beyond his house, and message while passing over them, are not within the protection of the Fourth Amendment."

CASE SIGNIFICANCE

Although the *Olmstead* decision no longer serves as controlling precedent, it was the prevailing rule of law guiding the use of electronic eavesdropping devices until the Court revisited the issue some four decades later in *Katz v. United States.* Initially, the decision as to whether or not electronic eavesdropping constituted a search turned upon a strict interpretation of the language contained in the Fourth Amendment. Under such an approach, officers were allowed to gather oral/conversational evidence against suspects which could later be admitted at trial so long as there was no physical intrusion into a protected area. Today, however, such tactics are no longer permissible, and any form of electronic eavesdropping—even in the absence of a physical trespass—constitutes a search protected by Fourth Amendment standards.

ON LEE V. UNITED STATES
343 U.S. 747 (1952)

FACTS

While out on bail pending trial for federal narcotics violations, On Lee was approached by an old friend who engaged him in conversation regarding the criminal charges. As it turned out, the friend was really an undercover federal agent who was wired with an electronic device capable of transmitting the conversation to a remote listening device. The incriminating statements that were obtained by this tactic were introduced at trial over On Lee's objection and he was convicted. The conviction was affirmed by a federal court of appeals, and the U.S. Supreme Court then granted certiorari.

ISSUE

Does a violation of the Fourth Amendment occur when a "friend" allows authorities to listen in on a conversation by way of using an electronic eavesdropping device?

HOLDING

No. The Fourth Amendment does not prohibit the use of an electronic eavesdropping device (i.e., a "wire") that is worn by the "friend" of a criminal suspect for purposes of gathering incriminating evidence.

RATIONALE

The petitioner, On Lee, argued before the Court that the evidence against him was improperly admitted insofar as it had been obtained in violation of the Fourth Amendment under the standard established in *Olmstead v. United States.* In *Olmstead,* the Court ruled that electronic eavesdropping does not constitute a search under the Fourth Amendment unless there occurs a physical trespass into a protected space. In the present matter, it was argued that the agent who was "wired" committed such an intrusion, thereby rendering the evidence inadmissible under the exclusionary rule. The Court rejected this assertion for several reasons. First, it was noted that as a "friend" of On Lee, the agent committed no trespass when he entered the location where the incriminating conversation took place. Second, the fact that the agent/friend engaged in behavior that On Lee would have objected to and would most likely have resulted in immediate expulsion from the property, does not constitute a de facto instance of trespassing ab initio (from the beginning). Rather, the Court ruled that the doctrine of trespass ab initio applied only to civil liability cases. Also rejected was an argument by On Lee that the agent's entrance onto the property constituted a trespass because permission to do so was obtained by fraud—that is, pretending to be a "friend" of the petitioner. The Court also observed that even if it were to overturn the *Olmstead* wiretapping decision, it still would not apply to On Lee's case because the evidence at issue was obtained by altogether different means (i.e., an agent wearing a "wire" as opposed to agents "tapping" a phone line). Finally, the Court rejected On Lee's request to overturn the conviction and throw out the evidence as a means of disciplining and thereby deterring law enforcement from engaging in such deceptive behavior.

CASE SIGNIFICANCE

The *On Lee* decision was the mechanism that allowed the authorities to obtain evidence against a suspect by electronic mean so long as they have the consent of at least one of the parties involved. In other words, if the police can convince an individual to wear a "wire" and obtain incriminating statements from another person, those statements may be admitted at trial. Obtaining an incriminating oral statement from someone by "wiring another for sound" is thus legally permissible under the Fourth Amendment. While it no doubt remains difficult for the police to obtain incriminating oral statements from a suspect through conventional interviewing strategies, the decision in this case allows authorities to employ more creative yet legally permissible methods for accomplishing the same objective.

BERGER V. NEW YORK
388 U.S. 41 (1967)

FACTS

Berger was convicted for attempting to bribe a public official. The chief evidence used against him was gathered by way of using an electronic eavesdropping device or "bug." The device was planted pursuant to a state law authorizing prosecutors or police officials at the rank of sergeant or above to issue a "bugging" order which would be valid for up to two months. The statute did not, however, require the state officials to detail specific information regarding the content of the conversations, nor did it provide guidelines for a "return" of the gathered information. The New York appellate courts upheld the constitutionality of the statute and affirmed Berger's conviction, and the U.S. Supreme Court granted certiorari.

ISSUE

Did the statute authorizing state officials to eavesdrop on private conversations by way of using a "bugging" device violate the Fourth Amendment protection against unreasonable searches and seizures?

HOLDING

Yes. Electronic eavesdropping constitutes a search, which in the absence of clearly limited guidelines regarding the information sought and how it is to be "returned," violates the Fourth Amendment prohibition against unreasonable searches and seizures.

RATIONALE

In concluding that the evidence used to convict Berger was illegally obtained, it was first noted that the use of electronic devices to monitor private conversations constitutes a search within the meaning of the Fourth Amendment. Thus, any such law or action by the state must comply with the standards set forth therein. For example, the Fourth Amendment requires officers to particularly describe the person or things to be seized. Because the New York law did not comply with this prerequisite, it was constitutionally defective. In the absence of this requirement, officers would possess "roving" authority to seize any and all private conversations. Yet another defective element of the law was that which authorized officers to listen in on conversations for up to two months. The Court equated this characteristic to a series of conventional searches conducted pursuant to a single showing of probable cause. Still other defective elements included: (1) the power of extension up to two additional months without any further showing of probable cause; (2) the absence of a specific termination date; (3) no requirement for a showing of exigency; and (4) no provision for "return" of the warrant and disclosure of how the obtained evidence would be used. In light of the breadth and gravity associated with these defective characteristics, the law in question was deemed unconstitutional under both the Fourth and Fourteenth Amendments.

CASE SIGNIFICANCE

This case is important on several grounds, not the least of which is that it is one of two electronic eavesdropping decisions rendered by the Court in 1967 (see *Katz v. United States*). Additionally, the cased clarified the requisite elements for an eavesdropping statute to pass constitutional scrutiny. First, the law must particularly describe the conversations to be surveilled. Second, probable cause to believe that criminal activity is afoot must be established. Third, the duration of the eavesdropping must be limited—extensions may be made, however, where an adequate showing can be made. Fourth, the individual(s) whose conversations are to be monitored must be named in the judicial order. Fifth, a return showing what conversations were monitored and the intended use of any evidence must be made available to the issuing court. Last, the eavesdropping must cease once the desired information has been obtained. While these requirements for electronic eavesdropping may seem commonplace today, they were revolutionary when they were announced. In fact, it was only one year later that Congress enacted the Omnibus Crime Control and Safe Streets Act which more specifically addressed such matters. Although not widely cited or relied upon as precedent, the *Berger* decision may very well find renewed significance in today's era of rapid technological expansion characterized by dramatic increases in Internet and computer-based crime.

KATZ V. UNITED STATES
389 U.S. 347 (1967)

FACTS

Katz was indicted and convicted on federal charges for transmitting wagering (betting) information across state lines by way of telephone. The evidence used to convict was obtained by FBI agents who had attached an electronic eavesdropping and recording device to a public pay phone used by Katz. Naturally, Katz objected to the introduction of this evidence at trial, but his motion to suppress was denied. A federal appellate court affirmed the conviction on grounds that there was no physical intrusion into an occupied area. The U.S. Supreme Court then granted certiorari.

Issue

Is a public telephone booth constitutionally protected from electronic eavesdropping by the Fourth Amendment even where there is no physical intrusion?

Holding

Yes. Despite the fact that a telephone booth exists in public, individuals who make use of it possess a reasonable expectation of privacy. Thus, any electronic monitoring of the phone constitutes a search. No physical intrusion needs to occur in order for the Fourth Amendment to be triggered.

Rationale

In resolving this particular case, the Court was asked to first determine whether or not a public telephone booth is a constitutionally protected area under the Fourth Amendment. The second issue to be resolved was whether or not there must be an actual physical intrusion into the booth itself or, instead, if a nonphysical intrusion such as that which occurs with electronic eavesdropping can also trigger the Fourth Amendment. As to the first of these issues—whether or not a public telephone booth is constitutionally protected under the Fourth Amendment—the Court rejected the government's position that individuals have a diminished expectation of privacy when using public pay phones because the typical booth is at least partially walled by glass. Thus, the Court showed reluctance to accept the government's argument that just because an individual can be observed through the glass walls of a pay phone, the affairs he or she conducts therein automatically become public rather than remaining private in nature. The fact that an individual closes the door of the booth clearly indicates a desire to keep the details of his or her conversation confidential. On these and similarly related grounds it was ultimately concluded that an individual who uses a pay phone possesses a reasonable expectation that his or her conversation will remain private and not be broadcast to or listened in upon by others. Having resolved this issue, the Court turned its attention to the second issue—that of determining whether there must be an actual physical intrusion into the protected space or, instead, if a nonphysical intrusion such as that which occurs with electronic eavesdropping can also trigger the Fourth Amendment. With regard to this question, the Court changed its position established by two earlier cases—*Olmstead v. United States* (wiretapping does not violate the Fourth Amendment unless there is a physical trespass into a constitutionally protected area) and *Goldman v. United States*, 316 U.S. 129 (1942) (the Fourth Amendment is limited only to searches and seizures of tangible property). In opposition to these prior rulings, the Court now asserted that once it has been acknowledged that the Fourth Amendment governs not only the seizure of tangible items but extends to the recording of private conversations, its application cannot depend solely upon the relative presence or absence of a physical intrusion into a given enclosed space. Combined, these two lines of reasoning allowed the Court to conclude that public telephone booths are constitutionally protected from electronic eavesdropping by the Fourth Amendment even where no physical intrusion occurs.

Case Significance

The *Katz* decision is important in several regards. First, it served to overturn the decision previously rendered in *Olmstead v. United States* establishing the rule of law that wiretapping does not constitute a search unless there occurs some trespass into a constitutionally protected area. Thus, the Court's decision in this case broadens the Fourth Amendment's protective scope so that even in the absence of physical intrusion into a protected space, electronic eavesdropping constitutes a search. Beyond establishing a new rule of law, the decision also sets forth the notion that just because an individual conducts his or her business in public view (i.e., a partially glassed-in phone booth), this does not mean that he or she has a diminished expectation of privacy. As the Court pointed out, despite the fact that a phone booth has glass walls which allow others to see inside, the conversation or communication that occurs within the confines of the booth remains private. Given these distinguishing characteristics, the *Katz* decision remains the rule of law controlling police behavior in the area of electronic eavesdropping.

UNITED STATES V. KARO
468 U.S. 705 (1984)

Facts

DEA agents learned from an informant that Karo and two other individuals had arranged to purchase two cans of ether to be used for purposes of extracting cocaine from clothing that had been imported into the U.S. With the informant's consent and court approval, a homing device was affixed to one of the ether containers so that agents could track its movement. After being transported between several locations, the agents secured a search warrant for the residence where the container finally came to rest. Upon executing the warrant a quantity of cocaine was found and Karo, along with others, was charged with various drug-related offenses. During federal pretrial proceedings, Karo moved to suppress the evidence on grounds that the original warrant authorizing placement of the homing device was defective, thereby rendering all subsequent evidence inadmissible. The government unsuccessfully appealed the motion to suppress, and the U.S. Supreme Court granted certiorari.

Issue

Did the warrantless monitoring of the homing device inside a private residence violate the Fourth Amendment?

Holding

Yes. The warrantless monitoring of a homing device inside a private residence violates the Fourth Amendment.

Rationale

Although planting a homing device does not in and of itself violate the Constitution, monitoring its presence and movement inside a private residence does offend the Fourth Amendment. The Court reasoned that because a residence is not open to visual surveillance, the government's surreptitious use of the homing device to obtain information was akin to conducting a warrantless search. At the same time, however, the justices concluded that monitoring the movements of the container over the open roads provided ample probable cause to sustain the issuance of the second search warrant for the residence. In the end, the suppression order was reversed, allowing the evidence to be admitted upon retrial.

Case Significance

This decision is somewhat confusing insofar as it ruled the monitoring of the homing device to be in violation of the Fourth Amendment while at the same time reversing the suppression order on other grounds. Specifically, the justices objected to the monitoring of the device while it was inside a private residence. On the other hand, the Court held that tracking the movement of the container over the open road created enough probable cause by itself to render issuance of the residential search warrant valid. For day-to-day police operations, this decision means that the police are authorized to use homing devices in open areas (roadways, etc.), but not in private areas (residences, etc). They cannot, however, rely on its mere presence inside a private dwelling as probable cause for a search warrant because such places afford property owners a reasonable expectation of privacy under the Fourth Amendment. Once a container is inside such a location, a warrant authorizing its seizure must be predicated upon other known facts or elements of probable cause. ✦

Discussion Questions

1. Discuss how changes in technology are likely to influence future Supreme Court decisions in the area of electronic surveillance/eavesdropping.

2. Do individuals still have a reasonable expectation of privacy even though communications via cellular phone can be easily intercepted by a radio scanner? Why or why not?

3. Do individuals have a reasonable expectation of privacy in communications via the Internet (e.g., email, one-on-one chatting, chat rooms, etc.)? Why or why not? ✦

Chapter Sixteen

Pretrial Identification Procedures

United States v. Wade, 388 U.S. 218 (1967)

Foster v. California, 394 U.S. 440 (1969)

Kirby v. Illinois, 406 U.S. 682 (1972)

United States v. Dionisio, 410 U.S. 1 (1973)

Manson v. Brathwaite, 432 U.S. 98 (1977)

United States v. Crews, 445 U.S. 463 (1980)

INTRODUCTION

During the course of day-to-day police operations, officers frequently need to obtain eyewitness identification without the luxury of being able to organize and conduct a formal lineup at the stationhouse. In such instances, it would not be uncommon for the police to accomplish this pressing objective by one of two means: (1) transport a suspect back to the scene of a crime so that a victim or witness can make a positive identification; or (2) present the witness or victim with a collection of photographs, hoping that he or she will be able to positively identify the suspect of interest. In both cases, officers must proceed with extreme caution in order to avoid prejudicially influencing the victim/witness identification. At the same time, officers must be intimately familiar with other due process requirements related to pretrial identification procedures. Specifically, they must know when a suspect is or is not entitled to the assistance of counsel during such instances. To this important end, the cases briefed within this chapter outline the basic constitutional concerns that arise during pretrial identification procedures.

Contrary to popular belief, suspects who have not been formally charged with a criminal offense are not entitled to assistance of counsel during pretrial identification procedures. This principle of law may be directly traced to the Supreme Court's ruling in *Kirby v. Illinois*. While this decision clearly benefits law enforcement interests, there exist other cases that ardently protect the due process rights of criminal suspects. For example,

United States v. Wade established the principle of law that once an individual has been formally charged with a crime, s/he is entitled to have an attorney present during any subsequent police-orchestrated lineups. Furthermore, such procedures—be they photographic collages or actual lineups—may not be so suggestive as to make the resulting identification a foregone conclusion (e.g., *Foster v. California*). ✦

UNITED STATES V. WADE
388 U.S. 218 (1967)

FACTS

Wade, having been indicted on federal bank robbery and conspiracy charges, was placed in a lineup without the benefit of counsel and, along with other participants, made to wear a disguise and repeat words like those reportedly used by the robber. Two bank employees identified him as having been involved in the robbery. This identification testimony was subsequently introduced at trial prompting Wade to enter a motion for acquittal on the grounds that the lineup procedures had violated his Fifth Amendment right to avoid self-incrimination as well as his Sixth Amendment right to counsel. The motion was denied and Wade was convicted. On appeal, the conviction was reversed on the grounds that although there had been no Fifth Amendment violation, his right to counsel under the Sixth Amendment had been abridged during the lineup. A new trial was ordered with instructions that the identification testimony be excluded, and the U.S. Supreme Court granted certiorari.

ISSUES

Does the Fifth Amendment prohibit the state from requiring a criminal defendant to appear in a postindictment lineup for identification purposes? Does the Sixth Amendment require the presence of a criminal defendant's attorney during postindictment lineups conducted for identification purposes? Are courtroom identifications of a criminal defendant that are the product of a postindictment lineup conducted without the benefit of counsel admissible at trial?

HOLDING

No, yes, and no. The Fifth Amendment does not prohibit the state from requiring a defendant to participate in a postindictment lineup conducted for identification purposes. However, the Sixth Amendment requires the presence of counsel during such procedures given their critical nature. Any identification testimony derived from a post-indictment lineup procedure in which a defendant was denied the right to counsel is violative of the Sixth Amendment and is thus inadmissible at trial.

RATIONALE

The Court has long held that the Fifth Amendment was intended to protect a defendant from being forced to testify against him- or herself or otherwise provide incriminating evidence of a "communicative" nature. For example, the Fifth Amendment does not protect a suspect from the state's demand that he or she submit to "fingerprinting, photography, or measurement, to write or speak for identification, to appear in court, to stand, to assume a stance, to walk, or to make a particular gesture." Thus, requiring Wade to repeat language allegedly used by the robber during the lineup procedure in no way violated his Fifth Amendment right to avoid self-incrimination. The question of whether or not the Sixth Amendment required the presence of counsel during a postindictment lineup was, however, an altogether different matter. Most importantly, the Court noted that "[a]s early as *Powell v. Alabama* (1932), we recognized that the period from arraignment to trial was perhaps the most critical period of the proceedings . . . during which the accused requires the guiding hand of counsel." This guiding principle, combined with the potential for unfairness inherent in most identification procedures, led to a conclusion that the best way to protect defendants from any risk of irreparable prejudice was to extend the right to counsel to postindictment lineups. Thus, any identification testimony derived from a postindictment lineup procedure in which a defendant was denied the right to counsel must be excluded from evidence at trial.

CASE SIGNIFICANCE

This case is important insofar as it established the general rule of law that criminal defendants have a right to counsel during any postindictment lineup/identification procedures. Under *Wade,* the filing of formal charges against a defendant was regarded by the Court as a "critical stage" of the adversarial process, thereby triggering this particular aspect of the Sixth Amendment. As a consequence of this determination, it is imperative that authorities know the "status" of a given case before requiring a suspect to participate in a lineup. Where formal charges have been filed, the state must not only give a defendant and his or her attorney advance notice of intent to conduct a lineup, but the attorney must also be allowed to attend in order to ensure that no unfair or prejudicial actions take place. It is worth noting that the opinion in *Wade* failed to specify whether suspects who have not yet been charged with a crime enjoy the same level of constitutional protection.

Instead, this question became the subject of a later case—*Kirby v. Illinois.*

FOSTER v. CALIFORNIA
394 U.S. 440 (1969)

FACTS

Foster was arrested and charged in connection with the armed robbery of a Western Union office after an accomplice turned himself in and confessed to police. Foster was made to appear in a lineup with two other, much shorter men but could not be positively identified as one of the robbers by a lone witness. The witness asked to speak separately with Foster so that he could be more confident in his identification. The two men confronted one another in a separate room, but the witness remained uncertain that Foster was the man who robbed him. A week or so later, a second lineup involving Foster and four other men was conducted. After viewing the participants this time, the witness stated that he was "convinced" Foster was the man. This identification evidence, in conjunction with testimony by the alleged accomplice, was admitted at trial and Foster was convicted. The Supreme Court granted certiorari to determine whether the lineup procedures resulted in a violation of Foster's constitutional rights.

ISSUE

Were the lineup and identification procedures relied upon in the present case so unnecessarily suggestive that they violated the defendant's right to due process?

HOLDING

Yes. Lineup procedures that are suggestive to the point that the resulting identification is all but inevitable violate the suspect's due process rights.

RATIONALE

As a general principle, the Court has previously held that lineup procedures may not be so suggestive as to present an irreparable risk of misidentification and denial of due process. Several factors within the present case led the Court to conclude that Foster's due process rights had been violated. For example, during the initial lineup Foster was made to appear with two men who differed in height. Even more disturbing to the Court was the face-to-face confrontation between Foster and the victim. Finally, the fact that Foster was the only individual from the initial lineup to make a "repeat" appearance in the second lineup was also regarded as highly prejudicial to the procedure's outcome.

CASE SIGNIFICANCE

The facts and decision in this case established threshold standards for determining whether or not a suspect's due process rights have been violated as the result of a prejudicial lineup or identification procedure. The Court's opinion left no doubt that a "lopsided" lineup in which the primary suspect is made to clearly stand out from others creates a prejudicial atmosphere. Further, face-to-face confrontations seem to receive little support as a reliable mechanism for making unbiased identifications. Lastly, the fact that Foster was the only person to appear more than once in any of the lineups had the effect of suggesting to the witness "this is the man!" Accordingly, authorities are strongly discouraged from using such tactics when seeking to obtain an eyewitness or victim identification of a suspect. Measures ensuring that a suspect is not unfairly set apart from other participants in a lineup should be followed. Face-to-face confrontations should also be avoided unless there exists some exigent circumstance precluding a more traditional lineup procedure (for example, the victim is near death or unable to come to the station). Certainly, where doubt as to the impartiality and fairness of a proposed lineup procedure exists, authorities are strongly encouraged to seek guidance from informed state counsel before proceeding. Otherwise, they run the risk of inadvertently violating a suspect's due process rights thereby causing the obtained identification testimony to be excluded at trial.

KIRBY V. ILLINOIS
406 U.S. 682 (1972)

FACTS

Petitioner, Kirby, and a companion, Bean, were stopped by Chicago police and asked for identification. Officers became suspicious when the two men produced documents (social security card and traveler's checks) belonging to another individual not in their immediate company. Unable to convincingly explain how these items came into their possession, the two were arrested and taken to the station house. Upon arrival, the arresting officers learned of a street robbery that had been reported just the day before. The victim, Willie Shard, reported that two men had stolen his wallet containing, among other items, his social security card and some traveler's checks. A police unit was dispatched to Shard's place of employment for purposes of bringing him in to make an identification of the two suspects. As soon as Shard entered the station house, he confirmed to an officer that Kirby and Bean were in fact the two men who had robbed him. At the time of this

identification, neither suspect had been informed of his right to counsel, neither had asked for assistance of counsel, nor was an attorney present in the station house. Kirby and Bean were subsequently indicted for the robbery, received appointed counsel, and pled not guilty. A pretrial motion to suppress Shard's stationhouse identification of the two men was denied and both were found guilty. Kirby's conviction was affirmed by a state appellate court, which found no error in the admission of Shard's testimony regarding how he had identified the two men to police. Specifically, the state appellate court held that the *Wade-Gilbert* per se exclusionary rule did not apply to preindictment lineups. The Supreme Court granted certiorari limited to this question.

ISSUE

Does the *Wade-Gilbert* per se exclusionary rule, which prohibits police from conducting post-indictment lineups in the absence of legal counsel, also apply to preindictment lineups? In other words, does the Sixth Amendment require the presence of a suspect's attorney at preindictment lineups?

HOLDING

No. The Sixth Amendment does not require that a suspect's attorney be present for any preindictment lineups conducted by the police for identification purposes.

RATIONALE

The *Wade-Gilbert* per se exclusionary rule stems from the guarantee of the right to counsel contained in the Sixth Amendment as it is applied to the states through the Fourteenth Amendment. Specifically, the *Wade-Gilbert* rule established the principle that criminal defendants are "entitled to the assistance of counsel at any critical stage of the prosecution, and that a postindictment lineup is such a critical stage. With very little elaboration on the matter, the Court flatly stated that it declined "to import into a routine police investigation an absolute constitutional guarantee historically and rationally applied only after the onset of formal prosecutorial proceedings." The Court noted, however, that its reluctance to apply a per se exclusionary rule to preindictment lineups should not be interpreted as a decision that condones unnecessarily suggestive or prejudicial lineup procedures. Instead, it issued a strong cautionary reminder that such actions were still strictly prohibited by the Fifth Amendment's due process clause.

CASE SIGNIFICANCE

The Court's refusal to extend the right to counsel to preindictment lineups conducted for identification purposes not only signaled a shift in its philosophy regarding suspects' rights but, more importantly, established a bright line standard for the point at which the right to counsel in criminal matters takes effect. Although the Court did not specifically mention the burden that would otherwise be imposed upon law enforcement had it decided to extend the *Wade-Gilbert* per se exclusionary rule to preindictment lineups, it nonetheless seems important to point out that many of the roadside identifications that no doubt occur on a day-to-day basis owe their permissibility to the decision in this case. Thus, it seems reasonable to speculate that had the Court extended the *Wade-Gilbert* per se exclusionary rule to preindictment identifications, the ability of law enforcement personnel to effectively combat crime would have been significantly hampered. Although suspects do not enjoy a right to counsel during preindictment identifications, law enforcement personnel must nonetheless remain cognizant of suggestive behaviors, influential factors, or inappropriate comments that may prejudice the outcome of a lineup. Otherwise, they run a considerable risk of losing the case not on Sixth Amendment grounds but, instead, on violations of the Fifth Amendment's due process clause.

UNITED STATES V. DIONISIO
410 U.S. 1 (1973)

FACTS

A federal grand jury subpoenaed roughly 20 individuals, informing each that he or she was a potential defendant in a criminal prosecution for alleged violation of federal gambling statutes. The witnesses were instructed to read aloud a transcript that would be recorded and compared for identification purposes to voice recordings already received into evidence. Dionisio and other witnesses refused to comply with the order on the grounds that doing so would violate their rights under both the Fourth and Fifth Amendments. The government filed petitions asking that a district court compel the noncooperating witnesses to provide the requested voice exemplars. The district court judge, rejecting Dionisio's argument, directed the witnesses to comply with the grand jury's request. When the witnesses again refused to furnish the voice recordings, they were held in civil contempt and taken into custody. The Seventh Circuit Court of Appeals

subsequently upheld and reversed in part the district court's ruling. Specifically, the court of appeals agreed with the lower court's finding that there was no violation of the Fifth Amendment because a voice exemplar, like a handwriting exemplar or fingerprint, does not constitute evidence of a testimonial or communicative nature. The appeals court did, however, disagree with the lower court's determination that no Fourth Amendment violation had occurred. Instead, it reasoned that the grand jury's request for the voice exemplar violated the Fourth Amendment's reasonableness standard on the grounds that it had subpoenaed such a large number of people in what appeared to be an exploitative abuse of its power. Because this holding by the Seventh Circuit contradicted that of another in the Second Circuit, the Supreme Court granted certiorari.

ISSUE

Does the compelled production of a voice exemplar violate any portion of the Fourth Amendment? Does the compelled production of a voice exemplar violate the Fifth Amendment privilege against self-incrimination?

HOLDING

No. The compelled production of a voice exemplar does not violate any portion of the Fourth Amendment. A grand jury subpoena does not constitute a "seizure." Consequently, a preliminary showing of reasonableness is not required when asking witnesses to provide voice and other noncommunicative exemplars. The compelled production of a voice exemplar does not violate the Fifth Amendment privilege against self-incrimination where such evidence is to be used for identification purposes and not for the testimonial or communicative content of the utterances.

RATIONALE

In reaching the determination that a grand jury subpoena does not constitute a "seizure" under traditional Fourth Amendment analysis, the Court noted that such an order falls considerably short of the detention accompanying formal arrest or even the brief inconvenience that occurs during an investigative stop. With regard to the Fourth Amendment's reasonableness standard, the fact that a grand jury has subpoenaed a large number of witnesses has no constitutional significance. In fact, the Court asserted, a grand jury can subpoena as many witnesses as necessary to meet the objective of returning only well-founded indictments. To otherwise restrict its subpoena powers unnecessarily limits its fact-finding mandate, which in turn impedes the wheels of justice. With regard to the Fifth Amendment issue, the Court largely relied upon its decisions in previous cases of a similar nature. For example, in *Schmerber v. California*, 384 U.S. 757 (1966), the Court held that extraction of blood from an unconsenting DWI suspect did not violate the privilege against self-incrimination. In *Gilbert v. California,* 388 U.S. 263 (1967), the Court held that handwriting exemplars were not protected by the privilege against compulsory self-incrimination. Lastly, in *United States v. Wade*, 388 U.S. 218 (1967), the Court found no constitutional error in requiring a suspect to repeat words used to commit a bank robbery during a lineup for identification purposes. Given that the preceding cases withstood constitutional scrutiny, the Court reasoned, there seemed no need to make an exception under the Fifth Amendment for voice exemplars that are used solely for identification purposes.

CASE SIGNIFICANCE

The Court's decision in this case solidified the principle of law that evidence of a noncommunicative nature (e.g., handwriting, fingerprint, blood/tissue, or voice exemplars) is exempt from the Fifth Amendment privilege against self-incrimination so long as it is used only for purposes of identification. It is important to point out that while police, prosecutors, and other investigative bodies such as a grand jury may lawfully compel a person to provide a voice exemplar, such evidence cannot be introduced as a "confession" or "statement" at trial. It is equally important to note that the Court did not address in the context of this particular case whether suspects were entitled to have legal counsel present when submitting a voice exemplar.

MANSON V. BRATHWAITE
432 U.S. 98 (1977)

FACTS

An undercover Connecticut state trooper assigned to the narcotics division was taken by an informant to an apartment building for purposes of buying drugs. The pair knocked on a third-floor apartment door and was met by an unidentified black male who exchanged drugs for money. During the transaction, the door was opened some 12 to 18 inches and the black male stood no more than two feet away from the trooper for a period of five to seven minutes. Upon leaving the building, the trooper radioed a physical description of the dealer to backup officers. Upon returning to work two days later, the trooper found on his desk a photo of the dealer that had been retrieved from local archives by one of his backup officers. The photo was used for pur-

poses of identifying Brathwaite as the dealer, a statement accepted into evidence without objection at his trial for possession and sale of heroin. Brathwaite was convicted and the state's supreme court affirmed his sentence. Brathwaite subsequently filed a petition for habeas corpus in district court claiming that admission of the identification testimony at trial violated his Fourteenth Amendment due process rights. The district court dismissed the petition. However, the U.S. Court of Appeals for the Second Circuit reversed this holding and ordered that a writ be issued unless the state expressed intent to retry Brathwaite within a reasonable period of time and absent the identification testimony. The U.S. Supreme Court then granted certiorari.

ISSUE

Does the Fourteenth Amendment's due process clause require the per se exclusion of a police officer's testimony where identification of the defendant was based upon a procedure that may have been unnecessarily suggestive?

HOLDING

No. The Fourteenth Amendment does not require the automatic exclusion of testimony based upon a police officer's identification of the defendant even if it was obtained as the result of a procedure that may have been unnecessarily suggestive.

RATIONALE

In the context of this particular case, the Supreme Court noted that there are two possible standards for determining the admissibility of identification testimony resulting from procedures that may have been biased or unnecessarily suggestive. A strict standard would require the automatic (per se) exclusion of any testimony obtained as the result of a biased or suggestive identification procedure. A second standard would determine admissibility of the testimony following consideration of the totality of circumstances surrounding the identification procedure in question. It was the latter of these two standards—one that considers the totality of circumstances—which the Court deemed most appropriate for cases of this nature. Under the totality of circumstances standard, the reliability of the identification is a critical factor. In other words, identification of a defendant arising from a biased or suggestive procedure does not have to be automatically excluded from evidence if it can be shown that the identification possesses certain qualities of reliability. Although these may be greater or fewer in number depending upon the facts of a given case, the Court enunciated five criteria that may be used to establish the reliability of an otherwise questionable identification. These include, but are not limited to: (1) the opportunity to view; (2) the degree of attention; (3) the accuracy of the description; (4) the witness's level of certainty; and (5) the time between the crime and the confrontation. Applying these five criteria to the facts in the present case, the Court concluded that: (1) the undercover trooper had ample opportunity to view the suspect (an elapsed time of several minutes) under adequate lighting; (2) the trooper was a trained observer cognizant of the fact that he would later be called upon to identify the suspect thus prompting him to take especially close note of Brathwaite's distinguishing features; (3) the trooper's oral description of Brathwaite to backup officers was so detailed that one was able to find a photo of him without even having seen him; (4) the trooper was absolutely certain in his identification of Brathwaite both in court and by photograph; and (5) the amount of time that elapsed between the trooper's exchange with Brathwaite and his viewing of the photograph was minimal as compared to days, weeks, or even months. In sum, the Court concluded that these factors created enough reliability to offset any unfairness or risk of error that may have occurred as the result of a suggestive identification procedure. Thus the Supreme Court reversed the decision of the court of appeals, which ultimately had the effect of letting Brathwaite's conviction stand.

CASE SIGNIFICANCE

This case represented an effort on behalf of the Supreme Court to resolve an apparent conflict among lower courts regarding the appropriate standard for determining the admissibility of questionable identification testimony. At the same time, it had important implications for law enforcement. Specifically, the case acknowledged that there will no doubt arise circumstances in which police—for one reason or another—are unable to conduct a lineup that is free from suggestive influence. For example, consider a situation in which the police have apprehended a suspect believed to be responsible for assaulting a victim who is hospitalized and perhaps not expected to live. The police do not have the time to wait for the victim to get better before asking him or her to make an identification. Similarly, they may not be able to bring the victim to the jail or other facility to make an identification because of his or her critical condition. Thus, the only reasonable alternative is to bring the suspect into the hospital room and ask the victim to try and make an identification. Clearly, such an approach is wrought with suggestive elements. However, the Court recognized through its opinion in the present case that an identification from such a procedure need not always be subject to automatic exclusion at trial. Instead, a more tempered approach—one which the Court embraced—allows these types of questionable identifications to be considered under a totality of circumstances to determine whether or not they possess qualities of reliability which offset any risk of misidentification. This is but one of several implications this case posed for law enforcement. The case also reaffirmed the notion that, where possible, investigators should incorporate procedures into the identification process that will negate the claim that a particular lineup was unfairly suggestive. Simple measures, such as ensuring that photo lineups consist of more than one picture (a montage) depicting subjects with physical characteristics roughly similar to those of the primary suspect, will help ensure the admissibility of critical identification testimony at trial. Identification procedures such as those at issue in the present case may be marginally acceptable, but they are not ideal.

UNITED STATES V. CREWS
445 U.S. 463 (1980)

FACTS

Immediately after being assaulted and robbed at gunpoint, the victim notified the police and gave them a full description of her assailant. Several days later, Crews, who matched the suspect's description, was seen by the police around the scene of the crime. After an attempt to photograph him proved unsuccessful, Crews was taken into custody, ostensibly as a suspected truant from school, and was detained at police headquarters, where he was briefly questioned, photographed, and then released. Thereafter, the victim identified Crews' photograph as that of her assailant. Crews was again taken into custody and at a court-ordered lineup was identified by the victim. Crews was then indicted for armed robbery and other offenses. On Crews' pretrial motion to suppress all identification testimony, the trial court found that the initial detention at the police station constituted an arrest without probable cause and accordingly ruled that the products of that arrest—the photographic and lineup identifications—could not be introduced at trial, but further held that the victim's ability to identify Crews in court was based upon independent recollection untainted by the intervening identifications and that therefore such testimony was admissible. At trial, the victim once more identified Crews as her assailant, and he was convicted of armed robbery. The District of Columbia Court of Appeals reversed, holding that the in-court identification testimony should have been excluded as a product of the violation

Chapter Sixteen ✦ *Pretrial Identification Procedures* 119

of Crews' Fourth Amendment rights. The U.S. Supreme Court then granted certiorari.

ISSUE

Should the in-court identification testimony have been excluded, since it may have been tainted by earlier illegal photographic and lineup identifications?

HOLDING

No. The in-court identification need not be suppressed as the fruit of Crews' concededly unlawful arrest but is admissible because the police's knowledge of Crews' identity and the victim's independent recollections of him both antedated the unlawful arrest and were thus untainted by the constitutional violation.

RATIONALE

The victim's presence in the courtroom at Crews' trial was not the product of any police misconduct. Her identity was known long before there was any official misconduct, and her presence in court was thus not traceable to any Fourth Amendment violation. Nor did the illegal arrest infect the victim's ability to give accurate identification testimony. At trial, she merely retrieved her mnemonic representation of the assailant formed at the time of the crime, compared it to the figure of Crews in the courtroom, and positively identified him as the robber. Insofar as Crews challenges his own presence at trial, he cannot claim immunity from prosecution simply because his appearance in court was precipitated by an unlawful arrest. Crews is not himself a suppressible "fruit," and the illegality of his detention cannot deprive the government of the opportunity to prove his guilt through the introduction of evidence wholly untainted by the police misconduct.

CASE SIGNIFICANCE

This case is important because it introduced the "independent source" exception to the exclusionary rule. Under this exception, an initial police illegality may not prevent the introduction of seized evidence, if the prosecution can establish that the police could have learned of the evidence through lawful means. Thus police misconduct may not necessarily bar the introduction of important evidence. ✦

DISCUSSION QUESTIONS

1. Why do suspects not enjoy the right to have an attorney present during pretrial identification procedures?

2. Why are suspects entitled to have an attorney present during identification procedures once they have been charged with a crime?

3. What measures can the police take to make sure that pretrial identification procedures are not unduly prejudicial?

4. What practical measures can be taken during a pretrial lineup to minimize claims of prejudicial influence when the suspect of primary interest has a unique identifying characteristic that clearly sets him or her apart from others (e.g., physical handicap, especially tall/short, hair color or style, etc.)? ✦

Chapter Seventeen
Right to Counsel

Powell et al. v. Alabama, 287 U.S. 45 (1932)

Gideon v. Wainwright, 372 U.S. 335 (1963)

Escobedo v. Illinois, 378 U.S. 478 (1964)

Massiah v. United States, 377 U.S. 201 (1964)

United States v. Henry, 447 U.S. 264 (1980)

INTRODUCTION

The right to counsel is specifically enumerated by the Sixth Amendment to the Constitution, which states in relevant part, "In all criminal prosecutions, the accused shall enjoy the right to . . . the assistance of counsel for his defense." Initially, this provision applied only to criminal trials. However, it has since been extended to other "critical stages" of the justice process. This chapter traces the evolution of this right from its initial application in *Powell et al. v. Alabama* to *United States v. Henry*.

In *Powell et al. v. Alabama*, also known as the "Scottsboro Boys" case, the Supreme Court held that the denial of legal counsel in a capital case violated the standards of due process. The issue was revisited three decades later in *Gideon v. Wainwright*, a case involving an indigent defendant who had been denied assistance of counsel during trial for felony burglary in Florida. In that matter, the Supreme Court reversed Gideon's conviction, concluding that the right to counsel applies not only to capital cases, but to felony prosecutions as well. *Escobedo v. Illinois* and *Massiah v. United States* were both decided the very next term. In *Escobedo*, the justices ruled that a suspect has the right to request and confer with an attorney during custodial interrogations. In *Massiah*, the Court held that the Sixth Amendment prohibits the government from surreptitiously eliciting incriminating statements once an individual has secured the assistance of counsel. More recently, the Court in *United States v. Henry* prohibited the government from enlisting the assistance of jailhouse informants for purposes of obtaining incriminating statements from a defendant.

Although limited in number compared to decisions in other areas of criminal procedure, the cases included in this chapter established the parameters of a very important area of the law. In particular, they defined the boundaries within which police and prosecutors must operate when seeking to obtain confessions lest their actions come into conflict with Sixth Amendment jurisprudence. Where such established rules are disregarded, even with the best or most naive of intentions, there exists likelihood that the obtained information will be later ruled as inadmissible. Accordingly, representatives of the government must remain keenly aware of these cases at the Supreme Court level, as well as those guiding state-level procedure. ✦

POWELL ET AL. V. ALABAMA
287 U.S. 45 (1932)

FACTS

Powell was one of nine black youths charged with the rape of two white girls. The judge presiding over the arraignment appointed all members of the local bar to serve as legal counsel for the boys although no specific attorney was named until the day of trial. All nine defendants were convicted and sentenced to death. The Alabama Supreme Court affirmed the convictions, and the U.S. Supreme Court granted certiorari.

ISSUE

Does the denial of legal counsel in a capital case constitute a violation of due process under the Fourteenth Amendment?

HOLDING

Yes. The denial of legal counsel in a capital case constitutes a violation of due process under the Fourteenth Amendment.

RATIONALE

In deciding this case, the Supreme Court first noted that criminal defendants should, at a minimum, be afforded the opportunity to secure their own legal counsel. Because Powell and his codefendants were financially unable to secure their own attorneys, combined with the fact that the trial court specifically appointed none, the men were effectively rendered incapable of protecting their liberty interest in what was certainly a serious criminal matter. Furthermore, an Alabama state law required that capital defendants who are unable to secure their own attorney be appointed legal counsel by the trial court. Given these circumstances, the U.S. Supreme Court reversed the nine convictions on Fourteenth Amendment grounds.

CASE SIGNIFICANCE

This early decision, which has since come to be known as the infamous "Scottsboro Boys" case, affirmed the constitutional principle that criminal defendants, especially those facing capital charges, are entitled to the assistance of legal counsel. Where a defendant is unable to secure an attorney it becomes the affirmative duty of the trial court to appoint one. An interesting aspect about this case is that it was decided not on Sixth Amendment grounds, as one might initially expect, but instead, on Fourteenth Amendment grounds; at the time the *Powell* case was heard, the Sixth Amendment and its attending rights did not apply to state criminal proceedings. Thus, the Fourteenth Amendment was the only mechanism available at the time to intervene in state judicial matters. Over the years and decades that have elapsed since this case was decided, the Supreme Court has selectively incorporated specific portions of the Bill of Rights to the states so that today such claims are more appropriately litigated on Sixth rather than Fourteenth Amendment grounds.

GIDEON V. WAINWRIGHT
372 U.S. 335 (1963)

FACTS

Gideon was arrested and charged with felony burglary. At trial, he requested that the court appoint legal counsel based upon his indigent status. The request was denied on grounds that Florida law only required appointment of counsel for indigent defendants charged with a capital crime. The trial proceeded with Gideon representing himself as adequately as possible. Pronounced guilty and sentenced to prison, Gideon filed an unsuccessful writ of habeas corpus with the state supreme court alleging violation of his Sixth Amendment right to counsel. The U.S. Supreme Court then granted certiorari.

ISSUE

Does the Sixth Amendment require that legal counsel be appointed to represent an indigent defendant in state felony prosecutions?

HOLDING

Yes. The Sixth Amendment requires the appointment of legal counsel to represent an indigent defendant facing prosecution on state felony charges.

RATIONALE

In deciding that indigent defendants are entitled to court appointed counsel in state felony prosecutions,

the Supreme Court overturned its previous ruling in the case of *Betts v. Brady,* 316 U.S. 455 (1942). In *Betts,* the Court held that a refusal to appoint counsel for an indigent defendant charged with a felony did not violate the due process clause of the Fourteenth Amendment. In making this shift, it was specifically asserted that "in our adversary system of criminal justice, any person haled [*sic*] into court, who is too poor to hire a lawyer, cannot be assured a fair trial unless counsel is provided for him." Consequently, the Sixth Amendment right to counsel in felony cases was deemed so fundamental to the American system of justice that it should also be applied to state prosecutions.

CASE SIGNIFICANCE

This landmark decision applied the Sixth Amendment right to counsel to state felony prosecutions. Not only did this mean that defendants are entitled to legal representation in such cases, but that an attorney must be provided free of charge for those who cannot afford one on their own means. This protection was afforded on a limited basis to defendants in capital cases as a result of the Court's previous decision in *Powell et al. v. Alabama. Powell,* however, was decided on Fourteenth Amendment grounds, whereas *Gideon* is based squarely on the Sixth Amendment. Thus, the *Gideon* case serves as an example of how the protections contained in the Bill of Rights have been selectively incorporated to the states by a judicially active and liberal Supreme Court. Finally, it is important to note that the Court did not specifically define what level of income (or lack thereof) constitutes "indigence" for purposes of determining whether or not an individual qualifies for court-appointed representation.

ESCOBEDO V. ILLINOIS
378 U.S. 478 (1964)

FACTS

Escobedo was arrested by police in connection with the shooting death of his brother-in-law. Escobedo was never informed of his right to remain silent and, although his attorney was present in the building at the time of questioning, his repeated requests for assistance of counsel were refused. An incriminating statement made to a government attorney was admitted at trial and Escobedo was convicted of murder. The state supreme court initially reversed the conviction, but later accepted the state's motion for a rehearing whereupon it allowed the conviction to stand. The U.S. Supreme Court then granted certiorari.

ISSUE

Does the Sixth Amendment require that police allow a suspect to confer with an attorney if one has been requested during the course of a custodial interrogation?

HOLDING

Yes. The police must allow a suspect to speak with an attorney if one is requested during the course of a custodial interrogation.

RATIONALE

In determining that suspects are constitutionally entitled to request and speak with an attorney during custodial interrogation, the Supreme Court considered several important factors. For example, it was noted that the investigation centered squarely on Escobedo as a primary suspect. Secondly, he was subjected to questioning in an environment intended to elicit incriminating statements. Finally, Escobedo was not informed of his absolute right to remain silent. These findings, taken into consideration with one another, amounted to a violation of his Sixth Amendment right to counsel requiring reversal of the conviction.

CASE SIGNIFICANCE

This landmark decision is credited with forming the nexus between the Fifth Amendment right to remain silent and the Sixth Amendment right to counsel during custodial interrogation that would later culminate in *Miranda v. Arizona,* 384 U.S. 436 (1966). Although some regarded the *Escobedo* decision as an important step forward in protecting the rights of suspects during custodial interrogation, others criticized the ruling on the grounds that it unduly complicated law enforcement efforts. Part of the reason that *Escobedo* is today overshadowed by *Miranda* is that it left several important issues unresolved, primary among them being the question of exactly when and under what types of circumstances the right to counsel becomes applicable. Does it apply only to serious crimes such as rape, robbery, and murder or does it also apply to petty offenses such as vandalism, shoplifting, and the like? What exactly constitutes a custodial interrogation and, similarly, at what point does one become the "focus" of an investigation? Because of these and other lingering questions, the decision is not as routinely relied upon today as it was initially. Instead, as noted earlier, it is credited with laying a foundation for the Court's decision in *Miranda* and its progeny.

MASSIAH V. UNITED STATES
377 U.S. 201 (1964)

FACTS

While employed as a merchant marine, Massiah conspired with others to smuggle drugs into the country aboard a U.S. vessel. Acting upon this information, federal customs officers boarded and searched the ship when it arrived in port. The expected cache of drugs was discovered, leading to Massiah's indictment. He was arraigned, retained a lawyer, pled not guilty, and was released on bail. Several days later one of Massiah's coconspirators began cooperating with the government by allowing agents to electronically eavesdrop on a postindictment conversation between the two men. During the conversation, Massiah made incriminating statements that were introduced over objection at trial. Massiah was convicted in federal district court and a federal court of appeals affirmed. The U.S. Supreme Court then granted certiorari.

ISSUE

Do incriminating statements surreptitiously elicited by the police from a suspect who has already been charged with a crime and retained an attorney violate the Sixth Amendment right to counsel?

HOLDING

Yes. The Sixth Amendment prohibits the police from surreptitiously obtaining incriminating statements from a suspect who has previously been charged with a crime and retained an attorney.

RATIONALE

In holding that the surreptitiously obtained incriminating statements violated Massiah's constitutional rights, the Court referred to its prior decision in *Spano v. New York,* 360 U.S. 315 (1959) overturning the petitioner's conviction on grounds that he had confessed to murder after being indicted and without the benefit of legal counsel. Also cited was the case of *Powell et al. v. Alabama,* in which the Court reversed the capital conviction of nine defendants on grounds that they had been denied legal counsel during trial. Although these two cases were decided on Fourteenth Amendment grounds, it was reasoned that the need for assistance of counsel during postindictment activities such as those in the immediate matter was so great that it could not reasonably be ignored. Accordingly, the Court ruled that the Sixth Amendment right to counsel was directly applicable to the facts present in Massiah's case resulting in reversal of the federal conviction.

Case Significance

This case prohibited the police from surreptitiously gathering incriminating evidence from a suspect who has already been indicted for a crime. Once charged, the police cannot elicit incriminating statements from a suspect without his or her attorney being present. If, however, the suspect has not been charged, the government behavior prohibited by this ruling would have otherwise been deemed constitutionally acceptable. One last point to note is that this case involved the use of an electronic eavesdropping device, thereby also raising a Fourth Amendment issue. However, the Court did not address this particular issue because of the manner in which it resolved the case. Instead, this issue has been addressed by an altogether different line of cases beginning with *Katz v. United States,* 389 U.S. 347 (1967).

United States v. Henry
447 U.S. 264 (1980)

Facts

Henry was indicted on federal bank robbery charges and was being held in jail awaiting trial when he made incriminating statements to a jailhouse informant operating under the guidance of government agents. The informant testified against Henry, who was convicted. Henry moved to have the senteced vacated on grounds that his Sixth Amendment right to counsel had been violated as a result of the informant's actions. A federal district court denied the motion but the court of appeals reversed, citing *Massiah v. United States* as controlling precedent. The U.S. Supreme Court then granted certiorari.

Issue

Does the use of a jailhouse informant operating under guidance of government for purposes of gathering incriminating information from a criminal defendant violate the Sixth Amendment right to counsel?

Holding

Yes. The government cannot enlist the assistance of a jailhouse informant for purposes of gathering incriminating information from a criminal defendant.

Rationale

The Supreme Court's decision that the government cannot enlist the assistance of a jailhouse informant for purposes of gathering incriminating information was predicated on two factors. First, it was concluded that the informant acted as an agent of the government. Secondly, Henry was under indictment when the informant gathered the incriminating information, thereby rendering his statements inadmissible under *Massiah v. United States.*

Case Significance

This case limited the use of jailhouse informants by police. More specifically, it prohibited the police from actively enlisting the assistance of jailhouse informants for purposes of gathering incriminating information from other prisoners. It should be noted, however, that the decision did not appear to prohibit the use of such information so long as the government does not actively solicit individuals to work on its behalf. Equally important, if not more so, is the fact that once an individual is charged, he or she may not be "questioned"—even by another prisoner—without having an attorney present. ✦

Discussion Questions

1. Why is the right to assistance of counsel of such vital importance in capital cases as compared to misdemeanor cases? Where should the line be drawn? That is, to what types of cases should the right apply and, conversely, to what types of cases (if any) should it not?

2. In constitutional terms, what is the major difference between the police prompting a jailhouse informant to obtain incriminating evidence or statements from a defendant, as compared to a situation in which the informant gathers the incriminating evidence on his or her own without having been asked to do so by agents of the state?

3. Describe and discuss the Supreme Court's rationale in extending the Sixth Amendment right to include felony prosecutions when in the past this right had only applied to capital cases.

4. Discuss how the Supreme Court's decision in *Escobedo* relates to the decision in *Miranda v. Arizona.* How are the two cases related to one another in chronological, constitutional, and practical terms? ✦

Chapter Eighteen
The Development and Scope of the *Miranda* Warnings

INTRODUCTION

With little room for disagreement, *Miranda v. Arizona* has been one of the most influential criminal procedure cases decided by the Supreme Court in recent history. The practical effects of this 5–4 decision on day-to-day police operations have been so profound that it has taken almost 50 years to decipher exactly how far and in what contexts the decreed protections actually apply. Contrast this enduring need for clarification against the fact that average members of the public can generally recite key phrases of the decision with amazing accuracy, and it is not surprising to find that many police officers widely bemoan its perceived restraining effect on their ability to fight crime.

The cases included in this chapter are of two broad types—those affirming the *Miranda* decision, and those weakening it. A history of the warnings' development is traced through cases such as *Brown v. Mississippi* (confessions obtained by torture are not admissible), *Edwards v. Arizona* (officers may not reinitiate contact with a suspect who has previously invoked the right to remain silent), and *Michigan v. Jackson* (the police may not interrogate a suspect who has asked for assistance of counsel until he or she has had an opportunity to meet with an attorney). By comparison, a number of decisions eroding the warnings' protective intent are briefed as well. These include cases such as *New York v. Quarles* (concern for public safety outweighs strict adherence to the *Miranda* decision), *Duckworth v. Eagan* (it is not necessary for the warnings to be recited exactly as they appeared in the original case), and *Pennsylvania v. Muniz* (the police ask routine questions of DWI suspects and videotape the responses without having to inform arrestees of their *Miranda* rights).

In summarizing these and the dozen or so other decisions highlighted within this chapter, three important points bear mention. First, the clearly diverse array of cases that follow have contributed to the development of an extremely confusing area of the law—one that requires constant updating and review by law enforcement personnel in all types of investigative and enforcement assignments. Second, unlike the exclusionary rule whose application is at least somewhat tempered by the "good faith" exception, the judiciary rarely gives latitude to officers who are blasé or haphazard in their respect for a suspect's right to remain silent. Last, whether or not one agrees with the *Miranda* decision and its progeny of related cases, the established principles it stands for now serve as immutable facts of life in police work. ✦

Brown v. Mississippi
297 U.S. 278 (1936)

Facts

Brown was confronted at his home by a deputy sheriff who asked that he accompany him to another residence where a murder had taken place. Once at the scene, Brown was accused of the crime and twice hanged from a tree until he was ready to talk. Once lowered to the ground, Brown was tied to the tree and whipped before being set free. Several days later the deputy returned to Brown's residence and placed him under arrest. The deputy beat Brown again while en route to the jail until he finally confessed to the murder. Unbeknownst to Brown, two other men were also arrested and beaten until they confessed. Despite testifying that the confessions had been beaten out of them, the three men were convicted and sentenced to death. The Mississippi Supreme Court affirmed the conviction and the U.S. Supreme Court granted certiorari.

Issue

Were the confessions, obtained by way of physical torture, properly admitted into evidence?

Holding

No. Confessions that are obtained by way of physical torture, coercion, or brutality on the part of law enforcement officials are not admissible at trial under the Fourteenth Amendment's due process clause.

Rationale

In deciding that physical brutality automatically renders a confession inadmissible at trial, the Supreme Court noted that although states are generally free to run their courts as they see fit, they are nonetheless required to observe certain fundamental constitutional principles. Chief among these is the right of a defendant to be free from physical torture aimed at obtaining a confession. Similarly, the state may not deny a defendant the assistance of legal counsel. The absence of such fundamental protections in Brown's case, the Court reasoned, amounted to a clear denial of due process, requiring reversal of the conviction.

Case Significance

This case, decided in 1936, established the principle of law that confessions obtained by way of physical torture, coercion, or brutality on the part of law enforcement officials are inadmissible at trial under the Fourteenth Amendment's due process clause. Although representing a clear step toward eliminating coerced confessions, it was not until the Supreme Court rendered its decision in *Miranda v. Arizona* some 30 years later that the full weight of the Constitution would be brought to bear. It is important to note, however, that the Court prohibited only those confessions obtained by physically coercive means as compared to those more subtly obtained by psychologically coercive means. Despite this limitation, the *Brown* decision stands as a landmark case upholding the rights of criminal defendants to be free from the injustice suffered as a result of being physically coerced into making a false confession.

Miranda v. Arizona
384 U.S. 436 (1966)

Facts

Miranda was taken into police custody in connection with a kidnapping and sexual assault. Interrogated at length by detectives, he eventually provided a full written confession that was admitted at trial resulting in conviction on both charges. Miranda appealed, but the state court upheld his conviction. The U.S. Supreme Court then granted certiorari.

Issue

Must the police inform a suspect of his or her dual constitutional rights to legal representation and protection from self-incrimination during custodial interrogation?

Holding

Yes. The police must inform a suspect of his or her constitutional right to legal representation and protection from self-incrimination during custodial interrogation. Any incriminating statements obtained in violation of these rights are inadmissible at trial.

Rationale

In ruling that prosecutors are constitutionally prohibited from introducing incriminating admissions obtained during custodial interrogation from an individual who has not been advised of his or her right to avoid self-incrimination under the Fifth Amendment and to legal representation under the Sixth Amendment, the Supreme Court scrutinized the coercive conditions under which such statements are generally obtained. Specifically, the Court reviewed a litany of questionable tactics employed by investigators to "persuade" a suspect to talk about and/or confess to involvement in a given crime. Given the long history with which the Fifth Amendment's privilege against self-incrimination had been applied to trial proceedings, it seemed only reasonable to extend its protection to settings such as custodial interrogation where it was also needed. In conjunction with extending the Fifth Amendment privilege against self-incrimination, the Court spelled out the language of the warning that must be given to suspects prior to custodial interrogation. Specifically, a suspect must be informed that: he or she has the right to remain silent; anything he or she says will be used against him or her in court; he or she has the right to consult with a lawyer and to have the lawyer present during interrogation; and if he or she cannot afford an attorney one will be appointed.

In addition to this language, the Court admonished officers that if a suspect invokes the right to remain silent prior to or during the interrogation, all questioning must immediately cease. In the event that a suspect chooses not to invoke these rights and allows the interrogation to proceed without requesting an attorney, the government bears the burden of proving that these rights were both knowingly and intelligently waived. Finally, the option to rescind a waiver of these rights rests with the suspect so that, at any time, he or she may invoke the privilege to avoid self-incrimination and request the presence of an attorney. Where any of these rights are violated, the obtained statements will be inadmissible at trial.

Case Significance

Arguably one of the most significant rulings of the due process revolution, *Miranda* is so widely recognized by the general public that many can recite portions of its language from memory. Unfortunately, however, a considerable degree of misconception surrounds its provisions despite the uncommon specificity with which the opinion was written. For example, many believe that *Miranda* applies in its entirety any time they are approached by the police. It is thought that officers must always warn an individual before asking even the most innocuous of questions. This is, of course, not true. Instead (and as other cases in this chapter illustrate), the police are required to warn individuals only during custodial interrogation—*Miranda* does not apply to roadside questioning during a traffic stop, nor when asking routine questions as part of the booking procedure. This misinformation, attributable in large part to the popular media and fictionalized television portrayals, leads to much controversy between the police and those with whom they come into contact. Finally, although the decision is widely looked upon by crime-control advocates as unnecessarily hindering the law enforcement mission, it has nonetheless served to curtail otherwise questionable tactics previously used to extract confessions, thereby enhancing ethical standards within the profession.

Edwards v. Arizona
451 U.S. 477 (1981)

Facts

Edwards was arrested by police on a warrant for the offenses of robbery, burglary, and first-degree murder. Having been informed of his *Miranda* rights upon arrival at the stationhouse, Edwards willingly submitted to questioning regarding his involvement in the alleged offenses. The officer conducting the interrogation told Edwards he had been implicated by another suspect also in custody. Edwards gave a taped statement denying his involvement but nonetheless offered to "make a deal." Lacking the authority to enter into such an agreement, the officer allowed Edwards to call a county attorney. The record does not provide any details regarding the nature of this call other than to indicate that after a few brief moments Edwards hung up and stated, "I want an attorney before making a deal." The investigating officer dutifully ceased the interrogation and returned Edwards to his cell. The following morning, two altogether different detectives arrived at the jail requesting to see Edwards, who stated that he did not want to talk to anyone. The jailer conveying the message told Edwards that "he had" to talk to the detectives. The pair of officers informed Edwards of his *Miranda* rights a second time, followed by a request that he talk with them about the alleged offenses. Edwards asked that he be allowed to hear the taped statement of his accomplice. The officers played the tape for several minutes, whereupon Edwards agreed to make an oral statement on the condition that it not be recorded. The detectives informed him that it was irrelevant whether or not the statement was recorded since they could still testify in court as to anything he said. Edwards stated that he would tell the detectives whatever they wanted to know but reaffirmed his demand that the statement not be recorded. Detectives accommodated this condition and Edwards offered information implicating his involvement in the crimes. Prior to trial, Edwards moved to suppress the statement on the basis that officers had violated his *Miranda* rights by returning to question him a second time without allowing him access to counsel. The trial court granted the motion to suppress, but later reversed the ruling when presented with a controlling decision by a superior Arizona court. The statement was admitted at trial and Edwards was convicted. The state's supreme court, considering the matter on appeal, determined that Edwards had indeed invoked his right to remain silent and have counsel present during the initial interrogation. Because the altogether different pair of detectives who visited Edwards the next morning correctly informed him of his rights which he then voluntarily waived, the Arizona Supreme Court upheld the decision of the trial court to allow his confession into evidence and the convictions were affirmed. The U.S. Supreme Court then granted certiorari.

Issue

Are officers prohibited from reinitiating contact with a suspect once he or she has invoked the right to remain silent and have the assistance of counsel during custodial interrogation?

HOLDING

Yes. Officers may not reinitiate contact with a suspect who has previously invoked the right to remain silent and have the assistance of counsel during custodial interrogation. In other words, once a suspect states that he or she desires legal representation during the course of custodial interrogation, the questioning must stop immediately and may not resume until the request has been satisfied even if only to inquire whether or not the individual has had a change of mind and wants to confess. The conviction was overturned.

RATIONALE

The Court's decision in *Miranda* established the principle of law that criminal suspects not only have the right to remain silent, but also to have legal counsel present while undergoing custodial interrogation by state agents. Once these rights are invoked, all questioning must immediately cease until such time as an attorney is present. In the event that a suspect chooses to waive these rights, the burden of demonstrating that this decision was both informed and voluntary is placed upon the state. In the immediate case, neither the trial court nor the state supreme court undertook an inquiry to determine if Edwards had made the waiver in an informed and voluntary manner. Instead, both courts erroneously assumed that the waiver met these criteria based solely upon the fact that Edwards was responsive to a police-initiated follow-up interrogation. Consequently, the decision of the Arizona Supreme Court that Edwards had knowingly and freely waived his right to the presence of counsel during the second interrogation was overturned.

CASE SIGNIFICANCE

The Court's decision in the *Edwards* case had several notable implications. First, it clearly reaffirmed the *Miranda* decision and its progeny to the extent that once a suspect invokes the right to remain silent and requests the presence of legal counsel, all questioning must immediately cease until such time as an attorney is physically present. Second, it established "bright line" procedures for how state agents are to act in these types of situations. More specifically, the case established the clear and unequivocal standard that once these joint rights are invoked, officers are prohibited from reinitiating contact and inquiry with the suspect even if they again inform him or her anew of his or her *Miranda* rights. For courts and the judges who preside over them, the decision helps clarify previously estab-

lished guidelines for determining whether or not a suspect's waiver of these rights was both voluntary and informed. Third, the decision serves as a prophylactic that protects suspects from the pressures inherent in the custodial environment. In the absence of such protection, the Court feared that suspects will eventually waive their rights and confess to police in the absence of counsel during follow-up interrogation sessions simply because they have been worn down. Thus, one might imagine a situation in which a suspect invokes the right to remain silent and have counsel present during questioning. The interview might then stop only to be resumed at a later time by other officers who again read the *Miranda* warning and proceed with questioning until such time as the rights are again invoked. Still later, other officers might again do the same until such time as the suspect waives his rights because he senses that he will never be presented with an attorney during the interrogations. A fourth implication specifically noted in the Court's opinion centers upon the issue of initiation—that is, who undertakes the subsequent contact in which the rights are waived and a confession is proffered. Writing for the Court, Justice White noted that the protections established by *Edwards* would not apply in situations where the suspect initiates subsequent contact, conversation, or communication with the police. In the final analysis, this decision prevents police and state agents from repeatedly interrogating a suspect who has invoked the right to remain silent and have counsel present during such questioning, even if they inform him or her of his or her rights anew each and every time. It also has the effect of prohibiting the police from even checking in on a suspect who is in custody to see if he or she has had a "change of heart" about wanting to talk.

SOUTH DAKOTA V. NEVILLE
459 U.S. 553 (1983)

FACTS

Neville was stopped by officers for running a stop sign. Unable to satisfactorily perform a series of field sobriety tests, he was arrested, informed of his *Miranda* rights, and asked to submit to a blood-alcohol test. Neville refused, stating that he was too drunk to pass the test. Under South Dakota law, the fact that a DWI arrestee refuses to submit to a blood-alcohol test may be introduced into evidence at trial. In Neville's case, however, the trial court judge suppressed such evidence on the grounds that officers had failed to inform him of the consequences for refusing to take the test. The state supreme court affirmed the suppression order on grounds that the introduction of such evidence would violate the Fifth Amendment protection to avoid self-incrimination. The U.S. Supreme Court then granted certiorari.

ISSUE

Does the Fifth Amendment privilege against self-incrimination prohibit the state from introducing evidence that a DWI defendant refused to take a blood-alcohol test? Does an officer's failure to inform a DWI suspect that refusal to take a blood-alcohol test may later be introduced as evidence at trial constitute a violation of due process?

HOLDING

No. Admission into evidence of a DWI defendant's refusal to take a blood-alcohol test does not violate the Fifth Amendment right to avoid self-incrimination. The failure of an officer to inform a DWI suspect that refusal to take a blood-alcohol test may be introduced at trial does not constitute a violation of due process.

RATIONALE

The U.S. Supreme Court overturned the South Dakota Supreme Court's decision prohibiting prosecutors from introducing into evidence the fact that a DWI defendant refused to take a blood-alcohol test. Specifically, the Court reasoned that such evidence does not violate the Fifth Amendment right to avoid self-incrimination due to the fact that an officer's request to take the blood-alcohol test is not of a coercive nature. Because the Fifth Amendment is limited to prohibiting the use of physical or moral compulsion exerted on the person asserting the privilege, its protection does not apply to the facts in Neville's case. In other words, an officer's request that a DWI suspect take a blood-alcohol test is no different than asking someone to submit to fingerprinting. A suspect who refuses to be fingerprinted may have this evidence introduced against him or her at trial without violating the Fifth Amendment. The same rules apply to the present case. Finally, the Court also ruled that it is not fundamentally unfair for the prosecution to use a suspect's refusal to take the blood-alcohol test as evidence at trial even though he or she was not specifically warned of its potential use. This finding stems from the fact that the defendant's right to refuse the test is a matter of grace bestowed by the state legislature, and an officer's failure to warn the suspect of its potential use does not constitute a promise that the refusal will not be used as evidence at trial.

CASE SIGNIFICANCE

The decision in this case not only endorsed the growing practice among states to require that DWI suspects provide a sample of their blood, breath, or urine for purposes of determining blood-alcohol content, but it also permitted the introduction of one's refusal to submit a sample as evidence suggesting guilt at trial. Consistent with the trend to more harshly deter and punish DWI, offenders are now left with no choice in the matter—either submit a sample and run the risk of disclosing one's guilt, or refuse the request and run the risk of refusal being used as suggestive evidence of guilt when the case comes to trial. A second implication raised by this decision involves day-to-day police procedure in the processing of DWI cases and evidence. Specifically, it clarified the fact that officers are not required to inform DWI suspects of all potential consequences of the decisions they make during the documentation stage.

BERKEMER V. MCCARTY
468 U.S. 420 (1984)

FACTS

An Ohio state trooper observed McCarty's vehicle being operated in an erratic manner consistent with drunk driving. Once stopped, the trooper asked McCarty to exit the vehicle—a request that was fulfilled despite considerable difficulty maintaining balance on the operator's part. The trooper decided that McCarty would be taken into custody and was not free to leave the scene but did not announce his intention until McCarty had clearly failed several standardized field sobriety tests. When asked if he was under the influence of drugs or alcohol during the course of this roadside detention, McCarty admitted that he had recently consumed two beers and smoked some marijuana. McCarty was placed under arrest and transported to jail, where a subsequent test failed to detect any alcohol in his bloodstream. The trooper continued asking questions of McCarty, who made incriminating statements about his condition in the absence of being given the *Miranda* warnings. McCarty was charged with a misdemeanor offense for operating a vehicle under the influence of drugs and/or alcohol. At trial, McCarty entered a motion to have the incriminating statements excluded from consideration on the basis that he had not been informed of his rights under *Miranda*. The trial court rejected this claim, McCarty pled no contest to the charges, and he was convicted. The conviction was affirmed on appeal by the county court and the Ohio Supreme Court denied review. Seeking habeas corpus relief in federal district court, the petition for review was denied but then reversed by the Sixth Circuit Court of Appeals, which held that the *Miranda* warning must be given to all individuals prior to custodial interrogation regardless of whether or not the offense alleged is a felony or misdemeanor. The court of appeals vacated the conviction but failed to specify which statements, if any, made by McCarty could be admitted at retrial. The U.S. Supreme Court then granted certiorari.

ISSUES

Two issues were at stake in this case: (1) Must the *Miranda* warning be given to a suspect prior to custodial interrogation regarding involvement in a misdemeanor offense? In simple terms, do the police have to read misdemeanor suspects their rights before asking them questions about their involvement in the offense?; and (2) Does the roadside questioning of a motorist who has been lawfully detained for a traffic violation trigger the *Miranda* doctrine? In simple terms, do police officers have to read motorists the *Miranda* warning every time they make a traffic stop?

HOLDING

Yes, and no. As to the first issue, the Court held that suspects are entitled to the procedural safeguards established under *Miranda* any time they are exposed to custodial interrogation regardless of whether the offense alleged is classified as a felony or misdemeanor. As to the second issue, the Court held that the roadside questioning of a motorist who is detained pursuant to a lawful traffic stop does not constitute a custodial interrogation. Consequently, officers are not required to inform traffic violators of their *Miranda* rights.

RATIONALE

In *Miranda v. Arizona,* the Supreme Court announced a principle of law designed to protect criminal suspects from the coercive pressures inherent in custodial interrogations that might otherwise give rise to self-incrimination—a protection specifically guaranteed by the Fifth Amendment. This principle has been affirmed over the years by a number of associated cases. In this particular matter, the Court was asked to create an exception to the general rule that suspects must be informed of their constitutional rights under *Miranda* when exposed to custodial interrogation related to involvement in a misdemeanor offense. The Court flatly rejected making such an exception on the basis that doing so would "substantially undermine" the simplicity of the *Miranda* rule. Furthermore, the Court reasoned, there often arise situations in which officers at the time of arrest or interrogation may be uncertain as to which charge (e.g., a felony or misdemeanor) is most appropriate. The example provided by the Court to illustrate this point is one in which an intoxicated driver is involved in a motor vehicle accident. Depending upon

the facts surrounding the accident and its outcome, the driver might be charged with a misdemeanor if the behavior in question is determined to be only negligent in intent. Alternatively, if someone dies as a result of the accident or the behavior in question is determined to be reckless in its intent, then a felony charge is in order. In such ambiguous situations, officers might have to ask probative questions that, if answered by a suspect in the absence of being read the *Miranda* warning, could be self-incriminating. Another scenario envisioned by the justices was one in which a seemingly minor offense gradually escalated into one of a more serious nature. The question would then become one of determining the point at which the *Miranda* Rule should be applied. Last, the Court also expressed reluctance to create the proposed exception on the basis that doing so would create a situation in which affected cases would have to be so closely scrutinized that they would be disruptive of the law enforcement function. Thus, the Court did not see fit to alter the existing rule's simplistic nature. Accordingly, the court held that officers must inform criminal suspects of their *Miranda* rights when conducting a custodial interrogation regardless of the severity of the alleged offense.

In seeking to resolve the second issue—that of determining whether or not traffic stops constitute a form of custodial interrogation thereby triggering the requirement that officers inform motorists of their *Miranda* rights—the Court concluded that such encounters do not create the type of situation in which individuals will be forced to divulge information they might not otherwise disclose. In simple terms, the Court decided that a traffic stop does not constitute a custodial interrogation. In reaching this conclusion, the Court cited two factors that serve to mitigate the danger that a person might be forced to make self-incriminating statements. First, a vast majority of traffic stops are brief in duration. Motorists likely know that eventually they will be sent on their way after answering a few questions. The type of questioning that occurs during a routine traffic stop, the Court asserted, is considerably different than that which occurs at the stationhouse when a person is brought in for detailed and more considerably prolonged questioning. And, although an armed uniformed officer projects an undeniable air of authority that may be intimidating to some, this concern is offset by the fact that traffic stops, unlike stationhouse interrogations, generally occur in public so that officers are deterred from employing less than legitimate means for extracting information from the detained motorist. Given these mitigating considerations, the Court ruled that motorists who are temporarily detained during a lawful traffic stop are not the subjects of a custodial interrogation requiring recitation of the *Miranda* warning.

CASE SIGNIFICANCE

The implications of this case for day-to-day law enforcement were multifold. First, in the event that there was ever any doubt, the decision expanded the *Miranda* Rule to all custodial interrogations whether they involve a felony or misdemeanor offense. Thus, individuals who are subjected to custodial interrogation for misdemeanor offenses are covered by the protections afforded under *Miranda*. While this ruling may appear to some observers as an impediment to effective law enforcement, it is counterbalanced by the finding that officers do not have to read the *Miranda* warning each and every time they make a lawful traffic stop and request information of a driver. Still in question, however, is the issue of determining exactly when is one deemed to be "in custody" for purposes of triggering the *Miranda* Rule. The Court openly acknowledged that lower courts would still be forced to answer this question almost on a case-by-case basis. In the present instance, the state trooper decided in the early stages of the traffic stop to take McCarty into custody but did not verbally articulate this intention. Thus, in the trooper's mind McCarty was under arrest almost from the outset. McCarty, on the other hand, may very well have been under the impression that he would soon be free to leave and the notion of being in custody may have never entered his mind. Situations like this, which likely characterize countless traffic stops on a daily basis, remain ambiguous and will continue to elude precise definition. Fortunately, however, the Court has provided some guidance to lower courts in resolving such dilemmas. Specifically, the Court stated that "a policeman's unarticulated plan has no bearing on the question of whether a suspect was 'in custody' at a particular time." Rather, what is most important in making such a determination "is how a reasonable man in the suspect's position would have understood his situation." One additional implication of the present decision is the contention that exempting traffic stops from the *Miranda* Rule will induce officers to conduct their interrogations on the roadside rather than in the stationhouse. That is, some are fearful that this decision will result in offices exploiting the fact that traffic stops do not constitute an "in-custody" interrogation and delay the arrest of an individual with an eye toward obtaining self-incriminating information they might not otherwise discover if the suspect is placed into immediate custody. Unfortunately, there appears to be no easy solution to this possibility other than to say that the facts surrounding such eventualities will be given consideration in hindsight and, where necessary, remedied through exclusion of the statements in question.

NEW YORK V. QUARLES
467 U.S. 649 (1984)

FACTS

Two officers were approached by a female who informed them that she had just been raped by an armed man who was last seen entering a nearby supermarket. Spotting an individual who matched the description given, one of the officers gave chase. Once cornered, the suspect was frisked and found to be wearing an empty shoulder holster. Asked where the gun was, he nodded toward some empty cartons and said, "The gun is over there." Quarles was placed under arrest and, having been properly informed of his *Miranda* rights, admitted to owning the weapon. At trial, both the weapon and Quarles' initial statement as to the gun's location were excluded on the basis that he had not yet been informed of his *Miranda* rights. Consequently, the statements that followed were also excluded on grounds that they were tainted by the *Miranda* violation. Both the Appellate Division of the New York Supreme Court and the New York Court of Appeals affirmed. The United States Supreme Court granted certiorari.

ISSUE

Should the trial court have accepted into evidence Quarles' admission regarding the gun's location and ownership? Does the concern for public safety outweigh strict adherence to the *Miranda* warning?

HOLDING

Yes. The lower courts erred in excluding Quarles' statement regarding the weapon's location and ownership, as well as his subsequent admission, as illegal fruits of the *Miranda* violation. The concern for public safety in this type of case clearly outweighs strict adherence to the principles of *Miranda*.

RATIONALE

The Supreme Court reversed the decision of the lower court, finding that the statement made by Quarles as to the gun's location should have been admitted at trial despite the fact that he had not been informed of his *Miranda* rights. In making this determination, the Court conducted a balancing test in which it weighed the public-safety interest against the suspect's right to avoid self-incrimination. In doing so, the Court noted that the doctrinal underpinnings of the *Miranda* decision do not require that the warnings be applied with total rigor to situations in which the police ask questions reasonably prompted by a concern for public safety. In other words, the Court acknowledged that had the officer taken time to inform Quarles of his *Miranda* rights, the cost associated with failing to immediately locate the gun would have been greater than the exclusion of evidence at trial. Thus, in the overwhelming interest of public safety, the Court concluded that officers are authorized to ask certain limited questions of criminal suspects without having to first read the *Miranda* warnings.

CASE SIGNIFICANCE

Narrowly applied, the *Miranda* decision prohibited authorities from asking any questions whatsoever of a suspect who is in custody until he or she has been informed of and waives certain rights extended under the Fifth Amendment. The facts of the present case, however, were substantially different from the day-to-day situations in which officers interrogate suspects about crimes that do not pose an immediate threat to others. Instead, this case clearly involved an encounter between the police and a suspect who was believed to have been both armed and dangerous. The fact that Quarles was found to be wearing an empty shoulder holster created an apparent and immediate concern not only for the safety of the officer, but for the safety of others as well. Thus, the primary significance of this case lies in the fact that it created a public-safety exception to the *Miranda* Rule. Interestingly, the Court did not identify other specific situations to which the exception might apply, but left the determination to the individual officer on the scene. Despite the fact that this decision weighed in favor of law enforcement and the public interest, due caution must be exercised so that the exception does not become the subject of abuse. Where this occurs with widespread pattern or frequency, the Court may retract the public-safety exception in favor of protecting the rights of suspects from arbitrary abuse.

OREGON V. ELSTAD
470 U.S. 298 (1985)

FACTS

Two officers went to the residence of Elstad's mother to arrest him on a burglary warrant. While explaining that he had been implicated in the alleged offense, Elstad openly commented to one of the officers, "Yes, I was there." Elstad was transported to the police station and, upon arrival, properly informed of his *Miranda* rights. He subsequently made a voluntary waiver of these rights, providing investigating officers with a written statement detailing his involvement in the crime. At trial, the state sought to introduce both Elstad's written statement and his initial unwarned comment to the arresting officer. The trial court ruled the unwarned oral statement inadmissible, but allowed the written confession. The Oregon Court of Appeals reversed and the U.S. Supreme Court granted certiorari.

ISSUE

Does a suspect's unwarned and unsolicited statement automatically render a properly obtained subsequent confession inadmissible?

HOLDING

No. A confession that is properly obtained subsequent to an unsolicited and unwarned statement is not automatically rendered inadmissible under the Fifth Amendment.

RATIONALE

In reaching the conclusion that a prior unwarned and unsolicited statement does not automatically render a subsequent properly obtained confession inadmissible, the Court rejected an assertion that the exclusionary rule's "fruit of the poisonous tree" doctrine should be broadly applied to such Fifth Amendment issues. Instead, a six-justice majority reasoned that while a failure to administer the *Miranda* warnings creates a presumption of involuntariness, there is no accompanying presumption that the information derived from otherwise voluntary statements be regarded as inherently tainted. In simple terms, the justices did not think it prudent to broadly apply the "fruit of the poisonous tree" doctrine to fact situations such as those in the present case. Absent any evidence to suggest that the police deliberately coerced or tricked Elstad into making the initial unwarned statement, the fact that they later took care to properly warn him of his *Miranda* rights remedied the condition that otherwise made it inadmissible. Lastly, the Court noted that not only was Elstad's fully warned confession knowingly and voluntarily given, but so too was his first, within the meaning of the Fifth Amendment.

CASE SIGNIFICANCE

The decision in this case partially eroded the rigors of *Miranda* insofar as it allowed a suspect who has previously responded to unwarned questioning to subsequently confess after being properly informed of his or her rights. In practical terms, this means that trial courts are not required to automatically exclude confessions that are obtained after a suspect has "let the cat out of the bag," as occurred in this case. Prior to this decision, lower courts would frequently suppress such evidence as fruit of the poisonous tree. Thus, a suspect who makes an incriminating statement without having first been read his or her *Miranda* rights can still be questioned later by the police so long as he or she is properly warned at that time. While the initial unwarned statement might not necessarily be admissible at trial, under this ruling the second warned statement certainly should be.

MICHIGAN V. JACKSON
475 U.S. 625 (1986)

FACTS

This case was decided in conjunction with *Michigan v. Bladel* (1986). In both matters, the defendants appeared for arraignment on unrelated murder charges, at which time each requested appointed counsel. Between the time this request was made and the time the defendants first met with appointed counsel, officers informed them of their *Miranda* rights, conducted interrogations, and obtained confessions. Although both defendants objected to the admission of their statements at trial, both were convicted. On appeal, the guilty verdict in one case was remanded for retrial while the other was allowed to stand. Upon reaching the Michigan Supreme Court, both cases were considered simultaneously and it was determined that the confessions were obtained in violation of the Sixth Amendment and, therefore, should not have been admitted at trial. The U.S. Supreme Court then granted certiorari.

ISSUE

Does the protection afforded under the *Edwards* rule extend to situations in which a suspect has requested assistance of counsel at arraignment but in the interim is interrogated by police before being allowed to confer with appointed counsel?

HOLDING

Yes. The police may not interrogate a suspect who is in custody and has asked the court for assistance of counsel until he or she has had an opportunity to meet with an attorney. If officers initiate an interrogation, even without specific knowledge that a suspect has previously requested assistance of counsel during arraignment proceedings, any incriminating information obtained from such an encounter is inadmissible at trial.

RATIONALE

Recall that in *Edwards v. Arizona,* the Supreme Court held that once a suspect has invoked the right to counsel, state agents are prohibited from initiating further interrogation until the individual has had an opportu-

nity to meet with an attorney who must also be present during any subsequent encounters. The same protections hold true for defendants who request assistance of counsel during arraignment proceedings. The major difference in *Edwards* and the immediate pair of companion cases lies in the basis for each claim. In *Edwards,* protection from repeated requests for information by the police was extended under the Fifth Amendment. In the present matter, protection from police interrogation before being allowed to meet with counsel was extended under the Sixth Amendment. As might be expected, this discrepancy was brought to the Court's attention but was summarily discounted on the basis that "the Sixth Amendment right to counsel at a postarraignment interrogation requires at least as much protection as the Fifth Amendment right to counsel at any custodial interrogation." Writing for the majority, Justice Stevens further reasoned that "after a formal accusation has been made—and a person who had previously been just a 'suspect' has become an 'accused' within the meaning of the Sixth Amendment—the constitutional right to the assistance of counsel is of such importance that the police may no longer employ techniques for eliciting information from an uncounseled defendant that might have been entirely proper at an earlier stage of their investigation." In an attempt to sway a majority of the justices' opinion on the matter, the state of Michigan asserted that there are likely to be times when investigating officers are wholly unaware of a defendant's prior request for legal assistance/representation. In response to this line of reasoning, the Court stated that Sixth Amendment jurisprudence requires that the state's knowledge on such matters be imputed from one state actor (the court) to all others (the police). Thus it is unacceptable for police officers to claim ignorance of a prior request for assistance of counsel by a defendant that occurred out of their immediate presence.

CASE SIGNIFICANCE

This decision extended additional protection to criminal defendants insofar as it prohibited the police or other agents of the state from initiating contact with an individual who has requested the assistance of counsel during arraignment proceedings. The basis for this decision stemmed not from the Fifth Amendment right to avoid self-incrimination, but rather from the Sixth Amendment right to counsel. In practical terms, this decision has at least one very important implication for law enforcement procedure. Specifically, the decision requires that any state agent seeking to initiate contact with an accused must first make absolutely certain that he or she has not invoked the right to counsel under the

Sixth Amendment during an arraignment or proceeding. Where such measures are not taken and the police initiate contact with a suspect who has requested assistance of counsel, any information will be ruled inadmissible under the Jackson rule. Simply claiming ignorance of the fact that the individual has invoked his or her Sixth Amendment right to counsel will not suffice. Thus, law enforcement agencies must develop policies for ensuring that such information is properly communicated to anyone seeking to initiate contact with an accused.

COLORADO V. CONNELLY
479 U.S. 157 (1986)

FACTS

Connelly approached a Denver police officer and confessed to a murder. The officer promptly advised Connelly of his *Miranda* rights, but he nonetheless insisted on talking about the crime in order to clear his conscience. Upon arrival at police headquarters, Connelly related his story in full detail and eventually accompanied officers to the crime scene. The following morning, Connelly became visibly disoriented and claimed that he was hearing voices, whereupon he was taken to a state hospital for psychiatric evaluation. In a pretrial hearing on the murder charge, the defense moved to suppress Connelly's statements on grounds that his psychotic condition had prompted him to confess. The trial court accepted this argument and ordered the initial statements suppressed although the police had done nothing coercive to obtain them. The Colorado Supreme Court affirmed and the U.S. Supreme Court granted certiorari.

ISSUE

Can a suspect who is lacking a fully rational state of mind validly waive his or her *Miranda* rights?

HOLDING

Yes. A suspect who is lacking a fully rational state of mind may validly waive his or her *Miranda* rights and, in the absence of any coercive police behavior, any incriminating statements are admissible under state rules of evidence.

RATIONALE

A majority of the Court, led by Chief Justice Rehnquist, asserted that incriminating statements made by an individual lacking a fully rational state of mind but who has been properly informed of his or her *Miranda* rights should not be subject to automatic exclusion. In reaching this decision, the majority reasoned that in order for a violation of due process to occur, there must be evidence of coercive police activity. In the present case, there was none—Connelly freely confessed without any pressure from police. Consequently, neither the taking of his statement nor its admission into evidence constituted a violation of his due process rights.

CASE SIGNIFICANCE

This case stands as yet another example of a ruling weakening the *Miranda* decision. The basis for this assertion is found in the Court's conclusion that the Fifth Amendment privilege against self-incrimination applies only to evidence that is obtained by coercive means. Because the police did not coerce Connelly into making the statement, there was no Fifth Amendment violation. Finally, the fact that Connelly apparently lacked a fully rational state of mind was determined to have no bearing on the case—he was properly warned, gave a valid waiver, and freely confessed without any pressure from police. In the absence of any coercive activity by police, the admissibility of such statements is left to state rules of evidence. Although the frequency with which the police encounter such situations is unknown, officers are allowed to take an individual's statement so long as he or she is properly Mirandized and a valid waiver of the attending rights is obtained.

COLORADO V. SPRING
479 U.S. 564 (1987)

FACTS

Federal agents arrested Spring on charges of selling stolen firearms. Spring was given the *Miranda* warning but provided a written waiver of his right to remain silent. During the course of this initial interrogation, agents gradually refocused their questioning upon Spring's involvement in an unsolved Colorado homicide case. Colorado authorities, having again advised Spring of his *Miranda* rights, later questioned him about the murder, at which time he confessed to having aided the actual killer. At trial, Spring moved to have his confession to involvement in the murder suppressed on grounds that his waiver only extended to the agents' questions regarding the federal weapons charge. Because the agents had not given Spring advance notice that they would question him about the homicide, the defense argued that he had not waived his *Miranda* rights for that particular offense. Rejecting this assertion, the trial court found Spring guilty of first-degree murder. The Colorado Court of Appeals reversed and remanded the case for retrial, accepting Spring's argument in favor of suppression. The Colorado Supreme Court affirmed the reversal and the U.S. Supreme Court granted certiorari.

ISSUE

Must a suspect be given advance notice of all possible topics of interrogation in order for his or her waiver of *Miranda* rights to be valid?

HOLDING

No. The police are not required to provide suspects with advance notice of all possible topics of interrogation in order for a waiver of *Miranda* rights to be valid. In other words, the police do not have to tell a suspect which specific crime(s) they intend to ask questions about.

RATIONALE

In reaching the decision that Spring's initial waiver of his *Miranda* rights was valid, the Court first noted that there was no evidence to suggest that he had been unduly influenced or pressured by the police. To the contrary, the written waiver of these rights further demonstrated that Spring clearly understood that he retained the right to remain silent and that anything he revealed could be used as evidence against him at trial. The Court then went on to assert that no provision of the Constitution requires the state to inform a suspect of every possible consequence that might arise from a waiver of the Fifth Amendment right to remain silent. That the police did not specifically spell out in advance every topic of interrogation has no bearing on determining whether or not the waiver is valid—more important for making such a determination is whether the suspect did so voluntarily, knowingly, and intelligently. Absent any evidence to the contrary, the initial written waiver must be held valid and, therefore, admissible.

CASE SIGNIFICANCE

This case is important insofar as it established the general principle of law that police are not required to inform a suspect of all possible offenses about which he or she might be asked during an interrogation. Once the police have informed a suspect of his or her *Miranda* rights and these protections have been validly waived, the police may probe any area they choose. In the immediate case, government agents began the interrogation by asking Spring about his involvement in a minor offense, then shifted the focus of their inquiry to more serious matters (i.e., murder). On appeal, it was argued that the police should be required to provide a suspect with advance notice of all crimes about which he or she will be asked during the interrogation. This argument was rejected and it was instead concluded

that the police do not have to tell a suspect what areas they intend to explore.

CONNECTICUT V. BARRETT
479 U.S. 523 (1987)

FACTS

Barrett, a sexual assault suspect, was picked up and transported to a police station for questioning. Having been advised of his *Miranda* rights no less than three times, Barrett told the attending officers that he would not give a written statement until an attorney was present, but that he was willing to give an oral statement. At trial, the oral statement was admitted into evidence based on Barrett's self-defense testimony that he had understood the *Miranda* rights as they had been read to him at the time. Barrett was found guilty, but the Connecticut Supreme Court later set the conviction aside on grounds that his request for an attorney triggered the rule established in *Edwards v. Arizona,* that once a suspect requests the presence of counsel, police are barred from initiating further communications until such request has been fulfilled. The U.S. Supreme Court then granted certiorari.

ISSUE

Can a suspect validly waive his or her *Miranda* rights and give an oral statement to police while at the same time refusing to give a written statement until such time as an attorney is present?

HOLDING

Yes. A suspect may validly waive portions of his or her *Miranda* rights and any statements (oral or written) may still be properly admitted into evidence at trial.

RATIONALE

The Court held that the Fifth Amendment does not require suppression of an oral statement in situations where a suspect, having been properly informed of his or her *Miranda* rights, agrees to talk about an offense but refuses to make a written statement until such time as an attorney is present. In the immediate case, there was no evidence that Barrett was "threatened, tricked, or cajoled" by police into talking about the alleged offense. Rather, Barrett's intention to narrowly limit his statement to oral form was made clear to police who, in turn, restricted their behavior accordingly. Had there been evidence to suggest that Barrett was pressured into providing a written statement after expressing his desire not to do so, that statement would have been ruled as inadmissible. In the absence of any such evidence, the trial court properly admitted the oral statement and the state supreme court erred in its reversal of the original conviction.

CASE SIGNIFICANCE

The decision in this case helped guide investigators confronted with a situation in which a suspect agrees to provide an oral but not a written statement of guilt. Somewhat weakening the *Miranda* decision, this ruling allowed officers to take an oral statement from a suspect so long as he or she was properly warned and there was no evidence of coercion. In turn, the oral confession may be introduced into evidence at trial. Furthermore, there is no need to obtain a written confession in order to make the oral confession valid. Again, the appropriate test for determining the validity of a confession—written or oral—is whether: (1) the suspect was properly Mirandized; (2) the rights were properly waived; and (3) there is no evidence of coercive police behavior.

PATTERSON V. ILLINOIS
487 U.S. 285 (1988)

FACTS

Patterson, who had been indicted for participation in a gang-related murder, began to make a statement about the homicide to an attending officer. The officer promptly interrupted Patterson and presented him with a waiver form clearly spelling out five provisions of the *Miranda* warning. Patterson read and signed the form and then gave the officer, and later a state attorney, an incriminating statement regarding his involvement in the murder. These statements were introduced over objection at trial and Patterson was convicted. On appeal, it was argued that the statements should have been excluded on grounds that the Sixth Amendment requires a higher standard for showing waiver of the right to counsel than that which is required for *Miranda* waivers. The Appellate Court of Illinois affirmed the conviction and the U.S. Supreme Court granted certiorari.

ISSUE

Does a suspect's waiver of the Fifth Amendment right to remain silent under *Miranda* simultaneously waive his or her Sixth Amendment right to counsel?

HOLDING

Yes. A suspect who has been properly advised of his or her *Miranda* rights during post-indictment questioning is deemed to have also been sufficiently informed of the accompanying Sixth Amendment right to counsel. A valid waiver of the *Miranda* rights simultaneously implicates both the Fifth Amendment right to remain silent and the Sixth Amendment right to counsel.

RATIONALE

On appeal to the Supreme Court, it was asserted that Patterson should have received an altogether separate warning regarding his Sixth Amendment right to counsel. By a five-to-four vote, the Court rejected this argument on grounds that it was inappropriate to designate one right (the Sixth Amendment right to counsel) as "superior" or "more difficult" to waive than another (the Fifth Amendment right to remain silent). Instead, the Court concluded that the appropriate method for resolving such Sixth Amendment issues is one that examines the utility of counsel at the particular stage of proceedings in question. In the end, it was reasoned that the *Miranda* warnings were sufficient for protecting Patterson's Sixth Amendment right due to the fairly limited role played by counsel at that particular stage of the adversarial proceedings.

CASE SIGNIFICANCE

This case rejected the notion that suspects must be given two distinct sets of warnings and waive each prior to custodial interrogation. Specifically, Patterson argued that he should have received a separate warning regarding the Sixth Amendment right to counsel in addition to the standard *Miranda* warning dealing solely with the Fifth Amendment right to avoid self-incrimination. This argument was rejected on the basis that while suspects possess a right to counsel during custodial interrogation, the intent of this right is limited to protecting the individual from self-incrimination. For purposes of day-to-day law enforcement, officers are still required to read the *Miranda* warning to a suspect prior to custodial interrogation. They are not required to inform the suspect of any additional rights beyond those specifically contained in the language of the warning.

ARIZONA V. ROBERSON
486 U.S. 675 (1988)

FACTS

Roberson was apprehended at the scene of a burglary and, upon being informed of his *Miranda* rights by the arresting officer, stated that he "wanted a lawyer before answering any questions"—a fact noted by the officer in his report. Three days later, Roberson was approached by a different officer who was unaware that he had previously invoked the right to assistance of counsel. The officer advised Roberson of his *Miranda* rights and then proceeded to interrogate him about his involvement in a separate burglary offense. During the interrogation, Roberson disclosed information that incriminated him in the second, unrelated offense that was of interest to this particular officer. At trial for the second burglary offense, Roberson's statement was suppressed under the *Edwards* rule establishing that once a suspect expresses a desire to deal with the police only through counsel, he or she may not be subjected to further interrogation until such time as the request is fulfilled or the accused initiates further communication with the authorities. Recall, however, that in *Arizona v. Edwards* the suspect was repeatedly questioned about his involvement in a single offense without the benefit of counsel being present, whereas in the immediate matter Roberson was subjected to questioning about his involvement in two separate, unrelated offenses. The U.S. Supreme Court granted certiorari.

Issue

Does the *Edwards* rule prohibit officers from initiating an interrogation with a suspect regarding an unrelated offense if he or she has invoked the Fifth Amendment right to assistance of counsel in a previous interrogation conducted by other officers?

Holding

Yes. The Supreme Court held that the previously established *Edwards* rule prohibits officers from initiating repeated interrogations of a suspect once he or she has invoked the Fifth Amendment right to counsel even if the subsequent interrogation focuses on an altogether separate offense.

Rationale

The state of Arizona asserted that the rule previously established under *Edwards* prohibiting police from conducting repeated custodial interrogations of a suspect who has invoked the Fifth Amendment right to counsel should not be applied to the facts in the immediate matter on two grounds. First, the state pointed to the Court's earlier decision in *Michigan v. Mosley*, 423 U.S. 96 (1975), holding that the police may question a suspect about an unrelated offense even if he or she has previously cut off communications where two conditions are met: (1) a significant amount of time passes; and (2) the suspect is again informed of his or her *Miranda* rights. This argument, however, was rejected by the Court on the basis that "a suspect's decision to cut off questioning, unlike his request for counsel, does not raise the presumption that he is unable to proceed without a lawyer's advice." In effect, the Court drew a distinction between suspects who simply refuse to talk

with police and those who refuse to talk without the benefit of counsel. A second argument raised by the state was premised upon the Court's earlier decision in *Connecticut v. Barrett*, 479 U.S. 523 (1987) involving a suspect who refused to give the police a written statement without assistance of counsel but did, however, agree to continue "talking" with them about the incident in question. In this particular case, the Court determined that Barrett himself had drawn a distinction between oral and written statements thereby voluntarily allowing officers to continue their questioning of him. The state asserted that Roberson's request for counsel was similarly limited so that it applied only to questions regarding his involvement in the burglary for which he was initially arrested. The Court, however, viewed this argument to be flawed on both legal and factual grounds. On legal grounds, a suspect's request for counsel creates the presumption that one is unable to deal with the pressures of custodial interrogation alone. This presumption, the Court continued, "does not disappear simply because the police have approached the suspect, still in custody, still without counsel, about a separate investigation." On factual grounds, it may be recalled, Roberson told the arresting officer that he "wanted a lawyer before answering any questions." In a literal sense then, the police were prohibited from asking further questions given Roberson's specific use of the term "any."

Case Significance

The Court's decision in this case is significant to the extent that it not only affirmed the *Miranda* decision, but also expanded the prophylactic measures created under *Edwards*. Naturally, the majority's decision drew sharp criticism from dissenting justices who acknowledged the realities of day-to-day law enforcement where suspects are frequently wanted in connection with multiple offenses. The *Roberson* decision, the dissenters astutely noted, effectively "bar(s) law enforcement officials, even those from some other city or other jurisdiction, from questioning a suspect about an unrelated matter if he is in custody and has requested counsel to assist in answering questions put to him about the crime for which he was arrested." Thus, crime-control advocates often criticize the Court's "broad brush" expansion of the *Edwards* rule on the basis that it unnecessarily impedes effective law enforcement. Furthermore, the decision requires arresting officers to pay very close attention to detail. Specifically, officers must carefully note whether a suspect states that he or she does not want to answer questions about the specific offense for which he or she has been arrested or, as did Roberson, states that he or she does not want to answer "any" questions whatsoever. Perhaps most importantly, this information must be conveyed to any and all investigators who wish to interrogate the suspect. In the event that this information is not specifically conveyed, such a breakdown in communication may very well lead to a situation in which any or all incriminating statements are ruled inadmissible at trial.

DUCKWORTH V. EAGAN
492 U.S. 195 (1989)

FACTS

Prior to questioning Eagan in connection with a stabbing, Indiana police read him a *Miranda* waiver form, including the provision that a lawyer would be appointed "if and when you go to court." Eagan signed the form and provided investigators with an incriminating statement that was later admitted into evidence at his trial for attempted murder. Eagan was convicted and, upon exhausting available state-level appeals, filed a writ of habeas corpus in federal court. The writ was denied in district court but granted on appeal by the Seventh Circuit on grounds that the language contained in the warning was constitutionally defective. The U.S. Supreme Court then granted certiorari.

ISSUE

Did the waiver form, which included the phrase "if and when you go to court," violate the requirements of *Miranda v. Arizona*?

HOLDING

No. It is not necessary for the *Miranda* warnings to be presented or recited exactly as they appeared in the original case.

RATIONALE

The Supreme Court reversed the judgment of the Seventh Circuit Court of Appeals, ruling that the warning given to Eagan was adequate for purposes of satisfying the intent of the *Miranda* decision. In reaching this decision, a five-justice majority first noted that the Court had never insisted on the warnings being given in a specific or exact form. Rather, the underlying objective has been to ensure that officers "reasonably convey" to a suspect his or her constitutional rights during custodial interrogation or its functional equivalent. To the extent that this objective is reasonably satisfied, no violation has occurred. The fact that the warning in question included language not found in the original *Miranda* opinion simply serves to clarify for the suspect other stages of the process when he or she can expect to have the assistance of counsel. Finally, the Court fur-

ther clarified that the police are not required to provide a suspect with counsel upon demand as might be inferred from a literal reading of the *Miranda* decision. Instead, all that is required is that the police cease questioning until such time as an attorney has been made available to the suspect by whatever procedural mechanism has been put in place.

CASE SIGNIFICANCE

This case is important for law enforcement purposes on two grounds. First, it resolved the question of whether the police must inform a suspect of the *Miranda* warning verbatim or, instead, if minor variations are acceptable. In clarifying this issue, the Court ruled that police officers do not have to inform suspects of their *Miranda* rights verbatim. This means that minor variations of the warning are acceptable so long as its substantive meaning remains the same. A second question resolved by this decision was whether or not the police must immediately produce an attorney for a suspect once one is requested. This issue was resolved by the Court's ruling that police are not required to immediately produce an attorney once a suspect has requested one. In simple terms then, this case stands for two principles of law: First, the police are not required to inform a suspect of the *Miranda* warning verbatim so long as its substantive meaning remains intact; and second, the police are not required to immediately produce an attorney once a suspect has requested one.

MINNICK V. MISSISSIPPI
498 U.S. 146 (1990)

FACTS

Minnick, wanted on capital murder charges in Mississippi, was arrested in California and held for extradition. While awaiting arrival of Mississippi officials, Minnick was questioned by federal agents who terminated their interrogation upon his request to speak with an attorney, which he was allowed to do two or three times. Upon arrival, the deputy sheriff from Mississippi resumed interrogation and told Minnick that he could not refuse to talk. During the course of being questioned by the deputy, Minnick confessed to involvement in the murder. At trial, a motion to suppress the confession was denied whereupon Minnick was convicted and sentenced to death. The Mississippi Supreme Court rejected Minnick's appeal alleging that the confession had been obtained in violation of his Fifth Amendment right to counsel. Specifically, the state's high court reasoned that the *Edwards* rule, which prohibits the police from reinitiating interrogation of a suspect until counsel is made available, was not applicable in Minnick's case because his request for representation had been granted before the deputy resumed questioning. The U.S. Supreme Court then granted certiorari.

ISSUE

Does protection established under the *Edwards* rule cease to exist once a suspect has consulted with an attorney? In other words, if a suspect asks for counsel during interrogation and this request is granted, may the police later resume the interrogation?

HOLDING

No. When, during the course of custodial interrogation, a suspect asks for counsel, all questioning must immediately cease and may not resume until such time as counsel is present in the room.

RATIONALE

In this case the Supreme Court clarified its earlier ruling in *Edwards* and, in doing so, expanded the scope of Fifth Amendment protection afforded suspects during custodial interrogation. In particular, the Court's Majority interpreted the requirement in *Edwards* that counsel be made available to the accused upon request to mean that before questioning by police may resume, an attorney must be physically present in the room. Thus, "the requirement that counsel be made available to the accused refers to more than an opportunity to consult with an attorney outside the interrogation room." The Court felt this expansion was necessary given that "[a] single consultation with an attorney does not remove the suspect from persistent attempts by officials to persuade him to waive his rights, or from the coercive pressures that accompany custody and that may increase as custody is prolonged." At one point, the State contended that a suspect could simply reinstate his or her desire for assistance of counsel during subsequent interrogations. The Court noted, however, that such a formulation would likely create unnecessary confusion by allowing the rule to pass in and out of existence multiple times. Thus, in the interest of protecting suspects' Fifth Amendment rights while at the same time maintaining *Edwards*' "bright line" standards, Minnick's conviction was reversed and remanded.

CASE SIGNIFICANCE

This case poses significant implications for law enforcement on several grounds. First, it clearly establishes the standard that once a suspect under custodial interrogation requests assistance of counsel, all questioning must immediately cease and be held in abeyance until such time as an attorney is physically present in the room. It is not adequate to simply allow the sus-

pect to communicate with an attorney by phone before resuming the interrogation; officers must refrain from asking any questions whatsoever until the suspect's attorney arrives at the location where the interrogation is being conducted. Any effort whatsoever by officers from any jurisdiction to reestablish communications with the suspect without his or her attorney being present is also strictly forbidden. As might be expected, this expansion of the Fifth Amendment by the Court's majority drew sharp criticism from the dissenting justices, who noted that even if a suspect genuinely and freely desired to do so, he or she could never consent to an interview with police unless an attorney is present. Thus, a criminal who is truly repentant cannot confess to a crime without waiting for an attorney to arrive on the scene. As the dissenting justices stated: "The value of any prophylactic rule must be assessed not only on the basis of what is gained, but also on the basis of what is lost." In effect, the dissenting justices suggested that although increased protection for criminal suspects has indeed been gained as a result of this decision, that which has been lost—a certain measure of power on the part of police to find those who have violated the law—may be of greater cost in the end.

PENNSYLVANIA V. MUNIZ
496 U.S. 582 (1990)

FACTS

Muniz was arrested for drunk driving and transported to a booking center where officers, as a matter of practice with such suspects, videotaped the intake procedure. During this procedure, Muniz responded to routine questions about his name, address, date of birth, etc. One particular question asked of Muniz was the date of his sixth birthday, which he was unable to correctly answer. While attempting to perform a variety of standardized sobriety tests, Muniz openly commented on his state of inebriation. He also refused a request to submit a sample of his breath for analysis. Muniz was then informed of his *Miranda* rights for the first time, signed a waiver of those rights, and admitted on video to driving while intoxicated. The booking video was admitted into evidence at Muniz's bench trial and he was convicted. An appeal for retrial was granted by a superior court on grounds that the audio portion of the tape violated Muniz's Fifth Amendment protection against self-incrimination insofar as he had been asked questions without having first been properly warned. The Supreme Court of Pennsylvania denied the prosecution's request for review, and the U.S. Supreme Court granted certiorari.

ISSUE

Did the police violate Muniz's Fifth Amendment protection against self-incrimination by videotaping the booking procedure without first advising him of his right to remain silent?

HOLDING

No. Not only may the police ask routine questions of DWI suspects during booking procedures, but they are also allowed to videotape the responses without having to first inform the arrestee of his or her *Miranda* rights.

RATIONALE

In resolving the claim that police violated Muniz's Fifth Amendment protection against self-incrimination by videotaping his responses to routine booking questions without having first properly Mirandized him, the Supreme Court reversed and remanded the case for further proceedings. More specifically, a majority of the justices agreed that Muniz's Fifth Amendment rights were violated by admitting into evidence that portion of the tape in which he was unable to correctly provide the date of his sixth birthday. Aside from this limited portion, however, the remainder of the tape was properly admitted. Those portions of the video depicting the sobriety test as well as Muniz's refusal to provide a sample of his breath had been properly admitted into evidence. The Fifth Amendment protects suspects from being compelled to provide the government with incriminating evidence of a testimonial or communicative nature. The fact that Muniz's speech was slurred and he apparently lacked muscular coordination constituted "nontestimonial" components of the recorded responses that fall beyond the protective scope of the Fifth Amendment. Furthermore, Muniz's statements during the sobriety tests as well as the refusal to provide a sample of his breath were all voluntary insofar as they were not elicited as the result of a custodial interrogation.

CASE SIGNIFICANCE

This case is important for law enforcement purposes insofar as it authorizes officers to interview DWI suspects and videotape their responses without first having to inform them of their *Miranda* rights. It is important to note, however, that the questions must be a "routine" part of the booking procedure (i.e., questions such as name, age, height, weight, place of residence, etc.). Thus, questions that are not part of the regular booking protocol may not be admitted unless the suspect has been properly warned (i.e., questions regarding how much alcohol he or she has consumed, where the individual had been drinking, etc.). From a due process perspective, the decision in this case reinforces the notion that the Fifth Amendment protects suspects from being compelled to provide self-incriminating evidence of a testimonial or communicative nature. Because Muniz lacked muscular coordination and manifested slurred speech—evidence of a physical rather than communicative nature—the Fifth Amendment was deemed inapplicable to the videotaped evidence.

ARIZONA V. FULMINANTE
499 U.S. 279 (1991)

FACTS

While incarcerated in a New York federal prison, Fulminante befriended a fellow inmate, Sarivola, who was acting as a paid informant for the FBI. Sarivola, having heard rumors that Fulminante had killed his 11-year-old stepdaughter while residing in Arizona, approached him and offered protection from the other inmates on the condition that he confess. Fulminante confided that he had indeed killed the girl and disclosed several details about the crime. After his release from prison, Fulminante was traveling by car to Pennsylvania with Sarivola and Sarivola's wife the latter of the two asked why he was going to Pennsylvania instead of returning to Arizona. In response, Fulminante freely cited the murder of his stepdaughter as the reason that he could not return and proceeded to provide even greater detail about the crime than he had to her husband while in prison. Fulminante was subsequently indicted for the young girl's murder, presumably as the result of Sarivola's relationship with the FBI, and held for trial. Prior to trial, Fulminante moved to suppress both confessions on the basis that the first was coerced while the second was a "fruit" of the first. The trial court denied the motion and both confessions were admitted, whereupon Fulminante was convicted and sentenced to death. On appeal to the Arizona Supreme Court, Fulminante claimed that the admission of both confessions violated his due process rights under the Fifth and Fourteenth Amendments. The Arizona high court initially held that Fulminante's prison confession was coerced given the totality of the circumstances (i.e., fear that if he did not confess in exchange for protection that he would be the target of attack by other inmates). At the same time, however, the court determined that the confession's admission at trial amounted to a "harmless error" because, even in its absence, there existed enough evidence to convict. Thus, Fulminante's conviction was initially allowed to stand. Upon motion for reconsideration, the state supreme court later changed its position, reversed the conviction, and ordered that Fulminante be retried without the use of the confession. The U.S. Supreme Court then granted certiorari.

ISSUES

Was Fulminante's prison confession "coerced" for purposes of Fifth Amendment analysis? Does the "harmless error" doctrine apply to cases involving involuntary confessions later admitted at trial? Was the admission of Fulminante's prison confession a "harmless error" that had no bearing upon his conviction?

HOLDING

Yes, yes, and no. As to the first issue, the Court held that Fulminante's prison confession to Sarivola was coerced under traditional Fifth Amendment analysis. As to the second issue, the Court held that the "harmless error" doctrine is applicable to cases involving the improper admission of an involuntary confession at trial. As to the third issue, the Court held that the introduction of Fulminante's prison confession at trial was more than a "harmless error," and thus required reversal of the conviction.

RATIONALE

The first order of business addressed by the Court was a determination of whether or not the Arizona Supreme Court had applied the appropriate test in reaching its conclusion that Fulminante's prison confession to Sarivola was coerced under traditional Fifth Amendment analysis. On this point, the justices held that the applicable standard was one that considered the totality of the circumstances. Because this was the standard the lower court had applied, its finding that the confession had not been freely given was deemed to be without error. In particular, the justices seemed receptive to the Arizona Supreme Court's acknowledgment that "[T]he confession was obtained as a direct result of extreme coercion, and was tendered in the belief that the defendant's life was in jeopardy if he did not confess. This is a true coerced confession in every sense of the word." Next, the Court considered the question of whether or not the "harmless error" rule established under *Chapman v. California*, 386 U.S. 18 (1967) was applicable in situations where an involuntary confession was improperly admitted at trial, as had occurred in Fulminante's case. Under considerable criticism by four dissenting justices, a majority of the Court nonetheless determined that the rule should be extended to such situations on the basis that it had previously been applied to numerous other types of trial errors. This extension of the rule is counterbalanced, the majority argued, by placing a burden upon the state to prove that

the error in question was harmless beyond a reasonable doubt. Last, the Court sought to determine whether the admission of Fulminante's coerced confession at trial constituted a harmless error or, instead, so adversely affected the proceedings as to render the outcome unfair. Referring again to its previous decision in *Chapman*, the justices concluded that the state did not, as required, adequately carry its burden of demonstrating beyond a reasonable doubt that the error was of harmless consequence. In so deciding, the majority recognized that "[a] confession is like no other evidence" in that it comes straight from the defendant him- or herself and can have such a dramatic impact on the minds of the jurors that they would likely not be able to disregard it even if told to do so. Because Fulminante's prison confession was coerced and because its introduction was deemed harmful to the trial's outcome, a majority of the justices affirmed the state supreme court's decision to grant him a retrial in which the tainted statement was not to be admitted.

CASE SIGNIFICANCE

This case presented multiple issues, and raised at least as many implications for criminal procedure. First, the decision affected the manner in which police use prisoners for purposes of gaining confessions from other prisoners. Specifically, when police use jailhouse informants for purposes of obtaining incriminating statements from other prisoners, they must be certain that the informants do not elicit confessions under coercive conditions. Where jailhouse informants create in the minds of other prisoners the belief that unless they confess to the act in question, something bad will happen to them, statements become inadmissible under the Fifth Amendment. Thus, state agents must be absolutely certain that jailhouse informants understand that they cannot engage in language or behavior that amounts to coercion. A second implication of this case is to be found in its application of what is known as the "harmless error" doctrine. In particular, the *Fulminante* decision established the procedural rule that the improper admission of an involuntary confession into evidence does not require an automatic reversal upon appeal. A third implication arising from this centers upon whether or not Fulminante's confession amounted to a "harmless error," or was so grave as to constitute a violation of procedural due process. Because the Court found that Fulminante's confession was both improperly admitted and amounted to more than harmless error, the conviction required reversal on procedural due process grounds.

McNeil v. Wisconsin
501 U.S. 171 (1991)

Facts

McNeil was arrested for armed robbery. He requested and received representation by a public defender at a bail hearing on the charge. While still in detention, McNeil was approached by an officer seeking information regarding his involvement in a murder and other related offenses that occurred in a nearby town. McNeil was properly Mirandized, waived the attending rights, and made incriminating statements. At trial for these offenses, McNeil moved to suppress the statements on grounds that his request for a lawyer during the bail hearing on the armed robbery charges constituted an invocation of his *Miranda* rights and thereby prohibited further police interrogations. The motion to suppress was denied and McNeil was convicted. An appeal to the Wisconsin Supreme Court was equally unsuccessful. The U.S. Supreme Court then granted certiorari.

Issue

Does a request for assistance of counsel at a bail hearing constitute an invocation of the Fifth Amendment right to counsel under *Miranda* for other uncharged offenses?

Holding

No. A request for assistance of counsel at a bail hearing does not constitute an invocation of the Fifth Amendment right to counsel under *Miranda* for other uncharged offenses.

Rationale

In *Edwards v. Arizona,* the Court held that once a suspect asserts the right to counsel during custodial interrogation, not only must all questioning stop until an attorney has been made available, but the police are also barred from approaching the suspect regarding any other offense unless an attorney is present. In other words, the right to counsel afforded under *Miranda* is not "offense-specific." The same does not hold true, however, for the Sixth Amendment right to counsel, which *is* offense-specific. Thus, the Sixth Amendment right to counsel cannot be broadly invoked as a protective shield from future questioning about other offenses that have not yet been charged. To do otherwise, the Court reasoned, would unnecessarily frustrate public interest and impede law enforcement investigations.

Case Significance

In this case, McNeil claimed that his request for counsel at a bail hearing simultaneously triggered his Fifth Amendment *Miranda* rights, thereby precluding officers from questioning him about other offenses for which charges had not yet been filed. The Court rejected this assertion, instead concluding that the Sixth Amendment right to counsel is "offense-specific." This decision thus authorized officers to question a suspect about other crimes that have not yet been charged even where he or she has requested assistance of counsel during pretrial proceedings. Naturally, the police are prohibited from asking the suspect additional questions about the offense charged unless his or her attorney is present. Equally clear is the requirement that before asking questions about other offenses not yet charged, the suspect must be properly Mirandized and validly waive all attending rights.

Davis v. United States
512 U.S. 452 (1994)

Facts

While serving as a member of the U.S. Navy, Davis was identified by the Naval Intelligence Service (NIS) as a murder suspect. Brought in for questioning, Davis was properly informed of but nonetheless waived his *Miranda* rights. Approximately an hour and a half into the interrogation Davis remarked, "Maybe I should talk to a lawyer." The NIS agent tried to clarify what Davis meant by this comment, and concluded that he had not specifically asked for a lawyer. The agent then reminded Davis of his rights and the questioning resumed for another hour until Davis made the comment again, whereupon the interview immediately ceased. During court-martial, Davis' motion to have the statement suppressed was denied on grounds that not only had the agents properly sought to determine what he had meant by the comment, but that his statement had not taken the form more closely associated with such a request. Davis was convicted and both a court of military review as well as the U.S. Court of Military Appeals affirmed. The U.S. Supreme Court then granted certiorari.

Issue

If a suspect has knowingly and voluntarily waived his or her *Miranda* rights and then, during the course of questioning, makes a comment that does not qualify as an unambiguous invocation of the right to counsel, must the interrogation immediately cease?

Holding

No. Authorities may continue to question a suspect who has knowingly and voluntarily waived his or her

Miranda rights until such time as he or she clearly asks for assistance of counsel.

RATIONALE

The U.S. Supreme Court affirmed Davis' conviction by a five-to-four vote. The Court first noted the critical assumption that military tribunals are governed by the same rules of evidence as civilian criminal courts. Where this assumption is met, the Court continued by stating that the general rule of law created under *Edwards v. Arizona* requiring the police to respect a suspect's request for counsel during custodial interrogation would become distorted beyond utility by requiring officers to cease questioning every time a suspect made an ambiguous statement along such lines. Thus, not only did the Court conclude that an interrogation may continue until a suspect clearly requests assistance of counsel, but it also added that officers are not required to stop and clarify what is meant by otherwise ambiguous comments such as those in the present case.

CASE SIGNIFICANCE

In this case, the Supreme Court slightly relaxed the rule established by *Edwards v. Arizona* requiring that all questioning immediately cease once a suspect invokes the right to counsel. The basis for this retraction is to be found in the specific language a suspect uses. In *Edwards,* the suspect's unequivocal request for an attorney required immediate cessation of the interrogation. By comparison, Davis did not specifically ask for an attorney but, instead, only vaguely remarked that he should probably talk to one. While Davis' comment may strike some as a valid request for counsel, the Court apparently regarded it as a slippery slope with the potential to distort the *Edwards* rule beyond utility. Thus, instead of requiring an interview to cease each time such an ambiguous statement is made, the appropriate standard for determining whether or not the right has been invoked is from the perspective of a reasonable interrogator. Where a reasonable interrogator would interpret a suspect's request for counsel as unambiguous, all questioning must immediately cease under the *Edwards* rule. Where, however, the request is vague, questioning may continue until such time as the suspect clearly invokes the right to counsel. The practical implication of this decision lies in the need to adequately document a suspect's exact language during interrogation in the event that questions are raised at trial regarding the clarity of any such requests. ✦

DISCUSSION QUESTIONS

1. Why is it a good idea for police officers to always read the *Miranda* warnings from a preprinted card or other prepared source rather than just "winging" it from memory? How might this affect admissibility of a suspect's statement at trial? How might it influence juror behavior?

2. How would you explain to a group of skeptical officers that the *Miranda* warnings actually promote a professional image of the police?

3. Why is it important for law enforcement agencies to develop internal procedures for communicating information regarding a suspect's prior invocation of the right to remain silent?

4. What practical measures can be taken to document that a suspect has been properly Mirandized in the field?

5. What special considerations arise when informing a suspect with diminished mental capacity (e.g., mental retardation or intoxication) of his or her *Miranda* rights? ✦

Chapter Nineteen

What Constitutes Interrogation?

Brewer v. Williams, 430 U.S. 387 (1977)

Rhode Island v. Innis, 446 U.S. 291 (1980)

Arizona v. Mauro, 481 U.S. 520 (1987)

Introduction

As a practical matter, one of the most confusing aspects of the *Miranda* decision involves determining exactly when and under what circumstances an officer must read a suspect his or her rights. This confusion is exacerbated by a pervasive belief among members of the general public that the police must inform suspects of their rights anytime the most innocuous of questions is put forth. Contrary to this misguided perception, however, officers are not required to read the *Miranda* warnings every time an individual is questioned but, instead, must do so only during the course of a custodial interrogation.

The task at hand thus becomes one of defining exactly what constitutes a custodial interrogation. As implied, two conditions must be met—the person must be in custody and he or she must be subjected to interrogation. "Custody" occurs when an individual is significantly deprived of his or her freedom to leave. "Interrogation" occurs when officers ask probative questions about an individual's involvement in a particular crime. Where these two conditions are met—the individual is not free to leave and he or she is being questioned about a specific crime—then, and only then, must the warnings be given.

A word of caution is appropriate at this point, especially where broad interpretation is given to the above definition of custodial interrogation. For example, it might reasonably be argued that the *Miranda* warnings must be given during traffic stops, insofar as the motorist is compelled to remain on the scene and answer questions about his or her involvement in a criminal traffic offense. Eventually, the Supreme Court resolved this issue in *Berkemer v. McCarty,* 468 U.S. 420 (1984) by ruling that the roadside questioning of a motorist detained pursuant to a lawful traffic stop does not con-

stitute a custodial interrogation. Consequently, officers are not required to inform traffic violators of their *Miranda* rights.

In spite of this clarification, problematic situations arise for police officers almost daily. For example, an officer dispatched to the scene of a domestic violence call notes that a physical assault has clearly taken place. Must the *Miranda* warning be given before any questions are asked of a suspected assailant, or is it permissible for the officer to ask general questions in order to first find out what occurred? While there exists no universal protocol for these and other types of conceivable situations the police frequently encounter, the safest bet is to warn suspects in order to prevent a subsequent claim that their rights were violated. To this important end, the cases included in this chapter illustrate problematic situations where officers conducted custodial interrogations (or the functional equivalent thereof) that were later scrutinized for constitutional appropriateness by the Supreme Court. ✦

Brewer v. Williams
430 U.S. 387 (1977)

Facts

Williams surrendered to police in Davenport, Iowa, on charges stemming from the abduction and murder of a 10-year-old Des Moines girl. While awaiting transport from Davenport to Des Moines, he was twice advised by two separate attorneys to refrain from speaking with officers about the alleged offense. Furthermore, Williams was arraigned before a judge in Davenport who informed him of his *Miranda* rights. Before leaving the courtroom, Williams consulted with yet a third attorney, who reiterated what the other two had already told him. When Des Moines detectives arrived, they too informed Williams of his *Miranda* rights. Thus, not only had Williams been twice informed of his *Miranda* rights by state agents, but he was also advised by three separate attorneys to remain silent if asked any questions about the alleged crime. While driving back to Des Moines, one of the detectives remarked to Williams that they should probably stop and locate the young girl's body so that her parents could provide her with a "Christian burial." Williams conceded and directed the transporting detectives to her body. He was eventually tried for first-degree murder and the state's supreme court allowed the conviction to stand. A federal district court granted Williams' petition for habeas corpus review on grounds that the evidence in question had been wrongly admitted at trial. The Eighth Circuit Court of

Appeals affirmed the petition, and the U.S. Supreme Court granted certiorari.

ISSUE

Did the officer's appeal for information regarding the whereabouts of the young girl's body violate Williams' Sixth Amendment right to counsel?

HOLDING

Yes. Officers are prohibited from appealing to a suspect's moral or religious beliefs for purposes of soliciting incriminating statements in the absence of legal representation.

RATIONALE

The officer's appeal for information regarding the whereabouts of the young girl's body violated Williams' Sixth amendment right to counsel on at least two grounds. First, judicial proceedings had formally been initiated against Williams, thereby triggering his right to counsel during any custodial interrogations. Second, the officer's statement regarding the need for a "Christian burial" was tantamount to a custodial interrogation. Consequently, a five-to-four majority of the Court ruled that the officer consciously and knowingly set out to violate Williams' Sixth Amendment right to counsel as well as his Fifth Amendment privilege against self-incrimination.

CASE SIGNIFICANCE

This decision is important in two regards. First, it served to remind officers that once formal proceedings have been initiated against a suspect, he or she is protected by the Sixth Amendment right to counsel so that no questioning about the offense may be undertaken unless an attorney is physically present. Second, the decision clarified the conditions that amount to custodial interrogation. Thus, although there was no direct questioning of Williams, the officer's reference to a "Christian burial" and reference to the suspect as "Reverend" nonetheless created a coercive environment violative of his right to counsel.

RHODE ISLAND V. INNIS
446 U.S. 291 (1980)

FACTS

Police arrested Innis after he was identified by a robbery victim. He was advised no less than three times of his *Miranda* rights by the patrol officer and two supervisory personnel on the scene. A prior robbery victim had been killed with a sawed-off shotgun. While en route to the jail, one of the transporting officers expressed concern to another that children from a nearby school for the handicapped might find the weapon and accidentally harm themselves. Overhearing this comment and apparently sharing similar concern, Innis told the officers to turn the car around so that he could show them where the weapon was hidden. Upon arriving back at the scene of his arrest, Innis was again informed of his *Miranda* rights. Indicating that he understood these rights, he nonetheless led officers to a nearby field where the gun was recovered. Innis was subsequently convicted of kidnapping, robbery, and murder. On appeal, the Rhode Island Supreme Court set aside the conviction on grounds that the transporting officers had interrogated Innis without the benefit of counsel while transporting him to the jail. The U.S. Supreme Court then granted certiorari.

ISSUE

Did the conversation overheard by Innis that led him to disclose the shotgun's location constitute an interrogation for purposes of Sixth Amendment analysis?

HOLDING

No. The conversation between the two officers did not constitute an interrogation or its functional equivalent as the suspect was not directly involved in the exchange. Therefore, no Sixth Amendment right was either implicated or violated.

RATIONALE

The U.S. Supreme Court reversed the Rhode Island Supreme Court's ruling that the transporting officers had interrogated Innis and thereby violated his Sixth Amendment right to counsel. In reaching this decision, the Court first reviewed the various procedural safeguards established by its decision in *Miranda v. Arizona*. Specifically, it was noted that the term "interrogation" refers not only instances of express questioning, but also to any words or actions undertaken by the police which are reasonably likely to elicit an incriminating response from the suspect. Given this definition, which places greater emphasis upon the perception of the suspect rather than the intent of the police, a majority of the justices concluded that the conversation that had transpired between the officers did not constitute an interrogation insofar as there had been no direct questioning of Innis. Furthermore, the conversation fell short of an interrogation on grounds that at no time did the officers attempt to elicit a response from Innis. Finally, the majority also observed that there was no indication that the two officers were specifically aware of and intentionally sought to exploit Innis' concern for the safety of nearby handicapped children.

CASE SIGNIFICANCE

This case is important in that it helped clarify those police behaviors that constitute an interrogation and those that do not. Recall that in the earlier matter of *Brewer v. Williams* the Supreme Court ruled that an officer's direct appeal to a suspect for information regarding the whereabouts of a murder victim's body so that the parents could provide her with a "Christian burial" constituted an interrogation for purposes of Sixth Amendment analysis. In the present matter, however, the Court concluded that the behavior of the two officers did not constitute an interrogation for purposes of Sixth Amendment analysis on the grounds that they did not directly engage the suspect in conversation—they were speaking only among themselves and did not ask him any questions. Although the distinction between these two cases may seem clear, the use of such tactics to obtain information remains risky given that the situation will be assessed not from the perspective of the officers but, instead, from that of the suspect. If the case can be made that a defendant believed he or she was being actively interrogated by the police, then most courts will rule in favor of the defendant's Sixth Amendment interest.

ARIZONA V. MAURO
481 U.S. 520 (1987)

FACTS

Seeking information about the murder of his son, officers informed Mauro of his *Miranda* rights, whereupon he declined to make any statements until an attorney was present. Officers promptly terminated the interview. Later, however, they allowed Mauro's wife to meet with him. Also present in the room during this meeting was an officer who openly laid a tape recorder on the desk between the two. During the course of their conversation, Mauro made incriminating statements to his wife. These statements were later introduced at trial and Mauro was convicted. The Arizona Supreme Court reversed the conviction finding that the tape-recorded conversation violated Mauro's right to avoid self-incrimination under the Fifth Amendment. The U.S. Supreme Court then granted certiorari.

ISSUE

Does the tape recording of a conversation between a suspect and his or her spouse that occurs in the presence of a police officer violate the Fifth Amendment privilege against self-incrimination?

HOLDING

No. The self-incrimination privilege of the Fifth Amendment does not forbid the introduction of incriminating statements made by a suspect to his or her spouse in the presence of a police officer, especially in instances where the suspect was not subjected to any compelling influences, psychological ploys, or direct questioning generally characteristic of custodial interrogation or its functional equivalent.

RATIONALE

By a five-to-four vote, the Court ruled that Mauro's incriminating statements were admissible on several grounds. First, the attending officer did not ask Mauro any questions about the alleged crime. Second, Mauro chose to speak openly with his wife knowing full well that a tape recorder was being used. Third, the police did not orchestrate the meeting between Mauro and his wife—she approached them and asked for the meeting with her husband. Finally, there existed no evidence to suggest that Mauro was coerced to speak to his wife or to make incriminating statements against his will during the course of their meeting. In contrast, the dissenting justices argued that the incriminating statements were obtained through use of a powerful psychological ploy set into motion at a time when it was reasonably likely to produce such evidence.

CASE SIGNIFICANCE

This case eroded the rights of criminals insofar as it allows authorities to tape record verbal exchanges between a suspect and others so long as no compelling influence, psychological ploy, or direct questioning is involved. Consistent with the facts of the present case, officers may sit in on or even record the conversation between a suspect and visitor so long as such measures are openly undertaken. The suspect cannot be coerced or tricked into giving the information under false pretenses. So long as the environment in which the information is disclosed does not constitute the functional equivalent of an interrogation, such tactics for obtaining information are constitutionally permissible. ✦

DISCUSSION QUESTIONS

1. Why do so many members of the public think that the police must read the *Miranda* warnings, even in situations where it is not legally required?

2. How should officers respond when confronted by an individual who demands to be given the *Miranda* warnings, even though they may not be legally necessary?

3. Must an arrestee be informed of his or her *Miranda* rights before being asked routine questions during the booking process? Why or why not?

4. What were the major differences in the facts and circumstances surrounding the *Brewer* case as opposed to the *Innis* case? In other words, why did the Supreme Court decide that Brewer's confession was not admissible but that Innis' confession was?

5. Why is it arguably a bad idea for the police to engage a suspect in casual conversation about even the most nonincriminating matters? ✦

Chapter Twenty

Entrapment

Sherman v. United States, 356 U.S. 369 (1958)

United States v. Russell, 411 U.S. 423 (1973)

Hampton v. United States, 425 U.S. 484 (1976)

Mathews v. United States, 485 U.S. 58 (1988)

Jacobson v. United States, 503 U.S. 540 (1992)

INTRODUCTION

Numerous defenses to criminal liability can be asserted by a defendant, including self-defense, insanity, and involuntary intoxication. Criminal law texts cover these in detail. One defense that straddles the line between criminal law and criminal procedure is *entrapment.* While it is a defense in the criminal law sense, it is one of the few that calls into question law enforcement's role in the instigation of a crime, and so it is almost always brought up in the realm of criminal procedure. Entrapment is an affirmative defense, which means it can easily be raised at trial.

It is important to note that the entrapment defense can be asserted even if the person charged with the crime refuses to admit all its elements. For example, if a defendant refuses to admit that he or she intended to commit a crime, he or she can still assert an entrapment defense, as decided by the Supreme Court in *Mathews v. United States.*

The entrapment defense is based on the principle that people should not be convicted of a crime that was instigated by the government. In its simplest form, the entrapment defense arises when government officials "plant the seeds" of criminal intent. That is, if a person commits a crime which he or she would not have committed but for the government's conduct, an entrapment defense will probably succeed. Entrapment is a frequent topic in both criminal law and criminal procedure. In the legal sense it is a defense; in the procedural sense it places restrictions on government actors by discouraging them from encouraging people to violate the law.

Despite its apparent simplicity, the entrapment defense has been a contentious one. In particular, there has been disagreement in the courts over what role the offender's predisposition plays, and how far the government can legally go in luring a person into criminal activity. When entrapment decisions are based on the offender's predisposition, this is known as a "subjective" inquiry. By contrast, a focus on the governmental conduct presumably responsible for someone's decision to commit a crime is known as an "objective" inquiry.

The American Law Institute's Model Penal Code takes an objective approach with regard to the entrapment defense: if the government "employ[ed] methods of persuasion or inducement which create a substantial risk that such an offense will be committed by persons other than those who are ready to commit it," then the defense is available regardless of the offender's initial willingness to offend. The Supreme Court, however, has opted to focus on the (subjective) predisposition of the offender instead of the government's role in instigating the crime in question (*Hampton v. United States*).

In *Sorrells,* the defendant was charged with violating the National Prohibition Act. When, after two unsuccessful attempts, a law enforcement agent convinced the defendant to sell him whiskey. Chief Justice Hughes noted that "artifice and stratagem" are permissible methods of catching criminals, so entrapment did not occur. Instead, it was the defendant's predisposition to offend that was significant.

In the next leading entrapment case, *Sherman v. United States,* the Supreme Court reached the opposite conclusion, but still adhered to the predisposition test. In *United States v. Russell,* the Court continued to focus on the defendant's predisposition. In *Russell,* a narcotics agent posed as a narcotics manufacturer and offered the defendant a difficult-to-obtain ingredient used to manufacture methamphetamine. The defendant accepted and was convicted. Justice Rehnquist, author of the majority opinion, observed that there was sufficient predisposition on the part of the defendant, and the entrapment defense did not apply. A similar decision can be found in *Jacobson v. United States,* a case we also brief.

In *Hampton v. United States,* the Supreme Court once again focused on the defendant's predisposition. In that case the defendant was convicted of distributing heroin supplied to the defendant by a government informant. The Court stated that "[i]f the police engage in illegal activity in concert with a defendant beyond the scope of their duties the remedy lies, not in freeing the equally culpable defendant, but in prosecuting the police under the applicable provisions of state or federal law." In other words, it is the defendant's predisposition that matters in the context of the entrapment defense, not the government conduct.

To suggest that the Supreme Court has ignored the role of government conduct is not entirely true. In a concurring opinion cited in *Hampton,* Justices Powell and Blackmun argued that government behavior that "shocks the conscience" could conceivably violate due process. In their words, "there is certainly a limit to allowing governmental involvement in crime. . . . It would be unthinkable . . . to permit government agents to instigate robberies and beatings merely to gather evidence to convict other members of a gang of hoodlums."

The Supreme Court has yet to affirmatively recognize a due process–based defense to government entrapment, but some lower courts have. Generally, if government officials use violence, supply contraband that is wholly unobtainable, or engage in a "criminal enterprise," defendants in such cases often succeed with the entrapment defense based on a due process argument. For now, the Supreme Court has said that it is unacceptable for police to create a person's disposition to a crime (*Jacobson*). ✦

SHERMAN V. UNITED STATES
356 U.S. 369 (1958)

FACTS

A government informant met Sherman in a doctor's office where both were being treated for drug addiction. During several subsequent meetings the informant asked Sherman if he knew of a source for buying drugs. Sherman initially avoided the subject, but eventually, after the informant asked several times, Sherman supplied the informant with drugs. The informant notified the FBI of the transactions and also set up several more narcotics transactions, which agents observed. Sherman was arrested and convicted of narcotics offenses. He appealed, and the U.S. Supreme Court granted certiorari.

ISSUE

Does entrapment occur when the government induces a person to commit a crime that he or she would not have otherwise committed?

HOLDING

Yes. The defendant will succeed with an entrapment defense where he or she can show that (1) the government induced the crime; and (2) the crime would not have otherwise been committed.

RATIONALE

"The case at bar illustrates an evil which the defense of entrapment is designed to overcome. The government informer entices someone attempting to avoid narcotics not only into carrying out an illegal sale but also returning to the habit of use. Selecting the proper time, the informer then tells the government agent. The setup is accepted by the agent without even a question as to the manner in which the informer encountered the seller. Thus the government plays on the weakness of an innocent party and beguiles him into committing crimes which he otherwise would not have attempted. Law enforcement does not require methods such as this."

CASE SIGNIFICANCE

This case was responsible for the standard still in use today: Entrapment occurs when the government induces innocent and nonpredisposed parties into the commission of a crime. It is difficult, even for the staunchest law enforcement advocate, to disagree with the Court's decision, because Sherman was seeking treatment for his narcotics addiction.

UNITED STATES V. RUSSELL
411 U.S. 423 (1973)

FACTS

Russell was under suspicion for the manufacture and sale of methamphetamine. Shapiro, an undercover law enforcement officer, approached Russell and offered to supply phenyl-1-propanone, a legal substance necessary to manufacture the drug. Russell then showed Shapiro his laboratory where he manufactured the drug. Russell was later tried and convicted of manufacturing and selling methamphetamine. He appealed his conviction, arguing that because the government supplied an essential ingredient, he should be found not guilty. The U.S. Supreme Court granted certiorari.

ISSUE

Can one succeed with an entrapment defense if one was already predisposed to commit the crime in question?

HOLDING

No. The defense of entrapment requires a showing that the defendant was not predisposed to commit the crime. In this case there was substantial evidence presented to show that Russell had manufactured methamphetamine before and after he received the ingredients from Shapiro.

RATIONALE

"While we may some day be presented with a situation in which the conduct of law enforcement agents is so outrageous that due process principles would absolutely bar the government from invoking judicial process to obtain conviction, the instant case is distinctly not of that breed. Shapiro's contribution of propane to the criminal enterprise already in process was scarcely objectionable. The chemical is, by itself, a harmless substance and its possession is legal. While the government may have been seeking to make it more difficult for drug rings, such as that of which Russell was a member, to obtain the chemical, the evidence described above shows that it nonetheless was obtainable. The law enforcement conduct here stops short of violating that 'fundamental fairness, shocking to the universal sense of justice,' mandated by the due process clause of the Fifth Amendment."

Case Significance

This case is important because it placed limits on the entrapment defense. Based on this decision, if a defendant was predisposed to offend, an entrapment defense will fail. The Court downplayed the role of the government, instead focusing on the conduct of the accused—particularly predisposition. The Court did intimate, however, that if the government's conduct was "outrageous," it could violate due process even if the defendant were predisposed.

HAMPTON V. UNITED STATES
425 U.S. 484 (1976)

Facts

Hampton bought heroin from a DEA informant and was convicted on narcotics offenses. He claimed that he was entrapped because the drugs he bought were supplied by the informant, and the U.S. Supreme Court granted certiorari.

Issue

Was Hampton entrapped when he bought drugs from a government informant?

Holding

No. Entrapment did not occur because the defendant was predisposed to commit the crime. Had the government planted the seeds of intent in the defendant's mind, then entrapment would have occurred.

Rationale

"Here . . . the police, the government informant, and the defendant acted in concert with one another. If the result of the governmental activity is to 'implant in the mind of an innocent person the disposition to commit the alleged offense and induce its commission,' the defendant is protected by the defense of entrapment. If the police engaged in illegal activity in concert with a defendant beyond the scope of their duties, the remedy lies not in freeing the equally culpable defendant but in prosecuting the police under the applicable provisions of state or federal law."

Case Significance

This case differed from *Russell* insofar as the government (through an informant) supplied the defendant with drugs, not just an ingredient used to manufacture drugs. To those on the left side of the political continuum, this decision was controversial because it seemed to permit questionable conduct on the part of the police. However, to the law enforcement community, *Hampton* was a step in the right direction because it permitted police to engage in buy-bust operations, arguably an essential method of waging war on drugs.

MATHEWS V. UNITED STATES
485 U.S. 58 (1988)

Facts

A government informant working for the FBI requested a loan from Mathews in exchange for Small Business Association benefits. When the two met to exchange the money, Mathews was arrested for accepting a bribe. The trial court denied Mathews' motion seeking to raise the entrapment defense because he would not admit committing all elements of the crime. He was found guilty, appealed, and the U.S. Supreme Court granted certiorari.

Issue

Can a defendant assert an entrapment defense even though he or she refuses to admit all elements of a crime?

Holding

Yes. Even if the defendant denies an element of the crime, such as *mens rea* or *actus reas*, he may raise the defense of entrapment if there is a reasonable probability that the jury would decide in his favor.

Rationale

"There is no merit to the Government's contention that, because entrapment presupposes the commission of a crime, defendant should not be allowed both to deny the offense or an element thereof, and to rely on the inconsistent, affirmative defense of entrapment."

Case Significance

This case permits a defendant to assert the entrapment defense even if he or she disputes an element of the crime. For example, the defendant could argue that the requisite *mens rea* (criminal intent) was lacking in light of the government's conduct, so the entrapment defense should succeed. The government argued that an entrapment defense where the accused refuses to admit an element of the crime would confuse the court and interfere with justice. The Supreme Court disagreed, stating that the only requirement necessary for an entrapment defense to be raised is a reasonable probability that the jury could side with the defendant.

JACOBSON V. UNITED STATES
503 U.S. 540 (1992)

FACTS

At a time when it was legal, Jacobson ordered a book containing pictures of nude boys from an adult bookstore. Congress subsequently passed the Child Protection Act of 1984, criminalizing receipt by mail of sexually explicit depictions of children. The Postal Service found Jacobson's name on the store's mailing list and began mailing him letters and questionnaires from fictitious research and lobbying organizations and a fake pen pal. The mailings discussed and asked about Jacobson's tastes in pornography and views on censorship. Each time he answered, the next mailing was geared more toward his tastes. Two years later, the Customs Service, through a fictitious company, sent Jacobson a child pornography brochure. He placed an order, but it was never filled. The Postal Service, using a fake company, sent Jacobson a letter decrying censorship and claiming the media and the government were trying to keep its material out of the country. Jacobson requested a catalog, from which he placed an order. He was arrested on controlled delivery of the magazine. He raised an entrapment defense, and the case came before the U.S. Supreme Court.

ISSUE

Does entrapment take place when the government creates a person's disposition and then induces the crime?

HOLDING

Yes. Where the government creates a person's disposition to commit a crime, and then induces the person to commit the crime, entrapment occurs.

RATIONALE

"Had the agents in this case simply offered petitioner the opportunity to order child pornography through the mails, and the petitioner—who must be presumed to know the law—had promptly availed himself of the criminal opportunity, it is unlikely that his entrapment defense would have warranted a jury instruction. But this was not what happened here. By the time petitioner finally placed his order, he had already been the target of 26 months of repeated mailings and communications from Government agents and fictitious organizations. Therefore, although he had become predisposed to break the law by May 1987, it is our view that the Government did not prove that this predisposition was independent and not the product of the attention that the government had directed at the petitioner since January 1985."

CASE SIGNIFICANCE

The Court reversed Jacobson's conviction in this case, stated that the "prosecution failed, as a matter of law, to adduce evidence to support the jury verdict that Jacobson was predisposed, independent of the Government's acts and beyond a reasonable doubt, to violate the law by receiving child pornography through the mails." Unlike *Russell*, this case placed a fair amount of weight on the conduct of the government in determining whether entrapment takes place. Thus, while the success or failure of an entrapment defense still hinges in large measure on the defendant's degree of predisposition, the government cannot create that predisposition. ✦

DISCUSSION QUESTIONS

1. Identify situations where a person could validly claim entrapment.

2. Identify situations where a person could *not* validly claim entrapment.

3. Does the entrapment defense inhibit effective police work? Why or why not?

4. It is possible for the police to entrap a person to the extent that their conduct violates due process. This requires that police engage in conduct that "shocks the conscience." What would it take for the police to violate due process in the entrapment context?

5. Entrapment is a unique topic in criminal procedure. It is perhaps the only criminal law defense that pops up in the procedure context. Why, then, is entrapment often discussed in criminal procedure class? ✦

Chapter Twenty-One
Asset Forfeiture

United States v. Good, 510 U.S. 43 (1993)

United States v. Ursery, 518 U.S. 267 (1996)

Bennis v. Michigan, 516 U.S. 442 (1996)

United States v. Bajakajian, 524 U.S. 321 (1998)

City of West Covina v. Perkins,
   525 U.S. 234 (1999)

Florida v. White, 119 S.Ct. 1555 (1999)

INTRODUCTION

The array of penalities the criminal justice system imposes on people convicted of a crime can be divided into two categories: monetary and nonmonetary. Nonmonetary penalties include probation, prison, home confinement, electronic monitoring, and similar sanctions. Monetary penalties include fines, fees, and forfeiture. Here we focus on forfeiture.

There are two types of forfeiture: civil and criminal. Each will be addressed separately. For now, however, forfeiture needs to be distinguished from seizure. Simply put, the police can seize property (e.g., cash), but forfeiture is a separate action. When something is forfeited, ownership to it (if any) is relinquished. A seizure, on the other hand, implies a temporary action where ownership is *not* relinquished.

Criminal forfeiture proceedings are referred to as *in personam,* which means they target people. Criminal forfeiture can only follow a criminal conviction. If criminal forfeiture is sought, the prosecutor must prove beyond a reasonable doubt that the offender is guilty *and* that the property is subject to forfeiture. For example, if, in addition to securing a criminal conviction, the prosecutor can prove beyond a reasonable doubt that the defendant bought a house with the proceeds of the offense for which he or she is charged, the house can be forfeited. Thus, unlike fines and fees, forfeiture is used to minimize the financial gain associated with certain types of crimes, usually drug offenses.

Civil asset forfeiture, in contrast to criminal forfeiture, is *in rem,* meaning that it targets property. Civil asset forfeiture does not require a criminal proceeding, and it can be pursued altogether independently of a criminal proceeding. Civil forfeiture proceedings can be understood in much the same way as wrongful death lawsuits, which can be pursued independently (or in lieu) of a homicide trial. Indeed, all varieties of civil litigation can be pursued independently of criminal proceedings.

Because civil forfeiture does not require that formal criminal proceedings be initiated, the property owner's guilt is basically irrelevant. Because property owner's guilt or innocence is irrelevant in civil forfeiture proceedings, many people have criticized the practice. Critics of civil forfeiture argue that because property is targeted—as opposed to an actual defendant—forfeiture laws conveniently circumvent important constitutional protections.

Civil asset forfeiture is also controversial because, depending on state law, proceeds can be awarded to the law enforcement agency that initiated the forfeiture. In some states, local police agencies that are responsible for the seizure of large quantities of cash can receive the cash (to be used for law enforcement purposes) if ownership to it is forfeited. Critics of this practice have argued that civil asset forfeiture creates a conflict of interest between crime control and fiscal management.

What does it mean to suggest that civil forfeiture targets property? In civil forfeiture proceedings, the government essentially sues property. The parties to the typical forfeiture case include the government and a piece of property (e.g., funds in a bank account at a certain location). The result can be a case such as *United States v. One Mercedes 300E.* Property that can be sued includes cars, cash, funds in a bank account, real property or virtually any thing else of value. The only restriction is that the property targeted be used to facilitate or is derived from criminal activity.

The idea that property can somehow be guilty of crime traces its origins to the Bible. Exodus, Chapter 21, Verse 28 states, "When an ox gores a man or woman to death the ox must be stoned; the flesh may not be eaten. The owner of the ox, however, shall go unpunished." Modern forfeiture statutes can be attributed to this idea that property, even livestock, can manifest the will to inflict harm. The Supreme Court:

> Traditionally, forfeiture actions have proceeded upon the fiction that the inanimate objects themselves can be guilty of wrongdoing. Simply put, the theory has been that if the object is "guilty," it should be held in forfeit. In the words of a medieval English writer, "Where a man killeth another with the sword of John at Stile, the sword shall be forfeit as deodand, and yet no default is in the owner." The modern forfeiture statutes are direct descendants of this heritage. (*United States v. United States Coin and Currency,* 401 U.S. 715 [1971])

There are three varieties of civil asset forfeiture proceedings. The first is *summary forfeiture.* This is where law enforcement officials summarily, or on the spot, seize property. Property to which no one can claim ownership, such as contraband, is subject to summary forfeiture. "Ownership" of the contraband immediately vests with the police, because no one can claim legal ownership of property that is not legal.

The second type of forfeiture proceeding is called *administrative forfeiture.* Administrative forfeiture differs from summary forfeiture in that it requires a formal court proceeding. The process usually begins with the property's seizure. Next, the property owner is given a certain amount of time in which to challenge the seizure. Finally, a court date is set, but only if the property owner decides to contest the seizure. If the property owner decides *not* to contest, the property is forfeited.

Administrative forfeiture is a controversial practice because it *begins* with a summary seizure of the property in question. Administrative forfeitures are justified by the "relation-back" doctrine. The relation-back doctrine is embodied in 21 U.S.C. Sec. 881(h) and provides that "all right, title, and interest in property [subject to forfeiture] shall vest in the United States upon commission of the act given rise to forfeiture." Generally, the only burden the police must meet to seize property is probable cause. Whether the property actually facilitated or was derived from crime is determined in court, but, again, only if the property owner contests the seizure.

The third type of forfeiture proceeding is known as a *civil judicial proceeding.* Civil judicial proceedings are not preceded by a seizure, and are usually reserved for expensive property or real property, such as real estate, that cannot be moved. The prosecutor brings a civil action against the property. Then, as in an administrative forfeiture proceeding, the property owner is given a reasonable amount of time in which to prepare a defense. If the property owner fails to appear in court in order to contest the proposed forfeiture, the property is forfeited to the government.

Civil asset forfeiture has been criticized extensively by an unlikely coalition of critics. House Judiciary Chairman Henry Hyde, a conservative, along with the American Civil Liberties Union, a staunchly liberal organization, have both championed forfeiture reform. Their hard work contributed to the recent passage of the Civil Asset Forfeiture Reform Act of 2000 (CAFRA), which has minimized a number of the procedural controversies associated with civil asset forfeiture.

The Supreme Court has confronted the constitutionality of forfeiture on several occasions. We consider six important cases in this chapter. First, in *United States v. Good,* the Court held that unless exigent circumstances exist, the due process clause of the Fifth Amendment requires that the government provide notice to property owners and an opportunity to be heard before seizing real property. Second, in *United States v. Ursery,* the Court held that civil forfeiture in addition to criminal prosecution does not violate the Fifth Amendment's double jeopardy clause.

In *Bennis v. Michigan,* the Court held that civil forfeiture of property used for criminal activity can be constitutional even if the owner is not aware of its criminal use. However, if a state has an "innocent owner" defense, the decision may not apply. At the time *Bennis* was decided, Michigan had no innocent owner defense. Next, in *United States v. Bajakajian,* the Court held that forfeiture that is grossly disproportionate to the gravity of the offense is unconstitutional.

In another case, *City of West Covina v. Perkins,* the Supreme Court held that the due process clause of the Fourteenth Amendment does not require the police to provide owners of seized property with notice about how to secure return of their property. And in *Florida v. White,* the Court held that no warrant is necessary for the police to seize an automobile from a public place that is subject to forfeiture. ✦

UNITED STATES V. GOOD
510 U.S. 43 (1993)

FACTS

Police officers served a search warrant at Good's home. They found 89 pounds of marijuana, marijuana seeds, additional drugs, and drug paraphernalia. Good pled guilty to drug charges and was required to forfeit the $3,187 in cash that was found in his house during the search. More than four years after the search, the federal government filed an action against Good's house, seeking forfeiture of the house and land it was situated on. Ten days later in an ex parte hearing (a hearing where one party is excluded—in this case, Good), a federal judge ruled in favor of the government and ordered Good's property forfeited. Good never received notice of any court dates, and was therefore unable to defend the proposed forfeiture of his property. He appealed, and the U.S. Supreme Court granted certiorari.

ISSUE

Can the government, through civil asset forfeiture proceedings, seize a person's home without affording notice of its intent?

HOLDING

No. The Fifth Amendment's due process clause prohibits the government from pursuing forfeiture of real property without notice to the property owner, unless exigent circumstances exist.

RATIONALE

". . . [B]ased upon the importance of the private interest at risk and the absence of countervailing Government needs, we hold that the seizure of real property under [21 U.S.C.] Section 81(a)(7) is not one of those extraordinary instances that justify the postponement of notice and hearing. Unless exigent circumstances are present, the Due Process Clause requires the Government to afford notice and meaningful opportunity to be heard before seizing real property subject to civil forfeiture. . . . To establish exigent circumstances, the Government must show that less restrictive measures—i.e., a *lis pendens,* restraining order, or bond—would not suffice to protect the Government's interest in preventing the sale, destruction, or continued unlawful use of the real property. We agree with the Court of Appeals that no showing of exigent circumstances has been made in this case. . . ."

CASE SIGNIFICANCE

Civil asset forfeiture actions target property, such as real estate, cash, and automobiles. Because these actions target property instead of property owners, there have traditionally been few protections available to people whose property is targeted by the government. This decision is arguably a step in the right direction because it requires notice to property owners before their real property can be subjected to forfeiture. Importantly, this case does not address property other than *real* property. Indeed, cash, automobiles, and other items can generally be seized by police, say, during a lawful arrest. In such instances no notice of intent to forfeit is required. However, if the owner of the seized property can claim ownership of it, then the government must hold a hearing where the property owner can present his or her case.

UNITED STATES V. URSERY
518 U.S. 267 (1996)

FACTS

Police found marijuana and growing equipment when searching Ursery's house. Ursery was prosecuted criminally, but the federal government also sought forfeiture of Ursery's house. Ursery filed a Section 1983 lawsuit against the government (see Chapter Twenty-

Two), claiming that the proposed forfeiture of his house would amount to double jeopardy, a violation of the Fifth Amendment.

ISSUE

Is a person placed in double jeopardy when he is criminally charged and civil forfeiture of his property is sought?

HOLDING

No. Civil asset forfeiture in conjunction with a criminal prosecution does not constitute double jeopardy. Civil asset forfeitures are directed against property and, as such, are not considered punishment. Prosecuting a property owner criminally and also seeking forfeiture of his property does not violate the Fifth Amendment's protection against double jeopardy.

RATIONALE

"The Double Jeopardy Clause provides: nor shall any person be subject for the same offense to be twice put in jeopardy of life or limb. . . . [I]n a long line of cases, this Court has considered the application of the Double Jeopardy Clause to civil forfeitures, consistently concluding that the Clause does not apply to such actions because they do not impose punishment. . . . It is the property which is proceeded against, and, by resort to legal fiction, held guilty and condemned as though it were conscious instead of inanimate and insentient. In a criminal prosecution it is the wrongdoer in person who is proceeded against, convicted, and punished. The forfeiture is no part of the punishment for the criminal offense. The provision of the Fifth Amendment to the Constitution in respect of double jeopardy does not apply."

CASE SIGNIFICANCE

This decision is significant not only because it permits criminal prosecutions and civil forfeiture actions against the same individual but because of the interesting argument it presents. The Court argued that because civil forfeiture actions target property, they don't constitute punishment. To critics of this decision, the Court's argument makes no sense. They claim that just as fines and criminal forfeiture are intended to punish people, so is civil forfeiture; even though civil forfeiture actions target property, the property still has an owner who would "suffer" from its loss. The government argued, however, that the reason behind civil asset forfeiture is to remove the "profit" from criminal activity. Why, the government and its supporters argue, should people be permitted to possess property that is used to commit crimes or is obtained from crime?

Bennis v. Michigan
516 U.S. 442 (1996)

Facts

Bennis and her husband were joint owners of a car in which the husband was caught with a prostitute. Based on a Michigan law, a court ordered the automobile forfeited as a public nuisance. Bennis was offered no compensation. She argued that she had no knowledge of her husband's activities and, as such, should receive compensation equal to her percentage of ownership in the car. The U.S. Supreme Court granted certiorari.

Issue

Can a person's property be subjected to civil asset forfeiture, even if the owner is not aware of its criminal use?

Holding

Yes. Certain civil asset forfeitures are permissible even if an innocent owner may not know of the property's facilitation of crime. A civil forfeiture of property used for criminal purposes is constitutional, even if the property's owner is not aware of its criminal use, but only if there is no innocent owner defense in place under the applicable forfeiture statute.

Rationale

". . . [I]t has long been settled that statutory forfeitures of property entrusted by the innocent owner or lienor to another who uses it in violation of the . . . laws of the United States is not a violation of the due process clause of the Fifth Amendment. . . . We conclude today, as we concluded 75 years ago, that the cases authorizing actions of the kind at issue are 'too firmly fixed in the punitive and remedial jurisprudence of the country to be not displaced.' The State here sought to deter illegal activity that contributes to neighborhood deterioration and unsafe streets. The Bennis automobile, it is conceded, facilitated and was used in criminal activity. Both the trial court and the Michigan Supreme Court followed our long-standing practice, and the judgment of the Supreme Court of Michigan is therefore affirmed."

Case Significance

This case is significant because it suggested that people whose property is put to criminal use, but who do not know as such, can be "hung out to dry." The Court referred to a long line of historical decisions in support of its position, but it can still be perceived as unfair that truly innocent owners have no recourse in civil forfeiture proceedings. This perceived unfairness has prompted several states as well as the federal government to provide statutory "innocent owner" defenses. For example, the Civil Asset Forfeiture Reform Act of 2000 permits any person whose property is targeted by a civil forfeiture action to assert a defense. In fact, this new legislation places the burden of proof—which is now a "preponderance of the evidence"—on the government (it used to be on the property owner), which serves to appease some of the Bennis decision's most vocal critics. One such critic is the lobbying organization Forfeiture Endangers American Rights (FEAR).

United States v. Bajakajian
524 U.S. 321 (1998)

Facts

Bajakajian and his family were at an airport, preparing to leave the country. Using "drug dogs" trained to detect traces of drugs on paper currency, customs inspectors discovered $230,000 in cash in Bajakajian's checked luggage. The inspectors then approached Bajakajian and told him that he was required to declare all money in excess of $10,000. Bajakajian stated that he had $8,000 in his possession and his wife had $7,000 and that they were carrying no additional cash in their luggage. A search of Bajakajian and his wife as well as all their luggage revealed $357,144 in cash. Bajakajian plead guilty to failing to declare the cash at the border. The government sought forfeiture of all the cash for failing to declare it at the border, and the case came before the U.S. Supreme Court.

Issue

Does a forfeiture that is grossly disproportionate to the underlying offense violate the Eighth Amendment's excessive fines clause?

Holding

Yes. A civil forfeiture that is grossly disproportionate to the underlying offense violates the Eighth Amendment's proscription against excessive fines.

Rationale

"The Eighth Amendment provides: 'Excessive bail shall not be required, nor excessive fines imposed, nor cruel and unusual punishment inflicted.' The Court has had little occasion to interpret, and has never actually applied, the Excessive Fines Clause. . . . The Excessive Fines Clause thus limits the government's power to extract payments, where in cash or in kind, 'as punishment for some offense' (*Austin v. United States*, 5098 U.S. at 609). Forfeitures—payments in kind—are thus 'fines' if they constitute punishment for an offense. . . .

We have little trouble concluding that the forfeiture of currency ordered by Section 982(a)(1) constitutes punishment. The statute directs a court to order forfeiture as an additional sanction when 'imposing sentence on a person convicted of a willful violation of Section 5316's reporting requirement.' The forfeiture is thus imposed at the culmination of a criminal proceeding and requires conviction of an underlying felony, and cannot be imposed upon an innocent owner of unreported currency, but only upon a person who has himself been convicted of a Section 5316 reporting violation. . . . Comparing the gravity of Bajakajian's crime with the $357,144 forfeiture the government seeks, we conclude that such a forfeiture would be grossly disproportional to the gravity of his offense" and is therefore in violation of the Eighth Amendment.

CASE SIGNIFICANCE

This case is significant because it limited the amount of property the government can seek to forfeit. The decision requires looking at the offense in question; serious offenses would be more likely to permit large forfeitures. The Court believed that failure to declare cash at the international border is not serious enough to warrant forfeiture of more than $350,000. Unfortunately, the Supreme Court failed to define what constitutes a "grossly disproportionate" forfeiture. For now, it is up to each individual court to decide.

CITY OF WEST COVINA V. PERKINS
525 U.S. 234 (1999)

FACTS

March, a suspect in a murder investigation, was a boarder at the Perkins house. Police officers obtained a warrant to search the Perkinses' home. No one was home when the warrant was served. The officers seized several items but did not find March. They posted a notice on the door as they were leaving, which included a copy of the warrant and the name of the judge who issued the warrant, among other information. The officers did not leave the warrant number because the case was still under investigation. After encountering difficulties getting their property returned, the Perkinses filed a lawsuit in an effort to secure return of their property, and the U.S. Supreme Court granted certiorari.

ISSUE

Are police required to provide detailed information to property owners as to how to secure return of their seized property?

HOLDING

No. The due process clause of the Fourteenth Amendment does not require the police to provide owners of seized property with notice about how to secure return of their property.

RATIONALE

"A primary purpose of the notice required by the Due Process Clause is to ensure that the opportunity for a hearing is meaningful. . . . It follows that when law enforcement agents seize property pursuant to [a] warrant, due process requires them to take reasonable steps to give notice that the property has been taken so the owner can pursue available remedies for its return. . . . No similar rationale justifies requiring individualized notice of state-law remedies which, like those at issue here, are established by published, generally available state statutes and case law. Once the property owner is informed that his property has been seized, he can turn to these public sources to learn about the remedial procedures available to him. The City need not take other steps to inform him of his options."

CASE SIGNIFICANCE

This case is one in a long line of Supreme Court cases dealing with civil asset forfeiture. The decision admittedly favored law enforcement, which is part of the reason the Supreme Court has been criticized for most of its forfeiture-related decisions. The Court did note that "individualized notice that officers have taken property is necessary in a case such as this one because the owner has no other reasonable means of ascertaining who is responsible for his loss," but additional notice as to what remedies are available to property owners is not required by the Fourteenth Amendment's due process clause.

FLORIDA V. WHITE
119 S.CT. 1555 (1999)

FACTS

The police observed White using his car to deliver drugs on several occasions. This made the car subject to forfeiture under Florida state law. Some months later the police arrested White on drug charges and seized his car without a warrant. During an inventory search the officers found cocaine in the ashtray. White was convicted of possession of a controlled substance. He appealed, and the U.S. Supreme Court granted certiorari.

ISSUE

Does the Fourth Amendment require the police to obtain a warrant before seizing an automobile from a public place when they have probable cause to believe that it is forfeitable contraband?

HOLDING

No. No warrant is necessary for the police to seize an automobile from a public place that is subject to forfeiture.

RATIONALE

"The principles underlying the rule in *Carroll* and the founding-era statutes upon which they are based fully support the conclusion that the warrantless seizure of White's car did not violate the Fourth Amendment. Although, as the Florida Supreme Court observed, the police lacked probable cause to believe White's car contained contraband, they certainly had probable cause to believe that the vehicle itself was contraband under Florida law. Recognition of the need to seize readily movable contraband before it is spirited away undoubtedly underlies the early federal laws relied upon in *Carroll*. This need is equally weighty when the automobile, as opposed to its contents, is the contraband that the police seek to secure. Furthermore, the early federal statutes that we looked to in *Carroll*, like the Florida Contraband Forfeiture Act, authorized the warrantless seizure of both goods subject to duties and the ships upon which those goods were concealed.... In addition to the special considerations recognized in the context of movable items, our Fourth Amendment jurisprudence has consistently accorded law enforcement officials greater latitude in exercising their duties in public places.... Here, because the police seized White's vehicle from a public area—White's employer's parking lot—the warrantless seizure also did not involve any invasion of White's privacy. Based on the relevant history and our prior precedent, we therefore conclude that the Fourth Amendment did not require a warrant to seize White's automobile in these circumstances."

CASE SIGNIFICANCE

This case is significant in that it addressed forfeiture of automobiles for civil asset forfeiture purposes. The Court's decision simply reinforced what was already known with regard to vehicle searches. White was arrested in a public place, which permits a search of the passenger compartment. Police did not search the passenger compartment incident to the arrest, which is their prerogative, but instead conducted an inventory search later. No Supreme Court decision prohibits this, so long as the search is conducted in accordance with departmental policy. The only difference, then, between this case and standard criminal procedure cases is that the police used the evidence seized against White at his criminal trial but also sought forfeiture under the Florida statute. Had the seizure taken place on private property, the Supreme Court would probably have decided differently. ✦

DISCUSSION QUESTIONS

1. Asset forfeiture is an especially controversial law enforcement practice by which law enforcement can "profit" from criminal activity. What is your opinion of asset forfeiture?

2. As part of plea agreements, defendants are often required to give up ownership to property (e.g., cash or conveyances). Do you agree with this practice?

3. In these times of tight budgets in public agencies, forfeiture is especially attractive as a method of compensating for budget shortfalls. Should it be?

4. Forfeiture laws are expanding in such a way that forfeiture can occur in a variety of criminal contexts. Do you agree with this progression?

5. By law, certain states do not permit forfeiture proceeds to go back to police agencies; however, if state and local agencies team up with federal officials, they can receive 80 percent of the forfeiture proceeds. These are known as "adoptive forfeitures." Do you agree with this practice? Why or why not? ✦

Chapter Twenty-Two

Civil Liability

INTRODUCTION

42 U.S.C. Section 1983 (hereafter referred to as Section 1983) provides a remedy in federal court for the "deprivation of any rights . . . secured by the Constitution and laws" of the United States. As such, it has been addressed by the Supreme Court on many occasions. Almost every case in this chapter deals with this important piece of legislation. Section 1983 states:

> Every person who, under color of any statute, ordinance, regulation, custom, or usage, of any State or Territory, subjects, or causes to be subjected, any citizen of the United States or other persons within the jurisdiction thereof to the deprivation of any rights, privileges, or immunities secured by the Constitution and laws, shall be liable to the party injured in an action at law, suit in equity, or other proper proceeding for redress.

Section 1983 was originally enacted as part of the Ku Klux Klan Act of April 20, 1871 (also known as Section 1 of the Civil Rights Act of 1871). The Act was designed to address atrocities being committed by Klan members in the wake of the Civil War, but it did not target Klan members as such. Instead, Section 1983 imposed liability on state representatives who failed to enforce state laws against illegal Klan activities. But the statute was rarely used and remained effectively dormant for some 90 years after it was signed into law.

Section 1983 enjoyed a resurgence in *Monroe v. Pape.* In that case, a group of police officers allegedly entered the home of James Monroe without warning, then forced the occupants to stand naked in the living room while the house was searched and ransacked. Monroe brought a Section 1983 action against the police officers and the city of Chicago. The case eventually reached the United States Supreme Court, where eight justices held that the alleged misuse of authority could support a Section 1983 action against the police officers—that is, the Supreme Court held that Section 1983 could be used as a vehicle to sue the police.

One of the requirements for a successful Section 1983 lawsuit is that the defendant, the person being sued, must have acted "under color of law." The Supreme Court has stated that someone acts under color of law when he or she acts in an official capacity (*Lugar v. Edmondson Oil Co.,* 457 U.S. 922, 937 [1982]). For example, a police officer who is on duty acts under color of law. By contrast, someone acting in a private capacity (e.g., an ordinary citizen) cannot be said to have acted under color of law.

To complicate matters, certain officials who act under color of law can nevertheless not be sued. In *Will v. Michigan Department of State Police,* for example, the Supreme Court held that neither states nor state officials, acting in their official capacity, can be held liable under Section 1983. However, state officials who are sued in their *individual* capacity can be held liable (see *Hafer v. Melo*).

What happens when it is unclear whether the defendant named in a lawsuit is a party who can be sued? The Supreme Court confronted this question in *McMillian v. Monroe County.* The specific question before the Court was whether a sheriff is a representative of the state or of the county. As a representative of the state, the sheriff could not be sued in his or her official capacity. As a representative of the county, he or she could. The Court held that it is necessary to consult individual state constitutions, laws, and/or regulations in order to make this determination.

The second requirement for a successful Section 1983 lawsuit is that a violation of constitutional rights take place. In determining whether constitutional rights have been violated the plaintiff(s) must establish that the defendant's (or defendants') conduct violated a specific constitutional provision, such as the Fourth Amendment.

Recently, the courts have begun to require that constitutional rights violations alleged under Section 1983 be committed with a certain level of culpability. That is, plaintiffs generally have to prove that the defendant(s) intended for the violation to occur. There is a very clear reason for this: Not all constitutional rights violations are (or should be) actionable under Section 1983, only the most egregious of civil rights violations. The level of culpability required for a constitutional rights violation varies depending on the type of unconstitutional conduct alleged by the plaintiff.

Typically, in Section 1983 cases, the plaintiff's lawsuit will target an individual officer, that officer's supervisor, the city or municipality for which the officer works, or a combination thereof. While the individual officer responsible for inflicting harm should arguably be held liable, plaintiffs are often attracted to "bigger fish" where there are larger rewards. Governmental entities, in particular, have deep pockets and are attractive targets for civil litigation. Individual officers can be sued, of course, because they are most directly responsible for constitutional rights violations, when they occur. The following paragraphs therefore discuss cases involving individuals as well as municipal or county liability.

Cities and counties can be held liable under Section 1983 if they adopt and implement policies or adopt customs that become responsible for constitutional rights violations (see *Monell v. Department of Social Services*). In general, a Section 1983 claim against a county or municipality will fail if a common practice is engaged in by lower-ranking officials who have no authority to make "policy" in the traditional sense of the term. For example, if a group of police officers regularly use excessive force, but do so on their own, with no authorization from the city or county, then the city or county could not be held liable for their actions.

In another city/county liability case, *City of Canton v. Harris,* the Supreme Court held that counties (and, by extension, cities) can be held liable for inadequately training their law enforcement officers. The facts of the case in *Canton* were that Harris was arrested and brought to the police station in a patrol wagon. On arrival, the officers found Harris lying on the floor of the wagon. She was asked if she needed medical attention, but she responded incoherently. After she was brought into the station, she slumped to the floor on two occasions. Eventually she was left lying on the floor; no

medical attention was summoned for her. Harris later sued, seeking to hold the city liable for a violation of her Fourteenth Amendment right, under the due process clause, to receive medical attention while in police custody. However, the Court held that "only where a municipality's failure to train its employees in a relevant respect evidences a 'deliberate indifference' to the rights of its inhabitants can such a shortcoming be properly thought of as a city 'policy or custom' that is actionable under [Section] 1983" (*City of Canton v. Harris*).

In *Board of the County Commissioners of Bryan County v. Brown* the Supreme Court revisited the city/county liability issue. In particular, the question before the Court was whether a single hiring decision by a municipality's policymaker could give rise to an inadequate hiring claim under Section 1983. In that case Brown's claim was fueled by the injuries she suffered at the hands of Bryan County Reserve Deputy Stacy Burns during a high-speed pursuit, and by the fact that Burns had two previous misdemeanor convictions for assault and battery, both of which were overlooked during the pre-employment screening process. Brown seemed to have a good case, but the Court's decision in *Bryan County* set the bar for a claim against a municipality for inadequate hiring rather high. Specifically, the Court held that "[e]ven assuming without deciding that proof of a single instance of inadequate screening could ever trigger municipal liability, Moore's failure to scrutinize Burns' record cannot constitute 'deliberate indifference' to respondent's federally protected right to be free from the use of excessive force (*Board of the County Commissioners of Bryan County v. Brown*).

Another Supreme Court case, *Collins v. City of Harker Heights,* also set the bar high. That case did not involve criminal justice officials but rather other city employees. The Court held that the city's failure to warn its employees concerning hazards in the workplace cannot lead to liability under Section 1983. What makes this decision distinctive is that the plaintiffs were city employees, not outside parties.

For a finding of individual liability, Section 1983 requires a plaintiff to demonstrate that his or her constitutional rights were violated by someone acting under color of state law. The constitutional rights most frequently claimed in Section 1983 lawsuits include those stemming from the Fourth, Eighth, and Fourteenth Amendments to the Constitution. We focus here on Fourteenth Amendment cases, as some of the others are discussed in a different context in other chapters (e.g., *Tennessee v. Garner* in Chapter Five).

The Fourteenth Amendment contains two primary components, both of which are actionable under Section 1983. These are the so-called "substantive" and "procedural" components. The essence of substantive due process is protection from arbitrary and unreasonable action on the part of state officials. A "shocks the conscience" standard has been used in cases involving allegations of Fourteenth Amendment substantive due process (*County of Sacramento v. Lewis*). There, the Supreme Court held that police officers will not be held liable for substantive due process violations unless their conduct shocks the conscience.

A different standard has been applied in procedural due process cases. At the risk of simplification, a procedural due process violation is one which violates a significant life, liberty, or property interest. To clarify, one court distinguished between procedural and substantive due process in the following way: "...substantive due process prohibits the government's abuse of power or its use for the purpose of oppression, and procedural due process prohibits arbitrary and unfair deprivations of protected life, liberty, or property interests without procedural safeguards" (*Howard v. Grinage*, 82 F.3d 1343 [6th Cir. 1996]).

Police officers enjoy qualified immunity, a defense to Section 1983 civil liability. Basically, qualified immunity shields individual police officers from liability for reasonably mistaken beliefs. One of the best examples of a reasonably mistaken belief was in the case of *Malley v. Briggs*. In *Malley* plaintiffs filed a Section 1983 suit alleging that a police officer applied for, and obtained, a warrant that failed to establish probable cause. Rather than focus on the probable cause issue, the Supreme Court stated that the "...question in this case is whether a reasonably well-trained officer in petitioner's position would have known that his affidavit failed to establish probable cause and that he should not have applied for the warrant." The Court went on to note that "[o]nly where the warrant application is so lacking in indicia of probable cause as to render official belief in its existence unreasonable will the shield of immunity be lost."

Importantly, the qualified immunity defense needs to viewed separately from the constitutional rights violation claimed by the plaintiff, as recently decided by the Supreme Court in *Saucier v. Katz*. There, the Court held that questions of whether excessive force is used and whether qualified immunity should be granted are to be kept separate and are not be fused into a single inquiry.

The term "qualified immunity" suggests that such immunity is not absolute. However, the Supreme Court declared in *Briscoe v. LaHue* that police officers *do* enjoy absolute immunity when testifying in court, even if their testimony is perjured, that is, untruthful. At the other extreme, municipalities and counties *cannot* claim absolute immunity, or even qualified immunity. Such was the Supreme Court's decision in *Owen v. City of Independence.* ✦

MONROE V. PAPE
365 U.S. 167 (1961)

FACTS

A group of police officers allegedly entered the home of James Monroe without warning, then forced the occupants to stand naked in the living room while the house was searched and ransacked. Monroe brought a Section 1983 action against the police officers and the city of Chicago, and the U.S. Supreme Court granted certiorari.

ISSUE

Can plaintiffs sue individual police officers for misconduct under 42 U.S.C. Section 1983?

HOLDING

Yes. 42 U.S.C. Section 1983 provides a cause of action against police officers for misuse of authority.

RATIONALE

Section 1983 provides that any "person" who "under color of" state law deprives another of "any rights, privileges, or immunities secured by the Constitution and laws shall be liable in an action at law, suit in equity, or other proper proceeding for redress." This provision, enacted as part of the Ku Klux Klan Act of 1871, can serve as a cause of action against police officers who misuse their authority.

CASE SIGNIFICANCE

This case has been described as the "fountainhead" of Section 1983 litigation. It effectively opened the door to Section 1983 litigation against law enforcement officials. Prior to *Pape*, Section 1983 was not used against law enforcement authorities who misused their authority.

MONELL V. DEPARTMENT OF SOCIAL SERVICES OF NEW YORK
436 U.S. 658 (1978)

FACTS

Female employees of the Department of Social Services filed a lawsuit against the Department and the City of New York (among other officials) under 42 U.S.C. Section 1983. They claimed that the city maintained a policy that compelled pregnant employees to take unpaid leaves of absence before such leaves were required for medical reasons. They further claimed that municipalities are considered "persons" for purposes of Section 1983. The U.S. Supreme Court granted certiorari.

ISSUE

Are municipalities considered persons within the meaning of 42 U.S.C. Section 1983?

HOLDING

Yes. Municipalities are considered persons within the meaning of 42 U.S.C. Section 1983, but they can only be held liable for constitutional violations that are sanctioned by policy or custom.

RATIONALE

"*Monroe v. Pape* is overruled insofar as it holds that local governments are wholly immune from suit under Section 1983. Local governing bodies (and local officials sued in their official capacities) can, therefore, be sued directly under Section 1983 for monetary, declaratory, and injunctive relief in those situations where, as here, the action that is alleged to be unconstitutional implements or executes a policy statement, ordinance, regulation, or decision officially adopted or promulgated by those whose edicts or acts may fairly be said to represent official policy. In addition, local governments, like every other Section 1983 'person,' may be sued for constitutional deprivations visited pursuant to governmental 'custom' even though such custom has not received formal approval through the government's official decisionmaking channels."

CASE SIGNIFICANCE

This case is significant because it opened the door to Section 1983 litigation against municipalities and, by extension, other units of local government. Prior to *Monell,* cities were not considered "persons" within the meaning of Section 1983. Of key importance in *Monell* is the Court's requirement that a policy or custom be in place before a city can be held liable for constitutional rights violations committed by its employees. Without this requirement, most cities and counties would have long ago gone bankrupt because of constitutional rights violations committed by their subordinates without their knowledge.

OWEN V. CITY OF INDEPENDENCE
445 U.S. 622 (1980)

FACTS

Amidst allegations that its police department was acting improperly, the city council of Independence, Missouri, discharged the police chief, giving no reason for the dismissal, and only sending the chief a notice that his position was terminated. The discharged chief brought an action under 42 U.S.C Section 1983 for violation of federally protected rights. Specifically, he claimed that he had been discharged without reason and without a hearing, in violation of his substantive and procedural due process rights under the Fourteenth Amendment. The district court and the court of appeals both found in favor of the defendants, deciding that even though the plaintiff's rights were violated, the defendants enjoyed qualified immunity because they acted in good faith. The U.S. Supreme Court then granted certiorari.

ISSUE

Are municipalities entitled to qualified immunity in Section 1983 actions?

HOLDING

No. Municipalities sued under 42 U.S.C. Section 1983 do not enjoy qualified immunity. "A municipality has no immunity from liability under Section 1983 flowing from its constitutional violations and may not assert the good faith of its officers as a defense to such liability."

RATIONALE

"We believe that today's decision, together with prior precedents in this area, properly allocates these costs among the three principals in the scenario of the Section 1983 cause of action: the victim of the constitutional deprivation; the officer whose conduct caused the injury; and the public, as represented by the municipal entity. The innocent individual who is harmed by an abuse of governmental authority is assured that he will be compensated for his injury. The offending official, so long as he conducts himself in good faith, may go about his business secure in the knowledge that a qualified immunity will protect him from personal liability for damages that are more appropriately chargeable to the populace as a whole. And the public will be forced to bear only the costs of injury inflicted by the 'execution of a government's policy or custom, whether made by its lawmakers or by those whose edicts or acts may fairly be said to represent official policy.' "

CASE SIGNIFICANCE

This case is important because it established that municipalities (and, by extension, counties) cannot assert immunity from liability. Only individual officials working for the city or county have this benefit. Importantly, this does not mean that cities and counties can be sued successfully very often. For a plaintiff to succeed with a Section 1983 lawsuit against a county or municipality, he or she must show that a policy or custom was responsible for some injury. Or, if the plaintiff alleges that the city or county failed to train its officers, he or she must show that the defendant acted with deliberate indifference to the plaintiffs' federally protected rights.

BRISCOE V. LAHUE
460 U.S. 325 (1983)

FACTS

After being convicted of burglarizing a mobile home, Briscoe brought suit against LaHue, a Bloomington, Indiana police officer. LaHue testified at trial that Briscoe was one of 50 to 100 people in the area whose thumb print would match a partial print found at the scene. Briscoe claimed that the FBI determined that the partial print was insufficient to identify the perpetrator. The lawsuit alleged that LaHue perjured himself on the stand at Briscoe's trial and that this perjury led to Briscoe's conviction. The U.S. Supreme Court granted certiorari.

ISSUE

Can police officers be held liable under Section 1983 for giving perjured testimony?

HOLDING

No. Police officers enjoy absolute immunity from testifying; they cannot be sued under Section 1983, even if their testimony is perjured.

RATIONALE

"In short, the common law provided absolute immunity from subsequent damages liability for all persons—governmental and otherwise—who were integral parts of the judicial process. It is equally clear that Section 1983 does not authorize a damages claim against private witnesses on the one hand, or against judges or prosecutors in the performance of their respective duties on the other. When a police officer appears as a witness, he may reasonably be viewed as acting like any other witness sworn to tell the truth—in which event he can make a strong claim to witness immunity; alternatively, he may be regarded as an official

performing a critical role in the judicial process, in which event he may seek the benefit afforded to other governmental participants in the same proceeding. Nothing in the language of the statute suggests that such a witness belongs in a narrow, special category lacking protection against damage suits."

CASE SIGNIFICANCE

On its face, this decision seemed to suggest that police officers can lie while testifying in order to assist the prosecution in obtaining guilty convictions. From a Section 1983 civil liability standpoint this is true; however, an officer who gives perjured testimony can be criminally convicted under the state penal code for giving such testimony. Thus, the risk of a criminal conviction helps ensure that police officers tell the truth while on the witness stand.

MALLEY V. BRIGGS
475 U.S. 335 (1986)

FACTS

A court-authorized wiretap intercepted a conversation between Driscoll and "Dr. Shogun." Based on information revealed in the conversation, police concluded that a marijuana party was taking place at Briggs' home. Arrest warrants were issued for Briggs and Driscoll, as well as 20 other people. Briggs was arrested, arraigned, and released. Extensive news coverage followed because Briggs was a prominent member of the community. The grand jury refused to return an indictment against Briggs, so all charges were dropped. He filed a Section 1983 lawsuit against Malley, the officer who was responsible for the wiretap, and the U.S. Supreme Court granted certiorari.

ISSUE

Is absolute immunity granted to police officers in Section 1983 actions?

HOLDING

No. Police officers do not enjoy absolute immunity in Section 1983 actions. Instead, they enjoy qualified immunity.

RATIONALE

"Although we have previously held that police officers sued under Section 1983 for false arrest are qualifiedly immune, petitioner urges that he should be absolutely immune because his function in seeking an arrest warrant is similar to that of a complaining witness. The difficulty with this submission is that complaining witnesses were not absolutely immune at common law. In 1871, the generally accepted rule was that one who procured the issuance of an arrest warrant by submitting a complaint could be held liable if the complaint was made maliciously and without probable cause. . . . Accordingly, we held that the same standard of objective reasonableness that we applied in the context of a suppression hearing in *Leon* [*United States v. Leon*, 468 U.S. 897 (1984)] defines the qualified immunity accorded an officer whose request for a warrant allegedly caused an unconstitutional arrest. Only where the warrant application is so lacking in indicia of probable cause as to render official belief in its existence unreasonable will the shield of immunity be lost."

CASE SIGNIFICANCE

This case is important because it no longer provided police officers absolute immunity from liability under Section 1983. Prosecutors, judges, legislators, and some other parties do still enjoy absolute immunity, however. Also, note that this decision did not overrule or even necessarily contradict *Briscoe v. LaHue*, discussed above. Officers still enjoy absolute immunity from giving perjured testimony, just not in other areas of their duties. Indeed, the bulk of police work takes place out of a courtroom, so this decision is one that benefits defendants and other individuals who find themselves subjected to police authority.

CITY OF CANTON V. HARRIS
489 U.S. 378 (1989)

FACTS

Harris was arrested by officers of the Canton Police Department and brought to the police station. When she arrived at the station Harris was found lying on the floor of the police wagon. When officers asked if she needed medical attention, she responded incoherently. After she was taken into the police station she slumped to the ground two more times. Officers finally left her on the floor to prevent her from falling again. She never received any medical attention at the stationhouse. Approximately one hour later she was released and taken to the hospital in an ambulance provided by her family. She was hospitalized for a week due to several emotional problems. She received outpatient treatment for nearly a year after that. She sued the city under Section 1983, claiming it failed to train its officers adequately.

ISSUE

Can a city be held liable under Section 1983 for constitutional violations resulting from failing to train its officers?

HOLDING

Yes. Cities can be held liable under Section 1983 for failure to train, but only if such failure amounts to "deliberate indifference."

RATIONALE

"In *Monell v. New York City Department of Social Services,* we decided that a municipality can be found liable under Section 1983 only where the municipality itself causes the constitutional violation at issue. *Respondeat superior* or vicarious liability will not attach under Section 1983. . . . [A] municipality can be liable under Section 1983 only where its policies are the 'moving force [behind] the constitutional violation.' Only where a municipality's failure to train its employees in a relevant respect evidences a 'deliberate indifference' to the rights of its inhabitants can such a shortcoming be properly thought of as a city 'policy or custom' that is actionable under Section 1983. . . . The issue in a case like this one, however, is whether that training program is adequate; and if it is not, the question becomes whether such inadequate training can justifiably be said to represent 'city police.' . . . But it may happen that in light of the duties assigned to specific officers or employees that need for more or different training is so obvious, and the inadequacy so likely to result in the violation of constitutional rights, that the policymakers of the city can reasonably be said to have been deliberately indifferent to that need."

CASE SIGNIFICANCE

This decision and one similar to it (*Board of the County Comissioners of Bryan County v. Brown,* discussed below) permit liability against cities and counties for failure to train, but only if deliberate indifference is shown. Importantly, if a plaintiff does not allege failure to train but, instead, argues that a city/county policy is responsible for the injury he or she suffered, a showing of deliberate indifference is not needed. That is, whether a city/county acts with deliberate indifference or, simply, no intent or culpability at all, it can be held liable for policies and customs that result in injuries of a constitutional nature. *Canton* is one of several recent decisions where the Supreme Court has forced plaintiffs to show that the defendant acted with a certain amount of culpability before a finding of liability will be returned.

WILL V. MICHIGAN DEPARTMENT OF STATE POLICE
491 U.S. 58 (1989)

FACTS

An employee filed a claim in Michigan Circuit Court against the Michigan Department of State Police and the Michigan Director of State Police in his official capacity, claiming that both parties denied promotion for an improper reason, in violation of 42 U.S.C. Section 1983. The Circuit Court remanded the case to the Michigan Civil Service Commission for a hearing, then the employee filed suit in the Michigan Court of Claims, raising the same Section 1983 claim as in his initial lawsuit. The circuit court held that: (1) the employee established a constitutional violation; (2) the state police and the director of state police were "persons" for Section 1983 purposes; and (3) although the circuit court action was prohibited by state law, the court of claims action could go forward. The Michigan Court of Appeals held that a state is not a "person" under Section 1983 and vacated the lower court's judgment. It then remanded the case for a determination as to whether the director of state police may enjoy immunity from suit. Finally, the Michigan Supreme Court held that neither the state nor a state official acting in his or her official capacity is a "person" under Section 1983. The U.S. Supreme Court then granted certiorari.

ISSUE

Are states and state employees acting in their official capacities considered "persons" within the meaning of 42 U.S.C. Section 1983?

HOLDING

No. Neither states nor state officials acting in their official capacity are "persons" within the meaning of Section 1983.

RATIONALE

"Our conclusion that a State is not a 'person' within the meaning of Section 1983 is reinforced by Congress's purpose in enacting the statute. Congress enacted Section 1 of the Civil Rights Act of 1871 . . . the precursor to Section 1983, shortly after the end of the Civil War 'in response to the widespread deprivations of civil rights in the Southern States and the inability or unwillingness of authorities in those States to protect those rights or punish wrongdoers.' . . . Although Congress did not establish federal courts as the exclusive forum to remedy these deprivations, . . . it is plain that 'Congress assigned to the federal courts a paramount role' in this endeavor. . . . Section 1983 provides a federal forum to remedy many deprivations of civil liberties, but it does not provide a federal forum for litigants who seek a remedy against a State for alleged deprivations of civil liberties. The Eleventh Amendment bars such suits unless the State has waived its immunity, or unless Congress has exercised its undoubted power under Section 5 of the Fourteenth Amendment to override that immunity."

CASE SIGNIFICANCE

This case only applies to state officials. In plain terms, the case prohibited lawsuits against states as well as state officials acting in their official capacities. States enjoy immunity and ". . . a suit against a state official in his or her official capacity is not a suit against the official but rather is a suit against the official's office. . . . As such, it is no different from a suit against the State itself." It is important to note that local units of government such as cities and counties can still be sued under Section 1983. Also, nothing prohibits plaintiffs from suing state officials in their individual capacities for damages, as the following case, *Hafer v. Melo*, attests.

HAFER V. MELO
502 U.S. 21 (1991)

FACTS

In 1988, Hafer successfully ran for election to the position of auditor general of Pennsylvania. During the campaign, she promised to discharge employees in the auditor general's office who supposedly obtained their positions by making payments to a former employee. Melo and several other employees whom Hafer fired sued her. All claims were dismissed on the basis of state immunity from suit, and the U.S. Supreme Court granted certiorari.

ISSUE

Can state officials be sued in their individual capacity under Section 1983?

HOLDING

Yes. State officials being sued in their individual capacity are considered "persons" within the meaning of 42 U.S.C. 1983, and may therefore be held liable for constitutional rights violations.

RATIONALE

"In *Kentucky v. Graham*, 473 U.S. 159 (1985), the Court sought to eliminate lingering confusion about the distinction between personal- and official-capacity suits. We emphasized that official-capacity suits 'generally represent only another way of pleading an action against an entity of which an officer is an agent.' A suit against a state official in her official capacity therefore should be treated as a suit against the State . . . because the real party in interest in an official-capacity suit is the governmental entity and not the named official, 'the entity's "policy or custom" must have played a part in the violation of federal law.' For the same reason, the only immunities available to the defendant in an official-capacity action are those that the governmental entity possesses. . . . Personal-capacity suits, on the other hand, seek to impose individual liability upon a government officer for actions taken under color of state law. Thus, '[o]n the merits, to establish personal liability in a Section 1983 action, it is enough to show that the official, acting under color of state law, caused the deprivation of a federal right.' . . . We hold that state officials, sued in their individual capacities, are 'persons' within the meaning of Section 1983. The Eleventh Amendment does not bar such suits nor are state officers absolutely immune from personal liability under Section 1983 solely by virtue of the 'official' nature of their acts."

CASE SIGNIFICANCE

This case is important because it held that state officials can be held liable under Section 1983 for constitutional rights violations they commit in their individual capacity, even when acting under color of state law. Thus, it behooves plaintiffs to sue state officials in their individual as opposed to official capacity, because the lawsuit cannot commence under the latter type of allegation. There is a barely perceptible distinction between official capacity and individual capacity. A state employee can act in his or her official capacity and individual capacity while on duty, acting under color of state law. Official-capacity suits are barred because the plaintiff essentially sues the office, not the person. Individual-capacity suits are permissible because they target an individual, not the office.

COLLINS V. CITY OF HARKER HEIGHTS
503 U.S. 115 (1992)

FACTS

Collins, a sanitation department employee of Harker Heights, died of asphyxiation in a manhole while trying to clear a clogged sewer line. His widow brought an action against the city under 42 U.S.C. Section 1983, alleging that Collins had a right under the Fourteenth Amendment's due process clause to be "free from unreasonable risks of harm." Further, she claimed that the city violated Collins' rights by failing to notify

him concerning the dangers associated with his job. The U.S. Supreme Court granted certiorari.

ISSUE

Does a city's failure to notify its employees about occupational hazards violate the due process clause of the Fourteenth Amendment?

HOLDING

No. The failure of a city to notify its employees concerning known hazards in the workplace does not violate the due process clause of the Fourteenth Amendment.

RATIONALE

"Petitioner's submission that the city violated a federal constitutional obligation to provide its employees with certain minimal levels of safety and security is unprecedented. It is quite different from the constitutional claim advanced by plaintiffs in several of our prior cases who argued that the State owes a duty to take care of those who have already been deprived of their liberty. . . . Neither the text nor the history of the Due Process Clause supports petitioner's claim that the governmental employer's duty to provide its employees with a safe working environment is a substantive component of the Due Process Clause."

CASE SIGNIFICANCE

This case did not deal with police directly, but the decision had implications for law enforcement. It is significant because local units of government (cities and counties) were not constitutionally required to advise their employees of occupational hazards. On one level the decision made sense; it would be burdensome to impose on cities and counties a requirement that they educate all their employees as to known work hazards. However, labor groups and unions probably disagree with this decision because it suggested that employees must "learn for themselves" the dangers of the workplace. Notice also that this decision applied to local governmental employers, not private employers. Private employers are not bound by constitutional restrictions in the same way that governmental employers are.

BOARD OF THE COUNTY COMMISSIONERS OF BRYAN COUNTY V. BROWN
520 U.S. 397 (1997)

FACTS

Brown was injured when Burns, an unarmed Oklahoma county deputy, pulled her from a truck which had been stopped after a high-speed pursuit. The passenger filed a lawsuit, claiming that the county, on the basis of the county sheriff's prior decision to hire the deputy, ought to be liable. The plaintiff claimed that Moore, the elected sheriff, had failed to adequately screen the deputy's background because he had a history of misdemeanor offenses, including assault and battery. The U.S. Supreme Court granted certiorari.

ISSUE

Can a county be held liable under Section 1983 for a sheriff's single hiring decision?

HOLDING

No. A county cannot be held liable under 42 U.S.C. 1983 for a single hiring decision made by one of its employees.

RATIONALE

"Even assuming without deciding that proof of a single instance of inadequate screening could ever trigger municipal liability, Moore's failure to scrutinize Burns' record cannot constitute deliberate indifference to respondent's federally protected right to be free from the use of excessive force. To test the link between Moore's action and Brown's injury, it must be asked whether a full review of Burns' record reveals that Moore should have concluded that Burns' use of excessive force would be a plainly obvious consequence of his decision to hire Burns. Respondent's showing on this point was inadequate because the primary infractions on which she relies to prove Burns' propensity for violence arose from a single college fight. A full review of Burns' record might well have led Moore to conclude that Burns was an extremely poor deputy candidate, but he would not necessarily have reached that decision because Burns' use of excessive force would have been a plainly obvious consequence of the decision to hire him. The District Court therefore erred in submitting the inadequate screening theory to the jury."

CASE SIGNIFICANCE

This case reduced the potential scope of earlier decisions. In *City of Canton v. Harris,* the Court held that counties can be held liable for inadequate training that amounts to deliberate indifference. Here, the Court held that single hiring decisions are not enough to hold counties liable for constitutional rights violations. So, counties can take a measure of comfort in the fact that their hiring decisions—assuming there is not a pattern of poor hiring—will be shielded from liability. However, once officers or deputies are hired, the city or county must adequately train them. Failure to adequately train—that is, failure that amounts to deliber-ate indifference to people's federally protected rights—can serve as a basis for Section 1983 civil liability.

McMillian v. Monroe County 520 U.S. 781 (1997)

FACTS

McMillian was convicted of murder and sentenced to death. His conviction was later overturned after a finding that investigators had suppressed exculpatory evidence, which amounts to a due process violation. He brought suit against the investigators, the sheriff, and Monroe County under 42 U.S.C. Section 1983. The case was based on the assumption that the sheriff was acting as a representative of the county when he and other investigators alleged suppressed the exculpatory evidence in question. The U.S. Supreme Court granted certiorari.

ISSUE

Is a sheriff in Alabama a representative of the county?

HOLDING

No. Whether a sheriff is a representative of the county or of the state is determined by the state's constitution, laws, or regulations. In Alabama, the sheriff is not a representative of the county.

RATIONALE

"In determining a local government's Section 1983 liability, a court's task is to identify those who speak with final authority for the local governmental actor concerning the action alleged to have cause the violation at issue (*Jett v. Dallas Independent School District,* 491 U.S. 701, 703). . . . In deciding this dispute, the question is not whether . . . sheriffs act as county or state officials in all of their official actions, but whom they represent in a particular area or on a particular issue. Ibid. This inquiry is dependent on the definition of the official's functions under relevant state law."

CASE SIGNIFICANCE

This case is important because it suggested that some sheriffs can be sued and others cannot. Where sheriffs represent counties, they can be sued. So can counties. However, where sheriffs represent the state, they cannot be sued in their official capacity, although they can be sued in their individual capacity.

COUNTY OF SACRAMENTO V. LEWIS
523 U.S. 833 (1998)

FACTS

On his way to a call to break up a fight, a police officer observed a motorcycle approaching at high speed. The officer turned on his lights, yelled for the motorcycle to stop, and unsuccessfully attempted to block the motorcycle by moving his cruiser close to that of a county sheriff's deputy. The deputy switched on his lights and siren and began chasing the motorcycle. During the chase, the motorcycle tipped over. The deputy was unable to bring his cruiser to a halt before hitting and killing the motorcycle's passenger. Representatives of the passenger's estate brought a Section 1983 action, alleging a substantive due process violation under the Fourteenth Amendment to the U.S. Constitution. The district court, granting summary judgment in favor of the deputy, suggested he was entitled to qualified immunity. The Court of Appeals for the Ninth Circuit reversed, suggesting that a "deliberate indifference" standard be applied to Fourteenth Amendment substantive due process claims, and the U.S. Supreme Court granted certiorari.

ISSUE

Is "deliberate indifference" the appropriate standard for judging Fourteenth Amendment substantive due process claims arising under 42 U.S.C. Section 1983?

HOLDING

No. A police officer will not be held liable for a substantive due process violation unless his or her conduct "shocks the conscience."

RATIONALE

"A police officer does not violate substantive due process by causing death through deliberate or reckless indifference to life in a high-speed automobile chase aimed at apprehending a suspected offender. . . . Lewis' allegations are insufficient to state a substantive due process violation. Protection against governmental arbitrariness is the core of due process, including substantive due process, but only the most egregious executive action can be said to be 'arbitrary' in the constitutional sense . . . ; the cognizable level of executive abuse of power is that which shocks the conscience. . . . In the circumstances of a high-speed chase aimed at apprehending a suspected offender, where unforeseen circumstances demand an instant judgment on the part of an officer who feels the pulls of competing obligations, only a purpose to cause harm unrelated to the legitimate object of arrest will satisfy the shocks-

the-conscience test. Such chases with no intent to harm suspects physically or to worsen their legal plight do not give rise to substantive due process liability."

CASE SIGNIFICANCE

Historically, in order to successfully state a claim under Section 1983, a plaintiff must show that he or she suffered a constitutional rights violation by a person acting under color of state law. Recently, however, the Supreme Court has begun to impose a culpability requirement on Section 1983 claims. The significance of this case is that for a plaintiff to succeed with a substantive due process claim, in addition to showing a constitutional violation by an official acting under color of law, the plaintiff must also prove that the official's conduct shocked the conscience. This is an exceedingly high standard, making it fairly difficult for people to succeed with Section 1983 substantive due process claims.

SAUCIER V. KATZ
533 U.S. 194 (2001)

FACTS

Katz, an animal-rights protestor, was taken into custody when he attempted to disrupt Vice President Gore's speech at a military base. Katz filed a *Bivens* action (the vehicle for Section 1983 lawsuits against federal officials) against Saucier, alleging that Saucier had violated his Fourth Amendment rights by using excessive force when arresting him. The District Court ruled that Saucier was not entitled to summary judgment on the claim of excessive force. The Court of Appeals for the Ninth Circuit affirmed, using a two-part qualified immunity inquiry. First, it found that the law governing Saucier's conduct at the time of the arrest was clear, so it moved to the second inquiry: whether a reasonable officer could have believed, given that the law was clear at the time of arrest, that his conduct was unlawful. The court concluded that the qualified immunity inquiry as well as the Fourth Amendment excessive force inquiry were the same and concluded that qualified immunity was inappropriate; the U.S. Supreme Court then granted certiorari.

ISSUE

Are the qualified immunity inquiry and the Fourth Amendment excessive force inquiry the same?

HOLDING

No. The questions of whether excessive force was used and whether qualified immunity should be granted are to be kept separate, not fused into a singly inquiry. The first inquiry should be whether a federal constitutional right would have been violated on the facts alleged. The second inquiry, assuming such a violation could be made out, requires determining whether the constitutional right was clearly established.

RATIONALE

"A qualified immunity ruling requires an analysis not susceptible of fusion with the question whether unreasonable force was used in making the arrest. The Ninth Circuit's approach cannot be reconciled with *Anderson v. Creighton,* 483 U.S. 637 (1987). A qualified immunity defense must be considered in proper sequence. A ruling should be made early in the proceedings so that the cost and expenses of trial are avoided where the defense is dispositive. Such immunity is an entitlement not to stand trial, not a defense from liability. . . . The initial inquiry is whether a constitutional right would have been violated on the facts alleged, for if no right would have been violated, there is no need for further inquiry into immunity. However, if a violation could be made out on a favorable view of the parties' submissions, the next, sequential step is whether the right was clearly established. This inquiry must be undertaken in light of the case's specific context, not as a broad general proposition. The relevant, dispositive inquiry is whether it would be clear to a reasonable officer that the conduct was unlawful in the situation he confronted. . . . The Ninth Circuit's approach—to deny summary judgment if a material issue of fact remains on the excessive force claim—could undermine the goal of qualified immunity to avoid excessive disruption of government and permit the resolution of many insubstantial claims on summary judgment."

CASE SIGNIFICANCE

This case addressed a somewhat narrow and controversial issue in police civil liability law: qualified immunity. The Fourth Amendment prohibits unreasonable searches and seizures. "Reasonableness" is determined by reference to what a reasonable police officer would have done under the circumstances. However, the courts also use a reasonableness test when determining whether qualified immunity should be extended to a defendant police officer. Just like the Fourth Amendment reasonableness analysis, qualified immunity considers how a reasonable officer would behave. The Ninth Circuit thought these two inquiries should be fused into one to avoid confusion. The Supreme Court disagreed, and held that two separate reasonableness tests should be conducted. First, in order to determine whether a Fourth Amendment violation has taken place, courts must consider whether a reasonable officer would have acted in the same way under the circumstances. Then, courts must move to the qualified immunity analysis, which requires determining whether a reasonable officer would believe the law surrounding the conduct in question was clear. In other words, if the law was unclear, and such a determination is reasonable, qualified immunity will be granted. Therefore, qualified immunity serves as a defense to officers who act on reasonably mistaken beliefs, even if their actions violate the Fourth Amendment. ♦

DISCUSSION QUESTIONS

1. Are civil lawsuits against the police an effective remedy when constitutional rights are violated?

2. When would it be more advantageous for a person to pursue civil litigation rather than some other remedy?

3. If civil litigation is not an option, aggrieved parties can file complaints with police departments' citizen complaint divisions. Is this procedure effective?

4. Clearly, we live in a litigious society where people are quick to sue one another. What is your opinion of this state of affairs?

5. Are jury verdicts against the police out of control? If not, where else in the world of civil litigation are they out of control? ♦

Chapter Twenty-Three

Where Do We Go From Here?

Police departments are responding to public fear of crime and calls to "get tough" on criminals and conduct a "war on drugs" by becoming more proactive in their approach to law enforcement. The result has been a dramatic increase in the type and number of police intrusions into the private lives of citizens. The Supreme Court in turn has repeatedly sanctioned these increasingly intrusive police practices, whether they involve the use of new technology or a new approach to circumventing the warrant requirement.

An example of how the Court has backed away from meaningful oversight of police practices is the development of the *Terry* "stop and frisk" doctrine. In *Terry v. Ohio,* 392 U.S. 1 (1968), the Supreme Court acknowledged that aggressive police patrol techniques and field interrogation procedures were often used to harass, humiliate, and control minorities in the inner cities, yet they legitimized forcible detentions on less than probable cause. Why?

Some have suggested that the Court decided it was the only way to maintain some sort of control over what the police were already doing (Juviller 1998; McGuire 1998). Some argue that *Terry* not only made sense at the time, but its later explication is logical and the extension of the doctrine to analogous situations such as car stops is appropriate, in light of changes in society and the crime problem (Saltzburg 1998). Others (Harris 1998) argue that whatever its initial validity, the *Terry* doctrine has been eroded by lower courts and the Supreme Court has permitted this erosion and at times (*Minnesota v. Dickerson,* 508 U.S. 366 [1993]) even facilitated it.

Terry has been changed from its original incarnation as a limited crime-fighting technique based on careful individual judgments to one based on categorical justifications that effectively widen police discretion to the point that they can stop anyone at any time, and can use the frisk as a tool to search for evidence. As one respected criminal justice scholar has recently noted (Skolnick 1998), the police constantly interpret the rules and fabricate events to comply with those rules. Skolnick notes, as an example, that there are not as many *Terry* stops today, because police are using "community policing" tactics instead, as courts routinely accept any police activity if it is based on some legal basis, even if the subjective intent of the officer is to investigate crime, not "help" someone.

An example of how the Supreme Court has accepted more intrusive police practices as necessary is the Court's refusal to require police officers to notify a suspect that he or she has the right to refuse consent. As the Ohio Supreme Court in *Ohio v. Robinette,* 519 U.S. 33 (1996) and the dissent in *Florida v. Bostick,* 501 U.S. 429 (1991) pointed out, people routinely give consent when doing so is clearly not in their best interest. The only logical conclusion to draw from this behavior is that people do not understand that they have the right to refuse consent. In *Miranda v. Arizona,* 384 U.S. 436 (1966) the Court required police to give a detailed explanation of a suspect's rights, and subsequent studies revealed that this requirement neither reduced the confession rate nor significantly impeded the investigatory process. But in *Robinette* the Court claimed that requiring a police officer to inform someone that a detention was over, or that the person had a constitutional right to refuse to consent to a search was "impractical"—this in the face of *Miranda,* and the reality that such a warning would take a few seconds at most. Clearly, the Court feared that if police inform suspects of their right to refuse consent, the likelihood of consent being given will be reduced.

The Supreme Court repeatedly endorses the existence of a constitutional right, but in a manner which effectively protects that right only for the privileged few, while as a practical matter denying it for the less privileged (Cole 1999). This leads to a gap between rhetoric and reality in criminal procedure decisions (Smith 1997). The Supreme Court has used a number of interpretive techniques, such as creating flexible exceptions to a rule, making bright-line rules vague, or limiting the opportunities for meaningful post-conviction review (Smith 1997). This so-called "symbolization of rights" in essence allows the Court to have its cake and eat it too—it is still seen as the champion of individual rights while actually advancing conservative justices' pro–law enforcement preferences.

It has been argued by a number of commentators that the criminal justice system has undergone a paradigm shift away from individual-focused justice to the regulation of aggregates, utilizing the language of social utility, systems management, and risk management (Feeley and Simon 1994; Vaughn and del Carmen 1997). This has been referred to as "actuarial justice," and involves making the criminal justice system more efficient and well managed, while reducing the concern with justice in the individual case—the focus is on offender groups rather than an offender.

A result of this move toward "actuarial justice" is the targeting of high-risk (in police opinion) groups, such as juveniles, gang members, parolees, and minority motorists. Constitutional limitations on police conduct obstruct this targeting, so the police have sought to overcome or avoid them. Here, too, the Court is helping. An example is the "special needs" exception (Vaughn and del Carmen 1997), as well as the acceptance of pretext stops, the refusal to require consent, limitations on the exclusionary rule, and increased use of the balancing test.

In addition, the Court is exploiting (or at least refusing to recognize) the inequality inherent in modern American society. An example is the Court's continued claim that warrants are preferred in all but a few limited, "exigent" circumstances. While continuing to maintain a preference for warrants, the Court has repeatedly held that it is permissible for police officers to seek consent to search at any time, without probable cause or even reasonable suspicion of involvement in criminal activity. This tactic is disproportionately employed against young black men (Harris 1998). If it were used against white men, there would be more public comment and outrage at the police intrusion into the lives of "innocent" persons. The Court rhetoric is that we protect rights of all, but the reality is that law enforcement prerogatives generally prevail over the rights of minorities and the poor (Cole 1999). The result, again, is that the police are freed to conduct the war on crime as they see fit, with little meaningful judicial oversight.

While the Supreme Court is the ultimate *decision-making* body with regard to criminal procedure, the Court is limited in its ability to *implement* its decisions (Horowitz 1977). Courts make policy decisions and announce them to the populations below them, which include the "interpreting population" and the "implementing population" (Canon and Johnson 1999).

The interpreting population is that set of actors which responds to Court decisions by refining the announced policy. In criminal justice this includes actors such as state attorneys general and police administrators. They are also in a sense interpreters, as they interpret the decisions of the Court and can either expand or limit its reach and meaning. They provide the "official" interpretation of a court decision for those in the criminal justice system.

The police on the street are what Canon and Johnson refer to as the implementing population—those authorities whose behavior is reinforced or sanctioned by the interpreting population. They apply the system's rules to persons subject to their authority. This population, along with the interpreting population, has received the message from the Supreme Court that all is fair in the drug war—virtually every criminal procedure decision of the past decade has been an endorsement of police practices, even as these practices have become increasingly intrusive. Consequently, the police continue to "push the envelope" in the drug war, trying new and ever more intrusive practices. Where this trend will end is anybody's guess.

According to the Supreme Court, the central meaning of the Fourth Amendment is reasonableness—that is, the Amendment merely requires that police officers act rationally and pursue reasonable goals when they intrude upon individuals (Maclin 1993). There is no requirement that police officers always have a warrant, or even probable cause in some instances. The Supreme Court since *Camara v. Municipal Court*, 387 U.S. 523 (1967) and *Terry* has utilized a balancing test of the individual's privacy interest against the legitimate interests of law enforcement to determine what constitutes "reasonable" police behavior. In the words of the Court in *Camara:* "There is no ready test for determining reasonableness other than by balancing the need to search or seize against the invasion which the search or seizure entails." Unfortunately, a balancing test is inherently subjective, and thus tends to deprive the Fourth Amendment of its meaning and weaken it, as well as producing inconsistent results (Strossen 1998).

Since *Camara* and *Terry* the Court has also moved away from requiring a warrant except in exceptional circumstances, and instead permits warrantless searches in a multitude of circumstances. The Court now insists that "reasonableness is the touchstone of the Fourth Amendment" (*Florida v. Jimeno,* 500 U.S. 248 [1991]), and that the warrant clause of the Fourth Amendment is just an example of one—but not the only—way to determine whether a particular search or seizure is reasonable. The Supreme Court has moved away from the Warren Court's concern with remedying the disadvantages of the poor and minorities and controlling abuse by public officials, and turned to an emphasis on truth finding and accurately separating the guilty from the innocent.

The result of the Court's relaxation of the warrant requirement and reasonableness standard has been a pronounced tendency by the Court to uphold virtually all police investigatory practices, based on expediency and the necessities of fighting the drug war. This is unfortunate, as the Fourth Amendment "reflects experience with police excesses" (*Davis v. United States,* 411 U.S. 233 [1944], Frankfurter dissenting). The Fourth Amendment makes plain, perhaps more directly so than any other Amendment, that the Constitution does not tolerate a police state. The central meaning of the Fourth Amendment is distrust of police power and discretion (Maclin 1993).

The Warren Court during the civil rights era was concerned with the treatment of blacks in the criminal justice system. This concern with race relations served as the "unspoken subtext" (Sklansky 1998) of many criminal procedure decisions. Today, this concern has disappeared from Fourth Amendment jurisprudence. Current cases show little or no concern for the intangible, insidious damage of police investigatory practices. Racial issues, as the *Whren v. United States,* 517 U.S. 806 (1996) opinion makes clear, are essentially irrelevant to the determination of "reasonableness" under the Fourth Amendment.

Scholarly complaints about the Court's treatment of the Fourth Amendment have generally fallen on deaf ears outside the legal academic community. This may be because society has become so unified in its fear of crime, and increased its trust of the police since the tumultuous 1960s. As Justice Douglas noted in dissent in *Terry v. Ohio* in 1968: "There have been powerful hydraulic pressures throughout our history that bear heavily on the Court to water down constitutional guarantees and give the police the upper hand." Douglas's concern was with the weakening of the probable cause standard, and his concern has proven true.

And as Justice Marshall declared in a dissenting opinion in 1991, "Power, not reason, is the new currency of this Court's decision-making" (*Payne v. Tennessee,* 501 U.S. 808 [1991]). The spate of recent Supreme Court decisions regarding criminal procedure reflect little more than a shared set of conservative, pro–law enforcement preferences and the ability to enact them into law (Burkoff 1984; Green 1992). Decisions are no longer based on an analysis of law and facts, as the conservative majority knows it has the votes for its desired pro–law enforcement outcome (Sklansky 1998). The Court, in its rush to uphold police actions, stretches existing doctrine to accommodate them. Exceptions to the warrant requirement are expanded, and bright-line rules are adopted (or not) based on law enforcement expediency. If the police can identify any plausible goal that promotes law enforcement interests, the Court is likely to hold that the challenged policy is reasonable (Maclin 1998). And the message appears to be getting through to the police—in the war on drugs, just about anything goes.

REFERENCES

Burkoff, J.M. (1984). "When Is a Search Not a 'Search'? Fourth Amendment Doublethink." *The University of Toledo Law Review* 15:515–560.

Canon, B.C., and C.A. Johnson. (1999). *Judicial Policies: Implementation and Impact.* Washington, D.C.: Congressional Quarterly Press.

Cole, D. (1999). *No Equal Justice.* New York: The New Press.

Feeley, M., and J. Simon. (1994). "The New Penology: Notes on the Emerging Strategy of Corrections and Its Implications." *Criminology* 30:449–474.

Green, B.A. (1992). " 'Power, Not Reason': Justice Marshall's Valedictory and the Fourth Amendment in the Supreme Court's 1990 Term." *North Carolina Law Review* 70: 373–415.

Harris, D.A. (1998). "Car Wars: The Fourth Amendment's Death on the Highway." *The George Washington Law Review* 66:557–591.

———. (1998). "Particularized Suspicion, Categorical Judgment: Supreme Court Rhetoric Versus Lower Court Reality Under *Terry v. Ohio.*" *St. John's Law Review* 72.

Horowitz, D.L. (1977). *The Courts and Social Policy.* Washington, D.C.: The Brookings Institution.

Juviller, M.R. (1998). "A Prosecutor's Perspective." *St. John's Law Review* 72:741–748.

Maclin, T. (1993). "The Central Meaning of the Fourth Amendment." *William and Mary Law Review* 35:197–249.

McGuire, R.J. (1998). "*Terry v. Ohio:* A Police Commissioner's Musings." *St. John's Law Review* 72:1249–1254.

Saltzburg, S.A. (1998). "*Terry v. Ohio:* A Practically Perfect Doctrine." *St. John's Law Review* 72:911–974.

Sklansky, D.A. (1998). "Traffic Stops, Minority Motorists, and the Future of the Fourth Amendment." In *The Supreme Court Review 1997,* Dennis J. Hutchinson, David A. Strauss, and Geoffey R. Stone, editors. Chicago: The University of Chicago Press.

Skolnick, J.H. (1998). "*Terry* and Community Policing." *St. John's Law Review* 72:1265–1270.

Smith, C.E. (1997). "Turning Rights Into Symbols: The U.S. Supreme Court and Criminal Justice." *Criminal Justice Policy Review* 8:99–117.

Strossen, N. (1988). "The Fourth Amendment in the Balance: Accurately Setting the Scales Through the Least Intrusive Alternative Analysis." *New York University Law Review* 63:1173–1267.

Vaughn, M.S., and R.V. del Carmen. (1997). "The Fourth Amendment as a Tool of Actuarial Justice: The 'Special Needs' Exception to the Warrant and Probable Cause Requirements." *Crime and Delinquency* 43:78–103. ✦

Glossary of Key Terms

42 U.S.C. Section 1983: A federal statute providing for civil litigation against law enforcement officials acting in their official capacity. The statute states "Every person who, under color of any statute, ordinance, regulation, custom, or usage, of any State or Territory, subjects, or causes to be subjected, any citizen of the United States or other persons within the jurisdiction thereof to the deprivation of any rights, privileges, or immunities secured by the Constitution and laws, shall be liable to the party injured in an action at law, suit in equity, or other proper proceeding for redress."

absolute immunity: An official who cannot be sued under any circumstances enjoys absolute immunity.

apparent authority: When the police reasonably believe a third party has authority to grant consent.

appellant: The person who appeals.

appellee: The person who is appealed against. The appellee is sometimes called the "respondent."

armspan rule: The requirement that a search incident to arrest be limited to the area "within [the] immediate control" of the person arrested, that is, "the area from within which he might have obtained either a weapon or something that could have been used as evidence against him."

arrest: The taking of a person into custody for the commission of an offense as the prelude to prosecuting him or her for it.

arrest warrant: Judicial authorization to arrest a particular person. If no name is available, a "John Doe" arrest warrant can be issued.

articulate/articulable: To express, formulate, or present one's thoughts in clear and effective fashion.

checkpoints: A law enforcement practice of briefly stopping people at fixed locations, such as on highways or in airports.

civil asset forfeiture: A legal method for the government to take possession of property used to facilitate or obtained by a criminal act.

civil litigation: A lawsuit.

closely regulated business: A business subject to strict licensing and monitoring requirements (e.g., a firearms dealership).

color of law: When a law enforcement officer acts in his or her official capacity, he or she is said to have acted under color of law.

common authority: Mutual use of property by persons generally having joint access or control for most purposes.

concurring opinion: A different reason for the court's decision offered by another judge or justice.

consent search: A search based on a voluntary waiver of one's Fourth Amendment rights.

culpability: Intent.

custodial interrogation: Questioning initiated by law enforcement officers after a person has been taken into custody or deprived of his or her freedom in any significant way.

deadly force: Physical force that is reasonably likely to cause death. A gun is an instrument of deadly force.

defendant: The person charged with a crime.

dissent: Much like an opinion, but written in opposition to the court's opinion.

distinguish: When a previous decision does not apply to the current facts, a court will hand down a "new" decision. A distinguished case is one where *stare decisis* does not or cannot apply.

district courts: Federal trial courts. There are 94 federal district courts in the U.S. as of this writing.

drug-courier profiling: The act of looking for individuals who fit the characteristics of people who transport illegal narcotics.

due process: A concern with people's rights and liberties; a perspective that gives significant weight to human freedom. The due process perspective closely resembles a liberal political orientation.

***Edwards* rule:** A decision stating that once a suspect expresses a desire to deal with the police only through counsel, he or she may not be subjected to further interrogation until such time as the request is fulfilled or the accused initiates further communication with the authorities.

Eighth Amendment: "Excessive bail shall not be required, nor excessive fines imposed, nor cruel and unusual punishments inflicted."

exclusionary rule: The rule that evidence obtained in violation of the Constitution cannot be used in a criminal trial to prove guilt.

exigent circumstances: Emergencies.

Fifth Amendment: "No person shall be held to answer for a capital, or otherwise infamous crime, unless on a presentment or indictment of a Grand Jury, except in cases arising in the land or naval forces, or in the Militia, when in actual service in time of War or public danger; nor shall any person be subject for the same offense to be twice put in jeopardy of life or limb; nor shall be compelled in any criminal case to be a witness against himself, nor be deprived of life, liberty, or property, without due process of law; nor shall private property be taken for public use, without just compensation."

Fourteenth Amendment: "All persons born or naturalized in the United States, and subject to the jurisdiction thereof, are citizens of the United States and of the State wherein they reside. No State shall make or enforce any law which shall abridge the privileges or immunities of citizens of the United States, nor shall any State deprive any person of life, liberty, or property, without due process of law; nor deny to any person within its jurisdiction the equal protection of the laws."

Fourth Amendment: "The right of the people to be secure in their persons, houses, papers, and effects, against unreasonable searches and seizures, shall not be violated, and no Warrants shall issue, but upon probable cause, supported by Oath or affirmation and particularly describing the place to be searched, and the persons or things to be seized."

frisk: A pat down of the outer clothing to locate weapons or other dangerous instruments.

"fruit of the poisonous tree" doctrine: The exclusionary rule applies not only to evidence obtained as a direct result of a constitutional rights violation, but also to evidence indirectly derived from the constitutional rights violation.

"good-faith" exception: If an honest and "good faith" mistake is made during the course of a search or seizure, any subsequently obtained evidence will be considered admissible at trial.

habeas corpus: A judicial order used to determine whether or not a prisoner is being restrained of his or her liberty without due process.

harmless error doctrine: A judicial rule stating that the admission of illegally obtained evidence by a trial court need not automatically require reversal of a conviction where it can be established that the error in question caused no real harm.

hot pursuit: An emergency situation in which police chase a fleeing suspect.

house: Any structure that a person uses as a residence (and frequently a business) on either a temporary or long-term basis.

immediate area/span of control: That area within a suspect's ready reach where a weapon, evidence of criminal activity, or implements of escape may be located.

immediately apparent: The requirement that the police have probable cause (more than 50 percent certainty) to sieze evidence under the plain view doctrine.

incident to arrest: Events or actions taken after an arrest has been made.

independent source: An exception to the "fruit of the poisonous tree" doctrine which provides that evidence provided by a neutral third party (or other source) in no way connected with the police will be admissible.

indigence: A state of impoverishment. An indigent defendant is one who lacks funds or the ability to hire legal defense.

inevitable discovery: An exception to the "fruit of the poisonous tree" doctrine which provides that evidence that would inevitably have been discovered will be admissible even if it was obtained in an unconstitutional fashion.

inspection: A "search" to ensure compliance with some set of rules or regulations. Inspections are not intended for detecting evidence of criminal activity.

jailhouse informant: An individual who assists authorities by providing incriminating evidence against another prisoner.

justification: A term used synonymously with "cause." It is usually part of a question: did the police have *justification* to search?

"knock and announce" requirement: The common law requirement that police officers first knock and announce their presence before serving search or arrest warrants.

lawful access: The requirement that the police be lawfully in the place where evidence is to be seized under the plain view doctrine.

neutral and detached magistrate: A judge or magistrate who is: (1) objective and not working with anyone in the executive branch of government; and (2) not receiving financial compensation for the issuance of warrants.

nondeadly force: Physical force that is *not* reasonably likely to cause death. Pepper spray is an instrument of nondeadly force.

objective reasonableness: The proper course of action as viewed by a "reasonable person."

opinion: The "voice" of the court containing the reasoning for a decision.

papers and effects: Personal items such as business records, letters, diaries, and memos.

particularity (in a search vs. arrest warrant): Particularity refers to the person to be arrested, the location to be searched, and/or the items to be seized. Particularity in a search warrant requires that the warrant specify the place to be searched *and* the items to be seized. Particularity in an arrest warrant is satisfied with the arrestee's complete name or a sufficiently detailed description of the suspect.

photo lineup: A photographic collage of individual "mug shots" generally assembled for purposes of identifying a particular criminal suspect from an array of other individuals.

"plain view" doctrine: A Court-created doctrine that permits warrantless seizure of evidence by the police when: (1) the police are lawfully in the area where the evidence is located; and (2) the items are "immediately apparent" as subject to seizure.

police-probation partnerships: The most common form consists of the pairing of police officers with probation officers for the purpose of conducting spot checks on probationers.

precedent: A rule of case law, i.e., a decision by a court, that is binding on all lower courts as well as the court issuing the decision.

prima facie: On the face of, at first glance.

pro se representation: Representing oneself in a legal proceeding.

probable cause (in a search vs. arrest warrant): Probable cause is, simply, more than 50 percent certainty. The officer applying for a search warrant must show probable cause that the items to be seized are connected with criminal activity *and* probable cause that the items to be seized are in the location to be searched. The probable cause showing in an arrest warrant requires that the officer applying for the warrant show probable cause that the person to be arrested committed the crime.

procedural due process: Protection from arbitrary and unfair deprivations of protected life, liberty, or property interests without procedural safeguards.

prosecutor: A representative of the government charged with presenting evidence against the defendant.

protective sweep: A cursory visual inspection of those places in which a person might be hiding.

"purged taint" exception: An exception to the "fruit of the poisonous tree" doctrine which provides that unconstitutionally obtained evidence may be admissible if the "taint" of the unconstitutional act has been significantly reduced, such as by a significant time lapse.

qualified immunity: A judicially created defense that does not appear in the language of Section 1983, or in any other statute. Qualified immunity can serve as more than an affirmative defense, and in some cases affords immunity from suit.

reasonable expectation of privacy: An individual's expectation of privacy that society is prepared to recognize as reasonable. The reasonable expectation of privacy is commonly contrasted with a *subjective* expectation of privacy, one that an individual believes is reasonable.

reasonable suspicion: A standard of justification that falls below probable cause but above an unarticulated hunch. It is the standard of justification necessary for stops and frisks.

reasonableness clause: The reasonableness clause consists of the following text from the Fourth Amendment "The right of the people to be secure in their persons, houses, papers, and effects, against unreasonable searches and seizures, shall not be violated."

remand: When a case is remanded it is sent back to the trial court for further action consistent with the appellate court's decision.

return (of warrant): The act of a law enforcement officer delivering back to a presiding court official a judicial order which he has executed along with a brief account of his or her doings under the order.

reverse: To nullify a trial verdict. A reversal is not the same as an acquittal.

school disciplinary search: A search of students' lockers or personal effects for evidence of rule violations.

search: A governmental infringement on a reasonable expectation of privacy.

search incident to arrest: A search conducted in close temporal proximity to an arrest, usually directly afterward.

search warrant: Judicial authorization to look for evidence of criminal activity.

seizure (of a person vs. of evidence): To interfere with a person's movement to the extent that he or she is not free to leave and/or to interfere with his or her possessory interest in property.

Sixth Amendment: "In all criminal prosecutions, the accused shall enjoy the right to a speedy and public trial, by an impartial jury of the State and district wherein the crime shall have been committed, which district shall have been previously ascertained by law, and to be informed of the nature and cause of the accusation; to be confronted with the witnesses against him; to have compulsory process for obtaining witnesses in his favor, and to have the Assistance of Counsel for his defense."

sovereign immunity: The rule that states and state officials acting in their official capacities cannot be sued in federal court.

standardized field sobriety test: Any number of widely accepted tasks used by law enforcement personnel to make a preliminary determination that an individual is intoxicated (e.g., horizontal gaze nystagmus).

stare decisis: A Latin term which means to abide by or adhere to decided cases.

statutes: Legal codes, such as the penal code.

stop: A stop occurs when the police question or communicate with a person and a reasonable person would believe that he or she is not free to leave.

stop and frisk: The detention of an individual for investigative purposes. The ensuing frisk or "pat down" is limited to the individual's outer clothing for purposes of confirming the presence of a weapon that may be used to harm an officer or another person.

subjective reasonableness: The proper course of action as viewed by the individual engaged in an act.

substantive due process: Protection from arbitrary and unreasonable action on the part of state officials.

Title III of the Omnibus Crime Control and Safe Streets Act of 1968: Federal legislation that sets forth specific requirements for electronic surveillance activities.

totality of circumstances: All of the facts and circumstances surrounding a case.

U.S. Supreme Court ("the Court"): The highest court in the United States. Appeals from state supreme courts or U.S. courts of appeals may be appealed here if they raise a federal constitutional question.

vacate: To set aside a lower court's verdict.

vehicle inventories: To take note of and document the contents of an automobile, usually after an arrest of a suspect and/or impoundment of the vehicle.

warrant clause: The warrant clause consists of the following text from the Fourth Amendment: ". . . and no Warrants shall issue, but upon probable cause, supported by Oath or affirmation and particularly describing the place to be searched, and the persons or things to be seized."

Warren Court: The Supreme Court under Chief Justice Earl Warren. The Warren Court handed down many due process–oriented decisions.

wingspan: That area within a suspect's immediate control where he or she may gain control of a weapon, evidence, or the implements of escape.

writ of certiorari: An order by the Supreme Court requiring the lower court to send the case and a record of its proceedings up for review. ✦

Index